OUTSOURCING INFORMATION TECHNOLOGY, SYSTEMS, AND SERVICES

Chapter Contents by

Robert Klepper

Southern Illinois University at Edwardsville

Practitioner's Perspective, Interviews of Outsourcing Experts, and Appendix Examples by

Wendell O. Jones

To join a Prentice Hall PTR Internet mailing list, point to:
http://www.prenhall.com/mail_lists/

Prentice Hall PTR
Upper Saddle River, NJ 07458

ISBN 0-13-281578-8

90000

9 780132 815789

Library of Congress Cataloging-in-Publication Data

Klepper, Robert, 1941-

    Outsourcing information technology, systems, and services /
chapter contents by Robert Klepper; practitioner's perspective,
interviews of outsourcing experts, and appendix examples by Wendell
O. Jones.

      p. cm.
    Includes index.
    ISBN 0-13-281578-8
    1. Information technology--Management. 2. Contracting out.
I. Jones, Wendell O.II. Title.
T58.5.K63 1997
658.4'038--dc21   97-38716
                                              .CIP

Editorial/production supervision: *Dawn Speth White*
Art design director: *Jayne Conte*
Cover designer: *Bruce Kenselaar*
Manufacturing manager: *Alexis R. Heydt*
Marketing manager: *Stephen Solomon*
Acquisitions editor: *Michael Meehan*

©1998 by Prentice Hall

Published by Prentice Hall PTR
Prentice-Hall, Inc.
A Simon & Schuster Company
Upper Saddle River, NJ 07458

Prentice Hall books are widely used by corporations and government agencies
for training, marketing, and resale.

The publisher offers discounts on this book when ordered in bulk quantities.
For more information, contact: Corporate Sales Department, Phone: 800-382-3419;
Fax: 201-236-7141; E-mail: corpsales@prenhall.com; or write: Prentice Hall PTR,
Corp. Sales Dept., One Lake Street, Upper Saddle River, NJ 07458.

All products or services mentioned in this book are the trademarks or service marks of their respective companies or organizations.

Printed in the United States of America
10 9 8 7 6 5 4 3 2 1

ISBN   0-13-281578-8

Prentice-Hall International (UK) Limited, *London*
Prentice-Hall of Australia Pty. Limited, *Sydney*
Prentice-Hall Canada Inc., *Toronto*
Prentice-Hall Hispanoamericana, S.A., *Mexico*
Prentice-Hall of India Private Limited, *New Delhi*
Prentice-Hall of Japan, Inc., *Tokyo*
Simon & Schuster Asia Pte. Ltd., *Singapore*
Editora Prentice-Hall do Brasil, Ltda., *Rio de Janeiro*

To Nancy and Adam, my closest companions on the road of life.

Robert

To Grace for many years of support, encouragement, and love
and to Tyler and Ryan who keep us young.

Wendell

Outsourcing means the transfer of responsibility to an external organization for the provision of an internal service or facility.

Contents

Foreword

Bruce Caldwell
Senior Writer - IT Outsourcing
InformationWeek

F aster, better, and cheaper is the perennial slogan of computing, and it doesn't apply only to the hardware. It also applies to the management of computing, and this book tells how.

The practice of computer outsourcing, or contracting for services normally performed by employees, began in 1954 when the first computer was applied to a business process. That was in 1954, when General Electric Corp. wanted to automate its payroll, material scheduling and inventory control, and other processes at its new appliance plant in Louisville, Kentucky. Because it was the first time a Univac had been used by a corporation, outside help was needed. GE contracted with Arthur Andersen for the firm's expertise in automating processes with the tabulating equipment that preceded the Univac, the first modern computer.

When insurance companies followed in GE's footsteps, the shortage in computer skills and the high cost of computers served to advance outsourcing to the next stage, where both skills and assets were outsourced.

It was called timesharing then. Businesses without the money to own the new thinking machines paid for the use of another company's computer during hours when the owner didn't use it. Businesses also backed each other up, agreeing to run each other's programs whenever they couldn't use their own computer for any reason.

As the spread of computers proved that IBM's Thomas J. Watson was wrong about the world needing no more than five of the room-sized machines, information systems departments started populating organizational charts. The "glass house," the sealed room that housed the computers and put them on display as examples of corporate might behind plate-glass windows, became a status symbol.

Consequently, timesharing fell into disrepute among business executives, as though anyone who didn't have their own computers were poor cousins. "Still timesharing, Johnson? Too bad, too bad. But computers are troublesome to own, you know. We've outgrown our glass house at company headquarters. Have to spend $20 million to build a special building just to house the computers now. All sorts of staff needed. You may actually be better off!"

Computers became the measure of corporate machismo. That is, until Eastman Kodak Co., a household name and a corporate heavyweight, signed its landmark outsourcing deals with IBM, Digital Equipment Corp., and Businessland in 1990. That deal, as this book explains, shook up corporate boardrooms everywhere.

If Kodak didn't need to own and staff its computers, the line of reasoning went, why do we? The spotlight was put on the IS organization, which, unable to justify its spending, attempted to defend its fiefdom by asserting that outsourcing equaled loss of control.

That argument failed to impact the sudden trendiness of outsourcing. A sort of herdlike mentality came into play. Waves of outsourcing contracts swept through industry after industry. The downturn in the economy during the early 1990s helped. When the outsourcing contract was signed, the customer unloaded hundreds of technical specialist employees, got a nice fat check from the outsourcing vendor in payment for the computer equipment and facilities acquired from the customer, and saw a constantly growing budget converted to a 10-year plan of easy installment payments. Outsourcing just looked too good to resist for many corporations.

So good, in fact, that the Office of the Comptroller of Currency cracked down on the practice of struggling banks selling their computer assets through outsourcing contracts to goose their bottom lines.

While outsourcing had become more respectable and mainstream, there was still the undercurrent of suspicion that outsourcing was only for the financially needy. Indeed, in addition to ailing banks, companies overburdened with debt were typical of the customers immediately following Kodak.

Kodak's deal came at a time when companies in every industry were slashing and burning through their organizations in desperate efforts to survive the economic downturn. To emphasize the positive, outsourcing customers often portrayed savings as secondary to outsourcing's loftier goal—which even Kodak expressed—of freeing companies from drudgery to focus on their core competencies, the things that they did best and that made a real difference in the competitive wars.

But as PCs and distributed computing began undermining the importance of the data center—the old glass-house technologies of mainframe computers that had been outsourced—and as companies changed the nature of their business through reengineering or mergers and acquisitions or downsizing, the old warning about loss of control came back to haunt outsourcing. The rigidity of some contracts meant that some companies weren't able to take advantage of falling costs for computer processing, or move as quickly as they would like to take advantage of new technologies and new business opportunities.

Companies are now starting to renegotiate outsourcing contracts signed three and five years ago because of changes in business and technology. Some are terminating contracts and bringing in new outsourcing vendors to obtain better terms and more flexibility. And new kinds of outsourcing relationships are emerging that are more like business partnerships or joint ventures, with clearly defined performance metrics and objectives, or even shared risks and rewards.

The co-authors of this book, Wendell Jones and Robert Klepper, work well together as a team to explain the world of outsourcing relationships clearly and comprehensively. While this is not the first book written on outsourcing, it is the first this writer has seen that can serve as a friendly advisor and guide for both business and information systems executives who want to know what they can expect from outsourcing, and how to get the most out of it.

Jones, who was instrumental in awarding and then managing one of the first megadeals, McDonnell Douglas Corp.'s 10-year, $3 billion outsourcing contract with IBM, contributes his experience and that of other practitioners. Klepper, possessing a doctorate in economics and a masters in management information sciences, brings the best academic thinking and research on outsourcing to the discussion. Together, they have produced a seasoned and well-informed book that helps the reader, step-by-step, take the appropriate actions for the desired business results.

The shortage of technology skills drives many outsourcing contracts today. But a shortage of outsourcing procurement, negotiation, and management skills also exists. This book can help make up for any deficits in those skills on your outsourcing team. It's worth keeping close at hand.

Preface

This book provides the background and insight necessary to make outsourcing decisions. We neither favor nor oppose outsourcing. Our purpose is to provide practical advice to general managers and information systems managers on outsourcing decisions and management of outsourcing relationships. The approach is based on both real-world experience and on theory from the academic world. Corporate executives and senior level information systems managers will be the major beneficiaries of the first-hand treatment of information systems outsourcing provided in this book.

Outsourcing is now a common phenomenon in corporate America and it is growing in Europe and Asia. Many business functions are candidates for outsourcing — information systems, included.

While outsourcing is decidedly trendy, a headlong rush to outsourcing can spell disaster. Information systems outsourcing is unique in a number of ways, and this uniqueness demands a level of management expertise and caution that outsourcing in other functional areas of a business may not require.

First, the size of information systems outsourcing deals can be quite large relative to outsourcing in many other business support functions. Billion dollar contracts have been written in the recent past between client companies and IT outsourcing vendors.

Second, the complexity of the applications-technology-management mix in information systems demands that careful attention be given to the issues of what to outsource, to whom to outsource, and how to manage the outsourcing relationship. Modern business depends on having the right information, at the right place, at the right time. Outsourcing should enhance this potential, not compromise it.

Finally, the substantial costs of getting out of information systems outsourcing contracts makes the choice of the right vendor all the more important. Careful management of the outsourcing relationship is necessary to insure outsourcing is cost-effective and requirements are satisfied.

This book addresses management considerations in all phases of information systems outsourcing. It offers specific recommendations to managers every step of the way, from decisions on whether information systems outsourcing is right for your organization to renegotiation of outsourcing contracts and decisions connected with the termination of an outsourcing arrangement.

The book takes advantage of the available academic theory on outsourcing from the management information systems literature and from the management literature in general. But this is not a book on theory. Real-world, practical aspects of outsourcing come first; theory is used as a supplement. Furthermore, pains have been taken to make the theoretical discussions easy to understand and easy to apply.

Chapter 1 provides a high-level outline and executive summary of the material in the book. It should be read by all managers concerned with information systems outsourcing decisions.

With the road map provided by the first chapter, senior managers may wish to read other portions of the book selectively, as it suits their needs.

Chapters 2 and 3 set the stage in terms of broad trends that favor outsourcing and specific motives and risks associated with outsourcing. The remaining chapters lay down the management issues in outsourcing in the order these are encountered in most outsourcing situations. High-level outsourcing feasibility issues are addressed in Chapter 4. The Request for Proposal and the analysis preceding it is the topic of Chapter 5. Chapters 6 and 7 deal with contract negotiation and contract provisions. Chapters 8 and 9 treat the transition to outsourcing and management of the ongoing outsourcing arrangement.

The partnership option is addressed throughout the book. Chapter 4 lays out the conditions under which partnerships are appropriate. Chapter 10 outlines methods for developing and sustaining partnerships.

Chapter 11, the last chapter, addresses the end of outsourcing contractual relationships in all the variations from premature termination to normal expiration with and without renewal. Thus the book addresses all stages in the outsourcing life cycle from methods for developing outsourcing ideas to the end of an outsourcing relationship.

The authors can be reached in the following ways: Robert Klepper, mail: CMIS Department, Box 1106, Southern Illinois University, Edwardsville, IL 62026; voice: 618-692-2432, fax: 618-692-3979, email: rkleppe@siue.edu and Wendell Jones, 206 Holmard Street, Gaithersburg, MD 20878; voice: 301-330-1518, email: jonesga@erols.com.

Acknowledgments

Many people have contributed to our knowledge of outsourcing. Although it is impossible to name all of them here, several individuals who directly contributed to this book deserve special mention.

First, we would like to acknowledge the unique contributions of each other in the creation of this book. Robert Klepper completed the review of the outsourcing literature, wrote each chapter, and served as the moving force for meeting the publication deadlines. Wendell Jones provided the practicing IT manager's perspective in the review and editing of each chapter and conducted the interviews of senior IT executives, outsourcing consultants, attorneys, and other leading outsourcing practitioners whose interviews are included throughout the book.

Second, we express appreciation to all of the experts who provided interviews. These busy people took the time to share their insights and in doing so greatly enhance the value of the book. They are:

- Michael Corbett, Co-founder of the Outsourcing Institute and President of Michael F. Corbett and Associates.
- Lance Eliot, PhD, President of Eliot & Associates in Huntington Beach, California.
- Cinda A. Hallman, Global Vice President, Integrated Processes and Systems for DuPont, Wilmington, Delaware, with responsibility for Information Systems and Continuous Business Improvement. In addition, she is in charge of Global Sourcing (Purchasing) and Business Process Modernization.
- David Kepler, Director of Global Information Systems, Dow Chemical Company in Midland, Michigan.
- Ellen Kitzis, PhD, Vice President and Lead Analyst for Dataquest's Worldwide IT Services Group. Dataquest is a Gartner Group Company.

- Jill Klein, formerly Senior Vice President and CIO of Riggs Bank, and now an executive with AETEA Information Technology in Rockville, Maryland.
- William P. Martorelli, Vice President of Giga Information Group, an industry research firm in Cambridge, Massachusetts.
- Pete Mounts, Vice President of Sales and Marketing for HBOC's Outsourcing Services Group.
- Edward Pisacreta, a Partner in the firm of Brown Raysman Millstein Felder & Steiner LLP, New York City.
- Richard Raysman, Partner with the New York City firm of Brown Raysman Millstein Felder & Steiner LLP.
- Robert Rubin, Vice President and Chief Information Officer of Elf Atochem North America.
- Grover Wray, Director of Contract Services, Arthur Andersen.

Special thanks goes to Bruce Caldwell, Senior Writer — IT Outsourcing at *InformationWeek*, for contributing an excellent foreword. Special thanks also to Norton Hoffman, an IT manager of uncommon insight, who provided many useful comments on an earlier draft.

This project would not have succeeded without the encouragement and nurturing of our editor, Michael Meehan, and the production skills of Dawn White, both of Prentice Hall PTR.

Lynette Wilson and Liz Burdette of the National Association of Securities Dealers in Rockville, Maryland assisted with the production of the interviews and appendices.

Robert Klepper and Wendell Jones

July, 1997

About the Authors

Robert Klepper is Professor of Management Information Systems in the School of Business at Southern Illinois University at Edwardsville. Dr. Klepper conducts research into the nature of outsourcing relationships between client and vendor firms and the processes by which partnerships can be developed in outsourcing. Other research interests include the mass media potential of the World Wide Web, the role of information systems in the transition to market economies in the countries of Eastern Europe, and productivity enhancement in software development. His outsourcing papers have been read at international outsourcing conferences, and his articles have been published in *The Communications of the ACM*, *Information & Management*, *The Journal of Information Technology*, *Data Base*, and *Computer Personnel Research*.

Dr. Klepper is a consultant to industry on outsourcing issues and information systems project management. He holds Ph.D. and M.A. degrees in economics from the University of Chicago, an M.S. degree in management of information technology from Washington University, and a B.A. degree from Westminster College.

Wendell Jones, has more than thirty years of management experience in the securities, aerospace and defense industries, is a leading practitioner of outsourcing, and presently leads a professional services firm located in Gaithersburg, Maryland which specializes in IT management and outsourcing consulting. As General Manager of McDonnel Douglas Aerospace Information Services Company, he led the evaluation, negotiation, implementation, and management of a $3 billion 10-year outsourcing contract with IBM. Recently, as Senior Vice President NASD/Nasdaq Stock Market, he implemented an offshore outsourcing agreement for applications maintenance with a company in Bombay, India. He anticipates in late 1997 to assume responsibility for Digital's worldwide outsourcing delivery services as a Vice President of Digital Equipment Corporation.

His education includes M.B.A. and Ph.D. degrees in management and management information systems from the University of Georgia, a post-doctoral fellowship at Cornell University, and a B.S. from the University of Arkansas.

1

Overview and Executive Summary

This chapter is an overview and executive summary of the material in the book. Senior managers should read it for the general ideas and management practices that lead to successful outsourcing. Managers in charge of outsourcing and outsourcing decision making should read it for an overview of and entry points to the detailed content of the book.

1.1 SENIOR MANAGER RESPONSIBILITIES

Senior managers have their own set of responsibilities in information systems outsourcing. They are often the champions and initiators of outsourcing efforts. The ultimate success of outsourcing depends on their guidance and oversight of the outsourcing process. Outsourcing has a better chance of success when senior managers:

- Put the best, most capable managers in charge of the outsourcing evaluation and management of the outsourcing arrangement. Outsourcing decision making and management are substantial responsibilities with important consequences in terms of the information that supports an organization's functioning. Outsourcing requires good people.
- Don't let vendors go around the disciplined process. Vendors sometimes try to by-pass the outsourcing decision-making process by going directly to senior managers who might then be tempted to make outsourcing decisions without good analysis and support.

- Engage consultants if you don't have the knowledge necessary to make informed outsourcing decisions and to level the playing field when dealing with vendors. See Appendix A for more information on consultants.

- Negotiate a sound contract. A good outsourcing contract is clear about what is to be done, who does it, who owns it, who pays, and what happens if it is not done correctly. A good contract should be a win-win arrangement for both parties. But remember that the relationship with a vendor involves more than a contract.

- Consider the key issues when evaluating and negotiating an outsourcing contract. These include defining the business issues, scope, desired results and metrics; determining the change-management process and who will be responsible for what. Contracts involve agreeing on a schedule and cost algorithms; resolving personnel issues; determining how to manage the relationship; and others.

- Encourage ownership of outsourcing at the business unit level. The business units will be the primary users and bill payers. Take-charge business units will manage usage and adjust charges.

- Revisit the outsourcing decision from time to time to see that it still makes sense. Changes in business conditions or changes in technology can change the benefits, costs, and risks of outsourcing.

Senior executives can't abdicate responsibility for outsourcing results. Delegate responsibility for outsourcing evaluation and management, but follow up and take the steps necessary to see that the whole effort is undertaken in a way that meets the organization's outsourcing objectives.

1.2 A GUIDE TO THE REAL-WORLD EXPERIENCE IN THIS BOOK

The analysis and managerial guidelines that follow are based on and rounded out by real-world experience in the form of interviews with experts in information systems outsourcing, examples of real-world outsourcing experiences, and a sample Request For Proposal and outsourcing contract. These amplify and extend an understanding of the management practices for good outsourcing.

Two-thirds of the chapters conclude with interviews of outsourcing experts. These are people who have vast experience with outsourcing, either as information technology (IT) executives who have outsourced in the past or as consultants and attorneys with expertise in aspects of outsourcing decision making and practice. All the interviews are worth reading on their own for the insight they provide.

Each interview begins with biographical information about the expert being interviewed. The topics, experts, and chapter locations of interviews are as follows:

- Trends in Outsourcing: An Interview with Ellen Kitzis (Chapter 2)
- Trends in Outsourcing: An Interview with William P. Martorelli (Chapter 2)
- Outsourcing in The Healthcare Industry: An Interview with Pete Mounts of HBOC (Chapter 2)
- Outsourcing Myths: An Interview with Dr. Lance B. Eliot (Chapter 3)
- Managing the Human Resource Issues: An Interview with Grover Wray (Chapter 5)
- The Dow Chemical and Andersen Consulting Alliance: An Interview with David Kepler (Chapter 6)
- Outsourcing Contract Issues: An Interview with Richard Raysman (Chapter 7)
- Employment Law and Outsourcing: An Interview with Edward A. Pisacreta (Chapter 8)
- Managing the Outsourcing Relationship: An Interview with Michael F. Corbett (Chapter 9)

Several Chief Information Officers shared their experiences and perspectives on outsourcing, and these are woven into the content of various chapters:

Cinda A. Hallman is Global Vice President, Integrated Processes and Systems for DuPont, with responsibility for Information Systems and Continuous Business Improvement. In addition, she is in charge of Global Sourcing (Purchasing) and Business Process Modernization. Ms. Hallman is a member of DuPont's corporate Integrated Operations Committee and the corporate Operations Network and is chair of DuPont's Business Information Board. She is a member of many information industry advisory committees and the recipient of many industry awards. As CIO she led DuPont into an innovative global alliance with two of the world's leading information technology (IT) firms — Computer Sciences Corporation and Andersen Consulting — to support the growth strategies of DuPont's businesses and to increase shareholder value. By working together with the "best of the best" in the IT industry, DuPont plans to strengthen and build on its competencies and meet the needs of the dynamic, global business environment in which it competes.

Jill Klein, who from 1987 to 1993 served as Vice President, Corporate Operations and later Senior Vice President and CIO of Riggs Bank, provides information on a major outsourcing deal between Riggs and IBM. Klein led the evaluation, negotiation, and implementation of the outsourcing agreement which is now in its seventh year. She is presently an executive with AETEA Information Technology in Rockville, Maryland. In addition to Riggs, her prior experience includes positions at the Advisory Board Company as a Managing Director and at IBM.

Robert Rubin is Vice President and Chief Information Officer of Elf Atochem North America and is responsible for all computer services, business process engineering, and certain administrative processing functions such as payroll and accounts payable. His views on outsourcing are included at several points.

The all-important Request For Proposal is addressed in Chapter 5. The topics to be included in an RFP are outlined in Appendix C, and an example RFP is included as Appendix D.

The importance of a good contract is stressed repeatedly. In addition to the interview at the end of Chapter 5, an example outsourcing contract is included as Appendix E.

Additional material to aid the manager concerned with outsourcing can be found in the form of advice on obtaining consultants in Appendix A, a list of information systems outsourcing deals in Appendix B, and a list of major information systems outsourcing vendors in Appendix F.

1.3 CHAPTER-BY-CHAPTER OVERVIEW

The overview that follows hits the high points of each chapter. It provides guidelines to issues like the following: What can be outsourced? How do you decide if it's a good idea to outsource? To what vendor should you outsource? What kind of relationship do you need with the vendor? How do you write a good contract with a vendor? How do you manage the vendor relationship? What happens when the contract ends or needs to be renewed?

Chapter 2 lays some historical ground work for outsourcing and reasons why interest in outsourcing is likely to continue. The remaining chapters, 3 though 11, set out a disciplined framework of five steps for making outsourcing decisions and managing an outsourcing relationship.

- First, be clear on the objectives and risks of outsourcing and make a high level determination that outsourcing is feasible before proceeding to more detailed evaluation. Chapter 3 outlines the motives and the risks of outsourcing. Chapter 4 introduces concepts of total and selective outsourcing and high-level screens to determine the initial feasibility of outsourcing.

- Second, proceed with a detailed analysis and evaluation of alternatives. Chapter 5 presents guidelines for evaluation of outsourcing requirements, benefits, costs, and risks and how to develop a Request For Proposal and evaluate vendors who respond.
- Third, design the relationship. Chapter 6 on contract negotiation and Chapter 7 on contract provisions provide a framework for designing and negotiating the contractual side of the outsourcing relationship.
- Fourth, implement and operate the outsourcing relationship. The transition to outsourcing is the topic of Chapter 8, and management of the ongoing relationship is the topic of Chapter 9. Chapter 10 deals with developing and managing partnership outsourcing relationships.
- Finally, the relationship (with the same or a different vendor) is renegotiated at the time of contract expiration or the contract terminates prematurely. These are the issues addressed in Chapter 11.

The remainder of this chapter takes up each subsequent chapter. Each chapter summary concludes with a brief section on critical success factors, or the things to do and the things to avoid in outsourcing and outsourcing management.

1.3.1 Trends Favoring Outsourcing (Chapter 2)

Various forms of information systems outsourcing have been in existence since computers first entered businesses fifty years ago, but the use of outsourcing services has exploded in the last 10 years.

Outsourcing can give an organization the flexibility required in a quickly changing global economy. It also allows an organization to focus on its core competencies in highly competitive marketplaces.

Vendors often have advantages of economies of scale, experience, and expertise with the latest technology that may be hard to duplicate in the information systems departments of individual organizations.

Outsourcing may be attractive from the client side (a) when information products and services are commodity like and not central to the competitive success of the business, (b) when information systems can easily be separated from the rest of the business, and (c) when outsourcing offers cost savings.

The successful negotiation of some large and visible outsourcing deals has brought attention to information systems outsourcing and made it respectable in the corporate world.

Although some commentators see information systems outsourcing as a fad, Chapter 2 presents arguments that strongly suggest it is not.

Since information systems outsourcing is likely to be a prominent feature of the business landscape in the future, the issue is how to do it right and manage it effectively. That is the topic of the book.

Critical Success Factors

Don't outsource because other firms or organizations are outsourcing.

Outsource because your organization has good business reasons for outsourcing that are clearly understood.

1.3.2 The Rewards and Risks of Outsourcing (Chapter 3)

Outsourcing may be driven by one motive, but often it is done for multiple reasons. Chapter 3 lays out a diverse range of motivations for outsourcing grouped into categories of cost saving, organizational finances, services and responsiveness, technology and skills, personnel issues, organizational change, and organizational politics.

Academics advance various theoretical rationales for outsourcing and find empirical support for their theories, including resource-based theory, resource-dependency theory, and transaction cost theory. The last, transaction cost theory, provides a framework in which to understand and analyze the kind of relationship that is best to develop with an outsourcing vendor. This framework is introduced in Chapter 4 and is used throughout the book to help guide appropriate management action.

A close relationship with a vendor, or partnership, is one of the options, and many vendors propose a "partnership" when courting clients. But transaction cost theory strongly suggests that partnerships are relevant only under particular, limited conditions. Partnerships usually make sense only when resources of client and vendor are paired in reinforcing ways that produce a unique capability.

The risks involved in outsourcing are real and are often neglected or underestimated. Chapter 3 catalogs the risks starting with the most fundamental, which is loss of control.

Control has to do with responsibility. When information services are produced in-house, IT managers have responsibility for their delivery. When information services are outsourced, the vendor takes responsibility for providing the services, but managers in the client organization must take responsibility for managing the vendor relationship and seeing that the vendor performs according to requirements. Vendor responsibilities are defined, in the first instance, by the outsourcing contract.

Academic studies have looked into the nature of information system outsourcing — what is being outsourced, why it is being outsourced, and how it is being outsourced. The picture is one of great variety. Many functions are being outsourced, for many reasons, and in many ways.

There is no single, best outsourcing formula. What is best depends on the circumstances of your organization. The main purpose of this book is to help you sort out what is best for your organization.

Critical Success Factors

Outsourcing decisions should be the outcome of a careful decision-making process. What's best for your organization may not be relevant to other organizations, and vice versa. It is necessary to understand your circumstances and evaluate outsourcing accordingly.

Outsourcing to rid the organization of a troubled IT function will probably fail. First you must understand how information services should support the organization and the exact capabilities and performance a responsive IT function exhibits. In other words, reform begins before outsourcing can be successful.

If the risks of outsourcing are unacceptably great or can't be managed, outsourcing should be avoided. If the risks are not too great relative to the expected benefits of outsourcing and/or can be managed, outsourcing can be considered. If the decision is made to proceed with outsourcing, manage the risks throughout the outsourcing process.

1.3.3 The Feasibility of Outsourcing Ideas (Chapter 4)

The disciplined, managerial approach to outsourcing outlined in this chapter parallels in many ways the phased approach to developing information systems with stages of feasibility study, detailed analysis of requirements, design of the relationship with a vendor through contract negotiation and contract provisions, building and implementing of the relationship, ongoing operation of the relationship, and expiration of the relationship with its renewal in a succeeding contract, if appropriate.

Outsourcing can be divided into two general categories. Total outsourcing involves contracting out 80 percent or more of the IT function to vendors. Selective outsourcing involves outsourcing a few functions that total less than 80 percent of the whole. Methods for identifying functions that might be selectively outsourced include opportunistic, problem-focused approaches and more methodical planning approaches.

Chapter 4 addresses feasibility issues by means of screens that every outsourcing idea should pass before further, detailed evaluation.

The first screen is *core competency*. If the IT function to be outsourced contribute in central ways to the organization's competitive success, it probably should not be outsourced.

The second screen is the *cost of controlling a vendor*. Vendors are controlled through governance mechanisms that can be termed a "relationship." The contract is a critical part of control and of the relationship. If complete contracts can't be written that anticipate all future contingencies, other means will be needed to control the vendor and see that the outsourced work is successfully completed. Chapter 4 develops a framework for determining the kind of vendor relationship most appropriate to various circumstances. Possible relationships run a continuum from those in which complete contracts can be written (market relationships) to relationships that can't depend on complete contracts or even a single contract (partnerships). Intermediate contracts have some aspects of market relationships and some aspects of partnership and occupy the middle of the outsourcing relationship spectrum. Outsourcing should not be undertaken when the costs of governance are too high relative to the benefits.

Other screens in the feasibility analysis phase of outsourcing evaluation are the following: (a) new technology that poses very significant risks, (b) organizational readiness for outsourcing, (c) the availability of appropriate vendors, and (d) a sufficient quantity of outsourcing work to interest vendors.

If the outsourcing idea or ideas pass the initial screens, planning can proceed for the detailed outsourcing evaluation that follows.

The fact that outsourcing is being considered should be made known to your employees in the absence of compelling reasons not to do so. Secrecy is hard to maintain; openness is preferred.

Critical Success Factors

Before serious evaluation of outsourcing ideas can take place, you should have complete clarity on the objectives of outsourcing and the scope of what is to be outsourced.

Never outsource all of IT management. Even in total outsourcing, keep a cadre of managers to (a) manage ongoing outsourcing relationships with vendors, (b) oversee and pass on vendor technical decisions, (c) develop experience with outsourcing and help make future outsourcing decisions, (d) negotiate and enforce future outsourcing contracts, (e) develop the technology strategy of the organization for the future, and (f) keep overall IT strategy in alignment with overall corporate strategy as it evolves over time.

Determining the most appropriate relationship to establish with a vendor is critical to outsourcing success. Effective control depends on the appropriate relationship.

Don't "partner" with a vendor unless the circumstances clearly warrant it.

Carefully consider the costs of controlling a vendor as part of the total costs of outsourcing. When there is a good chance the costs will outweigh the benefits, don't outsource.

Outsourcing a troubled IT function may not help. Part of the problem may lie outside the IT department or in parts of the IT function that won't be outsourced. It's necessary to understand the problem and correct any aspects that will remain inside your organization before outsourcing can proceed.

Outsourcing a function that has many interrelationships with other functions poses problems.

Don't outsource an information systems function that is part of your organization's core competency.

1.3.4 Detailed Analysis and the Request for Proposal (Chapter 5)

Clear outsourcing objectives are necessary for setting the parameters of a detailed analysis, collecting appropriate information for the analysis, formulating a good RFP, and evaluating vendor responses. Clear objectives are also necessary for analyzing and resolving trade-off issues in outsourcing.

Develop a baseline of current costs for the function or functions to be outsourced so that these can be compared with vendor proposals. Carefully define service requirements with sufficient depth to make them measurable. Develop both costs and service requirements in light of expected technological and business change (which may be interrelated) over the expected life of the outsourcing arrangement.

Analyze issues of personnel, hardware, and software transfer to a vendor. Consider data conversion and other transition issues. Estimate the costs of all of these, and determine your position on who will bear each cost — your organization or the outsourcing vendor.

It generally costs more to administer an outsourcing arrangement than it costs to administer the same function in your organization. Consider these costs that vary with the size and complexity of the function to be outsourced and with the nature of the governance arrangements necessary to control the vendor.

Develop estimates of the benefits of outsourcing.

Outsourcing involves the usual risks of information systems projects and operations plus the risks of doing the work through a vendor. Do a risk analysis to identify, analyze, and prioritize risks. Consider how the risks might be eliminated or reduced. Also consider the costs of risk management over the life of the outsourcing arrangement. Determine whether the risks change the feasibility of the outsourcing project. If they do, consider changing the project to reduce the risks, or avoid outsourcing. A risk analysis provides the foundation for risk management throughout the life of an outsourcing arrangement.

Develop a Request for Information, term sheet, and Request for Proposal to gather information about and from vendors. Encourage vendor competition throughout this process, evaluate vendor responses, consider trade-offs, decide whether outsourcing is still desirable, and, if it is, proceed to contract negotiations with one or more vendors.

Critical Success Factors

Clear outsourcing objectives are essential.

Requirements should be as detailed and measurable as possible.

Stating requirements in terms of the performance of your organization and its business and tying vendor compensation to your business performance can be a powerful way of aligning the vendor's objectives with the objectives of your organization.

The relevant costs and requirements in outsourcing are future costs and requirements. Without a good idea of future needs and the costs of meeting those needs, it is not possible to outsource effectively and efficiently.

Be certain to identify all the costs. Some costs may be in user budgets or in vendor charges.

Size, complexity, the need for flexibility, and newness to outsourcing raise the costs of managing an outsourcing relationship and raise the risks.

Risks can be interrelated with nonlinear consequences.

Don't let a vendor short-circuit the disciplined outsourcing evaluation and decision-making process by going directly to senior managers or user managers for quick decisions.

Foster competition between vendors from initial contacts through contract signing.

Jill Klein, who led an outsourcing effort at Riggs Bank, sets out her critical success factors: Be clear and complete in the RFP; you get what you ask for and no more. Keep the process simple but rigorous. Give each vendor the opportunity to present their proposal in person and answer questions. Set deadlines and enforce them; otherwise, you and the vendor will waste a lot of time and money.

Cinda Hallman of DuPont emphasizes the following factors for success: Tell candidates everything they need to know to effectively respond. Ask vendors to respond to everything you need to know to make a sound decision. Emphasize a win-win attitude from the outset. Set a schedule and insist that you and the vendors stick to it. Check their customer references. Require them to provide customer contacts with whom they have less than an excellent relationship, and check those too. Require full disclosure from both sides.

1.3.5 Contract Negotiations (Chapter 6)

While contracts are critical for successful outsourcing, contracts can't guarantee control over the vendor when there is uncertainty and when there are problems with knowing and measuring what the vendor does. Consequently, the relationship with a vendor involves more than a contract.

Choosing vendors based on reputation overcomes some of these difficulties. Other approaches include incentives and contract provisions that allow review of vendor work, changes in requirements, and even renegotiation of the contract.

Contract negotiation should be based on a clear view of the type of relationship appropriate to the outsourcing. Contracts should be complete in market-type relationships. Contracts should attempt to address uncertainty and information problems in intermediate and partnership relationships.

Preferred vendor relationships may be appropriate when the outsourcing work is marketlike but with a continuing need for the same kind of work. Preferred vendor programs qualify vendors as eligible to complete for future work based on current investments that improve their future capabilities.

Pricing issues are addressed at several points in this chapter. Pricing arrangements can vary between fixed prices, on the one hand, and time-and-materials arrangements at the other extreme. Prices should reflect the circumstances surrounding the outsourcing work and give vendors proper incentives.

Project versus process work and the implications of these differences for contracts is also addressed in this chapter.

What can be accomplished in contract negotiation depends in part on bargaining power. Power depends on relative dependency. The party more dependent on the other party has less power; the party less dependent on the other party has more power. The chapter outlines methods that can be used to increase bargaining power in contract negotiations.

Negotiation should start from a clear view of your interests and the type of vendor relationship that will further those interests.

Bargaining strategies can be win-win or win-lose. The chapter discusses the use of each and various other tactical aspects of bargaining, including fall-back positions, competition between vendors, focus in negotiations, and impasses.

Critical Success Factors

Control over a vendor can be accomplished by monitoring vendor output or monitoring vendor behavior (how the vendor works). Monitoring behavior is often more expensive than monitoring output. When vendor output is difficult to observe or measure, there may be no alternative to monitoring behavior.

Negotiate complete contracts or contracts as complete as possible. Complete contracts are possible in market relationships with vendors. Complete contracts are not possible in intermediate and partnership relationships; these contracts need provisions to help handle uncertainty and to address problems with information and measurement.

Develop a negotiation strategy before sitting down at the table with vendors. A term sheet (see Chapter 5) defines the essential issues for negotiation.

Never accept a vendor's standard contract without employing competent counsel to carefully scrutinize it and change it.

You can specify in the RFP that contract negotiations will not start with the vendor's standard contract. Use your term sheet instead.

Don't allow a vendor to begin work before a contract is completed and signed.

Cinda Hallman outlines success factors for negotiations at DuPont. Keep a win-win attitude, open communications, attention to detail, and a realistic, but firm schedule. It is also important to have the right people on the team. DuPont's negotiating team was led by its vice president of corporate initiatives and received constant input from a CIO with a clear vision of outsourcing objectives.

It is Jill Klein's view that success in negotiating a contract revolves around, "Knowing what really matters most to your company. Winning every point is not your objective. You want to win those that truly matter. Pick a vendor you trust whose culture seems compatible with yours. Trust your gut instincts in this regard. Stay dedicated to the process. This is not a part-time job. It demands 110 percent dedication from your people on the team. Demand the same dedication from the vendor."

1.3.6 Contract Provisions (Chapter 7)

This chapter provides an overview of some important outsourcing contract issues, but it is no substitute for obtaining expert legal counsel familiar with outsourcing contract issues.

The contract must have a specification of requirements as complete as possible, and requirements should be stated in measurable terms. The contract should make the vendor responsible for meeting requirements.

Build flexibility into a contract so that some change in requirements can be accommodated. Contract provisions should allow for growth associated with business expansion. If changes in technology are anticipated, the contract should accommodate these as well.

Some changes can't be anticipated, particularly in intermediate and partnership type relationships with vendors. Contracts should then specify a process for identification and authorization of additional work, and might also contain formulas for the pricing of additional work in various categories.

Outsourcing contracts for systems development work should establish ways of reviewing or auditing the work as it proceeds. Incentives might be used to reward on-time and quality performance by the vendor. Provision should also be made for some limited amount of change in requirements while the system is under construction, with additional compensation to the vendor for the additional work.

Pricing should reflect the goals of outsourcing. Fixed price arrangements are preferable when the goal of outsourcing is control of costs. Variable pricing arrangements are preferable when the goal is flexibility or enhanced service.

Pricing arrangements may need to address inflation, growth in service, and changes in technology that alter the underlying costs of providing services. Invoicing and payment provisions should be included.

Incentives and sharing arrangements can be written into contracts. These are particularly important in partnerships.

Chapter 7 addresses a host of resource transfer issues for transfer of personnel, hardware, or software to a vendor. Contracts should also set out the plan for conversions of systems when these are transferred to a vendor.

The outline of a management structure for the outsourcing arrangement should be part of a contract. The complexity of management structures should vary with the size, complexity, and nature of the outsourcing relationship. The contract might specify the individuals who will represent the vendor and give your organization some control over changes in vendor personnel.

Contracts should establish basic processes and procedures to be followed during the life of the arrangement, the rights for review and audit of vendor work, and dispute resolution procedures.

Every outsourcing contract needs provisions for the normal expiration of the contract and provisions for premature termination. The objective in both cases is to make a smooth transition to another contact (perhaps with another vendor) or a smooth transition to bringing the outsourced function back inside your organization.

The need for penalties and sanctions, control over subcontractors the vendor might use, confidentiality, warranties, insurance, and so forth should also be reviewed and included in the contract as needed.

A risk analysis can be done to determine the exposure to loss that accompanies a contract. Top-down analyses estimate the maximum damage from a vendor default. Bottom-up analyses look at the potential damage, clause by contract clause.

Critical Success Factors

Outsourcing contracts are the foundation of an outsourcing relationship. A poor contract jeopardizes the relationship before it begins. Avoid haste and contract carefully.

Contracts should be as complete as possible for the type of outsourcing relationship undertaken. Complete contracts should be possible in market relationships. Intermediate and partnership relationships are ones in which complete contracts are not possible, but contracts in these cases should attempt to anticipate and allow for change.

Beware of change of character clauses in outsourcing contracts. Depending on how these are worded, a change of character clause could allow a vendor to introduce new technology, claim that your organization is receiving increased functionality, and charge you more for what are essentially the same services.

Revise the cost-benefit-risk analysis in light of contract negotiations and the contract terms that can be negotiated. Despite the effort that may have gone into evaluation and contract talks, don't outsource if the analysis now shows outsourcing to be of doubtful or marginal net benefit.

1.3.7   The Transition to Outsourcing (Chapter 8)

Client and vendor organizations must achieve some level of integration from the outset of an outsourcing arrangement. The integration necessary for success is minimal in the case of market relationships and extensive in the case of partnerships.

Integration occurs at multiple levels — at the interfaces between client and vendor organizations, between units within the two organizations, between people in the two organizations, and between systems in the two organizations. All these interfaces must be managed.

Integration issues include getting started on the right foot, planning, scheduling, management structures, management control mechanisms, management skills, interpersonal relationships, communication with employees and with the vendor, and dispute resolution processes.

The contract sets out some procedures necessary for outsourcing management, but others may be necessary. These should be developed as part of the transition process.

All outsourcing involves people and management of people affected by a transition — those transferred to the vendor, those retained, and those terminated. Careful attention to communication and proper incentives are needed to successfully move key people to the vendor and to retain the people you want to retain.

Managing outsourcing is different than managing an in-house IT function and requires a different mix of skills. The team members put in charge of an outsourcing arrangement need negotiation, technical, financial, operational, and contract management skills specific to managing a vendor. Put good people in charge, and be sure they have the necessary skills.

Good conflict resolution processes clarify interests rather than positions, sustain a good working relationship between client and vendor, invent win-win ways to resolve differences, foster good communication, lead to good solutions, and are seen as fair by both sides. While the contract provides the basis for dispute resolution, day-to-day handling of disputes depends on outsourcing managers.

Critical Success Factors

If outsourcing involves multiple vendors, integration issues are much more challenging. Develop management structures and working relationships to ease this task and make it more effective.

Even if the vendor has more power in the outsourcing relationship than your organization, try to cultivate good personal relationships with higher level managers in the vendor organization so your outsourcing needs get more attention.

The skill set necessary to manage an outsourcing relationship differs somewhat from the skill set of a good manager in managing an internal IT function. Outsourcing managers may have to acquire contract and vendor management skills.

Designate one point of contact through which all official communication with the vendor takes place so that issues and issue resolution with the vendor can be controlled and documented. In large outsourcing deals, multiple points of contact may be required. These might be organized by outsourced function.

If possible, co-locate the outsourcing managers from your organization and the vendor's organization so communication is enhanced. Frequent face-to-face communication is the most effective.

The success of outsourcing can be seriously jeopardized by poor management of the people involved.

Client and vendor outsourcing managers should discuss and attempt to reconcile differences in their approaches to conflict management as part of the transition process. This helps to develop a unified and cooperative approach to resolving disputes.

The way initial problems are handled sets vendor expectations. Insist the vendor meet contract requirements from the outset.

1.3.8 Management of the Ongoing Outsourcing Relationship (Chapter 9)

The relationship with an outsourcing vendor requires discipline on the one hand and flexibility and cooperation on the other. Discipline is paramount in market outsourcing relationships and flexibility is much more important in partnerships. Monitoring and control is the classic method for enforcing discipline.

In addition to monitoring and control of the vendor, outsourcing managers should monitor and control other stakeholders in outsourcing — the users of information services, senior managers in the client organization, and the IT personnel who remain in the client organization.

Contract requirements are the starting point for monitoring the vendor. Client outsourcing management has responsibility for developing the procedures and methods to undertake this task.

Contract requirements for vendor performance are also the basis for control. However, contracts may be incomplete. Cooperation on the part of the vendor is necessary for effective control, particularly in intermediate and partnership outsourcing relationships.

Vendor cooperation is gained in positive ways through the vendor's sharing of your goals and in negative ways through sanctions and law suits to force vendor performance of contract terms. Positive motivation is preferable to negative motivation and can be fostered by giving a vendor an understanding of its services in the context of your business objectives, offering incentives, establishing good personal relationships with vendor managers, reminding the vendor of its need to uphold its reputation for good service, and rewarding good performance with promises of future work.

Outsourcing rarely goes forward without disputes of some kind. Good conflict resolution methods stress getting away from emotions and posturing and getting down to the real issues, looking for win-win ways to resolve differences, and using objective criteria that both sides respect.

Manage systems development work undertaken by an outsourcing vendor as you would well-managed systems development work in your own organization. Conduct reviews with appropriate persons in attendance. Follow up on problems. Exercise effective change control.

Critical Success Factors

The risks identified during the analysis phase of outsourcing evaluation must be managed throughout the life of the arrangement. Preventive measures and monitoring to detect problems arising from risk factors should be ongoing.

Monitoring and control have benefits and costs. Outsourcing managers need to balance the costs and benefits of monitoring and control to achieve cost-effectiveness in these activities.

Attempt to resolve disputes at lower levels and avoid contractual dispute escalation procedures, if possible.

Cinda Hallman of DuPont says of dispute resolution, "We resolve every issue at the lowest possible level. We will be disappointed if any dispute must be resolved higher than the CIO level and terribly disappointed if we find it necessary to go back to the negotiation table to resolve issues."

Watch for patterns in dispute resolution over time. Try to encourage the positive patterns and curb the negative patterns.

Train outsourcing managers in dispute resolution methods.

Think twice about using a power advantage that you may enjoy over the vendor to resolve disputes in your favor. Habitual use of power erodes cooperation in outsourcing.

1.3.9 Partnerships (Chapter 10)

Only a small proportion of all outsourcing deals work effectively as partnerships. The costs of partnerships are high because of the considerable communication and integration that goes on between client and vendor. The risks are high because partnerships involve investments that can't be recovered if the partnership fails. Therefore, the benefits of partnerships must be high to outweigh the considerable costs and risks.

Benefits that sustain partnerships are usually those that arise from combining client and vendor resources and abilities in ways that are unique and generate some measure of competitive advantage.

Partnerships are based on the following:

- Reciprocal, mutually supportive actions so that both gain over time.
- Trust that the other partner will take positive actions and refrain from opportunistic actions.
- A long-term perspective and the willingness to give-and-take, resolving differences as they arise and sharing gains, risks, and losses.

- Reputation as the most significant sign of reliability with a reduced need for monitoring. The desire for continued participation in the gains of the partnership limits opportunism.
- Performance monitoring, more through a peer review process than explicit measures.
- Mutual consent instead of formal rules and procedures.
- A meshing of processes in the two organizations and a blurring of the line between them.

A single contract cannot be the basis for a partnership arrangement; partnerships must last for long periods of time and multiple contracts to achieve the benefits. Contracts don't play the same role in partnerships as they do in intermediate and market relationships. A contract serves a useful function as a commitment to short run investments and behavior that support the partnership and as a safety net through its provisions for transitions and distribution of assets should the partnership fail.

To succeed, partnerships need long-term goals that involve sharing of mutual gains. But the long run is made up of a series of short runs. What builds and sustains partnerships in the short run is the sharing of knowledge across organizational boundaries, mutual dependence on distinctive competencies that each partner possesses, and linkages between the two organizations at the level of information, processes, and people.

Partnerships can't be successful without a joint vision on the part of client and vendor firms, complementary strengths, ways of effectively combining those strengths, and ways of building and sustaining trust.

Building a partnership takes time because mutually supportive behavior and trust are foundations that can't be erected immediately. However, if conditions are right the elapsed time can be less depending on how actively senior managers in both firms pursue partnership.

Five processes act to build, deepen, and sustain partnerships over time. (a) Attraction is the direct reward available from a partnership with the other party. (b) Communication is the open revelation of needs, the honest declaration of intentions, and the honest revelation of strengths and weaknesses. (c) Bargaining that goes forward with comparative ease and fairness is another factor. (d) Use of power differences in ways that are mutually beneficial is also a requisite. (e) The development of norms, or shared standards of behavior, foster acceptable behavior and help limit partnership-threatening behavior. All five factors work together to build, deepen, and sustain partnership arrangements.

Senior managers in client and vendor organizations set partnerships in motion by developing a joint vision and guiding the process. The vision of partnership may not be complete at the outset and may evolve over time. The partnership concept must be sold in both organizations. Buy-in has to occur to advance the necessary information and knowledge sharing and to undertake closely interrelated activities of the two organizations.

Monitoring and control activities are much more cooperative and decentralized and much less structured and disciplined than they are in market and intermediate outsourcing relationships. However, measurable short-term goals and indicators of success are important for demonstrating the mutual benefits of partnership, getting buy-in, and keeping the partnership on track.

The high level of integration required in partnerships requires considerable effort to achieve. Education, careful design of communication mechanisms, joint planning teams, co-location of personnel and rotation of personnel between the two organizations, and substantial top management commitment are ways to promote integration.

The greatest threats to successful partnerships are changes in the business environment that erode the gains from partnering activity. Long-run partnership goals can sometimes be worked around to accommodate environmental change, and sometimes not.

Critical Success Factors

Never partner with a vendor simply because the vendor suggests it is advantageous to do so. Analyze the benefits, costs, and risks carefully.

Don't rush into partnerships. Groundwork that builds mutual trust is necessary first.

Dispute resolution must be very effective in partnerships. Escalation should rarely occur. Prevention is a key.

While contracts are not the primary foundation for a partnership, do not neglect to write contracts with good termination provisions.

1.3.10 Contract Expiration and Termination (Chapter 11)

Outsourcing relationships can expire in a normal way at the end of the contracting period, or they can terminate prematurely.

In normal expiration, renewal of the contract may be your objective or you may want to outsource the same work to another vendor. In either case, review the experience of the current outsourcing relationship for desirable changes to incorporate in the next contract.

When the work is to be transferred to another vendor or brought back inside your organization, you need a plan for the transition of the outsourced function to a new organizational home. The planning should begin in the analysis phase of the current contract when requirements for transfer are identified. Elements of the plan should be incorporated in the contract so that the vendor provides the resources and help necessary to make a smooth transition.

Unless the contract is written to allow termination at will, termination can entail very steep costs, not only in termination charges and legal fees, but in the threat to continuity of information services if a vendor fights the termination and does not cooperate. Consider the costs, benefits, and risks of termination carefully before proceeding.

If the contract is an unbearable burden but the costs of termination are high, consider renegotiation of the contract with the vendor. Vendors may be open to this possibility if their own costs of termination are high or if they want to retain your business.

Critical Success Factors

In intermediate relationships, your current vendor has an advantage over other vendors in getting your outsourcing work at the time of contract renewal. This results from the vendor's knowledge of your organization, your work, and your ways of doing things. However, foster competition with other vendors if you can.

In market relationships, there is little or no reliance on the last vendor that did the work. Competition between vendors should definitely be encouraged as a new contract is let.

Moving an outsourced function back inside your organization is much more easily done if you retain a small IT management cadre.

When to tell a vendor you intend to terminate a contract depends on how much the vendor wants your business. A vendor keen to keep your business may improve service in the hopes of keeping you. A vendor who is less dependent may give you short shrift after termination is announced. Tell all in the former, and keep it a secret as long as possible in the latter case.

Don't use a threat of termination simply as a way to get better vendor performance. The vendor may call your bluff.

Beware of end-games in outsourcing relationships. When the vendor knows the relationship will end without renewal of the contract, it may be tempted to cut corners and otherwise take advantage of the end-of-contract situation.

1.4 SUMMARY

Cinda Hallman of DuPont gives her views on the sources of outsourcing success: "(a) Do not outsource any function that you do not fully understand. In fact, make it the strongest and best managed that you can, then turn to best-of-class service providers to make it even better. (b) Know your business. Do not rush into outsourcing just because others are doing it. Every company is different with different needs. (c) Evaluate, negotiate, and manage the relationship with strong teams of highly competent people. (d) Get top outside experts to advise and assist you throughout the outsourcing process. (e) Keep your management and employees involved continuously along the way."

Jill Klein, formerly of Riggs Bank and now with AETEA Information Technology adds: "(a) Keep your eye on the business value of the decision. Decide to outsource or not to outsource based on the business case and not concerns for protecting your turf. (b) Keep your people informed all along the way. Treat your people fairly. (c) Maintain vendor competition. (d) Negotiate a sound win-win contract. (e) Put in place an effective process and structure to manage the relationship. (f) Measure vendor performance. (g) Encourage continuous improvement of vendor performance and of the relationship. In my view, the continued success of this relationship is a result of well-meaning management on both sides."

2

Trends Favoring Outsourcing

Outsourcing is now seen as a valuable option by managers. The forces that brought outsourcing issues to the center of management attention are likely to continue. The outsourcing of information systems services is and will be an important method of meeting information systems needs into the foreseeable future. This chapter puts outsourcing in a broader historical context and explains why it will continue to be important. It concludes with several interviews of experts close to the trends in information systems outsourcing. Ellen Kitzis of Dataquest and William P. Martorelli of Giga Information Group address the broad trends in IT outsourcing and Pete Mounts of HBOC's Outsourcing Services Group gives an industry perspective for healthcare.

The wisdom of a decision depends on the circumstances. There are appropriate and inappropriate outsourcing decisions, and there are good and bad outsourcing arrangements with vendors. Subsequent chapters erect a framework for making good, sound management decisions at every step along the outsourcing road. The downside, as well as the upside, of outsourcing is discussed, and tools and methods are provided for making appropriate decisions and minimizing the downside.

2.1 SOME HISTORY

Information systems outsourcing has been around for a long time. In the age when mainframes ruled the earth, the services of these expensive machines were available through time-sharing. Hiring contract programmers is a thirty-year-old phenomenon. The list goes on:

- Service bureaus, like Automated Data Processing, have been in the payroll business for decades, and have expanded more recently into accounting. Facilities management has been available for data centers for decades.
- Ross Perot's Electronic Data Processing and the Big Six Accounting Firms entered the systems planning, design, and turnkey software businesses more than 25 years ago.
- Network sharing is also decades old.

From the birth of business data processing, companies have looked to entities with specialized talents and abilities to handle the computer-based information systems function, or some of its subparts.

While outsourcing is not new, it has taken on an increased importance in the thinking of managers who have been influenced by underlying changes in the business environment.

2.1.1 Global Competition

In many ways the 1980s represented a period of pivotal change in the way U.S. managers think, and much of this was occasioned by changes in competitive realities.

The United States rose to superpower status during and after World War II. Its manufacturing prowess was built through mass production of standard goods. Low-cost production was achieved with long production runs of standardized products and integration. Integration ran backward to sources of inputs and raw materials and forward into distribution, marketing, and service.

The bulk of U.S. manufacturing output was consumed in internal markets. Foreign markets did not drive major design, manufacturing, and marketing decisions.

Managerial mindsets shaped by World War II and its aftermath got a good shaking with the steep rise in global competition of the 1970s and 1980s. Firms from countries that previously were no threat entered the U.S. market with higher quality products, a greater variety of products more closely attuned to the tastes of more affluent and more discriminating consumers, and with less expensive products based on more efficient foreign technology and cheaper labor. Shoe and apparel manufacturing went abroad, Japanese autos ran U.S. vehicles off the road, the U.S. steel industry was in tatters. Some pundits were forecasting the demise of manufacturing in this country and the rise to dominance of service industries.

As this book is being written, U.S. manufacturing is in a revival. U.S. automobiles are successfully competing against the Japanese. What is left of the steel industry is hanging on. It looks like the United States will remain a manufacturing nation after all.

What turned the tide were major changes in management thinking that resulted in completely new ways of doing business from one end of the value chain to the other. U.S. managers learned quality; they learned product diversity; they learned to design for manufacture; they learned flexible manufacturing; they learned just-in-time supply; they learned outsourcing.

With the help of exhortations from Tom Peters and others, U.S. managers learned that change will always be with us and we must constantly innovate to survive. Peter Drucker speaks of the "New Society of Organizations" where, in a world in which knowledge is a factor of production along with land, labor, and capital, "every organization has to build the management of change into its very structure" (Drucker, 1992). The insularity and stability of the immediate Post War II period will not return.

2.1.2 Bigger Is Not Necessarily Better, Neither Is Smaller

Large size is no longer a necessary advantage to an industrial firm, neither is small size. Economies of scale no longer confer advantage for the production of many products; quality, flexibility, agility, and the ability to meet diverse consumer demands count for more. As Drucker puts it, "Whatever advantages bigness by itself used to confer on a business have largely been canceled by the universal availability of management and information," and, "whatever advantages smallness by itself conferred have largely been offset by the need to think, if not to act, globally" (Drucker, 1989).

2.1.3 Some Decentralization Is Better than
a Lot of Centralization

The General Motors and DuPonts of the 1920s and 1930s were classical highly integrated firms that encompassed everything from production of many raw materials through the production process, sales, delivery, and after sales service. Business success in the classical model was measured, in part, on the extent to which a company was vertically integrated. Whether to function as a highly integrated organization or whether to design a much smaller organization more reliant on suppliers, is a function of a firm's technology, its strategy, and its markets. Global competition now demands rapid response and flexibility — virtues that large, integrated firms find hard to cultivate.

The prophets of change decry hierarchically structured organizations with many levels of management. They urge less centralized, more flexible, more responsive organizations structured around teams of knowledge workers each bringing specialized talents to the integrated design, engineering, production, marketing, and delivery of a product. The task should be the focus of organizational structure, not the division of the organization by function (Drucker, 1991).

Stuckey lays a portion of the blame for the many-layered organization at the feet of centralized information systems technology (Stuckey, 1993). The role of the mainframe in the post-war corporation was as a central repository of information. Computer-based information systems enabled managers to centralize authority and manage large organizations with decision making concentrated at the top.

A high degree of centralization is now taken as an indicator of a dysfunctional organization. Stuckey argues for "demassification" or the pushing down of decision making into many less central "pockets" of power, closer to the customer and closer to the internal workings of the organization. Desktop computers linked through networks to each other and to corporate databases are now a very effective enabler of a more decentralized structure.

2.2 OUTSOURCING, ALLIANCES, AND REENGINEERING

Walter Powell (1990) sees outsourcing, alliances, and reengineering as responses to the liabilities of vertical integration and large scale in the current business environment. Large, vertically integrated firms are unable to respond rapidly to competitive changes; their bureaucracies resist innovation and new products. Hierarchy also reduces motivation. The desire to advance up the promotion job ladder systematically leads those on lower rungs to avoid criticism of those above them. Initiative is stifled, and employee morale and motivation takes a hit.

Large organizations work well for very repetitive and predictable tasks. But repetition leads to formalization with rules and documentation that create information barriers and slow-downs that are dysfunctional when the need changes to quick information flow. Large organizations are ponderous in response to customer needs when change sweeps the business environment (Powell, 1990).

With greatly increased competition and a rapidly changing business environment, size becomes a liability. Firms respond by outsourcing, forming strategic alliances, and downsizing work units (Powell, 1990).

- When firms see the need for cost cutting and greater management control over allocation of resources, outsourcing is a rational response.

- When companies require world class skills and world class innovation, they may turn to alliances and collaborative relationships with other firms that have the requisite talent.

- When internal tasks are too slow and unresponsive, firms turn to reengineering, which entails rethinking and radically reorganizing business processes, often with reduction in the number of layers of management and substitution of information technology for labor.

Heightened competition, then, pushes firms to outsource the tasks that are standardized, search for alliances in tasks that involve high skill and innovation, and redesign internal processes to obtain flexibility, innovation, and faster response time.

2.3 KEEP THE BEST, MAKE IT BETTER, AND OUTSOURCE THE REST

Managers have seized outsourcing as a way of streamlining the organization. Contemporary thinking on outsourcing is summed up in several *Harvard Business Review* and *Sloan Management Review* articles.

James Brian Quinn, Thomas L. Doorley, and Penny C. Paquette (1990a) ask readers to think of a corporation as a collection of services that provide value. Even in manufacturing firms, most workers are in service type functions like research, logistics, maintenance, design, accounting, law, and the like. Services, they point out, account for about 75 percent of all costs in most U.S. industries. To think in terms of services is to concentrate on the activities that create most of the value. Value is added in style, image, durability, after-sales maintenance, and the like, as much as in the actual fabrication of a product. Porter's (1985) value chain provides a framework for organizing thinking about the services to perform in each value chain activity.

Quinn, Doorley, and Paquette argue that technological change in services offers strategic opportunities. Service companies have evolved that employ the most advanced technologies and industry standard practices. These suppliers offer their services at lower cost and with quality that is often superior to the same services generated inside the firm.

Theirs is more than a simple outsourcing strategy, however. The leverage comes in analyzing all the services that comprise the company, discovering which actually give or could give the firm its edge over competitors, concentrating on doing a world class job in delivering these strategic services internally and acting to "eliminate, limit, or outsource" the rest. Instead of analyzing market share, Quinn, Doorley, and Paquette urge managers to analyze the strength of the service components of their business relative to its competitors.

The indirect benefits of outsourcing may be the most important. By outsourcing nonstrategic activities, organizations can devote more time and attention to the core activities that give them competitive advantage. Outsourcing can reduce the size of the organization and make it less hierarchical, allowing focus on obtaining, developing, and motivating the people who create value. It can also allow a shift in management attention toward strategy, coordination, and the skills that promote competitive success (Quinn, Doorley, and Paquette, 1990b).

George Stalk, Philip Evans, and Lawrence E. Shulman (1992) use Walmart's logistics system as a capability that sets Walmart apart from a competitor like Kmart and gives strategic advantage. Unique capabilities confer competitive advantage. Capabilities are cross functional and almost always involve more than one activity in the value chain. Walmart's system uses a combination of point-of-sale data to illuminate trends in customer preferences, savvy buyers, just-in-time suppliers, super efficient warehouse facilities, and its own fleet of trucks to implement its strategy of everyday low prices and dependable availability of the products customers want.

The Stalk, Evans, and Shulman capabilities concept is synonymous with "business processes." The trick is to identify key processes and transform them into a competitive advantage through strategic investments in the underlying infrastructure that is both human and technological. It follows that non strategic processes, or components of processes, can be outsourced to the best vendor available.

These views of competitive advantage represent a shift in management thinking and open the door to what *Business Week Magazine*, in a cover story article, called "The Virtual Corporation." The virtual corporation produces world class products and delivers world class services by organizing suppliers and vendors to do many of the activities in the value chain or many of its business processes. The virtual corporation performs the services and processes that give it the edge and outsources the rest to a host of vendors.

2.4 WHY VENDORS HAVE AN ADVANTAGE

The critics of outsourcing often rest their arguments on assumptions that internal functions should be able to do what vendors do if they only applied good management practices and worked smart. Sometimes this is true, but in other instances it is not. Consider the ways in which vendors could hold an edge:

2.4.1 Scale

- Multiple clients allow a vendor to operate at a scale unattainable by any single organization.
- A large vendor can buy and fully utilize large, powerful, and more efficient equipment than clients who operate at smaller scale.
- A large-scale vendor has considerable advantage in negotiating price and service with providers of equipment and software.
- Large-scale vendors can maintain a bench of technical experts with greater range and depth than any of their clients because the vendor can utilize the expertise efficiently and effectively when spread over multiple clients on a flexible, as needed basis.
- Large-scale vendor management can specialize, focus, and gain repeated experience with management of tasks that would only come around once in the careers of many IT managers. Vendor management may be more skilled and experienced, as a result.

2.4.2 Experience

Because of the variety of clients and circumstances vendors encounter, vendors have a depth and range of experience that individual clients can't match. Vendors can go through multiple restructurings and conversions that could only happen once in the experience of your own in-house personnel. Just as the best surgeons tend to be those who do many operations of the same type, day-in and day-out, so too vendors who do the same difficult tasks repeatedly gain an advantage over those who do them infrequently or only once.

2.4.3 Specialization

The ability to specialize in skills also extends to experience with new technologies. Your people will only encounter conversion to a new operating system or a client-server architecture once, but through experiences with multiple clients, vendor personnel can have this experience numerous times and gain a real advantage in knowledge, speed, and efficiency.

Being on the cutting edge in technology and methods is a big attraction to hiring and retaining the most talented people. Vendors can often offer these experiences on a more consistent basis to its personnel than can the typical IT department. For this reason, vendors often have very good people with the latest experience, something difficult to reproduce in other organizations.

Vendors may also squeeze fringe benefits to employees, rely on temporary labor when advantageous, locate major facilities in lower wage areas of the country or the world, implement tough standards on employees to keep and employees to let go, exercise tight control over inventories, use leaner management, and hustle more. These tactics may be available to other firms, but some vendors may be better positioned to carry them out. (McFarlan and Nolan, 1995)

2.5 TRENDS THAT FAVOR OUTSOURCING

Clark, Zmud, and McCray (1995) identify factors in information systems technological change, technology management, and business change that favor outsourcing.

First, technological change expands options and enables outsourcing in the sense that:

- Many information products and services have become commodities as computer technology and its use matures. "A product or service can be considered a commodity when a common functionality exists across customers and/or clients, particularly firms within a specific industry, and when reliable, high-quality performance levels are widely available at competitive prices." The commoditization of information technology and systems has fostered economies of scale in their delivery and clear identification of their status as non strategic or utilities. Vendors who compete on both price and quality of service can often reach the scale necessary for minimum cost, and the non strategic status of many information systems functions allows them to be outsourced.

- Technology change also allows the separation of the management, operation, and delivery of information services that expands the choices available for outsourcing and reduces the risks of outsourcing.

Second, technological change enhances demand for outsourcing:

- The incredible increase in the performance-to-price ratio of information technology in the last 50 years has led to widespread and innovative use of information technology in all aspects of businesses. However, the same rapid technological change quickly makes older hardware and software obsolete. Organizations are, therefore, on a constant treadmill with an abundance of equipment and staff skills that are always becoming obsolete and a shortage of critical cutting edge skills and hardware.

Outsourcing provides an avenue for reducing the human and equipment resources that don't fit the strategic direction and for meeting the latest needs with up-to-date resources.

Third, changes in the management of information technology also foster outsourcing:

- Information systems budgets have grown along with the growth in the use of computer equipment and automated systems. It is often difficult to measure the benefit and justify the use of information technology. Senior managers are attracted to outsourcing as a way of making costs predictable and assuring that the organization is paying the "market price" for information systems services.
- Chief information officers often have business backgrounds as strong or stronger than their technology backgrounds. They are taking a business view, rather than a technology view, of outsourcing alternatives.
- Information systems control has been decentralized and dispersed in many organizations. What remains of the old corporate or centralized IT function often has excess capacity and resources that makes some of its functions possible targets for outsourcing.

Fourth, industry-level changes may also promote outsourcing:

- Rapid technological change often creates over capacity in certain functions in information intensive industries that leads to opportunities for outsourcing, resulting consolidation, and economics of scale. Clark, Zmud, and McCray give the example of routine data processing functions in banking that have been widely outsourced to third parties (sometimes other banks) as a way of achieving lower costs.
- The number and quality of outsourcing vendors offering price competitive and high-quality services has increased. Barriers to entry are low, and technological change creates discontinuities in needs that vendors can exploit. As new vendors enter the marketplace, competition increases and further reduces the price and increases the quality of service.
- Vendors are experiencing rapid growth in the demand for their services and can afford to snap up, reward, and promote some of the best technical talent in the industry, further enhancing their potential and the attractiveness of outsourcing.

Finally, firm level forces favor outsourcing in some instances:

- The corporate imperative to run "lean and mean" and cut costs has favored outsourcing for the reasons already mentioned above.
- Globalization of business in combination with technological change creates new needs for capabilities to address problems related to distance, size, and rapid change. The new needs may be better met through reliance on vendors with these capabilities.

These factors work in interrelated and reinforcing ways to account for the phenomenal increase in information systems outsourcing over the last decade. It is clear that technological change will continue unabated into the foreseeable future, and many of the organization and institutional factors that favor outsourcing are not likely to diminish.

The upswing in outsourcing coincides with a period in which evolving information technology is stretching the abilities and resources of IT departments. IT must struggle to cope with the ongoing operation of legacy systems while at the same time implementing new architectures. The new architectures support the move to flexibility in a global marketplace and involve networks that integrate computers internal to the company and connect the company's computers with computer systems of customers and suppliers. Outsourcing provides a means of sharing the combined burden of the past and the future (McFarlan and Nolan, 1995).

2.6 KODAK EFFECT

Loh and Venkatraman (1992) view outsourcing from a diffusion of innovations perspective, where the innovation was the highly publicized outsourcing by the Kodak Corporation of its four data centers to IBM in 1989. Outsourcing had been increasing throughout the 1970s and 1980s, but it accelerated after the Kodak deal. Kodak's initiative made a real difference in the way the information systems community viewed outsourcing major IT functions; it gave outsourcing legitimacy.

Some have criticized the Kodak effect as a "bandwagon." They condemn the IT managers following Kodak's lead as something akin to lemmings and traitors to the cause of IT management. And they warn that such behavior is dangerous to individual careers and to whole organizations.

Indeed, some outsourcing has been done for the wrong reasons and without proper thinking and safeguards. Shortly after Kodak, Lacity and Hirschheim (1993) did case studies of a number of total outsourcing deals in which a large part or the whole of the information systems function was outsourced. They found a significant portion of these deals to be politically motivated, preceded by inadequate study, and resting on questionable contracts.

Despite the problems, outsourcing surged ahead. In a real sense the market has spoken — outsourcing has a contribution to make, and many organizations have embraced it for that reason. "Outsourcing is no longer a taboo topic among senior managers, including IT professionals. The question is not whether to outsource but what to outsource, as companies redirect valuable internal skills and capabilities to high value-added areas." (Vankatraman, 1997).

2.7 EXAMPLE OF CONTINENTAL BANK

Huber (1993) provides insight into management thinking underlying the outsourcing of information services at Continental Bank, the first money center bank to do so. Information systems are usually seen as a core function in delivering services to banking clients, and, for this reason, might seem to be a last candidate for outsourcing. Continental Bank decided otherwise.

In the early 1990's, Continental was rethinking its competitive strategy against the backdrop of falling profitability. The top management team identified two broad areas of the bank's activities that generated profits and were essential to the bank's long-run competitive position: its core clients of businesses (many of which were privately held) and wealthy individuals and Continental's overseas investments. All other activities became candidates for outsourcing.

Continental outsourced activities in which it had no special expertise, such as legal services, food, security, and property management. Eventually information systems was added to this list. The bank's existing mainframe-based information systems infrastructure couldn't respond rapidly and flexibly to clients' changing needs. A host of desktop systems had grown up in an attempt to get around the limitations of the mainframes, but these were poorly integrated. The bank's information systems staff represented an inflexible asset, too small to effectively mount large development projects and too large to efficiently handle day-to-day operations and maintenance. The investment needed to straighten out its information systems problems was huge, and Continental management wasn't certain that the IT staff could succeed.

Continental saw its core competencies as keen insight into customer needs and excellent relationships with customers. It needed information technology to maintain both, but its competitive advantage was maintained by access to the best technology at an acceptable price, not ownership of the technology. In fact, its ownership of the technology had become an impediment.

Continental outsourced much of its information systems function. It developed a contract in which the fees it pays to the outsourcing vendor vary with the quantity of services provided. Continental expected to pay more for outside services during periods of high demand than it would if services were provided in-house. But the periods of high demand are expected to generate business that continues to produce revenues over periods of slow demand. Overall revenues are expected to increase and costs for information services to decline, making the deal profitable in the long run. Outsourcing also enabled Continental to rework information systems delivery making it more flexible and responsive to customer needs.

2.8 IS OUTSOURCING A FAD OR A FACT OF LIFE?

What of the future? Is outsourcing a bandwagon destined to roll to a stop? Or, will outsourcing continue to grow?

Management ideas seem to run in cycles and show some of the characteristics of fads. Outsourcing has been a very popular idea for some years, but the counter reaction is also evident. *Business Week* asks, "Has Outsourcing Gone Too Far?" (Byrne, 1996), and articles appear in business journals that stress "The Risks of Outsourcing IT" (Earl, 1996). Certainly there are outsourcing deals that make little or no sense, and the business and academic press will continue to offer reassessments (Lacity and Hirschheim, 1995).

There is currently a debate on outsourcing. In a series of recent strikes, unions have made outsourcing and job preservation a central issue. Jobs and preservation of jobs is an increasing political concern. Frederick F. Reichheld and Thomas Teal (1996) in their book, *The Loyalty Effect*, emphasize the positive aspects of the sustained loyalty of employees who are long-term employees of organizations. On the other hand, books on the future of jobs, like William Bridges' (1995) *Job Shift: How to Prosper in a Workplace Without Jobs*, contend that most workers will be independent contractors or work for outsourcing firms and providers of temporaries in the Twenty-First-Century. Jobs are an emotional issue, and so is outsourcing at some levels.

Public and managerial perceptions will also be shaped by performance in outsourcing contracts. But the media feeds at the trough of bad news. Very public and catastrophic outsourcing failures could lead to greater caution, and, perhaps, to some periods of time in which outsourcing is viewed less favorably.

How all this plays out in the future is not certain. It is quite possible that the pendulum will swing from time to time with some periods of go slow and caution on outsourcing. But the trend is probably toward more outsourcing over the long run for these reasons:

- Competition will not lessen; the nations of Southeast Asia and Latin America are providing the next challenge; cost pressures will not abate.
- Clients and vendors will find new ways to utilize and conduct outsourcing arrangements. See, for example, the interviews of outsourcing experts at the end of this chapter and their views on the trend toward using outsourcing to deliver business value, rather than simple utility-like IT services.
- Vendors of outsourcing services will get better and more numerous; their products and services will benefit from experience, improved management, and better technology. Even companies that are traditionally hardware-oriented are getting into services, and outsourcing services among them, because services offer potential growth and margins that aren't available in many product lines (Deutsch, 1997).
- Vendor alliances will become more common, combining the specializations and particular strengths of two or more vendors who offer their services as a package. Alliances present clients best-of-breed outsourcing services and a greater range of options with a better fit to their outsourcing needs. The interviews of experts at the end of this chapter expands on this theme.
- The performance-price ratio of information technology will continue its upward spiral for some decades to come, allowing vendors the opportunity to exploit economies of scale and provide outsourcing deals that lower costs for their clients.
- Managers will become more adept at managing client-vendor relationships, making repeat contracting for products and services more efficient.
- Trends in information technology are lowering the cost of coordination between firms that favor a shift toward obtaining products and services in the market place (outsourcing) over hierarchies (internal production) (Malone, Yates, and Benjamin, 1987).
- Many aspects of information systems services will continue to have a commodity like nature, unrelated to a company's competitive strategy, which make them good candidates for outsourcing.
- Partnerships and alliances, as Peter Drucker (1995) says, may be major vehicles for business growth in the future, where partnerships pair two or more businesses with complementary strengths to undertake ventures that neither could undertake independently. McFarlan and Nolan (1995)

see the willingness to undertake client-vendor partnerships and alliances as one of the prime movers for outsourcing information systems functions in the future.

- Virtual organizations will be more commonplace in the future (Grenier and Metes, 1995). Companies will outsource most of the functioning of the organization in the process of going virtual.

2.9 TRENDS IN OUTSOURCING: AN INTERVIEW WITH ELLEN KITZIS

Ellen S. Kitzis, PhD, is vice president and Lead Analyst of Dataquest's Worldwide IT Services Group. Dataquest, a Gartner Group Company, is the leading supplier of market research and consulting services to the IT industry. As the lead analyst, Dr. Kitzis is charged with identifying new opportunities in the services industry and helping clients build competitive value, revenue growth, and market differentiation. She regularly serves as an industry spokesperson on topics ranging from outsourcing, services marketing, and brand management, to quality principles and practices, and global IT services trends.

What are the major changes that have occurred in outsourcing over the last decade?
As information technology permeates customers' enterprises, the services industry has shifted from supporting products to supporting customers' business objectives — from maintaining systems availability to building enterprisewide, robust information architectures. Not surprisingly, outsourcing today is dramatically different than the origins of outsourcing, exemplified by facilities management and "glass house" outsourcing contracts.

Outsourcing has become one of the key service delivery models for helping customers manage the new information backbone. To meet this demand service providers have increased the components of the infrastructure that customers want to rely on outside providers to support. Hence outsourcers who previously only supported data centers are now providing comprehensive outsourcing solutions that address the distributed systems environment including data centers, networks, desktops, and more recently applications. This shift has allowed for the entrance of new players who have strong infrastructure management skills, as well as those who can support network enabled applications, business solutions, end users, as well as network backbones.

What are the future trends for outsourcing based on your research?
Dataquest is observing a significant shift from traditional IT outsourcing to
business process outsourcing (BPO). BPO holds the potential to become the
ultimate form of outsourcing. The key differentiator between traditional outsourcing and business process outsourcing is the management by the service
provider of the business process with the specific objective of improving business results. This is not an opportunity for all traditional outsourcers. To succeed
in this new outsourcing arena, service providers will be required to help customers reengineer their business processes and offer best practice methodologies for managing key business functions such as logistics, human resources,
internal audit functions, and customer care.

**What are some of the new opportunities in outsourcing that you are
recommending to your clients for competitive value, revenue growth,
and market differentiation?**
Dataquest believes that the outsourcing market continues to hold ample opportunity for existing players and new entrants. Outsourcing, like other services,
however is becoming increasingly a commodity-based service. To avoid the trap
of commodity-based margins, services providers will need to target opportunities that optimize the full range of their service capabilities and are more difficult for competitors to imitate. These opportunities will typically combine
outsourcing with consulting as well as application development and integration
capabilities. More importantly, competitive differentiation will require outsourcers to focus on specific business functions and offer customers a share of
the cost savings and ultimately future business opportunities.

Dataquest is also recommending that outsourcers become more strategic in
the customers they target and the solutions they offer. In practice, this means
understanding what characterizes the best customer for your company, the industries or business processes where you can offer a better solution, and the alliances
or partnerships that will help improve the total value customers can receive.

**What are the opportunities you see in the emerging markets
of Europe and Asia?**
Corporations in Europe, Asia, and Latin America like their North American
brethren also view outsourcing as a strategy for improving the management of
the IT function and allow them to focus on their own core competencies.
Global companies are often the first adopters in these markets, followed by
indigenous companies who want to expand rapidly or become global. Our
research shows that in terms of pure dollars the market is far larger today in

Europe than in Asia or Latin America, but the growth rates in these smaller markets have already overtaken the United States.

Not surprisingly, these emerging markets have become the target for global outsourcing companies, particularly the consultancies, independents, and systems vendors who already have well-established global service delivery capabilities. Scale, however, is not the only criteria for success. In order to achieve local acceptance, global players are partnering with smaller indigenous outsourcing companies that have an appreciation of cultural issues and existing relationships with potential customers.

What do you see as the future of strategic partnering among service providers?
It has become apparent from Dataquest's research that outsourcing vendors realize that they cannot possibly deliver the full range of services customers require alone. In order to meet the increasing expectations of customers for "best of breed" solutions, outsourcers are recognizing the need to align themselves in strategic relationships with other outsourcing providers. We see numerous examples of these relationships in recent outsourcing deals. Firms with strong business process and consulting skills are partnering with companies that have deep operations management capabilities. Providers with network management and desktop skills are partnering with companies that have helpdesk and call center management operations.

In addition to partnerships that focus on service delivery, we have also seen new models emerge. These newer models tend to take two forms. Co-marketing models whereby the companies go to market with side-by-side company logos and statements of combined value. The "two is better than one" approach to creating customer value. The second are co-development alliances. These relationships tend to go far deeper than the co-marketing relationships and are characterized by the integration of skills, resources, and proprietary methodologies. These alliances create new service offers and often result in the formation of a new company or merger.

2.10 TRENDS IN OUTSOURCING: AN INTERVIEW WITH WILLIAM MARTORELLI

William P. Martorelli is vice president of Giga Information Group, an industry research firm in Cambridge, Mass., responsible for worldwide research in the areas of outsourcing, systems integration, and IT management. Mr. Martorelli came to Giga from CSC Index's Research & Advisory Services unit. Previously he served as senior vice president, research, for New Science Associates.

What were the biggest trends in outsourcing during the last several years?
One of the biggest trends was the evolving nature of the deals at the industry's high end, which revealed a high degree of creativity and innovation, in some cases driven in large part by IT executives. Deals such as the J.P. Morgan award, the DuPont deal, Textron's network outsourcing award, indicate that leading IT organizations are succeeding in structuring outsourcing deals that seek to satisfy both overall corporate and IT goals.

However, these deals do not come without significant management challenges for both vendor and customer. Overall we see customers becoming much more selective and aggressive in sculpting their outsourcing solutions.

Other significant trends included the growth in desktop and network outsourcing, which have become significant portions of overall awards, as well as the basis for significant deals in their own. We've seen continued globalization, a broadened roster of players, and good prospects for significant deals in the coming years.

What industry growth are you predicting for the next few months?
We believe the IT outsourcing market itself will continue to expand, with growth accelerating primarily in the desktop, network, applications, and business process segments. However, the lines between the different segments are becoming less and less meaningful over time. More meaningful is the division between the high-end business process players and the IT commodity suppliers, which will take further shape in the coming years.

What are the most significant developments expected this year in the outsourcing industry?
We'll see continued jockeying for positions of greater strength on the customer value chain. This activity will include partnering, acquisition, and strategic alliances, all geared at achieving positions of higher potential value-add in the business enterprise, at correspondingly higher margins. This activity will be driven largely by ongoing margin pressures.

Margin pressures on commodity segments will intensify, particularly in the data center segment (driven in part by arrival of new players including defense-oriented suppliers) and desktop segment (driven by the increasing aggressiveness of players at the "low end" like Entex, Vanstar, and their competitors). Plus, customers are becoming more aggressive in seeking all potential cost reducing benefits and are increasingly likely to set up deals that are, in effect, ongoing competitive bidding exercises, which was true in both the DuPont (in part) and Citibank awards in 1996. The high cost of lengthening sales cycles (with some companies turning back at the end) also contributes to it. All of these factors will continue to heap the pressure on outsourcing suppliers, with the high-margin business process-oriented work being the most likely way out. Network outsourcing and managed network services will also solidify as service offerings.

What growth are you predicting for international outsourcing contracts?
We expect the international market to expand at a somewhat faster rate than the North American market, as outsourcing growth continues in Europe, Asia/Pacific/Australia, and other market segments.

Who will be the biggest players?
Today's leading firms, Andersen Consulting, AT&T Solutions, Computer Sciences Corp., EDS, and IBM Global Services will continue to achieve the preponderance of business, but the market as a whole is becoming more varied, and more complicated. You'll see continuing pressure from the low-end desktop suppliers and continuing evolution of the networking segment, with increasing activity. We're also looking for more business process experts to team with IT suppliers for business process outsourcing solutions. However, this reemergence of the IT "super service bureau" is still in its early phases. Andersen Consulting and the "Big Five" will also play increasingly in this space, usually in tandem with IT service suppliers on the back end.

What types of outsourcing activities do you expect?
We'll see a lot more deals where various levels of service delivery and different kinds of business value are intertwined. Some deals now combine motivations, including cost savings, capital redeployment, as well as tackling the Year 2000 crisis. Ultimately, outsourcing is becoming a way to position the enterprise for ongoing business and technical change.

What will be the biggest trends in the next few years?
We'll see more creative, multivaried deals in which different players will be enlisted for their core competencies and will work together in subcontracting relationships, as well as deals where different vendors are, in effect, forced to work with each other as peers, particularly at the high end of the market.

We also foresee a growing emphasis on business value creation through sourcing as cost savings becomes just one of many motivations for outsourcing. By business value creation we do not necessarily mean value pricing per se, but more emphasis on achieving customer satisfaction, expanding business options, and improving core business process competencies rather than improving IT processes only. We've already witnessed these tendencies, I believe, in some of the most significant deals of recent years. There will also be more blurring of the lines between IT outsourcing and business process outsourcing, which will be manifested in a variety of different deals.

Do you have any other important observations that you would like to share in regards to the outlook of outsourcing?

The growth in outsourcing has been quite significant, and this growth will continue. However, we notice an increasing sense of accountability as outsourcing becomes more of a legitimate business alternative and less of a phenomenon, less driven by dissatisfaction with IT and more by business needs. This transition is well along, but our research indicates that many customer satisfaction issues with outsourcing remain, particularly in some of the newer segments such as desktop. There is tremendous variability with regard to service provision, expectations management, and customer satisfaction. If outsourcing can be said to have "come of age," we'll need to see some improvement in these areas. Outsourcing suppliers, we believe, will increasingly be called to account for these discrepancies, even though not all of the issues are their fault, obviously. Inevitably, some large deals will go publicly awry. The drivers for outsourcing itself will remain in force. If anything, they will accelerate, but increasing customer sophistication will raise the bar for all suppliers.

2.11 OUTSOURCING IN THE HEALTHCARE INDUSTRY: AN INTERVIEW WITH PETE MOUNTS OF HBOC

Pete Mounts is vice president of HBOC's Outsourcing Services Group. His primary responsibility is the sales and marketing activities for healthcare IT outsourcing services throughout North America. Since joining HBOC in 1980, he has held a number of key positions and has witnessed the growth of the outsourcing business in the healthcare industry from its infancy.

How are the changes in the healthcare industry impacting IT and outsourcing?

Restructuring in healthcare has brought about some fundamental changes. Until a few years ago, the emphasis in healthcare was keeping patients in-house. Successful healthcare organizations were judged by number of beds rather than patient outcomes. The software technology to support those organizations reflected these measurements and processes and were mainly limited to charge-capture functions with minimal departmental functionality.

During the past few years, however, managed care has focused more attention on patient wellness and improving outcomes rather than increasing occupancy rates. The resulting competition has meant mergers and acquisitions among healthcare providers that have become integrated delivery networks (IDNs) comprising hospitals, clinics, physician practices, homecare agencies, at-risk affiliates, and more. To communicate patient information, these newly formed IDNs require technology that spans the healthcare continuum. With the emphasis now on improving patient outcomes, how patient information is accessed, processed, and used throughout the IDN or health enterprise is more critical.

Concurrent to the changes in healthcare, information technology has experienced its own changes. There's been a move to a PC-based, client/server environment. And, as the cost of technology overall has decreased, it has become available to more users. The cost of personal computers has decreased dramatically from thousands of dollars to only a few hundred dollars. So in healthcare, PCs can be found throughout the hospital in nurses' stations, on physicians' desks, and in the CEO's office. Consequently, the demands for IT software are greater, and the information to be extracted is more broad-based, coming from clinicians as well as administrative personnel.

All this gets back to the notion that IT department employees must be externally versus internally focused. They must understand and embody the customer service skills necessary to help users get over the hurdles of learning new software programs. They must also have the business acumen necessary to help users reengineer their daily processes to ensure they use information technology to its fullest capacity.

How has outsourcing in healthcare benefited from outsourcing in other industries?

Because outsourcing in healthcare has been slightly behind the trend of outsourcing in other industries, at least from an IT standpoint, it's benefited simply by learning from the missteps of other industries. For example, outsourcing IT in healthcare moved more quickly to performance-based contracts and incorporating "best practice" methodologies than other industries such as banking or insurance. Also, in healthcare, organizations are more quickly coming to regard IT outsourcing as an enabler to success rather than a necessary evil.

What are the major trends in outsourcing now and in the future?

Outsourcing tends to hit industries undergoing dramatic changes such as competitive pressures or other outside forces that affect supply and demand. The catalyst is that businesses in the affected industry usually are trying to do more with less. In healthcare, for example, the shift from fee-for-service to capitation and managed care has forced healthcare organizations to deliver high-quality healthcare with fewer resources — both from a people standpoint as well as capital funding. So they return to their core business — in this case, providing healthcare — while outsourcing support functions to vendors that specialize in those areas: food service, laundry, maintenance, and even strategic support services such as the information technology department.

Another trend is what the organization gets with outsourcing. By outsourcing the IT function, a healthcare organization wants to find a partner to share the risk of running that strategic department. It wants to capitalize on the outsourcing vendor's ability to institute business process reengineering so that it can improve work flow and become more efficient.

From the outsourcing vendor's perspective, a trend for the future is to partner with other outsourcing vendors for niche skill sets. Increasingly, one major vendor will take the lead in providing a range of outsourcing services and, in turn, outsource to others for specialty skills sets. HBOC has already done this successfully at one customer site. The contract calls for outsourcing support in the business office and in the medical records and IT departments. Our expertise lies in running the IT department so we have teamed with other specialty vendors to handle the other areas. HBOC has overall responsibility for the entire contract.

How has outsourcing changed during the course of your career?

During the past 10 years, the most significant changes have been a shift from headcount or FTE (full-time equivalent) based contracts to performance-based contracts, as well as the move from total IT department outsourcing to selective outsourcing. Also, specifically in healthcare IT outsourcing, there's been a dramatic departure from an internally focused department to an externally focused one.

In the past, outsourcing vendors negotiated contracts that depended on "throwing people at the problem." That is, the more employees — or FTEs — assigned to the outsourcing contract, the better. Now, however, contracts are negotiated with performance in mind. Use only the necessary amount of resources to get the job done.

Following along those lines, past outsourcing contracts were negotiated for entire departments. But there's been a realization — at least in healthcare — that the organization itself might be able to handle certain projects with its own resources, or it might want a vendor to handle large, one-time projects such as the installation of new computer systems. Outsourcing contracts now are unique to each customer's needs, both from human resource and scope perspectives.

Finally, in those cases involving IT department outsourcing, employees in the IT department are no longer internally focused, writing software programs or updating coding. Today, they must be out among their users — the caregivers — to help determine ways to maximize the information users get from IT systems. The role has shifted from programming to consultant.

2.12 REFERENCES

Bridges, William, *Job Shift: How to Prosper in a Workplace Without Jobs*, Reading, MA, Addison-Wesley, 1995.

Byrne, John A., "Has Outsourcing Gone Too Far?" *Business Week,* (April 1, 1996) 26–28.

Clark, Thomas D., Zmud, Robert W., and McCray, Gordon E. "The outsourcing of information services: transforming the nature of business in the information industry," *Journal of Information Technology*, 10 (1995) 221–237.

Deutsch, Claudia, H., "Services Becoming The Goods in Industry," *The New York Times,* (Tuesday, January 7, 1997) C1.

Drucker, Peter F., "The New Productivity Challenge," *Harvard Business Review,* (Nov.–Dec. 1991) 69–79.

Drucker, Peter F., "Peter Drucker's 1990s: The Futures that have already happened," *The Economist* (October 21, 1989) 19, 20, and 24.

Drucker, Peter F., "The Network Society," *The Wall Street Journal, (*March 29, 1995) A14.

Drucker, Peter F., "The New Society of Organizations," *Harvard Business Review,* (Sept.–Oct. 1992) 95–104.

Earl, Michael J., "The Risks of Outsourcing IT," *Sloan Management Review,* (Spring 1996) 26–32.

Huber, Richard, L., "How Continental Bank Outsourced Its 'Crown Jewels,'" *Harvard Business Review*, (January–February 1993) 121–129.

Grenier, Raymond and Metes, George, *Going Virtual: Moving Your Organization into the 21st Century*, Prentice Hall, Professional Technical Reference, Upper Saddle River, NJ, 1995.

Lacity, Mary C. and Hirschheim, Rudy, *Beyond the Information Systems Outsourcing Bandwagon: The Insourcing Response*, John Wiley & Sons, 1995.

Lacity, Mary C. and Hirschheim, Rudy, *Information Systems Outsourcing: Myths, Metaphors and Realities*, New York: John Wiley & Sons, 1993.

Lacity, Mary C. and Hirschheim, Rudy, "The Information Systems Outsourcing Bandwagon," *Sloan Management Review*, (Fall 1993) 73–86.

Loh, Lawrence and Venkatraman, N., "Diffusion of Information Technology Outsourcing: Influence, Sources, and the Kodak Effect," Information Systems Research, 3/2 (1992) 334–358.

Magnet, Myron, "The New Golden Rule of Business: It's Love Thy Supplier," *Fortune Magazine*, (February 21, 1994) 60, 61, and 63.

Malone, Thomas W., Yates, Joanne, and Benjamin, Robert I., "Electronic Markets and Electronic Hierarchies," *Communications of the ACM*, 30/6 (June 1987) 484–497.

McFarlan, F. Warren, and Nolan, Richard L., "How to Manage on IT Outsourcing Alliance," *Sloan Management Review*, (Winter 1995) 9–23.

Porter, Michael, *Competitive Advantage*, New York: The Free Press, 1985.

Powell, Walter W., "Neither Market Nor Hierarchy: Network Forms of Organization," *Research in Organizational Behavior*, 12 (1990) 295–336.

Quinn, James Brian, Doorley, Thomas L., and Paquette, Penny C, "Beyond Products: Services-Based Strategy," *Harvard Business Review*, (March–April 1990a) 58–67.

Quinn, James Brian, Doorley, Thomas L., and Paquette, Penny C.,"Technology in Services: Rethinking Strategic Focus," *Sloan Management Review*, Winter (1990b) 79–87.

Reichheld, Frederick F. and Teal, Thomas, *The Loyalty Effect, The Hidden Force Behind Growth, Profits and Lasting Value,* Cambridge, MA: Harvard Business School Press, 1996.

Stalk, George, Evans, Philip, and Shulman, Lawrence E., "Competing on Capabilities: The New Rules of Corporate Strategy," *Harvard Business Review*, (March–April 1992) 57–69.

Stuckey, M.M., *Demass: Transforming the Dinosaur Corporation*, Cambridge, MA: Productivity Press, 1993.

Vankatraman, N., "Beyond Outsourcing: Managing IT Resources as a Value Center," *Sloan Management Review*, 38/3 (Spring 1997) 51–64.

3

Rewards and Risks
of Outsourcing

While outsourcing yields benefits, there are also costs and risks. Therefore, outsourcing decisions should be the outcome of a careful management decision-making process.

The current chapter explores factors that underlie decisions to outsource and the variety of internal circumstances that may lead a company to favor outsourcing over providing its own information systems capabilities. It also addresses the risks. Some of the academic work on the characteristics of information systems outsourcing activity is summarized.

The chapter concludes with an interview of Dr. Lance B. Eliot on the myths of outsourcing.

The benefits, costs, and risks of outsourcing can only be interpreted and understood in the context of your particular organization and its circumstances. Something that may be of great benefit to another firm may not be important in your context and vice versa. As you read the trade press, you can't help but be impressed with the numerous outsourcing success stories and the very large deals that are being made. But it is extremely dangerous to assume that your organization is the same and that it can and should do what other organizations do, even in the same industry. This book provides the tools to assess your situation.

3.1 REASONS TO OUTSOURCE

This section outlines motives for outsourcing in major categories of meeting business objectives, cost saving, organizational finances, information services, technology and skills, personnel issues, organizational change, and organizational politics.

3.1.1 Motives Involving Business Objectives

- Use a vendor to manage an information systems dependent business process with the specific objective of improving business results.
- Reengineer business processes with the help of a vendor who offers best practice methodologies for managing key business functions.
- Link information systems service delivery and different kinds of business values using outsourcing as a way to position the enterprise for ongoing business and technical change. Increase customer satisfaction, increase business options, or improve core business processes in addition to improving IT processes.

3.1.2 Motives Involving Costs

- Provide services at less cost than the internal IT department.
- Make costs more predictable and better controlled when services are contracted for with a vendor.
- Transform information services from a fixed asset with fixed costs to a more variable cost so that information services can be more easily ramped up in times of business increase and profitability and cut back when business conditions dictate.
- Bring IT budgets in line when the rapid increase in the performance relative to price of computing is not reflected in costs.

3.1.3 Motives Involving Organizational Finances

- Transfer equipment and other fixed assets to the vendor in exchange for cash as a way of dressing up the organization's balance sheet. This can free up capital funds for investment in areas that are important to strategic success. It can also improve the financial measures routinely scrutinized by the investment community by eliminating the need to show return on investment in noncore areas of the firm.
- Outsource the capital intensive aspects of information systems as a way of avoiding discontinuous or lumpy capital investments in the future.
- Outsource to convert a fixed cost business into a variable cost business in firms that experience large year-to-year fluctuations in business and in firms that are downsizing.

- Outsourcing to get cash for a portion of a business unit that otherwise might not create value when sold or divested. McFarlan and Nolan (1995) found a number of banks that used this tactic when they anticipated being acquired in order to make the bank more attractive as a buyout candidate.

3.1.4 Motives Involving IT Service and Responsiveness

- Outsource mundane and routine information services to a vendor so that the IT department can better concentrate on the activities and applications that allow it to contribute real value to the organization.
- Outsource old technology and the functions and applications it supports to a vendor (for example, legacy mainframe systems) to allow concentration on a move to new technology that better serves customer needs (for example, client-server applications). Performance of in-house IT staff may improve when there is greater focus, a challenging and cutting edge project, and less hierarchy in IT structure allowed by outsourcing part of the information services burden. The new challenges may be strategic to the organization and allow it to focus on core competencies supported by or delivered by information systems technology.
- Outsource to improve service when vendors can provide better quality service than in-house information systems resources. Vendors may have the edge because of their greater range of services, more skilled and/or motivated staff, better technology, or superior management. Outsourcing part of the IT function may also increase the motivation of in-house IT staff through reorganization and a sharper focus.
- Outsource to increase flexibility and the ability to handle fluctuations in work load. Outsource when the demands on information services rise and peak, and cut back on outsourcing when demands fall. Maintain a core IT staff, and use vendors to absorb the fluctuations in demand on the information systems function. This tactic will increase responsiveness if the hiring and releasing of vendors or vendor staff can be accomplished more rapidly than similar fluctuations in internal resources.

3.1.5 Motives Involving Technology and Skills

- Outsource to reap the benefits of access to cutting-edge technology and skills.

- Outsource to gain the skills your firm cannot attract in the marketplace on its own accord.
- Outsource to gain access to resources available to outside equipment and service providers through the contacts and alliances established by these vendors that otherwise would not be available to or not as accessible to the IT department.
- Outsource to share the risks of new technology with a vendor or transfer the risks entirely to the vendor.
- Outsource to shift the risks inherent in obsolescence of technology and skills to a vendor for all or part of the organization's technological and human resource infrastructure. The potential gain here is in both access to resources and the ability to change these rapidly and flexibly as conditions require. Concentrate on only those areas of technology and skills that create real value or offer competitive advantage.

3.1.6 Motives Involving IT Staff

- Outsource to reduce fatigue and burnout of IT personnel when undertaking new ventures, mergers and acquisitions, embarking on new technology, or undertaking large new application development efforts.
- Outsource routine operations and maintenance and upkeep of legacy systems so that staff can learn new technology implementing new solutions, and not become technically obsolete.

3.1.7 Motives Involving Organizational Change and Politics

- Outsource information services in start-up companies as a way of reducing the initial investment and removing one potential headache from an already overloaded agenda.
- Outsource to facilitate mergers, acquisitions, and corporate restructurings by contracting some or all of the work to vendors. Vendors may have experience and special capabilities in what are one-time-only experiences for the client company and its staff. Vendors are often immune from internal political pressures that stand in the way of structural change. Reliance on vendors can diffuse, deflect, or nullify the politics that accompany mergers, acquisitions, and restructurings.
- Outsource to facilitate decentralization and corporate reengineering as a particular kind of restructuring that often involves information systems.

Outsourcing offers the potential to both provide the information systems resources and capabilities that underlie reengineered ways of doing business and of moving around political obstacles to the restructuring that reengineering often involves.

- Outsource in a partnership with a vendor to boost business performance while sharing the gains and risks of outsourcing with the vendor.

- Outsource to benchmark the internal IT department against external standards. Outsource (perhaps for a limited period of time) a portion of information systems work in order to compare quality and efficiency against an external source of service. This is essentially a tactic to keep the IT department motivated and on task.

- Outsource to control or completely remove a mismanaged and ineffective IT function.

- Outsourcing may also be a career enhancing move for the senior IT or general manager who champions and motivates it.

3.1.8 Politics as a Foundation for Outsourcing

Lacity and Hirschheim (1993) show that politics sometimes plays a major role in the outsourcing decision. The politics of information systems in organizations often involve the relationship between the CEO and the CIO (chief information officer). Michael Earl and David Feeny (1994) argue that the role of information systems in the organization and the chemistry between top IT managers and top corporate officers are interrelated. The difference between firms in which information systems are viewed as an asset and those in which information systems are viewed as a liability have to do with the strategy, political abilities, and performance of top IT managers and the predispositions of CEOs toward the IT function as an adder of value or spendthrift provider of inadequate services. The excellent IT executive builds esteem for the IT function by focusing information systems activity and resources on successful initiatives that make a real difference to the business. The successful IT executive also crafts relationships with top management and other functional heads that keep information services pointed toward real needs and at the same time sells IT successes. But top management must be receptive to this message. In firms with top managers not prepared to believe that IT can ever be more than a pain in the backside, the chances for IT glory are slim, even for the best IT managers.

When viewed in this context, Earl and Feeny stress that the choice of insourcing or outsourcing is largely irrelevant to information systems success. It's the mutual understanding between top management and IT executives on IT roles and the successful delivery of information services in support of business objectives that matters, regardless of whether the services are produced in-house or by outside vendors. Outsourcing in an attempt to cure fundamental mismatches between expectations and information strategy will probably fail. Politics alone is not a sound foundation for outsourcing.

3.1.9 Outsourcing and Strategic Advantage

Many of the motives listed above could be strategic, depending on the circumstances of the organization. For example, a bank under considerable competitive pressure might outsource data center functions to a vendor. In doing so, it could obtain several benefits that support a strategic plan of acquisitions and better customer service and focus. The bank benefits from the infusion of cash that could accompany the transfer of its computers and related equipment to the vendor aiding it in pursuing acquisitions. And the bank can use IT enhanced customer service to retain existing customers and attract new customers.

One variant on the use of outsourcing as strategy is to team with a vendor to create new revenue generating business opportunities. An example is the partnership of Caterpillar and Andersen Consulting to build a worldwide, high speed replacement parts delivery business by combining Andersen's information systems and Caterpillar's warehouse system. The alliance paired Caterpillar's worldwide warehouse infrastructure and its knowledge and skills in parts and parts inventory with Andersen Consulting's expertise in information systems. The system provides the right inventory at the right place at the right time. The partnership brought the relative strengths of the two organizations together to form a business venture that neither could successfully perform alone. It allowed the sharing of investment, investment risk, and investment returns. Chapter 10 addresses issues in forming and sustaining partnerships.

When constructing a strategic plan that includes information systems, an organization can view outsourcing as an option to be considered and debated for the competitive contributions it might make. The planning exercise should:

- Analyze how existing information resources support the existing strategy.
- Determine how information resources and services can be realigned to support a new strategic direction under a best case scenario, without regard to their provision inside or outside the organization.
- Explore and clearly define the gap between present support and future support necessary to redirect strategy.

- Analyze how outsourcing can be used to close the gap and facilitate and support the transition from existing support to the best-case support under the revised strategy. Do this by analyzing the comparative costs and benefits of in-house versus vendor provision of each of the changes necessary to close the gap between current information systems support and future, strategic support.

The next chapter addresses issues of discovering outsourcing opportunities in greater depth.

3.2 THEORETICAL VIEW OF THE MOTIVATION FOR OUTSOURCING

With the tremendous burst in outsourcing in recent years, academics have been working on new theories and reworking old theories to better understand the motives for outsourcing. Cheon, Grover, and Teng (1995) provide a useful summary of some of these.

One perspective is gained from resource-based theory that says that a firm gains a competitive advantage and above average profits in its industry by having distinct products or lower costs, which in turn depend on the distinctiveness of its resources and the way it combines them. To attain and keep this advantage a firm must acquire and deploy its resources according to a competitive strategy. Filling gaps in the resources it needs to pursue its strategy can sometimes take place through outsourcing. Outsourcing can be used to good effect when this allows the firm to fill out and extend its existing resource base. When existing information systems resources and capabilities don't meet what is required to undertake the firm's competitive strategy, outsourcing is an option to be explored.

A second perspective comes from resource-dependency theory. This theory views the firm as being involved in a network of relationships with other firms and organizations in its environment, some of whom provide the firm with resources necessary for its success and survival. But depending on others involves uncertainty. The uncertainty can be reduced to some extent by an on-going relationship that is one of interdependence. Outsourcing is one method of gaining access to needed resources. The degree to which a firm becomes dependent on an outside supplier of resources is a function of:

- How important the resource is to the firm's functioning and success.
- The power the firm has over the supplier of the resource.

- The degree to which alternatives exist in the form of other suppliers or other resources that can substitute and the ease of making a switch to other suppliers.

Cheon, Grover, and Teng put the resource-based and resource dependency theories to a test and found support for them. Outsourcing depends, at least in part, on the resources the firm needs and its strategy for obtaining them.

A third perspective comes from transaction cost theory. Organizations look for opportunities to lower their costs of production by outsourcing tasks to vendors who have lower costs — usually as a result of vendor economies of scale. But production cost savings are offset to a greater or lesser extent by the costs of negotiating a contract with a vendor, managing the vendor relationship, and making sure the vendor does what the vendor has contracted to do. These vendor-related contracting and management costs are called transactions costs. Transactions costs depend on:

- Asset specificity, or uniqueness of the resources involved and services provided in the outsourcing relationship. Asset specificity exists if the outsourcing work results in something that is unique to the outsourcing relationship in terms of a physical asset or knowledge so that another vendor could not immediately replace the first. If the relationships falls apart, your firm has to put time and money into finding another vendor or bringing the outsourced function back inside.

- Uncertainty raises transaction costs. Uncertainty springs from possible future changes in technology involved in the outsourcing deal, or the market for outsourcing services, or the business environment. With uncertainty, more work has to go into structuring a contract and administering a contract with a vendor that allows for change in the relationship when circumstances change.

- Infrequent contracting with the vendor also raises transaction costs. It's more work to structure a deal with a vendor you have never done business with before than a vendor you deal with all the time. Your experience with a vendor reduces the time and effort needed to set up a new contract and lowers the cost of managing the relationship when it is up and running. You know and trust the vendor people, and they know and trust you. You can more easily work out problems that arise because you understand how the vendor firm works. Dealing with an unfamiliar vendor raises the costs of setting up the contract and administering the relationship.

Transaction cost theory says when the gains exceed the costs (including transactions costs), it is advantageous to outsource. Empirical work from the academic world supports the validity of a transactions cost-perspective (Aubert, Rivard, and Patry, 1996).

Transactions cost theory is also useful for understanding the kinds of relationships that are possible with vendors and deciding which of these is most appropriate for outsourcing specific information systems functions.

3.2.1 Partnerships in Outsourcing

Transactions cost theory says that when asset specificity and uncertainty are high for particular tasks or functions that might be outsourced, it is sometimes advantageous to try to develop a partnership with a vendor. In partnering, you and the vendor firm intend to enter an ongoing relationship that involves multiple contracts over time. Gushing accounts of partnership success can be found in the trade press. On the other hand Lacity and Hirschheim (1993) take a dimmer view.

Grover, Cheon, and Teng (1996) tried to address partnership aspects of outsourcing success in their study of 188 large companies. They measured success as satisfaction with the strategic, technological, and economic aspects of outsourcing on the part of top IT management. They measured partnership dimensions of communication, trust, cooperation, and satisfaction with the outsourcing relationship. Their results show the establishment of partnership-type relationships often contribute to satisfaction and success in outsourcing, and the authors suggest that establishing partnerships at the beginning of an outsourcing relationship is a worthwhile tactic. However, they did not control for factors that determine the appropriateness of partnerships. Partnerships should be fostered where partnerships are appropriate and avoided where they are not. Chapters 4 and 10 address this issue in detail.

3.3 RISKS OF OUTSOURCING

The risks of outsourcing are many, and, as a result, the anticipated benefits of outsourcing may not come to fruition. It is necessary to analyze the risks, and if they are unacceptably great or can't be managed, outsourcing should be avoided. If the risks are not too great or can be managed, outsourcing should be considered.

This section gives several views of the risks inherent in outsourcing. For each risk a very brief, one-line managerial response to the risk is offered. Later chapters take up risk management strategies in depth.

3.3.1 A View of Risks from the Perspective of Control

The first and most fundamental risk of outsourcing is loss of control. As a manager you delegate all the time, giving responsibility to someone else to accomplish work that needs to be done, and you lose some measure of control each and every time you do so. The difference, of course, is that employees of outsourcing firms don't report directly to you. It follows that:

- Outsourcing can involve some loss of control over the timely delivery of services and the quality of services. But if contractual aspects of requirements are handled well, this risk can be minimized.
- Flexibility is reduced. Any change in requirements must be accomplished through and with the consent of the vendor. However, contract provisions can be formulated that allow for some flexibility in vendor services.
- Costs may creep. Clients are surprised when vendors present bills for extra charges. Good analysis of requirements and requirements change coupled with sound contractual measures can manage this risk.
- Corporate secrets and confidential information may be accessible to vendors and their personnel. Obviously these should be protected by contractual provisions.
- Your organization's intellectual property can also be at risk in outsourcing situations. Basic protective measures include legal copyright and nondisclosure.

Notice that a good contract is the basis for control in each instance. In outsourcing it is the legal document that makes vendors responsible. The contract as the foundation for an outsourcing arrangement is addressed in Chapters 5 through 7. Monitoring to see that vendors discharge the responsibilities given to them is a topic of Chapter 9.

3.3.2 A Second View of the Risks of Outsourcing

Lacity, Hirschheim, and Willcocks (1994) have been vocal and persistent Cassandras on the pitfalls of outsourcing. Based on interviews with IT executives in many companies, they have drawn up a list of potential problems. They also suggest remedies:

- Cost savings may not be realized if user-customers use discretionary money to go around the vendor and get information services from other sources. These costs may be largely hidden, so that it appears that outsourcing is saving money when it actually is not. The solution: work with user-customers to rank-order their requests, be sure needs are met, and prevent going to the outside.

- Up-front infusions of cash as vendors take over information services equipment and purchase company stock are often gained at the expense of long contracts, perhaps as much as 10 years. As the contract runs technological change continues to cause the price-to-performance ratio to continue to plunge. The company that outsources pays the same flat fee to the vendor year after year and fails to enjoy the improved economics of information technology. Obviously, this is trade-off that should be anticipated as the deal is structured, but if this outcome is not desirable, then a shorter contract of five years or less is the answer.

- The whole of the IT function is outsourced on the assumption that it is a utility so that the organization can focus on core competencies. But later it is realized that IT has valuable, strategic contributions to make. The solution: Before outsourcing IT, look at each IT function for its contribution to corporate competitiveness, and only outsource those functions that are not strategic.

- When IT has not kept abreast of and made a part of the decision-making process in mergers and acquisitions, there is too little time and too little attention paid to the meshing of information systems with resulting information systems malfunctions and disasters. The solution: Make IT part of the decision-making process, and hire a vendor with deep experience in merger work.

- Outsourcing information systems in start-up companies can fail if the customer can't foresee needs well enough to communicate these and put these in a contract with vendors. The solution: Set up short–term contracts with vendors that contain provisions for change, and put needs that emerge into new contracts as successor contracts are negotiated.

- The high service level and quick response that the vendor was expected to provide did not materialize; in some instances vendor service was worse than IT service before outsourcing. This problem often arises when the client firm does not understand that outsourcing economics dictates that the vendor make money. Vendors have the incentive to closely control costs and only deliver what the contract calls for. They centralize functions, sometimes at long distances from the sites of clients; they prioritize user requests; they use standardized equipment and software to gain economies of scale; and they run minimal staff to meet what they see as the anticipated demand for their services. The solution: Put together a contract that will guarantee service levels: Carefully define services and service levels; set penalties for nonconformance; specify vendor staff size, quality, and availability.

- The outsourcing company may assume the vendor will share new technology as it comes along, only to find the vendor continues to offer what is now outdated equipment and services. One solution: Negotiate a contract that anticipates new technology coming over the horizon; another: give the vendor contractual incentives to adopt and apply new technologies.

- IT managers may initiate an outsourcing evaluation as a way of proving the worth and value of the internal IT function only to find that senior managers distrust, ignore, or distort the results and move ahead with outsourcing despite the results of the internal study. Involving senior management in the evaluation process from strategy to construction and evaluation of bids is a way of avoiding this pitfall.

- Senior managers may also see outsourcing evaluations initiated by the IT department as a way to stall for time and a biased exercise. Involvement of senior management in the evaluation process and benchmarking IT performance against best-of-breed companies in the same industry are ways to avoid these traps.

- Outsourcing a troubled, poorly managed, and poorly understood IT function almost always leads to disaster. Outsourcing success demands that the outsourcing relationships be managed, so that the failure of management is likely to be carried over to management of the outsourcing relationship as well. And without a clear understanding of the function to be outsourced, it is not possible to structure and manage a successful outsourcing relationship with a vendor. Get information systems under control, then consider outsourcing.

- Outsourcing to get around the constraints of staff with outdated and inappropriate skills may boomerang. The vendor may not provide superior staff and superior skills. In fact, the outsourcing agreement that moves much of the client's staff to the payroll of the vendor may result in the same people, who are now disgruntled former employees, providing the service from the vendor's side. The solution: careful selection of the vendor, careful specification of service levels, careful selection of the persons to be transferred to the vendor's staff, and in some cases specific designation of certain individuals from the vendor's staff as persons to be assigned to your company.

3.3.3 A Third View of Outsourcing Risks

Michael Earl (1996) identifies other potential risks associated with outsourcing. Earl points out that there is "endemic uncertainty" in the information systems world. Technology keeps charging ahead and takes directions that are not well anticipated, as in the recent rise in the World Wide Web and Internet. The business environment also changes in unpredictable ways. The combination of the two compounds the uncertainty. How will information systems be required to support the business in the future when both the technology and the business are uncertain? And if your organization outsources, will it lose the capacity to innovate in ways that the business requires?

Earl also points out that learning about information technology and how it best applies in an organization is largely experimental; it is learning by doing and evolves through time. He gives the example of airline reservation systems that were initially developed to save clerical costs but eventually became competitive weapons. If you outsource to vendors, will they have the incentive to learn or be around long enough to learn the many ways to fit information technology to the business?

The response to Earl's first point is to give vendors incentives to incorporate innovations into the mix and *keep contracts short* so that changes can be incorporated in the next agreement. (It should also be obvious that effort must be put into assessing uncertainties and risks.) However, the managerial response to Earl's second point is to *keep contracts long* or structure long-term relationships with vendors so that vendor learning about your organization can take place. Under some circumstances, the appropriate response to this seeming contradiction is partnerships with vendors. Both parties build continuity in the relationship through mutual trust and undertaking a series of contracts.

Earl also warns of technological indivisibilities. Software, hardware, networks, and applications are so interrelated and interdependent that outsourcing one of these functions leads to mayhem as it becomes impossible to coordinate with a vendor in ways that keep all aspects of the technology functioning well together. He uses the example of desktop computers connected to LANs and wide area networks. The point is well taken. The solution is to outsource carefully; if interrelationships are strong, either outsource the whole or don't outsource at all.

Earl's fundamental criticism of outsourcing is that outsourcing to control information systems costs restricts the supply side of information services without carefully considering the impact this restriction has on the demand side. Yes, costs can be cut when vendors take over data centers, manage networks, and run help desks. But managers lose focus on the demand for information services and the benefits the organization derives through data centers, networks, and help desks. The result is compromise in the real effectiveness, and perhaps the competitive advantage, that can be obtained from the use of information services.

Earl's point is well taken. Outsourcing must be carefully done, and only for functions suitable for outsourcing. Through careful selection of vendors, a good contract, and vigilant management of the outsourcing relationships, it's possible to get good service in an outsourcing relationship.

3.3.4 A Fourth View of the Risks

Clark, Zmud, and McCray, (1995) present a summary of outsourcing risks. First, information systems costs may not be lower with outsourcing. Usually, it's the unforeseen and unaccounted for changes that result in higher cost. Here are some possibilities (there may well be others). In each case a solution is offered that involves anticipation of the problem and addressing it before the deal is signed:

- Employees are transferred to vendor, but unaccounted for vested pension and insurance benefits must be paid out resulting in a deal that costs more than it saves. The solution: account for all costs when analyzing the deal.
- Software license fees get passed to your organization as a cost of upgrading and continuing to run software that was handed over to the vendor to run. The solution: Recognize the possibility of such costs upfront and analyze them as part of the outsourcing deal.
- The time, effort, and labor necessary to manage the outsourcing arrangement with the vendor is large and only partially anticipated. The solution again is to make good, realistic estimates of outsourcing relationship and contract enforcement costs while analyzing the outsourcing arrangement and manage the outsourcing deal so that costs don't spiral out of control.

Second, risks arise from the nature of specific vendor firms and their behavior. In outsourcing, your organization depends on a vendor but doesn't have control over the behavior of a vendor in the way your organization has control over the behavior of its own employees. Here are the fundamental sources of risk where vendor behavior are concerned and responses to them:

- The vendor has to make a profit or it goes out of business. It follows that your organization and the vendor organization are fundamentally in conflict in the sense that you will want the vendor to do more and the vendor will want to do less. The vendor may not complete tasks as you would like and may not be as careful and prudent as you would be. A good definition of service requirements, measurable criteria for performance of services, and a good contract with suitable requirements and pricing arrangements alleviates this problem.

- Because you have a contract with the vendor and are dependent on the vendor (perhaps all your equipment and people have been transferred to the vendor) you are in a position of vulnerability. The vendor is in a position to take advantage of you. Vendor opportunism can be handled by choosing the right outsourcing relationship with a vendor and through contract provisions.

- The vendor's culture and ways of operating are different from those in your organization. There's a mismatch and resulting conflict and inefficiency. Good vendor screening should eliminate this possibility.

- The vendor firm is young and unseasoned; the vendor doesn't have the right mix of resources. It makes big mistakes while servicing your account in the process of learning or building up its resource base. Choose a seasoned, competent vendor.

- When you outsource to a vendor, the vendor might turn around and outsource part of your work to a third party, perhaps giving you much less control with resulting poor service. The answer is careful selection of a vendor not dependent on subcontractors for the services your organization requires or contract provisions that limit what a vendor can subcontract and control of the subcontractor through contract provisions.

Third, by outsourcing you cut your organization off from learning about new developments in technology and the application of the technology in your business. The solution is to retain people on your staff whose job it is to keep up with the technology you've outsourced and its application, not only in the vendor's operations, but in the larger realm of your industry, as well. Your costs will be higher as a result, and in fairness you should include these as costs of going the outsourcing route when making the decision to outsource.

Fourth and finally, you lose some flexibility by outsourcing. Clark, Zmud, and McCray identify three aspects of flexibility. The first is short term flexibility or the ability of your organization to reorganize its resources and to address changes in the business environment as they occur. Having some slack or excess resources and capacity is an important way to assure short run flexibility.

The second is flexibility needed in a short to medium time frame, or "adaptability." This is the ability to restructure business processes and strategy in new ways to address change. The ability to restructure includes information technology. Flexibility of this type requires new capabilities not previously possessed.

Evolvability is a third type of flexibility that is medium to long term in nature and arises when an organization transforms its technological infrastructure to take advantage of new generations of technology. Success here requires accurate forecasting of technological trends, business trends, and the ability to see the best alignment of the two. It also requires the funds necessary to experiment with, pilot, and install the new technologies.

When one or more IT functions are outsourced any or all of the above types of flexibility might be compromised, depending on the nature of the contract and the relationship with the vendor. In addition, your organization incurs the following possible costs:

- You create a big hill to climb if you ever decide to insource and take it all back in the future. The longer the outsourcing contact, the more difficult it may be to insource, as your IT management capabilities may atrophy, and your organization develops a cultural dependence on the vendor as well as one based on the services provided by a vendor.
- You may also lose the ability to rapidly scale up or down in information systems operations or move in new technological directions depending on the nature of the vendor and the nature of the contract that defines the relationship with the vendor.

The answers to the problems raised in last area of risk are several:

- Maintain short-run flexibility by building provisions in outsourcing contracts that address change, growth, and need for additional requirements.
- Maintain medium term flexibility by giving vendors incentives to introduce new technology, when appropriate.
- Maintain long-term flexibility by keeping outsourcing contracts short to medium-term in duration. Restructure the outsourcing arrangement to address the changed business-technology mix when the contract is renegotiated.

3.3.5 Conclusion

In the above analysis, you can see that the responses to risk fall into main categories of controlling the outsourcing decision, choosing the right vendor, limiting opportunism on the part of the vendor by a good contract, and managing the out-sourcing relationship:

- When you choose to outsource, scrutinize the vendor closely before sign-ing. Make certain this firm knows its business, has the resources and peo-ple required to do the job, and a culture that is compatible with yours.
- Have a contract with the vendor structured to get the vendor behavior you want and need.
- The contract and the less formal aspects of the relationship with the ven-dor can guide vendor behavior, performance, and provide mechanisms for possible resolution of conflict.

In addition, there are so-called self-enforcing aspects of relationships with vendors that sometimes help:

- The vendor has a reputation to build and defend; this is a fundamental of business and is particularly true in a consulting business like out-sourcing. A bad relationship with your organization (particularly if your organization is large and influential in its industry) can be bad for the vendor's business with other firms.
- The vendor's need to protect its reputation also extends to future busi-ness with your own organization, and the more future business you have to offer, the more motivated the vendor will be to perform well on the current contract.

3.4 PRACTICAL PERSPECTIVE: WHO IS OUTSOURCING AND WHY?

Outsourcing has grown rapidly and continues to expand so that any survey results rapidly become outdated — particularly in terms of the number of firms involved in outsourcing and the size of the outsourcing market. Nonetheless, the existing studies are instructive for what they say about the characteristics of outsourcing.

Sobol and Apte (1995) surveyed the companies that make up *Computer-world*'s list of the premier IT departments in the United States, as chosen by their peers. It's not clear how this elite sample differs from the rest of the world in what and how it outsources, but the researchers found that 77 percent of top-ranked IT departments were outsourcing at least one information systems func-tion. McFarlan and Nolan (1995) report that over half of the companies they surveyed were outsourcing one or more functions.

3.4.1 Information Systems Functions Outsourced

In the Sobol and Apte study, equipment maintenance and service, training and education, disaster recovery, data entry, and systems integration tasks were the most frequently outsourced. None of the premier IT organizations were outsourcing the whole of the IT function.

While most outsourcing activity is in noncore, nonstrategic information systems functions in the cross industry study by Sobol and Apte, a case study research effort involving U.S. regional banks by McLellan, Marcolin, and Beamish (1995) found that in banking, top management viewed information systems as a core activity, important to competitive functioning, but were willing to outsource large parts of it nonetheless. Information systems resources alone provided no advantage, but when combined with their particular service strengths and market position, the banks could get an edge.

3.4.2 Advantages and Disadvantages of Outsourcing

Sobol and Apte found cost savings, cost predictability, reduction in the need for IT staff, focus on core competencies, and the wide choice of outsourcing vendors to be the major reasons for outsourcing. The greatest disadvantages of outsourcing were the cost of monitoring vendors (recall the concept of transaction costs from the discussion above on theories of outsourcing), the loss of control over the functions outsourced, communication difficulties with vendors, and the potential compromise of organizational secrets and intellectual property.

In their study of banks, McLellan, Marcolin, and Beamish found that the motivation for outsourcing was strongly based on finances. Five of their seven case study banks outsourced, even though they were financially strong and had strong top management teams. They did so to prevent future cost problems and as a way of giving a boost to performance. Outsourcing also allowed them to smoothly integrate new business into the company while growing through mergers and acquisitions. Weak IT departments that lacked good managers was another motivation for outsourcing; top management saw outsourcing as a way to increase information systems performance, and flexibility. A subset of the banks were also motivated by desires to restructure and transition their organizations to new forms and by desires to reduce technological uncertainty and to access new technology.

3.4.3 Initiation of Outsourcing

In 80 percent of Sobol and Apte's companies, the most important person taking the initiative in the outsourcing effort was an IT executive. Top management along with IT executives initiated outsourcing investigations in 8 percent of the cases and

IT executives and user managers in an additional 6 percent of the cases. Top managers initiated outsourcing in only 2 percent of the cases. This result, based as it is on the most revered IT organizations in the United States, may not be representative, and top managers may be more assertive and active in the general population of all IT organizations.

IT managers had the most influence in making the outsourcing decision in slightly over half their sample companies, top managers in about one-eighth of the cases, with the rest being made by a combination of IT and other managers, including top managers. Consultants, who are sometimes feared by IT managers for their proclivity of going over the heads of IT to get to top managers, were not important for the firms in this study. They were instrumental in initiating outsourcing in only 2 percent of the cases.

While Sobol and Apte found IT managers to have substantial control, case study research by Lacity and Hirschheim (1993) and by De Looff (1995) finds that much outsourcing is put in motion when top management mandates cost cutting and the IT department is unable to demonstrate that it can be as efficient and effective as outside vendors. Again, the top-drawer nature of the Sobol and Apte sample may bias their results.

3.4.4 Firm Size and Outsourcing

Sobol and Apte found that smaller companies and companies with smaller information services budgets are less likely to outsource than their larger counterparts, and smaller companies required greater relative cost savings to justify and undertake outsourcing. In their study, more than 40 percent of smaller firms required cost savings of 30 percent or more to undertake outsourcing while only 25 percent of large firms required such margins to initiate an outsourcing deal. The reasons may be:

- Large firms have more clout where vendors are concerned and may have less reason to fear that vendors will try to take advantage of them.
- Cost savings are often based on vendor economies of scale. When large firms outsource, their work may represent much higher incremental volume to vendors who can then offer their work at much lower cost than they can to smaller firms with less work.
- Transaction costs, or the costs of dealing with the vendor, probably don't scale up proportionally when the size of the outsourcing deal increases. This gives the edge to larger firms as they outsource.
- Alternative, smaller firms may require greater cost savings to justify outsourcing because the transaction costs of negotiating contracts and monitoring vendors is relatively fixed, so their smaller deals require greater savings to justify the relatively fixed transaction costs.

3.4.5 Other Firm Characteristics and Outsourcing

Firms with more decentralized information systems functions are more likely to outsource than more centralized firms. More than 90 percent of the most decentralized firms in the Sobol and Apte study outsourced versus two-thirds of the most centralized. Outsourcing is, in a sense, decentralization; so outsourcing may be a more attractive and natural step for decentralized information systems functions to make. Also, decentralized IT departments may not command the range of resources possessed by larger departments and may look to outsourcing as a way of meeting their resource needs.

This conclusion is reversed where outsourcing information systems work to foreign companies is concerned. Here organizations with centralized information systems functions were more likely to outsource to foreign vendors than organizations with decentralized information systems. Now, the greater transaction costs of doing international outsourcing may only be sustainable if the volume of work to be done is large, which is more characteristic of large, centralized IT departments.

They found outsourcing to be unrelated to the nature of information services as a strategic or nonstrategic resource in a company. One might think that companies that view information services as a core competency would want to outsource utility like information systems functions so that available staff and resources could focus on the strategic aspects of the information systems operation. This, apparently, is not true.

3.4.6 Motives for Outsourcing and the Nature of Outsourcing

The advantages and disadvantages of outsourcing, as seen by an organization, have some relationship to what is outsourced (Sobol and Apte, 1995):

- Companies seeking cost savings in technical labor categories were more likely to outsource integrated information systems work and data communications and networks — all highly technical work.
- Companies for whom overall cost reduction was most important outsourced support functions, such as data entry, disaster recovery, and education, and training, more frequently.
- Companies pursuing strategic aims by outsourcing were more likely to outsource software maintenance and integrated systems development to permit reallocation of resources to strategic concerns.

- When acquiring advanced technology was very important, the firm was more likely to outsource software maintenance.
- Firms who found the large number and variety of vendors to be a major advantage of outsourcing were more likely to outsource data entry and support operations.

Sobol and Apte found that manufacturing companies outsourced a bit more than service firms, but the difference was too small to be statistically significant.

3.4.7 Conclusion

The academic research results strongly suggest that the outsourcing marketplace now offers a variety of solutions to a variety of needs. There is no single reason or set of reasons for outsourcing. Many different information systems functions can be outsourced. Even when an information systems function is strategic and central to competition, it may be outsourced. The persons most responsible for initiating outsourcing and leading outsourcing efforts vary. The view is one of great variety.

3.5 OUTSOURCING MYTHS: AN INTERVIEW WITH DR. LANCE B. ELIOT

Lance Eliot is President of Lance B. Eliot & Associates, Huntington Beach, California. Dr. Eliot has assisted several clients with selective outsourcing evaluations, RFP preparation, and relationship management.

What is your background related to I/S outsourcing?
The topic of outsourcing has been of interest to me throughout my career. In the early stages of my career I worked for an outsourcer and gained valuable insights into providing I/S services to the marketplace. When I later became a Chief Information Officer, I made use of outsourcers for various subfunctions within my Department.

More recently, I have studied outsourcing as a professor, and currently consult to companies that are considering using outsourcing as a strategy for their firm. I would guess that I have advised several dozen firms about outsourcing issues, ranging from selective outsourcing (outsourcing a particular subfunction) to outsourcing the entire IT function itself.

What kind of outsourcing advice do you provide to companies?

Most companies need to be educated about the advantages and disadvantages of outsourcing. Often, management and non-management are not fully aware of the benefits and costs that are associated with outsourcing.

Also, outsourcing an I/S function involves proceeding through a life cycle of activities, starting with determining whether outsourcing is warranted and culminating with engaging and monitoring outsourced services if appropriate. I try to help companies safely and systematically make their way through the entire life cycle.

In your experience, what do companies most need to know?

I would say that the starting point for educating firms about outsourcing involves exploring the various myths that have emerged in the last several years. These myths are commonly found in the hallways of firms considering adopting outsourcing and also found among many outsourcers as well.

Can you give us an example of such a myth?

One popular myth involves the notion that outsourcing means simply making use of a service bureau. As I'll explain in a moment, contemporary outsourcing means much more than merely contracting with a service bureau.

For those managers who remember back to the 1970s and early 1980s, it was common to outsource selected aspects of a data center operation to a service bureau. If you wanted a few extra MIPS available for processing you could make a deal to buy additional processing power as-needed from a service bureau. You might even supplement your in-house operations staff with outside personnel to handle peak processing periods.

Marketplace changes of the late 1980s and now the 1990s have transformed the older style outsourcing arrangements to a new, closer relationship with an outsourcer that provides a wider range of services. The outsourcer becomes an integrated element of the I/S function, rather than an outside entity that is used only when extra capabilities are required.

I emphasize this distinction because the nature of reviewing outsourcers, contracting with them, and managing the relationship with them has changed radically from the earlier era. If a manager today were to go into a contemporary arrangement with the old style approach, both the I/S function and the outsourcer would undoubtedly suffer and be unable to succeed with the relationship.

Using an analogy, the question of casual dating with an outsourcer now becomes one of marrying with the outsourcer. The degree of commitment and extent of interdependencies is significantly heightened and altered from the way that things used to be.

Can you mention some other myths?

Another myth is that outsourcing means there is no need for a Chief Information Officer. In my view, any organization that does away with their CIO will be unlikely to succeed with outsourcing.

A CIO still plays an important role in an organization even if the entire I/S function is outsourced. The CIO serves as the company insider that can aid the organization during its strategic planning to determine how I/S can best support and drive the strategy of the firm. The CIO acts to oversee the outsourcer and ensure that the firm is making proper use of the outsourced services. And so on.

Note that the role of the CIO shifts away from operational and tactical matters and tends to move toward more strategic matters. Of course, the CIO still keeps abreast of operational issues, and serves as the internal voice for resolving tactical complications, but the relief from day-to-day headaches of operational management can allow a CIO to focus more clearly on strategy issues.

A firm that outsources all of I/S and removes the CIO role will become headless and will probably see its I/S function drift.

Can you quickly give us a few other common myths?

Several come to mind. Let me briefly mention a few.

One common myth is that outsourcing implies that the current I/S function is not efficient or effective. This is a myth because a company might have other valid reasons to embark upon outsourcing, such as turning the I/S function into an asset that can bring in quick cash or shedding a function that is not considered a core competency, and therefore a firm might do outsourcing even when the I/S function is world class caliber.

Another is that applications development should never be outsourced. This is a myth because a firm might intentionally want to outsource application development to gain rapid access to new technologies and new development skills. Or, a firm might outsource legacy application development and maintenance in order to free in-house staff to work on new systems development.

Another popular myth is the notion that outsourcing is an all or nothing proposition. The view seems to be that everything goes or nothing goes. It is a false dichotomy. Firms can outsource all, none, or some of the I/S function.

Outsourcing some of the I/S function is called selective outsourcing. A firm might decide to outsource the Data Center. Then, after some experience with such an outsourcing arrangement, might outsource their network. Next, if all goes well, the firm might outsource the Help Desk support. And so on.

Outsourcing in a selective, gradual fashion allows a company to become progressively experienced at outsourcing. And, note that the outsourcing does not necessarily have to continue to grow in size. A firm might discover that outsourcing is not a good alternative, and therefore move the outsourced subfunction back into the IT department.

Besides the myths, what other advice can you offer for our readers?

Treat outsourcing as a project. You want to plan the project, stating the appropriate timing needed to accomplish the project successfully. Firms often do not conceive of the outsourcing effort in project terms per se, but instead seem to think about the outsourcing issue as a single decision that needs to be made ad hoc.

The best way to avoid trouble is to systematically and carefully approach the outsourcing issue. Has the firm reviewed why outsourcing? Does the firm understand where their current problems exist? Has the company stated the desired goals from outsourcing? Has the firm prepared a tight, Request for Proposal that multiple qualified bidders can respond to? And so on.

When should a firm consider outsourcing?

Always. I believe that every IT department should continually be asking the question as to whether or not an outsourcer can be doing a better job, at lesser cost, at the same or higher quality. By making a comparison to the outsourcing option, IT departments are forced to remain on their toes and be competitive. In a formal sense, I recommend a look at outsourcing alternatives when updating an IT Strategic Plan.

When someone else in the firm asks the question: "Should we outsource some or all of I/S," I believe that the IT function should have an answer. Rather than resisting the outsourcing question, top-notch I/S groups can respond that they have already outsourced those sub-functions that make sense to outsource, or that they have determined analytically that the outsourcing option is not viable for their organization at this time. Notice that I said "at this time" since the outsourcing decision of a year ago may no longer be relevant due to changes in the company, changes in technology, or changes in the outsourcing marketplace.

Thank you for taking the time to talk with us.

I appreciate being given this opportunity to share some of my thoughts on the subject.

I advocate that firms should consider outsourcing as an alternative means of using IT in their organizations, and do so with their eyes open. I/S management and non-I/S management all need to increase their awareness about this vital topic.

3.6 REFERENCES

Aubert, Benoit A., Rivard, Suzanne, and Patry, Michel, "A transaction cost approach to outsourcing behavior: Some empirical evidence," *Information & Management*, 30 (1966) 51–64.

Cheon, Myun J., Grover, Varun and Teng, James T. C., "Theoretical perspectives on the outsourcing of information systems, "*Journal of Information Technology*, 10 (1995) 209–219.

Clark, Thomas D., Zmud, Robert W., and McCray, Gordon E. "The outsourcing of information services: transforming the nature of business in the information industry," *Journal of Information Technology*, 10 (1995) 221–237.

De Looff, Leon A., "Information systems outsourcing decision making: a framework, organizational theories, and case studies," *Journal of Information Technology*, 10 (1995) 281–297.

Earl, Michael J., "The Risks of Outsourcing IT," *Sloan Management Review*, (Spring, 1966) 26–32.

Earl, Michael and Feeny, David F, "Is Your CIO Adding Value?" *Sloan Management Review*, (Spring 1994) 11–20.

Grover, Varian, Cheon, Myna Jung, and Teng, James T. C, "The Effect of Service Quality and Partnership on the Outsourcing of Information Systems Functions," *Journal of Management Information Systems*, 12/4 (Spring 1996), 89–116.

Lacity, Mary C. and Hirschheim, Rudy, *Information Systems Outsourcing: Myths, Metaphors and Realities*, New York: John Wiley & Sons, 1993.

Lacity, Mary, Hirschheim, Rudy, and Willcocks, Leslie, "Realizing Outsourcing Expectations: Incredible Expectations, Credible Outcomes," *Information Systems Management*, (Fall 1994), 7–18.

McFarlan, F. Warren and Nolan, Richard L., "How to Manage on IT Outsourcing Alliance," *Sloan Management Review*, (Winter 1995), 9–23.

McLellan, Kerry, Marcolin, Barbara, and Beamish, Paul W., "Financial and strategic motivations behind IS outsourcing," *Journal of Information Technology*, 10 (1995), 299–321.

Sobol, Marion G. and Apte, Uday, "Domestic and Global Outsourcing Practices of American's Most Effective IS Users," *Journal of Information Technology*, 10 (1995), 269–280.

Teng, James T., Cheon, Myun Joong, and Grover, Varun, "Decisions to Outsource Information Systems Functions: Testing a Strategy-Theoretic Discrepancy Model," *Decision Sciences*, 26/1 (January–February 1995), 75–103.

4

The Feasibility of Outsourcing Ideas

his chapter outlines an outsourcing methodology and discusses a few preliminary people issues. It then introduces total and selective outsourcing and general issues that can motivate each approach. It continues with a discussion of various screens that should be used to assess the feasibility of outsourcing ideas. The chapter concludes with some advice on preliminary planning efforts for the remainder of the outsourcing evaluation process.

4.1 OUTSOURCING METHODOLOGY

The disciplined outsourcing process parallels the phases of the time-honored waterfall application development methodology with its customary stages of feasibility and planning, analysis, design, build, implement, and operate. A brief description of phases follows:

- In the feasibility and planning phase, the objectives and scope of the outsourcing idea are defined and scrutinized and made to pass various criteria or screens before a decision is made to proceed. The ensuing effort is planned in terms of time, budget and resources needed.

- In the analysis phase, baselines are constructed, if needed, and the service levels required of vendors are specified. Relationships between the information system function(s) to be outsourced and other functions that will remain in-house are also clarified so that contracts with vendors are certain to include proper interfaces with IT performed in-house. The Request For Proposal is developed, responses are collected from vendors and analyzed and a vendor is chosen.

- In the design phase, negotiations go forward with the vendor and a contract is developed and signed.
- In the implementation phase, the transition from in-house provision of information systems services to outsourcing is made.
- In the operations phase the outsourcing relationship with the vendor is managed and any maintenance or changes in the outsourcing relationship are negotiated and implemented.
- At the end of the contracting period the decision is made to negotiate another contract with the vendor or a new vendor, and the cycle begins again. Alternatively a decision is made to bring the information systems function back inside the organization.

As in standard application development methodologies, phases can overlap to some extent, and there can also be some iteration back to earlier phases.

The methodology provides a discipline that leads to better outsourcing decisions, better outsourcing contracts with vendors, and better outsourcing results than a casual approach to outsourcing. It also provides a framework for management decision making. The method is scalable; for simple outsourcing situations, a simplified, quick version of the methodology suffices.

4.2 PEOPLE WHO MUST BE INVOLVED

Before work can begin on an outsourcing idea, persons must be identified who will take leadership responsibility and do the analysis and make the decisions. Those involved depend on what is to be outsourced and the circumstances surrounding the outsourcing decision.

An executive sponsor or champion is desirable, and in cases that involve organizational politics such support is absolutely critical. For larger outsourcing initiatives, top management must play a role. For smaller efforts, middle-level managers might do the heavy lifting with the support of higher managers.

Jill Klein, who was a leader in the outsourcing effort at Riggs Bank, explains the support she received from higher levels of management and how it evolved. "My EVP for Operations and Systems gained the interest of the Vice Chairman and two members of the Board. The Vice Chairman got the Chairman's ear and also influenced the CFO and President. Then throughout the outsourcing evaluation process, we spoke with banking industry executives whose opinions mattered to the Chairman. To my knowledge, none of the senior executives opposed the evaluation or the decision."

Cinda Hallman of DuPont explains how support was won for a very large outsourcing project: "At the time we began to consider outsourcing, we already had a strong and active Business Information Board chaired by our current CEO who at the time was the second highest executive in the company. Board members included senior vice presidents, vice president/general managers who ran the business units, other vice presidents of various functions, and, of course, myself, the CIO. We kept the Board informed and involved throughout the process. We also worked individually with business heads and operations leaders. Some executives expressed concern over the potential for high prices and exposure of proprietary information. All recognized the criticality of IT and knew that IT was a key enabler of DuPont's global leadership in the chemical industry. I think the three major factors that won the support of the executives who showed the most concern were the active interest of the Board and executive management, the decision to go with two providers instead of one, and the decision for DuPont to manage the Alliance. They saw this as not putting all our eggs in one basket while still retaining our IT management strengths. Also, the strong involvement and support of our IT leaders in the businesses were instrumental in obtaining support of business and corporate leadership."

The team needs a mix of managerial and technical talents and should also include representatives from user areas that will be directly and heavily impacted by the outsourcing under consideration. User views may be critical for setting scope and for assessing risks.

The size of the team depends on the scope and size of the project, but smaller teams are generally more effective. The team can be quite small in the feasibility phase and expanded when full-blown analysis begins. Teams with full-time members are often more focused and effective than teams composed of people who devote part-time effort. However, full-time allocation may make sense for big outsourcing projects. It helps tremendously to have persons experienced in outsourcing on the team for the insight they bring to the issues and the realism they bring to cost and benefit estimates.

Once the decision is made to outsource, IT managers, perhaps in consultation with other managers in the organization, should identify persons in the IT department who will be given responsibility for oversight and management of the outsourcing arrangement and vendor relations after the contract is signed. These managers should be part of the team that crafts the contract. Their inclusion is critical for several reasons. First, there is no better way to understand the issues involved in outsourcing than to be involved in all aspects leading up to the deal. Second, relationships with vendors start at the moment discussions begin. Being on the ground floor and having continuity in the relationship with people in the vendor organization contributes to success.

When outsourcing threatens to upset the status quo in an organization — as in instances of outsourcing motivated by high costs or poor performance of the IT department — it may not be possible to rely on internal sources for accurate estimates of internal costs or internal effectiveness. Under these circumstances, bring in objective outsiders to do some of the assessment work.

4.3 TOTAL OUTSOURCING AND THE CORE COMPETENCIES SCREEN

Total outsourcing transfers most equipment, staff, and responsibility for delivery of information services to a vendor, while selective outsourcing identifies specific functions or services to outsource. If your organization outsources functions that account for 80 percent or more of the information systems budget, you're engaging in total outsourcing (Lacity, Willcocks, and Feeny, 1996). Selective outsourcing is the outsourcing of one or a few selected information systems functions. The sum of what is outsourced is substantially less than total outsourcing.

Total outsourcing isn't easy because of the scope of the endeavor and because of the consequences if it isn't done well, or if, in retrospect, it shouldn't have been done at all. The stakes are high. A considerable sum of money is usually involved, not to mention the effectiveness of an information pillar that supports your organization's structure and performance.

Some organizations may be more predisposed to total outsourcing than others (McFarlan and Nolan, 1995). Factors include:

- Concerns about costs and quality: can outsourcing provide the same or better quality at lower cost.
- IT departments that don't deliver adequate service, or are perceived to deliver inadequate service.
- General managers and IT managers who are at loggerheads may look for a way of cleaning the slate and moving on to different, more arms-length relationships with vendors.
- Competitive pressure: the search for ways to concentrate on core competencies with the information systems function outside the core.
- Financial restructuring needs: cash generation by shifting information systems equipment to vendors.
- The need to restructure the IT department but without the internal political consensus to do so.

The stakes are high; total outsourcing is a major undertaking; no organization should do it without considerable thought for several reasons. First, these deals are often structured to last for long periods — usually more than five and often ten years. Vendors plan to make their margins on economies of scale and on replacing hardware in the future at costs that are substantially below hardware costs today. Total outsourcing arrangements only yield acceptable margins over longer periods of time.

Second, clients who enter into total outsourcing arrangements must spend considerable time, effort, and money analyzing the deal and contracting with a vendor.

Third, information systems flexibility may be considerably reduced. The long contracts involved in total outsourcing have obvious downsides. Technology will certainly change over a five or ten year period. The business environment will change leading to shifts in the role of information systems, yet it is hard to set contracts that allow for large changes in scope. If the arrangement with the vendor does not succeed, it is necessary to either contract with another vendor, which involves substantial costs and disruption, or it's necessary to bring the information systems function back inside the organization with all the attendant costs and problems. This is not to say that total outsourcing should never be considered, but it drives home the point that it should not be undertaken lightly.

There is no industry in which all firms have entered total outsourcing deals, so the circumstances that lead to total outsourcing must be specific relating to factors such as financial health, corporate strategy, or information systems performance. According to McFarlan and Nolan (1995), organizations better suited for total outsourcing likely have one or more of the following characteristics:

- Information systems functions that are focused on maintaining existing systems and developing new applications not critical to competitive success are more susceptible to being outsourced. The issue of loss of control diminishes under these conditions.

- IT departments with a portfolio of applications that are highly structured — that is applications with very well-defined and understood outputs and whose implementation does not involve significant organization change — are candidates for outsourcing. Contracting with vendors is easier and more straightforward under these circumstances. When these applications require specialized skills that are not abundant or are nonexistent in the IT department, outsourcing becomes even more attractive.

- Organizations whose past experience and learning gives them the ability and confidence to successfully manage relationships with vendors are more likely to consider outsourcing.

- Organizations wanting to accelerate change and catch up by sweeping away a backward and antiquated IT function are candidates.
- Organizations with highly differentiated and/or decentralized information systems functions are good candidates for outsourcing. Here parts have already been defined as separate from other functions, and the job of defining what is to be outsourced and how it relates to the rest of the organization has already been done. This makes it easier to define and write an outsourcing contract.

The business and trade press often publish lists of factors that supposedly indicate a need for outsourcing:

- Large backlogs of information systems projects.
- Escalating costs in information systems.
- Maintenance that is out of control.
- Poor information service quality.
- Turnover in IT management and staff.
- A lack of comprehensive information systems planning.

While these and other factors may be warning signs of trouble, no simple check-off of indicators is an adequate foundation for a total outsourcing decision. Given the considerable stakes involved in total outsourcing, a much more comprehensive analysis of the information systems function and the options is required.

4.3.1 The Core Competencies Screen

Once the idea of total outsourcing is raised, the feasibility phase begins. The first and most important feasibility issue and screen involves information systems as a core competency. Most outsourcing commentators warn against outsourcing information systems functions if they are core competencies. This is generally good advice. However, exceptions arise when clients enter strategic alliances or partnerships with vendors in which risks and gains are shared.

To determine if information systems are strategic and central to the organization's success, define the role of information systems as they must function to support the business in the future. Their future role may differ from their current role. The motivation to outsource may rest in large part on this difference and the fact that current and past information systems performance is at variance with what it must be if it is to adequately support the firm. Benko (1993) suggests four categories into which information systems support strategy can fall:

- Competitive advantage in which information systems are critical for profitability and overall success in competition against rivals in the same industry. Information systems help differentiate the organization's products and/or services.

- Low-cost provider in which information systems are critical for profitability by doing the routine transaction processing of the business at very low cost relative to the competition, thereby making an important contribution to overall low cost as a competitive strategy.

- Low-cost operator in which information systems are not a factor in the organization's competitive strategy, but the IT department is expected to be a competent, low cost provider of services — a utility function, if you like.

- High flexibility in which the firm is planning to acquire or spin off businesses thereby requiring an information systems function that can flexibly adjust, absorb, interface, integrate, or disengage from other information systems components and functions.

If information systems fall into the first category (critical for competitive success), total outsourcing will likely entail too much risk. Membership in the low-cost provider category might exclude total outsourcing of information systems functions but allow for selective outsourcing of certain information systems functions. Outsourcing when an organization is in the high flexibility category depends on the nature of the business changes contemplated.

4.3.2 Never Outsource All of IT Management

Perhaps it goes without saying, but it must be emphasized at the outset, that in total outsourcing no organization should outsource its capability to manage outsourcing and information systems technology strategy. Don't outsource all information systems responsibility to a vendor. Retain a small group of IT managers who: (a) manage ongoing outsourcing relationships with vendors, (b) oversee and pass on vendor technical decisions, (c) develop experience with outsourcing and help make future outsourcing decisions, (d) negotiate and enforce future outsourcing contracts, (e) develop the information systems technology strategy of the organization for the future as it relates to support of business needs, and (f) keep overall information systems strategy in alignment with overall corporate strategy as it evolves over time (Cronk and Sharp, 1995). Otherwise your organization is left at the complete mercy of vendors, and it will be difficult, if not impossible, to plot a course through the constantly changing technology waters.

Reflect for a moment on the changes in technology over the past 10 years to get a sense of the turmoil that the next 10 will likely bring. As new technologies break, your organization must have the managerial capacity to analyze and decide whether and how these will be used to support the business. Changes in the business environment can be equally dramatic. Someone must also negotiate contracts or renegotiate contracts with vendors to bring the promising new technologies into the mix. Because the future of technology can't be predicted with precision, it is not possible to specify all technological contingencies in a contract. Managerial competence must be retained to do the analysis and take the necessary steps with vendors or to implement some capabilities in new technology by insourcing.

An in-house information systems management function should also be retained to establish technology standards and ensure that essential organizational data is properly acquired, stored, backed-up, and accessed, even when the day-to-day processing is performed by a vendor.

Finally, the long term effectiveness of the information systems function depends on its proper alignment with corporate strategy. Corporate strategy evolves as the business environment changes. Information systems strategy must also evolve to keep the services aligned with the changing business strategy. This alignment function should not be outsourced to a vendor whose basic objectives are not the same as your organization's objectives.

4.4 SELECTIVE OUTSOURCING AND CORE COMPETENCIES

Like total outsourcing, selective outsourcing decisions require up-front thought and analysis. Simply because the IT department in your organization exhibits one or more of the symptoms of dysfunctional behavior listed in some trade publication doesn't mean outsourcing is the best course of action to take. A more comprehensive view leads to better outsourcing decisions.

The identification of functions or services that might be selectively outsourced can be initiated in either a systematic or an opportunistic manner:

- The opportunistic approach starts from a new need, a chronic information systems problem, or an ongoing pattern of high cost in information systems service delivery. Something indicates that close attention should be placed on some aspect of the information systems operation where one of the ways to solve the problem might be selective outsourcing.

- A systematic approach involves thinking through each and every information systems function as a candidate for outsourcing using one or more of the common motives for outsourcing summarized in the previous chapter, such as cost cutting, leveling the demand on in-house personnel, obtaining specialized skills from vendors, and so forth. The choice of motives depends on circumstances inside your organization and the pressures on and the priorities of the IT department.

- Another systematic method is to approach outsourcing from the standpoint of a regular information systems planning process — a strictly information systems planning process or as part of overall organizational strategic planning (Venkatraman, 1997).

4.4.1 Selective Outsourcing Decisions Made in a Planning Framework

Planning methodologies abound. The approach adopted here is one proposed by Kovacevic and Majluf (1993). Information systems planning is a subset of overall corporate planning, which is done with the active involvement of the IT department. The steps in the planning process are as follows:

1. Establish a strategy for the organization as a whole. This includes information requirements for the organization and its units, including some notion of the relative priorities of these requirements. The strategy is clearly stated in documentation created in the strategy formation process.
2. Look outside your organization and evaluate new technologies, new methods, and new applications of information technology that might have an impact on your organization and your industry, and sleuth out how your competitors are moving to use existing and new technologies to their advantage. Even if information systems isn't called into battle against competitive foes, it's still necessary to evaluate new trends for their relevance to information systems support of the business. The basis idea is to compare where you are to where your organization wants to be in the future, and then determine what has to change in information systems capabilities to support the transition from the present to the future.
3. An internal analysis follows in which information systems strengths and weaknesses are identified. Given the business environment, the information needs of your organization, the technology available in the marketplace, and your current information systems capabilities, what are your strengths and what are your weaknesses? What is needed in addition to or in place of current information systems resources to be successful in support of the business? How does your IT department stack up against the competition, if information systems is part of competitive strategy? Or, for an IT department that is in a support mode, how do information systems compare to industry benchmarks? Is the IT department efficient and effective? Does it have the resources (including the technology and skills) necessary for the next round of application development and service delivery?

4. With the background gathered in the preceding steps, define actions to be taken in the future. These include:

   4.1 Priorities for application development projects.

   4.2 Technology and skills necessary to make the strategy work.

   4.3 Changes in IT organization and structure that will make it more effective in support of the organization.

   4.4 **Sourcing decisions:** Should the provision of the necessary capabilities be done through in-house means or by outsourcing? This question is not limited to acquisition of new technology and new skills, but applies to existing stocks of technology and skills, as well. Would outsourcing be a more efficient and effective way?

   4.5 Decisions on relationships with suppliers and customers, including the nature of the relationship with outsourcing vendors.

   4.6 Changes in the structure of the IT department and its relationship to the rest of the organization. If outsourcing is an important component in the provision of overall information systems services, changes in IT organization should follow.

5. Resource allocation and budgets. Projects are evaluated and the most promising are selected. Resources are identified. Budgets are set.

6. Implementation is the final step. Identification of outsourcing vendors and establishment of contracts and vendor relationships are part of the implementation process, as is the ongoing management of contracts and vendor relationships.

   In this top-down approach, outsourcing decisions are part of a strategic planning process that starts with business needs.

4.4.2 Core Competencies and Selective Outsourcing

Regardless of the method used to identify selective outsourcing candidates, they should be screened for their contribution to your organization's competitive success. It is not wise to outsource information systems functions that confer a competitive advantage.

It may seem that instances of competitive advantage would be obvious, but it is best to be sure. Venkatesan (1992) suggests some practical tests for strategic functions in manufacturing subsystems that have applicability for information systems as well. For the information systems function identified as a possible outsourcing candidate, ask the following questions:

- First, does this function contribute substantially to what customers see as your organization's most important product or service attributes? Think of all the ways in which customers perceive your organization. A value chain analysis might assist here. Look at all activities in your organization's value chain and consider how information and information technology affects the customer's experience with your organization. This analytical task can also be approached by looking at the relationship between the information systems function under consideration and business processes. If the information systems function is integrated into or provides close and essential support to a business process that is critical to competitive advantage, then the function is essential to competitive position. By all means ask your customers or a sample of customers if you're not sure how the results of a business process or information systems function are seen by them.

- Second, does provision of this information systems capability involve skills or combinations of skills and other assets that are unique to your organization and not extant in competitor organizations and not easily duplicated by vendors to whom you might outsource?

- Third, as provision of this information systems capability evolves in your organization in the future, is it likely that your organization will develop skills and abilities not duplicated in other organizations or vendors? It is very important to consider the capabilities issue in terms of the future because your organization is constantly changing, as are competitors, vendors, and the business environment.

If the answer is "yes" to any of these questions, and particularly if the answer is "yes" to both the first and either of the second or third, you have identified an information systems capability that supports a competitive advantage, is a competitive advantage in itself, or could be a competitive advantage in the future. Think twice about outsourcing it.

Recognize that outsourcing decisions are often intensely political with factions working for and against outsourcing. Expect those who oppose outsourcing to mount arguments that claim more strategic or core competence in the outsourcing candidate than may actually be the case. On the other hand, those who favor outsourcing will downplay the competitive importance. Lacity, Willcocks, and Feeny (1996) argue that non-IT managers may assume an information systems function is not strategic, when in fact it is, because information systems are consistently treated as a cost rather than an investment and managers lose track of the benefits of information systems.

In the best of all possible worlds, the outsourcing feasibility team will be above politics. Realistically this is impossible. If upper management really intends the decision to be objective, their role as executive sponsor must include constant admonitions and watchfulness to see that the process is as unbiased as possible.

4.4.3 Using Outsourcing to Play Catch-Up or Leap Ahead

While it's generally not a good idea to outsource core competencies, outsourcing might be used to catch-up with or move in front of competitors in the technology that could underlie a competitive strategy.

For example, use of the World Wide Web for customer support and sales is exploding onto the information systems scene as this is being written. Many organizations lack the skills and experience to handle the security, site construction and maintenance, links to legacy databases, and reliable 24-hour per day service that commercial Web sites demand.

Various firms have outsourced some or all aspects of Web customer systems to vendor firms for the fast start this allows and the reliable, secure service it provides.

Some of these same organizations have decided to let vendor contracts terminate and insource commercial Web site functions now that it's clearer what the competitive strategy will be and the organization's own IT department has had time to move up the learning curve.

4.4.4 Competitive Necessities

Competitive necessities are information systems functions required to put your organization on a level playing field with other organizations in your industry. Competitive necessities don't confer a competitive advantage, but without them your organization is at a *competitive disadvantage*. Information systems functionality that was leading edge at one time in the history of an industry and provided competitive advantage often becomes a competitive necessity as other organizations copy it. An example is bank ATMs. The banks that innovated this customer service in the 1970s gained market share. Now nearly all banks offer ATM service, and ATMs are no longer a competitive advantage. But they are competitive necessities. A bank without ATM service is at a competitive disadvantage.

While there is risk in outsourcing a function that confers a competitive advantage, the risk in outsourcing competitive necessities is not so clear-cut. Consider outsourcing a competitive necessity if all of the following are true.

- Vendors offer industry standard services that fulfill a competitive necessity role.
- Vendors can perform the function more skillfully or at less cost.
- The vendors have good track records, are reliable, and lead or at least stay very current in the new developments in the technology or application that is a competitive necessity.
- A sound contract can be written and enforced for provision of these services.

The competitive necessities issue must also be considered in terms of the future. What is critical to business functioning now, may not be so critical in the future. If computer-based home banking and down-loadable cyber cash become the norm, ATMs may decline in competitive significance and gradually disappear or become concentrated in certain geographical areas. On the other hand, what is not critical now may become so in the future. Scan the future business and technical environments as they relate to competitive necessities. Outsourcing a competitive necessity or a function that will become a competitive necessity may be a cost-effective way of keeping up with advancing technology and changing functionality in applications that deliver services necessary to stay in the competitive running.

4.4.5 An Alternative Framework for Analyzing Selective Outsourcing

Another way to analyze the selective outsourcing issue is suggested by Lacity, Willcocks, and Feeny (1996). They look at an information systems function that might be outsourced in terms of two dimensions — its contribution to business positioning and its contribution to business operations. A function that is all-important to business position or competitive advantage is a "differentiator" while a function that doesn't contribute to competitive advantage is a "commodity." The same function can be categorized by the degree to which it is critical to business operations from "critical" at one extreme to "useful" at the other. Once categorized on these two dimensions, place the function in the two-by-two matrix shown in Figure 4–1.

Information systems functions in the northeast quadrant are critical differentiators that are both essential to competitive positioning and to support of business operations. These are functions that for reasons of control are best left in-house. Outsource this only when a joint business or strategic alliance that brings competitive advantage to both can be structured.

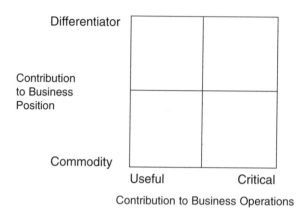

Figure 4-1. Selective Outsourcing Analysis Matrix

Critical commodities, the southeast quadrant, are the competitive necessities that all companies in an industry must have to be successful. They don't confer competitive advantage, but they must be done well to provide the essential services that keep a company in the race with others. These can be outsourced, but only if they pass the tests set out above for competitive necessities.

Useful commodities, the southwest quadrant, are the functions most amenable to outsourcing. Because they are commodities many vendors have the capability of performing them well, and they pose no real risk to competitive position when outsourced.

Useful differentiators, the northwest quadrant, is a null category of systems that should not exist. These are systems that make the business different from competitors but aren't critical as supports for business operations. Maybe the system was initiated with the hope of using it to win competitive advantage, but these hopes were not fulfilled. Maybe an enhancement of a commodity like system gives the business a capability that other competitors don't have but without conferring a competitive advantage. These are systems that can be terminated or migrated to some standard, low-cost method for provision, like package software. They are not candidates for selective outsourcing.

Michael Earl (1996) adds another dimension to be considered in a selective outsourcing decision and that is the level of performance of an information systems function by the IT department. When the IT department is performing a function poorly, Earl suggests the function is probably a good candidate for outsourcing as a way of improving performance if the function is a commodity. But core functions, or functions vital to business success, should first be put to a market test before outsourcing. Benchmark the function against industry standard performance as a way of determining whether outsourcing can be expected to lead to performance gains that will more than offset costs. If competitors and vendors do considerably better than internal IT, then seriously pursue the outsourcing option. If the market gains are too meager to offset the additional costs of outsourcing, then shake up and reform the internal IT operation to get performance comparable to the market.

4.5 CONTROL SCREEN, APPROPRIATE RELATIONSHIPS WITH VENDORS, AND INSOURCING

The second screen in an outsourcing feasibility study addresses control issues as they affect both total outsourcing and selective outsourcing decisions. Much of the outsourcing literature warns against giving vendors too much control. But the admonition "don't lose control" isn't very useful in itself. The issue of control comes down to the nature of the outsourcing arrangement with the vendor. Which outsourcing arrangements are safe and which are dangerous? What are the determinants of safe and dangerous arrangements?

Organizations can't function without controls. Controls are one of the glues that hold organizations together. The issue always is "What controls are necessary and at what cost?" When you delegate work to another person in your organization, you institute controls and depend on the controls to guide the effort of the worker. You depend on controls to achieve the desired work output or benefits.

If the nature of the work to be done is such that delegation necessitates very burdensome, expensive controls, you may be better off doing the work yourself. The same is true of outsourcing. If it will take too much effort and cost to insure that you get what you want from the vendor, do it yourself — insource.

4.5.1 Outsourcing Objectives

The starting point for analyzing the control issue is a clear understanding of the objectives of outsourcing and the scope of what is to be outsourced.

DuPont had clear sourcing objectives when it entered a four billion-dollar ten-year agreement with CSC and Andersen Consulting. It wanted business solutions for its manufacturing, marketing, distribution, and customer service functions. The sourcing arrangement was undertaken to enhance the range and speed of services for DuPont's businesses and improve its productivity through simplified business processes, integrated systems, and cost-effective operations. Cost reduction was not a primary objective. DuPont judged its IT functions as already cost-effective and world class. However, DuPont does expect continued productivity improvements throughout the life of the outsourcing arrangement.

Riggs Bank identified several motives to outsource before it entered a 10-year contract with IBM. The bank had had an aging data center infrastructure with a pressing need to invest in new storage devices at a time when the bank had no capital budget available for IT. It was having trouble attracting and retaining qualified IT skills. And there was no competitive barrier to outsourcing; IT was not viewed as a core competency. Data Center operations, systems programming, and voice and data communications were selected as functions to outsource. Elf Atochem North America outsourced the support of legacy systems that would be replaced by SAP in order to permit its staff to concentrate on the implementation of the new software.

Your organization needs to address and get agreement on the following issues:

- What is to be outsourced? Answer this question in high-level terms but with some precision. See the discussion of scope below.

- Why is it being outsourced?

- What are the expected benefits of outsourcing? Again, the original motive for outsourcing should help frame the benefits issue. Consider all the benefits that may be available from outsourcing. It would be a mistake to reject an outsourcing possibility out-of-hand for insufficient benefits because the analysis missed some collateral benefits that could make outsourcing work. If you're not certain, talk with vendors, your industry contacts, and perhaps consultants.

- Given the expected benefits, what are the expectations with respect to vendor performance? Answers to this question start with the motives for outsourcing but don't end there. If cost savings is the desire, then obviously a vendor is expected to save costs, but not, presumably with a great sacrifice in service levels. Think beyond the immediate issues that motivate outsourcing to the other issues that surround good performance and decide what a vendor must do to satisfy your organization in all these dimensions. Don't forget that outsourcing must please the ultimate business users of information services *as they perceive service*, not just the IT department.

4.5.2 Scope of the Function Being Outsourced

Understand and carefully define the scope of the function to be outsourced. Identification of an outsourcing candidate does not necessarily result in a crisp definition of the boundaries of what might be outsourced. Before discussions of relationships with vendors and ultimate decisions on whether to outsource can proceed, it's necessary to know the exact scope of the outsourcing proposal.

- "User support" is not a sufficient definition. Does this include support for customers? Does this include technical manuals and training? Does this include the building of end-user systems?
- "Maintenance programming" isn't a sufficient definition. Does it include enhancements — what kind of enhancements? Does it include defect tracking, reporting, analysis, and configuration control?
- Where are the boundaries of "network management" for a proposal to outsource this function?

When outsourced functions have many connections and interrelationships with other functions that remain in-house, the costs increase and the benefits may decline relative to outsourced functions without connections. Costs increase for vendor negotiation and contracting because it takes more effort to separate closely interrelated functions, specify what is inside and outside the contract, and how each must work together. Costs go up for managing a vendor because it takes more coordination time and effort between the people managing the in-house functions and the vendor managing the outsourced functions. Benefits may be harder to achieve because coordination between client and vendor is difficult and might break down at times.

Since the interrelationships in question are so important, this is the time, at the very outset of the outsourcing process, to get a clear idea of scope. Minimize interrelationships between outsourced and in-house functions to reduce coordination costs and increase the probability of achieving the desired benefits.

4.5.3 The Nature of the Relationship with a Vendor and Insourcing

Retaining control in an outsourcing relationship is critical. If outsourcing would cause your organization to lose control, it's better to insource.

Controls are embedded in governance arrangements. For example, you control subordinates through reporting and authority relationships that define much of the governance structure of your organization. In addition to the formal relationships, informal mechanisms also contribute to your control.

Outsourcing relationships also have governance structures. The formal part of outsourcing governance is the legal contract with the vendor. Other control mechanisms exist outside a single contract. Together the formal contract and the informal controls define the governance arrangements in outsourcing.

It may seem premature to address the relationship or governance structure to be developed with a vendor in the feasibility phase of an outsourcing evaluation, but it is not. In fact, failure to address this issue at an early stage is an important cause of ultimate difficulties in outsourcing. The choice has far-reaching consequences, including impacts on the benefits and costs of outsourcing and the risk incurred.

The relationship to develop with a vendor depends critically on the extent to which you can negotiate a complete contract at the outset (Apgar and Saharia, 1995; Klepper, 1994). "Complete" in this sense means a contract that covers all possible contingencies that can arise over the life of the arrangement. Consider two examples from everyday life that frame the extremes in relationships:

Supermarket purchases.

When you pay for groceries and take the sales receipt at the supermarket checkout counter, ownership of the goods in your shopping cart are transferred from the supermarket company to you. Although there are occasional returns, these business deals rarely go wrong. The reasons are as follows: (a) once the purchaser takes the goods away from the store, his or her use, consumption, and derivation of benefits from the goods is completely independent of the supermarket; (b) the purchaser typically has very good prior information on what he or she is buying and the purchaser has accurate expectations of how the products bought will perform in use or consumption; (c) the time between purchase and consumption is short and rarely does the environment change sufficiently to call into question the original reasons for making the purchase or raise regret that the conditions under which the goods are to be consumed has changed; and (d) if for any reason the customer is not satisfied, or simply as a matter of whim or convenience, the customer is not compelled to go back to the same supermarket for a future purchase. Injury or damage caused by use of the product is an issue between you and the manufacturer, not the supermarket.

Marriage.

"In sickness and health 'til death do us part," is the pledge in many marriage ceremonies. The circumstances surrounding marriage contracts are a lot different than supermarket sales in that (a) many commitments are made as a marriage progresses that are more or less specific to the marriage relationship (like buying a house or having children) so that continued enjoyment of some of the benefits of the marriage are dependent on the cooperation of one's spouse; (b) complete knowledge of the personality and behavior of a spouse over the life of a marriage is not possible at the outset, and the environment that surrounds the relationship can change dramatically (as when one or both partners get more education, change jobs, change careers, and when the couple moves to a new city, develops new friends and relationships outside the marriage, have children, etc.); and (c) if the relationship is to endure, it must be renewed or renegotiated as time goes on, a process that takes place consciously and formally or unconsciously and informally.

The fact that the courts hear few supermarket cases but many divorce cases suggests that doing a satisfactory deal with a supermarket is a lot easier than a marriage.

As absurd as the supermarket-marriage comparison may be, it points up the elements that underlie control or lack of control in contracts and how relationships can be structured to accommodate these elements.

4.5.4 Factors That Determine Control

The nature of the relationship developed with a vendor — contractual and otherwise — determines control. The emphasis here is on the extent to which complete legal contracts can be written and the measures to which you must resort if complete contracts cannot be developed.

The range of relationships that can be developed with a vendor extend from market relationships at one extreme to partnerships at the other. The factors that make one relationship more appropriate for control than another are asset specificity, uncertainty, and the need for repeated contracting with the same vendor. Each of these factors is now defined.

Asset specificity

Asset specificity refers to assets constructed as part of an outsourcing deal that are specific to the outsourcing arrangement with a particular vendor and whose productivity will be compromised if the deal falls apart. Outsourcing with a vendor for a good or service can necessitate (a) the development of some resource or asset that is specific to a certain physical place; or (b) a technological advantage that is specific to a particular interacting equipment, software, people, and data; or (c) knowledge that can't be separated from specific people or institutions; or (d) an advantage in delivering a service in a timely fashion that is specific to particular resources or capabilities developed in the deal between the two parties.

When any combination of these circumstances arise, the continued bene-fits to be derived from the work done depend on the continuity of the relation-ship between the two parties. Both parties depend on the other. The party making the investment, party A, can't recoup the investment if the other party, party B, abandons the relationship. Party B enjoys the benefits of A's invest-ment, does not have complete knowledge of how the investment is employed, and consequently becomes dependent on the relationship with A. Buying printer paper from a computer supply company involves no asset specificity. The stock of paper is worth just as much if the vendor goes out of business or the rela-tionship is severed in some other way. Having a vendor develop and operate a system that's critical to business functioning and based on specific knowledge of your business involves a lot of asset specificity. If the vendor goes out of business or the relationship rapidly terminates for some reason, it may not be possible to maintain the services of the system at levels adequate to support the business, and it could take another vendor a lot of effort and a long time to gain sufficient knowledge of the system to successfully replace the first vendor.

The following questions help clarify the existence of asset specificity (Ang and Beath, 1993):

- Will the work result in physical assets or software that can only be fully functional and useful if the vendor is around to operate, support, or maintain them?
- Will giving the vendor a full understanding of your requirements involve a lot of time and effort (and thus, cost) on your part and/or the vendor's part?
- Will the work require a lot of time and effort (and thus, cost) to your organization in learning the vendor's methods or ways of doing things?
- Will the work require a lot of time and effort (and thus, cost) to the ven-dor's organization in learning your organization's methods or ways of doing things?

Positive answers indicate asset specificity, and the more time or effort or cost that is involved, the greater the degree of asset specificity. When asset specificity is present, your organization is dependent on the vendor in a way that simply doesn't exist when asset specificity is absent.

Uncertainty

Uncertainty about the future causes other potential difficulties. The inabil-ity to foresee all changes that can occur in the environment makes it impossible to construct a contract with the vendor that anticipates all changes. If unforeseen circumstances do occur, you need assurance that the arrangement with the vendor can be satisfactorily modified to take account of the new conditions. For example, if you wrote a contract to outsource all networking in your company a few years ago, you probably could not anticipate the evolution of Internet and Intranet technology. If networking using Intranet technology now makes a lot of sense, can this be worked out with the vendor when the original contract has no provision for change of this sort?

Complex outsourcing needs may compound uncertainty because complexity increases the difficult in seeing exactly how future events can impact an outsourcing relationship.

Need for flexibility in the information systems function for business or other reasons also heightens the impact of uncertainty. The extent to which contracts can be complete is reduced and the cost of governing the relationships with a vendor is increased if your IT department is constantly adjusting to stay in alignment with changing business needs.

Repeated Contracting

If there are benefits in using the same vendor repeatedly for a service, you should put more effort into selecting that vendor initially and in maintaining the relationship as it progresses. The governance costs of the relationship are higher with repeated contracting. If the relationship doesn't work out beyond the first contract, you've lost the advantage that repeated contracting promises, and you incur the costs of searching for a new vendor. In other words, for some kinds of outsourcing you want a relationship that will endure for the greater benefits continuity provides, but the costs of governing such relationships will also be higher.

Maintenance programming is an example of a service that might best be performed by repeated contracting with the same vendor. If the vendor can guarantee some continuity in the people who fix your systems, these people gain knowledge of the systems they maintain and become more proficient. A new maintenance vendor hired every year or so is a situation in which the costs of finding and contracting with a vendor are incurred repeatedly.

4.5.5 Choosing the Right Relationship

Contracting relationships can be viewed as a range or continuum, as in Figure 4–2. At one extreme are marketlike relationships in which your organization has a choice of many vendors capable of performing the work, relatively short contract durations, and the ability to switch to another vendor at the end of a contract for future work of the same type with little or no cost or inconvenience. At the other extreme are long-term partnership arrangements in which your organization contracts repeatedly with the same vendor and develops a mutually beneficial relationship that lasts a long time. The middle of the continuum is occupied by relationships that must endure and remain reasonably harmonious until a major piece of work is completed; these are termed "intermediate" relationships in this book. Since it is a continuum, there are relationships that lie closer to market relationships and relationships that lie closer to partnerships, as well as those that are midway between the extremes.

Market   Intermediate   Partnership

Figure 4–2. Vendor Relationship Continuum

Market relationships cost the least to set up and administer and are relevant for work that is fairly simple and straightforward. Intermediate relationships cost more and are relevant for work that is more complex and has substantial benefits. Partnerships cost the most but are only relevant when the benefits of a close relationship with a vendor are substantial. Choosing the wrong relationship results in either excess costs or failures. The remainder of this section outlines the factors that determine appropriate contracting relationships.

The type of relationship to develop with a vendor depends on the asset specificity, uncertainty, and repeated contracting issues introduced above (See Figure 4–3). Market relationships are appropriate when the work can be done in a fairly short time with little chance that changes in the environment will upset requirements and when there is no real asset specificity, then it should be possible to write a contract that specifies all contingencies. Generally this describes generic services many vendors can provide and situations where one vendor can readily be substituted for another. The fact that complete contract terms can be specified and enforced and the fact that other competing vendors are waiting to take the business if the vendor of choice doesn't perform keeps your vendor in line. Short-term contract programming might be an example here.

Intermediate relationships are best if the work will (a) take some time to accomplish; (b) changes in the environment could change requirements; and (c) some asset specificity is present; but (d) there is no particular advantage to maintaining a relationship with the vendor once the work is completed. There needs to be durability in the relationship with the vendor. Durability can be obtained by developing a contract and general relationship with the vendor that recognizes events may occur that are not specified in the contract and outlines the ways your organization and the vendor will handle these when they arise. The law and economics literatures call this "neoclassical contracting." Since it's in an intermediate position between market relationships and partnerships, the more descriptive term, "intermediate relationships" is used here. Systems integration work that is handed over by the vendor when completed with no future need for vendor services is an example of an intermediate relationship.

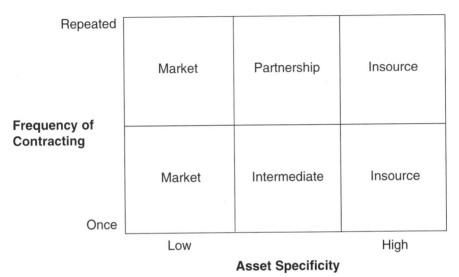

Figure 4–3. Contracting Relationships

Partnerships should be considered if (a) the time to do the work is longer in duration so that requirements could change with unforeseen fluctuations in the environment; (b) asset specificity is high; and (c) the need is one best addressed by repeated contracts with a vendor. The desired durability of the relationship is obviously much longer than in the second case. Here partnerships work best. In partnerships, continuity is obtained by trust and mutually beneficial behavior that is reciprocated by the other party. The governance costs and risks are high, so the gains from partnership must be substantial to offset these. A long term relationship between a client and vendor who undertake a profit making venture is an example.

Insourcing is the appropriate response when uncertainty and asset specificity are very high and the need for long-term continuity is great. Here the process of performing the function through an outside vendor probably involves so much setup and governance costs that it's cheaper to do it yourself.

The above analysis assumes the work to be done is project like with beginning and end points. When the task to be performed is a process, like operating a data center or network, the issues of uncertainty and asset specificity are still central, but there is no natural end point to a relationship with a vendor. As uncertainty increases, shorter contracts are desirable so that renegotiating can take place to address new circumstances. As asset specificity rises, longer contracts are best so that the assets built as part of the relationship with a vendor are protected by the continuing relationship. Under combinations of very high uncertainty and very high asset specificity, insourcing is the best option.

Examples abound of outsourcing arrangements toward the market end of the relationship spectrum. True partnerships are rarer. The deal between DuPont as the client and CSC and Andersen Consulting as the vendors is a partnership example. Like most partnerships, it has objectives that extend beyond the IT function to impact the business processes of DuPont. Its main objectives are to augment DuPont's growth and increase shareholder value.

4.5.6 An Alternative Framework

Lacity, Willcocks, and Feeny (1996) propose a somewhat different framework for contracting options. See Figure 4-4. They identify two dimensions that define the nature of contracts: (a) purchasing style, or the relationship with a vendor that runs from what they call "transactions" (and this book calls marketlike exchanges) to "relationships" (or what this book calls partnerships) and (b) purchasing focus or the desire to structure the contract to obtain either resources from the vendor that are then managed by the internal IT department or outcomes or results where the vendor provides the management of an outsourced function as well as the resources to undertake it. Lacity and her co-authors then define four contracting types:

(1) "Buy-in" — vendors supply resources, like contract programmers, to meet short-terms needs, and management is retained by the internal IT department. This corresponds to market-type relationships.

(2) "Preferred supplier" — longer-term relationships with a vendor for provision of services over more than one contract. This is structured to give the IT department more information on vendor resources and a chance to influence how the vendor does its business (for example, in selecting or training its staff). Each separate contract is marketlike, but the vendor's opportunity to win future business is contingent on undertaking efforts beyond those required in a single contract to be in the running for the next contract. This is a market-type contracting relationship with a second, implied contract the performance of which qualifies a vendor for future business.

(3) "Contracting out" — the requirements are quite clear-cut and a fairly complete contract can be written. This corresponds to intermediate contracting.

(4) "Preferred contractor" — the vendor supplies management and resources, and the two parties share risk by structuring the contract to give the vendor incentives to perform. Lacity, et al. use the example of a joint company formed to do data center operations as an example. These are longer term, repeat contracting situations that fall in the partnership category.

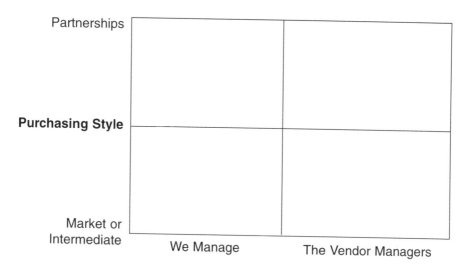

Figure 4–4. Contracting Options

Adapted from "The Value of Selective IT Sourcing," by Mary C. Lacity, Leslie P. Willcocks, and David F. Feeny, *Sloan Management Review*, Spring 1996, by permission of publisher. Copyright 1996 by Sloan Management Review Association. All rights reserved.

4.5.7 A Recap of Vendor Control and Relationship Issues

In this feasibility phase of the outsourcing process, it's only necessary to understand the nature of the outsourcing need and objectives in terms of asset specificity, uncertainty, and the desirability of repeat contracting. Do some early, up-front thinking about your candidate for outsourcing against the dimensions of asset specificity, uncertainty, and the desirability of repeat contracting so that further consideration of benefits, costs, and risks can be made with a clear view of how the relationship with a vendor will affect these.

Of the three main contracting options, market relationships are the least risky and the least costly in terms of finding a suitable vendor, entering a contract with the vendor, enforcing the contract, and coordinating with the vendor over the life of the contract. The kind of work suitable for market relationships is also the kind of work for which returns or benefits are usually most certain. The last option, partnerships, is the most risky and most costly. The benefits from partnerships are less certain. Intermediate contracting lies between the other two in risk, cost, and the certainty of benefits.

Outsourcing arrangements in the range of the continuum from intermediate relationships to partnerships are ones in which all necessary controls can't be put in a contract. To stay in control, your organization has to build a relationship with a vendor that keeps the vendor in line.

Some work should not be outsourced at all because it involves too much asset specificity, uncertainty, and need for continuity. There are no adequate governance mechanisms for controlling a vendor. It is wise to consider this early in the outsourcing decision process before incurring unnecessary costs.

Vendors may approach your organization proposing "partnerships." This can occur in the context of many different kinds of services, some of which meet the conditions outlined above for partnerships, and many of which do not. The meaning of the term "partnership" in everyday speech has been devalued. Reserve true partnerships for situations that demand them. Don't enter long-term relationships with vendors when the circumstances and facts do not support partnering. The details of partnerships and preferred vendor relationships are discussed in later chapters.

4.6 OTHER HIGH-LEVEL FEASIBILITY CONSIDERATIONS

Thus far two key issues and screens have been considered in assessing the feasibility of an outsourcing project, core or competitive competencies and control of the vendor through the nature of the relationship. Now it is time to consider other factors that a feasibility analysis should address.

4.6.1 Risks of New Technology

If outsourcing involves technology new to the marketplace, risk is always substantially higher. Outsourcing may be attractive because your organization has no experience with the technology, and you hope that outsourcing with a knowledgeable vendor can reduce the risk that the new technology presents. Be careful. Vendor magic may be limited where cutting-edge technologies are concerned. Investigate the available vendors who claim experience with the new technology and talk with some of their clients.

4.6.2 Organizational Readiness

The readiness of the organization for change is another early consideration in outsourcing decisions. Will outsourcing cause considerable disruption in the organization? Is the organization already in turmoil so that outsourcing will compound existing difficulties? Think through the consequences. For example, outsourcing some aspect of application development may break up close relationships between application developers in your internal IT department and users who have worked with and depended on these developers in the past. If new applications are critical for business support, this may not be the appropriate time to make changes that alter relationships and work patterns.

Outsourcing also has obvious impacts on the IT department. Depending on what is outsourced, there can be morale problems, turnover, and disruption in information systems functions left in-house.

Think through the organizational and human dimensions and impacts. It would be a mistake to assume that organizational response is unimportant or that it can be easily managed. Outsourcing can fail due to human factors. If outsourcing could be derailed by an organizational backlash, now is the time to reconsider.

4.6.3 Available Vendors

Outsourcing has grown dramatically over the last decade, and vendors have appeared to address almost every conceivable information systems requirement. But your need might be unique, or it may involve a combination of requirements that no vendor has experienced before. Perhaps this can be handled by taking on two or more vendors, perhaps not. It is best if more than one vendor is capable of and interested in doing your work so that there is competition for your business. Check to see that your outsourcing need can be met and there will be competition for your business.

4.6.4 Sufficient Scale

The selective outsourcing candidate function must be large enough to interest vendors. If the unit of work is too small, few vendors will bid for the work and/or the vendor that takes up the work may pay little attention to the work as it strives to satisfy accounts that are much more important in its total revenue stream. This problem might be lessened by finding smaller vendors to bid on the work. But this can limit the pool of vendors competing for the work, and it may force you to deal with vendors who have less capability and experience.

4.7 A PRELIMINARY DECISION AND PLANNING

Even at this early stage the main outlines of critical cost, benefit, and risk elements will be apparent. As Riggs Bank approached an outsourcing decision on data center, systems programming, and voice and data communications, Riggs identified the biggest benefit as a predictable cost structure with the elimination of capital expenditure spikes. The biggest risk was the potential inability of the vendor to perform as contracted. Also, there were significant costs to enter into the agreement, such as the time of the executives and others conducting the evaluation and negotiating, but these costs were judged to be insignificant compared to the data center's capital expenditure requirements.

At this point in the outsourcing process, a decision can be made to proceed to a more detailed evaluation of outsourcing. Because subsequent analysis will involve still more time and resources, it is appropriate at this stage to do some planning for that activity, particularly for large outsourcing projects.

4.7.1 Budget and Schedule

At this point you should have good knowledge of the objectives and scope of the outsourcing project. The next step is to make some estimates of the additional time and effort that will be necessary to:

- Perform additional analyses and prepare a Request for Proposal (RFP), including the details of services that a vendor must provide.
- Receive vendor replies and evaluate them.
- Choose a vendor.
- Negotiate and sign a contract.
- Transition from the current situation to outsourcing.

Understand the time constrains on the evaluation effort your IT staff will be concerned about the time to a decision, and sometimes top managers are anxious for outsourcing to proceed and will lose patience with a long, drawn-out evaluation exercise. Include senior management and selected staff in the planning process for the schedule and other aspects that are central to their concerns.

Use experience on past outsourcing projects of similar size, scope, and complexity to estimate the costs and the time necessary to complete the above activities. If previous experience with outsourcing is limited or nonexistent, get outside consulting help.

Key people from the user community, the ranks of technical people, or the executive sponsor may be needed to move the process forward. Confirm their availability and get their commitment to a schedule that will keep the outsourcing evaluation on track and on schedule.

Bring the analysis and planning work done thus far together in a document. Be certain that critical assumptions are clearly stated.

4.7.2 Leadership

The performance of the feasibility analysis team and its individual members should be evaluated. Normally the familiarity with the issues obtained by the team in the feasibility phase will argue for retaining this group to do the detailed analysis and development of an RFP in the next phase of the outsourcing process. However, if one or more team members is ill-suited for this purpose, now is the time to replace them with persons who are more capable.

4.7.3 Communication of the Evaluation to Employees

Complete secrecy in outsourcing feasibility and decision making is often impossible. IT staff and users will likely know that outsourcing is under consideration. Anxieties of various sorts arise and can be very counter-productive. Fear of outsourcing will result in a greater intrusion of politics into the outsourcing process than otherwise might be the case. Staff turnover may rise in anticipation of outsourcing. When attempts at secrecy fail, as they often do, rumors inevitably start. Rumors usually bear no relationship to reality, and rumors are almost always devoid of any of the benefits that change can bring.

Every organization must make its own decisions on how much of the deliberations over outsourcing are made public. However, in the absence of other reasons to close off the process, openness is advised. With more information, those who won't be affected can be relieved of all anxiety. With more information, the advantages of outsourcing can begin to be communicated to users who might be affected, and recall that user representatives should be part of the outsourcing decision process when their areas will be impacted by outsourcing. With more information, IT personnel who might be affected by outsourcing can be reassured.

Communication should take place by frequent dispatches through many communication modes — general meetings, small group meetings, newsletters, e-mail, and one-on-one conversations. Consider establishing a hot line that any employee can use to receive reliable and up-to-date information on the pending outsourcing initiative.

4.8 REFERENCES

Ang, Soon and Beath, Cynthia Mathis, "Hierarchical Elements in Software Contracts," *Journal of Organizational Computing*, 3/3 (1993), 329–361.

Apgar, Paul and Saharia, Aditya N., "Outsourcing Information System Functions: An Organization Economics Perspective," *Journal of Organizational Computing*, 5/3 (1995), 197–217.

Benko, Cathleen, "Outsourcing Evaluation," *Information Systems Management*, (Spring 1993), 45–50.

Earl, Michael, "The Risks of Outsourcing IT," *Sloan Management Review*, (Spring 1996), 26–32.

Klepper, Robert, "A Model of I/S Partnering Relationships," *Journal of Computer Personnel Research*, 15, 2 (July 1994), 3–9.

Kovacevic, Antonio and Majluf, Nicolas, "Six Stages of IT Strategic Management," *Sloan Management Review*, (Summer 1993), 77–87.

Lacity, Mary C., Willcocks, Leslie P., and Feeny, David F., "The Value of Selective IT Sourcing," *Sloan Management Review*, (Spring 1996), 13–25.

McFarlan F. Warren and Nolan, Richard L., "How to Manage an IT Outsourcing Alliance," *Sloan Management Review*, (Winter, 1995) 9–23.

Vankatesan, Ravi, "Strategic Sourcing: To Make or Not to Make," *Harvard Business Review*," (November–December, 1992) 98–107.

Vankatraman, N., "Beyond Outsourcing: Managing IT Resources as a Value Center," *Sloan Management Review*, 38/3 (Spring, 1997) 51–64.

Ward, John and Griffiths, Pat, *Strategic Planning for Information Systems*, 2nd edition, New York, John Wiley & Sons, 1996.

Willcocks, Leslie and Fitzgerald, Guy, "Market as opportunity? Case studies in outsourcing information technology and services," *Journal of Strategic Information Systems*, 2/3 (September, 1993) 123–242.

5

Detailed Analysis and the Request For Proposal Process

I f the outsourcing candidate passes the high-level screens discussed in the previous chapter, more detailed evaluation can begin. This chapter treats the analysis of costs, requirements, benefits, risks, and the preparation of a Request For Proposal (RFP).

In large outsourcing deals where the stakes are high, it's common to rely on outside consulting advice to be certain the analysis is correct and complete. DuPont used consultants extensively ensure that they had completely identified the potential costs, risks, and benefits. Smaller deals may not warrant this level of effort and expense, but attention should still be paid to the issues raised below.

An interview with outsourcing human resources expert Grover Wray concludes the chapter. Personnel issues often present the greatest problems in outsourcing and the management of the ongoing outsourcing relationship. Wray sets out ways to address these issues.

5.1 STRATEGY AND OBJECTIVES

To succeed in outsourcing, the strategy and related objectives to be met must be crystal clear. Clear objectives are the foundation for the outsourcing evaluation process at every stage:

- The first step is to know exactly what is wanted from outsourcing and what is most important.

- The second step is to analyze your organization in light of the objectives so good information is available on the current situation and the needs relative to objectives.
- The third is to formulate a complete Request For Proposal based on your objectives and issue the RFP to qualified vendors.
- The final step is to evaluate responses and negotiate with vendors in light of the objectives.

A clear sense of purpose is essential at every step for it focuses the study effort on the issues that matter most, and it's the foundation on which the Request For Proposal is structured. Knowing exactly what is needed guides the requirements and conditions in the RFP. It provides the basis for evaluating vendor responses, and clear purpose guides the inevitable trade-offs that must be made. If properly managed, this process leads to a sound decision on whether to outsource or not and provides the basis for success in selecting, negotiating with, and managing the vendor.

The motives for outsourcing set forward in Chapter 3 can be grouped into a few summary categories. One is business transformation or using outsourcing to improve both information systems services and related business processes. Another is efficiency or the desire to obtain information systems services at a lower cost. A third is effectiveness or the desire to obtain better service. A fourth is flexibility. A fifth is to shift the burden of information systems management from your organization to an outside vendor. A sixth is to change the financial structure of the organization by converting fixed to variable costs and obtaining cash for fixed assets. The last is political.

If multiple objectives exist, particularly if these fall into more than one of the major categories listed above, prioritize them. Be certain there is understanding and agreement among stakeholders. Trade-offs among objectives will likely be necessary. Without agreement on priorities, not only is there no basis for making trade-offs, but stakeholders will be pulling in different directions and major disagreements and misunderstandings may arise.

5.2 PEOPLE

At this point, the team that developed the initial high-level feasibility analysis can be expanded to include sufficient people with the requisite skills to perform a detailed analysis of the outsourcing proposal. While it may be necessary to expand the numbers, smaller teams are generally more efficient than larger teams. Again, both IT and user managers have a role. Technical people are needed to analyze technical issues. If transfer of personnel will account for a large part of the cost saving from the outsourcing deal, human resource people should be involved in the analysis.

In large outsourcing deals, including total outsourcing, a formal division of roles and responsibilities with reporting relationships is critical. Responsibilities might be divided by forming a technical group and a business group to which the technical group reports.

As DuPont evaluated its IT services needs prior to its $4 billion sourcing arrangement with CSC and Andersen Consulting, it relied on a large group of people. The project team consisted of approximately 25 full-time people and an additional 300 or so from every part of the company who served on various supporting teams. Focus groups with IT leaders from every region and business unit worked on the scope, objectives, and other component parts. Employee forums, held in most regions of the world, provided ongoing employee suggestions and feedback. DuPont brought in one of the top outsourcing consulting firms from the beginning to advise and assist with all aspects of the sourcing process. Top human resources consultants were engaged to assist DuPont in looking after the best interests of employees throughout the entire process. External outsourcing legal experts advised and assisted from the outset. The IT and other people participating were among the best in DuPont, and the outside legal and outsourcing experts were considered by DuPont to be the best in the business.

5.3 BASELINE ANALYSIS

The purpose of an outsourcing analysis is to set requirements and build a baseline to compare to vendor proposals. Without a baseline there is no rational way of knowing whether the proposal a vendor presents is better than keeping functions in-house.

What constitutes the baseline depends on what is to be outsourced and the motives for outsourcing. All baselines should start from service needs or requirements. Unless you know what you need, there is no way to ask a vendor for it. And most baselines will also include a measure of the costs of providing the required services in-house so that vendor proposals can be compared to the cost of doing the same things in your own organization. An exception might be outsourcing for new services or skills not currently available in-house. Other exceptions can arise when outsourcing is politically motivated. Here services and their related costs may take a back seat to any number of other agendas. The outsourcing objectives and scope should firmly set the boundaries of the needs and costs analysis.

The intended duration of the outsourcing arrangement also helps set the boundaries of the analysis. Going into the market to obtain contract programming labor by the month involves analysis of current conditions only. Developing an outsourcing deal to last 10 years requires consideration of many aspects of the business and technological future as part of a baseline and is much more difficult and time-consuming.

5.3.1 Analysis of Current Costs

Good estimates of the current costs of providing the function or functions to be outsourced are necessary. This is particularly true if cost savings is the main driver of outsourcing. Current costs are compared to vendor costs to provide a measure of the savings available from outsourcing.

It is best to view costs from the business unit perspective because the business unit users will still pay for the services and because the cost analysis is more understandable to users if done from that view.

If the scope of the work to be outsourced is broad, it will take a lot of effort to develop estimates of current costs. The work should be divided among several individuals or teams

Build a standard format or outline for recording costs by hardware platform, by software, by service, and facility type so there is consistency and the final results can be brought together more easily. Standard categories will also facilitate comparison with vendors' responses.

Be sure all the costs are reflected in the numbers put together as information systems budgets sometimes don't reflect all the costs. If part of the costs of providing the function or functions is in user budgets, don't forget to include these in the total. If some part of providing this function is already outsourced, don't forget to include these costs, as well. Interview IT and user managers close to the functions to be certain nothing is missed.

When vendor equipment will replace your organization's equipment in the provision of services, estimate current equipment costs from the depreciation on the equipment. If necessary, go to your accounting department for help on the value of the assets in question and the appropriate depreciation method. Your organization's equipment also has a cost of capital or the cost of borrowing the money to buy it; again, the accounting department can help.

Don't forget the cost of leased equipment, and don't forget hardware and software maintenance fees. Personnel costs should include benefits, as well as wages and salaries. To make a fair comparison with vendor costs, personnel costs should also include incentives like bonuses, training, and education expenses.

Make some adjustments in your cost baseline to bring it in line with the way a vendor will operate in outsourcing. For example, you may have several distributed data centers. When outsourced, these data center operations will be consolidated by the vendor into one operation. If your own consolidation of data centers would generate savings, then the relevant cost comparison is your consolidated data centers to the vendor's consolidated operation.

If an asset-for-cash swap is to be part of the outsourcing deal, estimate the current value of the information systems assets to be transferred by their current market value, book value, or other means.

Costs Based on Improved Information Systems Performance

If outsourcing is to be considered against the alternative of a revamped, improved, more efficient internal IT department, current costs must be altered accordingly. Two basic approaches can be taken. The first is to adjust current (and future) cost estimates to reflect intended improvements in internal performance. The second is to use industry benchmark data for performance of IT departments that are similar.

The second approach involves engaging an industry group or consulting firm with the relevant data. Hopefully these data will be disaggregated and available for the function or functions as defined by the scope of the outsourcing proposal. If not, the industry group or consulting firm may be able to do the disaggregation. Make the most informed estimate of the cost for the function or functions under consideration from the evidence available.

The first approach of adjusting current costs to reflect anticipated productivity gains is more problematic. Who is to say what is possible and reasonable? Hopelessly optimistic adjustments may result from leaving this exercise entirely in the hands of the IT department. Unnecessarily pessimistic adjustments may result if others are left in charge of this exercise. Sometimes it's possible to put this task in the hands of persons who command respect as unbiased. Sometimes this job can be put to a committee with representatives from differing views on what is possible. Sometimes it will be necessary to go outside the organization for consulting help to sort out these issues. Going to experienced consultants has the added advantage of tapping the knowledge of persons who have seen what is possible in improvement in information systems productivity in other organizations.

The credibility of cost estimates is of considerable importance. Certainly morale and motivation can suffer if persons on any side of an outsourcing issue feel the results are "cooked." Beyond the human resource implications, the soundness of the decision to outsource or not rests on these numbers. Bad numbers will likely result in a bad decision. Costs must be estimated accurately and thoroughly.

If the IT department is given the opportunity to make its own bid for the function or functions to be outsourced in competition with outsourcing vendors, the possibilities of bias discussed above are obvious. Such bids should be checked for accuracy and reasonableness by persons outside the IT department.

5.3.2 Analysis of Services to be Outsourced

Services are very different from products. They tend to be intangible and are often consumed as they are produced. This makes services more difficult to evaluate than products (Bowen and Schneither, 1988) and puts a premium on finding performance-based measures of services (Cronin and Taylor, 1992).

Complete understanding of the services to be outsourced is essential. An outsourcing contract should specify in detail what the vendor is to do, and this analysis must be driven down to a level that permits measurement. Service measures should provide a clear distinction between adequate and inadequate service. Without precise definitions and measures of the services involved in outsourcing, the necessary detail can't be put in a contract with the vendor, and you will find yourself negotiating with the vendor over the life of the contract on what is and is not covered in the deal and whether a service is being performed at an adequate level or not.

Elf Atochem's Request For Proposal included the terms of the expected contract and the measurements by which service quality would be tracked. Robert Rubin says, "We wanted to make sure that the potential suppliers understood our expectations."

If your organization has performance measures in place, start with them as a way of defining requirements, but don't be limited by them. If your performance measures are not complete, detailed, and measurable, you must extend this effort to prepare for outsourcing.

A detailed treatment of service levels is beyond the scope of this book. A good source to consult is the book by Andrew Hiles (1993) on service level agreements. The agreement or contract with a vendor should include the following where the description of a service is concerned:

- The organizational context of the service. How the organization is dependent on it; the priority of the service viewed against the business background; normal, critical, and peak periods for the service; and the business implications and costs incurred if the service is not available at normal and critical times. The analysis job, then, is to understand and characterize the service in its business setting as a support for the business. Complex services should be disaggregated into their component functions, and each sub-function should be addressed in the issues that follow.

- Where the service is delivered. Location can be important to quality delivery of a service. If location is important, analyze and document location issues.
- To whom the service is delivered. Document the recipients of services, which could include suppliers or customers of your organization as well as your own internal people.
- Transaction type. The kind of transaction undertaken by the service should be clearly specified. If one service process performs more than one kind of transaction, disaggregate the service further into its component transactions, or specify the requirements that follow in terms of each type of transaction.
- The output of the service or what the service contains or of what it consists. This needs to be specified in detail.
- The delivery time or periodicity of the service. Normal, critical, and peak times should be carefully defined and specified. If these do not occur at predictable intervals, measurable criteria should be established to distinguish one period of need from another.
- Availability of the service. Define what availability of the service means. Provide measurable targets or requirements for that availability.
- Throughput or capacity. What volume or capacity must the service be capable of handling, during normal times and during critical and peak periods?
- Response time. Within what period of time is it necessary to perform a service process, in normal, critical, and peak periods?
- Accuracy. If services are thought of as involving inputs, processes, and outputs, then what accuracy is required in each of these to constitute adequate quality? Make these requirements measurable, if possible.
- Security. What steps, if any, must be taken to secure the inputs to the service, the service process itself, or the outputs of the service?
- Backup and recovery measures, as necessary.
- Disaster planning and contingency measures, if necessary.
- Maintenance and downtime. If provision of the service entails scheduled maintenance or downtime for changes, these should be specified and the nature of the maintenance and/or changes must also be specified in a measurable way.
- Problem escalation. If problems occur in the provision of the service, how rapidly must these be corrected, in normal, critical, and peak times?

What procedure should be followed to ensure that correction takes place? The procedure should specify steps in an escalation process that requires attention by management in the vendor organization at successively higher levels as time proceeds.

- Penalties. The analysis can also address penalties due from the vendor for failure to correct within specified times and conditions.

- Reporting. What data must be reported to keep on top of the above aspects of service levels and at what frequency? What reporting is necessary in the event of problems and shortfalls? Should it include only numbers of incidents or also causes and related circumstances? What constitutes a problem? What form should reports take? (You shouldn't have to wade through a mountain of vendor paper to find what you want.)

- Any other requirements that are relevant to the quality of the service and its successful provision.

If particular services work in concert with each other in some ways, those relationships need to be specified in the requirements, and joint service levels should be defined.

Normal versus peak-period service levels have a few wrinkles that should not be overlooked. In most organizations during peak periods, resources are thrown at critical tasks leaving less critical jobs to sit undone until the peak is past. The same strategy might be adopted in outsourcing. The interrelated service levels of tasks in peak periods can be specified with specific degrading of some services in order to support others. Of course, you should expect vendor prices to be lower on this account since this approach spreads the work load over time.

Vendor reporting requirements can also include analyses of the root causes of faults. Requirements of this sort can force vendors to go to the bottom of problems and resolve them so that they don't occur again.

Service level targets should reflect expected improvements over time. Just as continual service productivity and quality improvements are goals in your organization, so vendor performance should improve over the life of an outsourcing arrangement, and these targets need to be established in requirements. If continuous improvement is required, vendor reporting should show performance trends.

Much of the information necessary to analyze services can only be obtained from users in your organization who depend on the services to support business functioning. It follows that knowledgeable user representatives must participate in the analysis effort.

Don't overlook necessary services. Documentation, report distribution, training, installation of new PC software, and many other tasks have the potential for being overlooked. Check each task in the function or functions to be outsourced very closely. Involve more than one person for the positive effects that two minds have over one. Simple process diagrams that account for inputs, processes, and outputs may help identify all elements of services.

Construct quantitative measures of all aspects of services and service requirements whenever possible; include these in the RFP; and include them in the contract and its exhibits. Vendor performance is much easier to determine if the measures are quantitative. Finding quantitative measures isn't always easy or even possible, but efforts should be made to do so. Consultants may have ideas that will help.

Specify how the vendor is to report service performance and problems and at what time intervals. Require that reports be to the point and tailored to your needs. Vendor standard reports may bury the numbers you need in voluminous documents. Put the responsibility for accuracy of reports on the vendor.

See the interview of David Kepler at the end of Chapter 6 for an example of some measures used by Dow Chemical in its outsourcing arrangement with Andersen Consulting.

5.3.3 Requirements Specified in Terms of Business Performance

When the motives for outsourcing fall into the category of business change and business performance, consider specifying requirements in business terms with related measures. Combining services specified in business terms with pricing or sharing formulas that reward vendors for meeting or exceeding the business targets is a particularly powerful way of aligning vendor incentives with the strategy and direction of your organization. For example, the requirement may be to provide your sales people with all the necessary infrastructure and information necessary to write a contract with a customer and book an order in real time, at customer locations throughout a sales region, using lap-top computers with dial-in capability. The measures could then be in terms of a reduction in order cycle time and customer satisfaction. If a vendor is given bonuses for making this work or if the vendor shares in some of the increased sales revenue that this approach might generate, the vendor has a very strong incentive to get your work done in the most effective way.

Partnerships usually involve anticipated bottomline business gains of substantial magnitude. Setting at least some requirements in business terms is likely in partner relationships. In its partnership arrangement with CSC and Andersen Consulting, DuPont aims to respond to the changing business environment with flexibility and speed, to gain rapid access to new technologies and skills, to continuously improve productivity, to maintain the ability to lead, manage, and renew, and to continuously improve operational reliability. Other important criteria for success are low unit costs, retaining stewardship of IT, maintaining a unified, global infrastructure, and continued fair treatment and development opportunities for its current and former employees.

5.3.4 Backlogs

If the function or functions that are candidates for outsourcing are plagued by persistent backlogs and one of the expectations for outsourcing is that backlogs will be reduced or eliminated, then some adjustment in current cost and service baseline numbers may be called for.

The hope is that the vendor's superior productivity will allow the work to be done with reduced backlogs and at lower cost than is currently incurred to provide these function(s) in your organization. However, if the problem is not one of productivity in your organization, but one of too few resources being applied to the problem, your cost numbers when compared to a vendor's proposal will be unrealistically low. Adjust actual cost and service levels upwards to realistic levels. Comparison with industry benchmarks for the function or functions under consideration should be helpful.

5.4 CHANGE: FUTURE REQUIREMENTS AND COSTS

Change is a constant in the information systems business. The analysis leading up to the Request For Proposal must address uncertain requirements and the possibility that requirements may change in ways that are not completely predictable.

5.4.1 When Requirements Are Less Certain

Some types of outsourcing have less certain requirements. Outsourcing to acquire and implement new technology is an example. Here the exact uses to which the new technology will eventually be put cannot always be completely specified upfront. The new technology may replace existing technology. The outsourcing vendor may be responsible only for the new technology, or the vendor may operate the existing, older technology as well. Despite the difficulties, outsourcing evaluation should attempt to define requirements as completely as possible.

An example might be outsourcing to replace an existing mainframe system or systems with a new solution implemented in client-server technology. It's unlikely that the analysis can predict the exact requirements and dimensions of the reengineered systems and accompanying client-server technology. However, the basic business information needs can be specified. Certainly the boundaries of the systems to be reengineered should be specified. To a large extent the sites and people who will be involved can be identified. It may also be possible to identify the kind of client-server technology that will be used, even if all aspects of the equipment and software cannot be specified.

It may also be possible in cases like these to think of the work to be done by the vendor as consisting of two stages — a first that does the analysis of the new systems and their design and a second project that builds and implements the systems. The dimensions of the first are more easily determined than the second. The RFP might then specify that the contract will cover the first project with an agreement, after some specified period of time and successful completion of the first project, to negotiate the second build and implement project. If the outsourcing vendor also takes responsibility for existing systems, the requirements for these systems can be very specifically determined and incorporated in an RFP and contract. The contract could specify two stages of the existing systems work — the first while the reengineering and client-server design project is completed, and the second involving a cut-over to the new systems by the vendor, contingent on the successful negotiation of the second project.

5.4.2 Analyzing the Potential for Change

Preparation for outsourcing contracts contemplated to last more than a year or two requires extrapolation of requirements into the future. Future needs are established by many factors but two of the most important where information systems are concerned are (a) business change and how information systems must alter to effectively support business change and (b) technological change that requires the adoption of new technology to support the business.

Projecting business change and technological change can be highly problematic. The further into the future one must project, the more uncertain the results become. This explains, in part, why critics of information systems outsourcing claim that an organization loses control through outsourcing. The contract written today can't possibly anticipate all future requirements because these will change as the business and technology change. What will the business and technology be in five years? In ten years?

Fortunately, it's possible to establish relationships with vendors and build provisions in contracts that incorporate mechanisms for addressing future change. The greater the likelihood of future change, the more toward the partnership end of the contracting spectrum a relationship with a vendor should be. The greater the likelihood of future change, the more contractual mechanisms for adjustment or renegotiation of the terms of the contract are required.

Do not forget to include personnel costs, including benefits, in your calculations. With newer and more advanced technology, the corresponding skill sets of technical people will change. Be realistic about the labor costs necessary to deliver services with the technology of the future.

Also bear in mind that in instances of selective outsourcing, you only analyze those aspects of your business that depend on the information systems functions under consideration for outsourcing. But because many parts of a business are interdependent, be sure the analysis is sufficiently broad to incorporate these interrelationships so that significant future change is not missed.

5.4.3 Business Change

First, estimate the expected rate of growth in your business in the years to be covered by the contract. Growth in business activity has consequences for information services. Do this by business segment or function because different segments and functions probably have different rates of growth. Look at how past rates of growth impacted the demand for information services and use these factors to estimate the impact of future growth on future services.

Second, check your organization's business strategy and plan and talk with user managers. Look for new initiatives. Look for mention of environmental factors that are likely to stimulate change. Convert these to impacts on the various business segments or functions with the help of business managers and roll these in with changes expected from the underlying rate of growth in the business.

Then, with the help of users in each business segment or function, project what these mean for information services necessary to support the change and translate these into requirements.

Adjust the cost baseline to reflect the support necessary to meet the anticipated changes in requirements. Also, adjust costs for anticipated future inflation. Do this year-by-year over the projected term of the contract. The year-by-year dollar estimates can also be discounted to the present for a summary measure.

In its preparations for outsourcing, Riggs Bank developed proformas based on historical budgets and projected major capital expenditures across 10 years with differing bank growth models. They also estimated fees based on different growth and reduction models with inflation protection.

5.4.4 Technological Change

Ten years ago, the World Wide Web and Intranets did not exist. Ten years ago, client-server computing was practically nonexistent. Projecting technological change and its impact on information services five or ten years into the future is a real act of faith. Much of the change brought by technology in longer time frames must be addressed through change mechanisms in a contract and in the relationship with a vendor. Still, effort devoted to technology forecasting is worthwhile. Even if the details of technical change can't be known, an idea of the sensitivity of baseline costs and requirements will help in the formulation of the change mechanisms in the contract.

Divide technology into categories that incorporate both technology type and the portions of the business supported by that type. Get information on the trajectory of each technology type from the trade press, from technology vendors, and from the consulting firms that are technology watchers.

Be alert for technological change that is likely to break the frame or radically change how information supports the business. It's easier to write a contract to accommodate incremental change in technology than radical change. The contract should address technology coming over the horizon that is likely to be important and specify mechanisms for dealing with it.

Use the results of the technology analysis to adjust cost estimates year-by-year. This analysis is also used to revise the requirements that vendors must meet. Don't forget to include in these requirements the documentation, training, and other support that users of the new technology will require. And don't forget that each round of technology upgrades, even that which is an extension of the existing technology set, involves configuration changes and user support.

5.4.5 Interrelated Business and Technology Change

In many industries and organizations, business change and technology support are interacting factors. Business change demands changes in technology. Technology change allows changes in business. The interrelationship makes forecasting more difficult, but also more compelling, if a good outsourcing contract is to be written.

Consider your organization from this perspective. Is new technology likely to change the way you do business creating whole new business options with accompanying technology requirements? Is business change going to spark the adoption of new technology sets not previously used in the business or even result in business-technology provider alliances that develop new technology?

5.4.6 Continuous Improvement

Continuous improvement in the delivery of information services may be part of your objective in outsourcing. If so, cast the analysis of the business and technological futures in continuous improvement terms, and set requirements that specify measurable goals in terms of productivity and quality improvement over time.

5.4.7 Future Cost and Services Evaluation Outcomes

The analysis should produce a business scenario, a related technology scenario, and corresponding cost baseline estimates and information systems support requirements with yearly detail. These are important starting points for construction of the RFP and negotiations with vendors.

5.4.8 Radical Change and Contract Circuit Breakers

If your organization's business and/or technological environment is uncertain, consider the possibility of structuring the Request For Proposal, the contract, and the eventual relationship with a vendor in terms that only hold if change is within some limits. If change exceeds prescribed limits, the contract requires that client and vendor renegotiate some or all of the contract and restructure their relationship accordingly. The analysis should identify good measures of business or technological change and the specific limits to change in the future. If change does exceed the threshold limits, a circuit breaker provision in the contract suspends contract terms (in part or for the whole of the contract) and specifies that renegotiation take place.

5.5 TRANSFERS OF PERSONNEL, HARDWARE, SOFTWARE, AND DATA

Outsourcing often involves transferring people, hardware, software under license, software developed in-house, or data to a vendor. The analysis leading up to the Request For Proposal should address each.

5.5.1 Personnel

When cost savings is a motivation, the effectiveness of personnel transfer is one key to realizing savings. The ability to manage an outsourcing deal is also affected by transfers. Therefore, a careful analysis of personnel is a requisite.

For the function or functions to be outsourced, make a list of all the employees involved. Don't forget employees who may be accounted for in user budgets. Then, determine which you want to transfer to the vendor, which to transfer to other parts of your organization, and which might be let go, if any.

Consider the cost and service ramifications of transferring your personnel to a vendor or replacing your people with vendor people. Some argue that your application systems maintenance people, with their first-hand and detailed knowledge of your systems and ability to fix and enhance these systems, are valuable resources that should not be transferred or let go if maintenance activity is important to the future quantity and quality of information services (Mylott, 1995). The same argument might be applied to application development staff in general. On the other hand, if you must let some people go to achieve the objectives of outsourcing, you should think through how personnel changes will affect services as against the cost savings or other advantages of the proposed outsourcing arrangement. There may be ways to keep the most indispensable people and still achieve most outsourcing objectives.

Consider the financial ramifications of all the options. Keeping an employee involves salary, benefits, and incentives, like bonuses. Transferring an employee may have substantial costs. The severance clauses in employee contracts need to be carefully checked; in some cases transfer to a vendor may be considered severance and trigger all kinds of severance payments and benefits. State laws may also have something to say about severance and if transfer is severance in outsourcing cases.

Management is also a consideration in who will be transferred. If the function or functions to be outsourced have one or more IT managers, the manager may be transferred to the vendor or retained in your organization to manage the liaison between your organization and the vendor. If the manager is transferred, another person must take responsibility for liaison. Consider personalities and attitudes. Keeping a manager to oversee the outsourcing deal who has contempt for outsourcing is probably not wise. And remember it's a mistake to outsource all of your information systems managerial knowledge and ability.

You may also consider the possibility of rotating people between your organization and the vendor's firm. This may be attractive to some people in your organization who don't want to sever ties completely. It may also be attractive to persons who see career and professional advantages in having experience on both sides of an outsourcing relationship. Such rotation arrangements may allow you to retain the services of key people who would otherwise seek employment elsewhere.

5.5.2 Analysis of Hardware Issues

Is hardware to be transferred to the outsourcing vendor? If so, an inventory of the affected hardware needs to be constructed, and research must be done on the hardware lease and maintenance agreements. Under what conditions can leases and maintenance agreements be transferred? What must be done? How much will it cost? How much lead time will it require? These are considerations that affect both the cost and the practicality of outsourcing.

The RFP should contain information on the hardware to be transferred and the terms and conditions under which it is to be transferred. Any payment from vendor to client as part of the transfer should also be determined and specified.

5.5.3 Analysis of Software Issues

Will it be necessary to transfer software so that the vendor can provide the required services? Do a careful analysis to find out; make an inventory. If so, does your organization own the software, or do you use it under license from a software vendor?

When the software is under license, significant problems may stand in the way of transferring the software to an outsourcing vendor. License agreements need to be checked carefully and, if necessary, lawyers consulted to uncover the constraints.

License agreements often prohibit disclosure, and transferring software to an outsourcing vendor is likely to be disclosure by the definitions used in licenses. Vendors of the software must be approached to see what can be done to get around the constraints; they often want more money, and the amount can be substantial.

Before caving in to software vendor demands, consider their bargaining position. Bargaining power tends to be less for vendors of generic systems and database software. It's typically much stronger for application software.

As part of this analysis, consider whether it might be cheaper to utilize completely different software when outsourcing the function or functions under consideration. Also, think through the time necessary to resolve the software-related issues. The analysis should pin down the dates on which licenses expire. Perhaps expiration presents opportunities for renegotiating with software vendors on terms that are favorable.

5.5.4 Conversions

Think through the costs of transferring your function or function to the vendor. In many instances the vendor will bear most of these costs, but even if this is the case, defining the costs is necessary to negotiating a contract that clearly specifies which costs belong to the vendor. Transition costs can include those associated with transferring and relocating people, transferring equipment and leases, and transferring software licenses. The vendor may need to train users in your organization if vendor systems are to be used. The vendor may also need to do data conversion and testing to see that systems that serve your organization will work in the vendor's environment. In most cases, these are the vendor's costs. Use the analysis of resource transfer issues to adjust overall outsourcing cost and time estimates.

Conversions must go smoothly to prevent disruptions in your business, and vendors should have the capability and experience to undertake these with confidence. The RFP process and its follow-up in negotiations with the vendor should probably include a test run of your data or a subset of your data on the vendor's system to see that the results are accurate and correspond to what your users anticipate.

Vendor systems may differ in many ways from your own — in interfaces and in various aspects of functionality. The differences may require changes in some of your business processes and almost certainly will require some training of the people who will use the vendor systems in your organization. Anticipate these needs, get information from vendors on differences as part of the RFP process, and include conversion costs, redesign of business process costs, and retraining costs as part of the costs of outsourcing.

Resources cannot be transferred overnight. Good service is often required on a more-or-less continuous basis, even during the period of transition. Often a phased approach is necessary with the transfer of resources and the assumption of vendor responsibility taking place over time

The RFP need not specify all aspects of transfers. Vendors have a lot of experience with transfers and will have good ideas about how to proceed with these.

5.5.5　International Issues

When the outsourcing deal will involve a contract that governs work in more than one country, the preparatory work is considerable. Your organization's legal department, or consultants hired for the purpose, need to research the laws of the countries involved to discover any statutes that govern the following and their relevancy:

- Transfer of employees and benefits.
- Transfer of data or data operations across national boundaries and other data issues.
- Encryption.
- Your particular industry or business.

- Ownership of computer assets.
- Technology exports and imports.

There are also money issues concerning where payment is to be made, in what currency, and how to handle exchange rate issues.

5.6 ADMINISTRATION COSTS IN OUTSOURCING

Outsourcing costs include the cost of finding a vendor, negotiating a contract, enforcing the contract, and managing the outsourcing relationship. The costs of negotiating and overseeing the outsourcing contract are usually higher than in-house management of the function to be outsourced, viewed from the same or similar levels of management.

Outsourcing administrative costs are higher for several reasons. First, no vendor must be found and no formal contract must be negotiated when the function is done in-house. Yes, some understandings must be reached when one function in an organization does work for another, but the time and effort involved in these cases is usually small relative to outsourcing. Second, outsourcing involves the risk that vendors will engage in opportunistic behavior; the vendor may try to take advantage of your organization.

When tasks are done in-house, less effort has to be put into assuring that the job is done. The risks of nonperformance are usually lower. The enforcement costs are much higher when the work is done by an outside vendor.

If your organization has previous experience with outsourcing, the best starting point is your own historical experience with outsourcing governance. Absent any experience in your organization, industry peers who have engaged in similar outsourcing or consultants are possible sources.

When Riggs Bank developed its outsourcing cost estimates, it interviewed a half dozen other banks and used their experience to determine the number of bank employees needed to manage an outsourcing relationship. The estimates were later validated by an outside consultant.

DuPont talked with other companies and with outsourcing experts to get an idea of the number of people required to manage their IT partnership with CSC and Andersen Consulting. They were careful not to err in the direction of being too lean.

Adjust historical costs for inflation, the size of the contemplated outsourcing deal, the relative complexity or nature of the function being outsourced, and the type of relationship with the outsourcing vendor. Inflation adjustments are straightforward; the others are not. Here are some considerations:

- Size and complexity adjustments should be nonlinear, just as in estimation of conventional application development projects. A deal twice the size of a deal in the past will likely involve much more than twice the cost where management of outsourcing is concerned. Greater size inevitably brings greater complexity with more interacting components, more parties involved in communication, greater opportunities for misunderstanding, and more resulting management overhead.

- For reasons mentioned above, some functions necessarily involve more complexity in the sense of more interconnections with other functions. Outsourcing the help desk is not as complex as outsourcing maintenance because the help desk function is relatively self-contained while changing code in one legacy system could have ripple effects through many other systems. Monitoring to detect possible problems and communication with the vendor to avoid problems is greater and more costly in the second case.

- Complexity can also be internal to the function being outsourced. Outsourcing the management and operation of networks with many components that do not work easily together involves a complexity that outsourcing of a smoothly functioning data center does not. Expect to incur more cost in monitoring and communicating with the vendor in the first case.

- Finally, the outsourcing relationship also impacts costs for reasons explored in the previous chapter. Straightforward market-type arrangements, where contingencies can be fully specified in contracts with a vendor, will involve much less management cost than intermediate or partnership outsourcing.

If your organization is new to information systems outsourcing, try to get help on estimates of the management costs from peers in your industry who have relevant experience, from consultants, or from organizations that track outsourcing, like the Sourcing Interest Group and the Outsourcing Institute. Since these costs increase nonlinearly with size, complexity, and the nature of the vendor relationship, the payoff from getting outside help also increases nonlinearly and should guide your determination to seek it.

It's standard procedure to build contingencies into application development project estimates, and the same holds for outsourcing. The less experience your organization has with analyzing outsourcing, the less experience it has with outsourcing the kind of function under consideration and with managing vendors, the better the argument for a contingency and the bigger the contingency should probably be.

5.7 OUTSOURCING BENEFITS

The above analysis will suffice when outsourcing is motivated by cost saving alone. But when increased effectiveness is a major motivation of outsourcing, some analysis of the expected benefits of outsourcing is warranted.

Sometimes effectiveness benefits are quite tangible and measurable, but often they are not. When quantitative justification for outsourcing initiatives is required and intangibles play a critical justification role, then try:

- Sensitivity analysis in which the minimum payoff needed from intangible benefits to make the outsourcing idea viable is calculated, or the range within which intangible benefits must lie to give the project the go-ahead is determined.

- Scenarios created to show in a plausible manner how events are likely to unfold with associated estimates of intangibles based on projections of other parameters in the scenario. This is particularly useful when variables are interdependent, and the magnitude of intangibles depend on other things.

- Build a case for the danger of not acting to outsource. Perhaps competitors can outsource to gain a cost advantage, and your organization must do the same to complete effectively. Clemons and Weber (1990) call this the "danger of the status quo."

5.7.1 Collateral Benefits

Consider collateral benefits as well. For example, the move to outsource maintenance programming can be undertaken to free up internal staff for mission-critical application development work, give staff more experience on state-of-the-art computing tools, provide focus, increase staff morale, and reduce turnover. Outsourcing maintenance to a vendor skilled in maintenance and maintenance management may also lead to better quality and performance in legacy systems and reduce maintenance costs. Take all the benefits into account.

5.8 RISK ANALYSIS

No information systems activity or function is risk free. Outsourcing has most of the risks of the same function done internally *plus* risks associated with working through a vendor. Clemons and Webber (1990) identify the following risks in information systems projects:

- Technical risk arises if what is to be accomplished requires a change to new, unproven technology.
- Project risk occurs when the project is large or complex relative to the resources in time, money, people, and skills available for it.
- Functionality risk is the risk that the project does what is specified but still fails because the specifications were in error or because what is actually needed exceeds what was specified for the project because of a changing environment.
- Political risk arises when persons or groups inside the organization act to undermine the project. These vary from vice presidents who might want to sabotage the outsourcing effort to persons on the lowest rung of the organization ladder who would resist the changes that outsourcing bring.
- Environmental risk results from actions of competitors, governmental bodies, or the economy that compromise the success of the project.
- Systemic risk is a very large shift in the environment that changes major conditions and assumptions and invalidates the analysis on which a project was originally based.

Outsourcing involves the following additional risks:

- Loss of control. Opening sensitive data to outsiders, compromising competitive secrets, and the other possible downsides of outsourcing addressed in Chapter 3.
- The transition to outsourcing is poorly handled causing alienation on the part of users of information services, or information systems personnel, or both.
- The outsourcing contract is incomplete and does not cover all contingencies.
- The nature of the relationship with the vendor is not appropriate to the function that is outsourced.
- The vendor takes advantage of your organization by underperforming, not performing, overcharging, stealing your people, stealing your data, and doing any of a great number of other things that are undesirable.
- The relationship with the vendor sours, great conflict with the vendor ensues, and raises the costs of managing the relationship.
- The relationship with the vendor falls apart and the issue winds up in the courts.

- It's necessary to find another vendor to replace the previous vendor or it becomes necessary to insource the function once more.
- Support of business functions is compromised because of problems with the vendor.

Management of outsourcing risk starts with an understanding of risk exposure. Risk is multiplied in any situation that involves a substantial departure from the past. Exposure is greater if:

- The technology is new to the marketplace (unless the purpose is to go to a vendor that has expense with the new technology as a risk reduction strategy).
- Your organization is completely new to outsourcing or has never outsourced the kind of function under consideration.
- Your organization is critically dependent on the information services to be provided through a vendor. Reliance on the outsourced function for competitive advantage or mission-critical functioning raises the risk level substantially.
- The function is large or complex. The service your organization requires from a large or complex function is likely to be more difficult to specify and include in a contract, and there is simply more possibility for misunderstanding, miscommunication, and conflict with a vendor. Total outsourcing falls in the large and complex category of outsourcing and represents a challenge for that reason alone.

If your organization demands flexibility in the function that is being outsourced, risk is also greater on this account, since future needs cannot be completely specified.

5.8.1 Evaluating Risk

Since outsourcing necessarily involves risk, risk evaluation should be part of the analysis phase before the decision to outsource is made. Risk evaluation consists of (a) identifying risks, (b) analyzing the significance of each identified risk, and (c) prioritizing the risks identified and analyzed (Boehm, 1991).

Historical experience is a good starting point for risk analysis. Organizations new to outsourcing, or new to outsourcing the particular type of function that is a candidate in this analysis, might seek the help of consultants.

Risk Identification

For the outsourcing arrangement under consideration, take each of the possible areas of risk outlined earlier in this chapter (technological, project, functional, political, etc.) and brainstorm possible sources of risk. Don't forget to include the business and technological change issues that surfaced during the requirements analysis phase.

Next, analyze risks that arise from the relationship with an outsourcing vendor. Uncertainty and the variance in governance costs increases along the contracting spectrum from market relationships to partnerships. As part of this exercise, also consider what would happen if the outsourcing relationship fails, and it becomes necessary to insource the function again. The probability of premature termination of outsourcing relationships also increases with the relationship type. It's lowest with market relationships and highest with partnerships.

Scenario analysis might be used to good effect if the environment of your organization could have a large impact on the success of outsourcing. Three scenarios might be developed. One that projects the future if present trends continue. A second that projects the environment and its effect on outsourcing under an optimistic set of assumptions that would tend to favor the outsourcing decision. And a third scenario that estimates the future under a pessimistic set of assumptions that would be unfavorable to the outsourcing route. Exploring scenarios gives a more robust and realistic picture of the risks involved.

Risk Significance

For each risk identified, analyze the sources or the underlying causes of the risk. If employees are likely to be unhappy with outsourcing, analyze the causes of this likely unhappiness. Further analyze the causes, going back in a causal chain until fundamental or root causes are identified. For example, fear of transfer to a vendor might have causes in fear of moving to a new locale, fear of reduced pay, fear of change in working or benefit conditions, and so forth.

Breaking down causes into further detail is extremely useful for more fully understanding the risks, estimating their probability and possible effect on the business, and for ultimately managing risks if the outsourcing project goes forward. A good tool for brainstorming and representing risk relationships is fishbone diagrams.

Try to quantify risk exposure for each risk identified, even if this can only be done in terms of categories like "high," "medium," and "low." Risk exposure is a combination of the effect of the risk and its probability of occurrence:

```
Exposure = Effect x  Probability of occurrence
```

Effects can include costs incurred because of the risk, losses that might result from the risk, and delays. Also, recognize that each risk exposure can have a time profile with little or no exposure at some times in the outsourcing experience and high exposure at another time. Exposure can increase or decrease with changes in both the probability of occurrence and the size of the possible effect. If exposure will vary with time, make estimates of the time profile as well. Simple diagrams that chart exposure by time aid in understanding the risk.

Don't overlook the fact that some risks may by interrelated. For example, new technology presents its own risks where getting the technology to work are concerned, but new technology may also unleash a set of political risks when persons inside the organization — even those who will not have to use the new technology — are uncomfortable with the technology. And adoption of new technology may cause a competitive rival in your industry to do the same, leading to a race with greater cost and risk than a case in which your organization adopts the technology alone.

Scenario analysis can lead to better estimates of exposure to risk — both the probability of the occurrence of unfavorable events and the magnitude of their effect.

Risk Prioritization

Finally, prioritize the risks. Discard those judged to be insignificant. Of those remaining, and starting with the most significant, make a reasoned guess at how successfully each risk can be managed and at what cost. If management can include preventive efforts, adjust the probabilities accordingly and include the management costs in the cost analysis. If monitoring to detect the occurrence of a risk and action to minimize the effect of the risk are feasible, rework the risk analysis and size of exposure to reflect this.

Also, remember that management of risk involves closer and more careful coordination with vendors, and this can raise the governance costs associated with an outsourcing relationship. Risk analysis that shows high coordination costs with vendors may even lead to a reappraisal of the nature of the relationship most appropriate for outsourcing. If risk analysis surfaces uncertainties that were not previously apparent, go back and reconsider the kind of relationship necessary to support outsourcing. If this relationship changes, revise the cost analysis to reflect the change.

If the outsourcing project is a large one, risk analysis might be confined to the essential aspects of the proposal in terms of functions and/or deliverables. Don't forget to think to the future and the changes in technology, business, and the combination of technology and business that might act to change your organization's risks of outsourcing.

Risk Management

After identifying the risks associated with an outsourcing idea, consider ways in which each might be managed. Risk management consists of (a) planning, (b) resolution by elimination or reduction, and (c) follow-up or monitoring (Boehm, 1991).

For each risk, think of approaches to managing it. Can the risk be avoided, or can it be reduced? If the risk can't be avoided, is it possible to transfer the risk to another bearer (the vendor)? Is it a good idea to make such a transfer? How much time and expense would be involved? Are the efforts one-time or continuing? How successful are management efforts likely to be?

People and Groups in Risk Evaluation

The persons to involve in risk analysis depend on the issues. For an outsourcing decision that is noncontroversial involving a very limited and stable function in a stable environment, minimal risk analysis is needed, and it can reasonably be undertaken in a meeting or two between a couple of persons on the outsourcing evaluation team. Always involve more than one person to guard against the blind spots we all have when considering possible problems in business decisions.

For larger, more complicated outsourcing decisions, expand the size of the risk analysis group. A group effort will ensure different perspectives that are necessary for good analysis. If the risk issue is highly technical or specific, bring in experts with the appropriate skills and insight.

When the stakes are high and differences of opinion are likely between members of the group that evaluates a risk or group of risks, a Delphi process might be followed. The Delphi technique is good for obtaining numerical estimates, like risk probabilities and effects, from underlying data that is essentially subjective. In a Delphi process, each member of the group is given the facts as they are known. Each writes his or her analysis and submits it anonymously to the rest of the group. The group votes on the issue or issues at hand without discussion so that particularly glib or politically powerful members can't sway the group. The results are tallied and presented to the group. At this point members are invited to submit a refinement of their analysis and rebuttal of other approaches. Successive rounds of voting take place up to some preagreed maximum of four or five or until the group reaches consensus, which might be defined as some percentage, say 75 percent or 80 percent of the group, agreeing with one analysis or another.

The Use of Risk Analysis Results

If numeric estimates of risk exposure and the costs of risk management are possible, these should be included in costs in the analysis of benefits and costs. If nonquantitative estimates of risk are the best that can be done, roll these in with other factors in a nonquantitative analysis of costs and benefits.

Consider changes to the outsourcing proposal that might reduce risk. Perhaps breaking up the proposal into several smaller ones to let to different vendors would reduce risk. Is it possible to keep functions that expose the organization to high risk in-house and outsource the rest? Perhaps contractual aspects of the outsourcing deal could reduce risk.

If exposure from one or a combination of risks is very high, even after possible management action to reduce risk exposure has been factored into the analysis, it may be better not to outsource.

5.9 REQUEST FOR PROPOSAL PROCESS

In the past, some major outsourcing deals were developed without the benefit of a Request For Proposal process. When Riggs Bank was considering selective outsourcing it invited IBM and EDS to submit bids. EDS declined, IBM responded, and the Bank then did a joint assessment of their needs with IBM. Looking back on this experience, Jill Klein who helped lead the outsourcing initiative at Riggs thinks a thorough RFP process is superior for the discipline it instills and the competition between vendors it promotes. On the other hand DuPont conducted a rigorous RFP process prior to outsourcing to CSC and Andersen Consulting.

Proceed with a Request For Proposal (RFP) and a comparison of the baseline to what vendors can do, unless the information gathered in the analysis phase indicates that the benefits are too limited or uncertain, the risks are too high, or the administrative costs of an outsourcing relationship are too burdensome. Now is the time to cut the losses and cease any further consideration of outsourcing. On the other hand, if the evidence favors outsourcing, follow the RFP process:

- The identification of potential vendors, perhaps with a Request For Information.
- Development of a term sheet.
- Development of a Request For Proposal.
- Distribution of term sheet and RFP to prequalified vendors and solicitation of proposals from vendors.
- Receipt and analysis of vendor proposals.
- Vendor presentations and visits to vendor sites, if appropriate.
- Selection of finalists.
- Complete due diligence.

- Reworking of the cost-benefit and risk analyses in the light of what vendors can do and what they will charge.
- Choice of a vendor or decision not to proceed with outsourcing.
- Contract negotiations and another decision to proceed or not.

The process should be planned and dates set in advance for each of the major stages identified above.

In the lead-up to its sourcing deal, DuPont initially identified 20 vendors based on their reputations as IT services providers. The list of 20 was narrowed to 11, then to four, then to two. The 20 potential service suppliers were analyzed based on DuPont's objectives, consultant input, and DuPont's own assessments. This preliminary analysis cut the list of 20 to 11. One key factor for making the list of 11 was that the provider have a global capability and presence. The eleven companies were brought in for a 30-minute presentation by DuPont followed by more detailed discussions with each of them about their strengths, industry experience, and understanding of DuPont and its industry. The 11 were then asked to explain why DuPont should do business with them. The list was narrowed to four vendors that seemed to have the strongest capabilities and best fit with DuPont's objectives, requirements for people, and its values. The RFP went to the final four, and the RFP process narrowed the field to two. Because DuPont was interested in a partnership arrangement with vendors, it issued two RFPs — one for the services to be provided and another to get vendor input on how the vendor expected to benefit from a relationship with DuPont, how the vendor could leverage that advantage worldwide, and how DuPont could share in the resulting gains.

5.9.1 Request for Information

A Request for Information (RFI) is a standard way of obtaining information on which to prequalify vendors who will receive the RFP. The following information is useful for judging which vendors might be serious candidates:

- Experience. Given your particular outsourcing need, does the vendor have depth of experience and a track record in this type of outsourcing? Has the vendor done work of a similar nature for other firms in your industry?
- Resources. Does the vendor have the material and personnel resources to do your work, in number, type, and skills?

- Location. Where is the vendor located, and where would the work you propose be done? If your work is international in nature, does the vendor have a presence in the necessary locations?

- Subcontracting. To what extent does the vendor rely on subcontractors, and what kind of control does the vendor exercise over subcontractors?

- Organization. How is the vendor organized to do the kind of work proposed by your organization? Would it undertake this as part of work it does for your industry? Does it have a department or division that does your kind of work? If your work is scattered over several countries, how is the vendor organized to undertake multinational commitments?

- Resource transfer. If you intend to transfer equipment, software, or personnel to a vendor as part of an outsourcing deal, does the vendor have experience with these types of resource transfers?

- Financial viability. Is the vendor financially stable? Is it established or an upstart? What share of the market does it have? Has it been growing or shrinking? Is it subject to any lawsuits, other litigation, or other claims?

- References. Ask for references to similar organizations for whom similar work has been done.

You also need information on the culture of the vendor organization. Unless a vendor's culture is a good match to the culture of your organization, outsourcing, particularly outsourcing toward the partnership end of the relationship spectrum, is not likely to be successful. Information on vendor culture is best obtained from past or present clients of the vendor.

Realize that vendors with different strengths and specialties sometimes form consortiums or alliances so that jointly they can address needs that as single firms they could not. If your requirements match the abilities of an alliance rather than a single vendor, you will want to direct your information gathering efforts to the group of vendors in the alliance, rather than a single vendor.

Vendors respond variously to RFIs. If your business is very attractive to the vendor, the RFI will be taken more seriously and you can insist that it be taken seriously. If your work is less interesting to the vendor, what comes back by return mail may be a packet of sales literature. In the latter case, it's often possible to do a little research of your own on potential vendors by having a meeting or conversation with a sales rep or by talking with the vendor's clients.

The vendors you know best are the vendors you've used before. Doing the research on vendors who have given good service in the past can be accomplished with much less time, effort, and money than vendors who are new, and it will generally be more accurate. Remember that transaction costs are lower for repeat contracting with the same vendor than with a succession of new vendors. However, there is the danger that your good working relationships with people in a familiar vendor organization will color the analysis, insert bias into the process, and lead to a bad decision. Guard against it.

Use information obtained through the RFI to develop a short list of vendors that seem well suited for your work.

5.9.2 Term Sheet

A term sheet is a document that establishes your organization's position on issues that will enter the contract to be negotiated with the chosen vendor. It's an up-front declaration of what you want in a contract as it relates to the issues addressed in the RFP. Think of it as the legal companion to the RFP and your organization's opening statement of what it wants in contract negotiations.

Some organizations prefer not to issue a term sheet with the RFP but to use it as a kind of internal statement of what it wants to achieve in contract negotiations. Others want the term sheet to accompany the RFP, so that the vendor knows as it responds to the RFP what the client's position is on the contractual aspects. Issuing the term sheet with the RFP puts the vendor on notice that the client is not interested in starting negotiations with the vendor's standard contract and allows the vendor to shape its response to the RFP to correspond to term sheet issues and stands.

Some organizations develop a term sheet in consultation with a vendor. Such was the case when Riggs Bank was negotiating with IBM in its selective outsourcing deal. However, since a term sheet sets out your contract negotiation approach, it's usually best to do this development independent of the vendor.

When the term sheet goes out with the RFP, the vendor must consider both. Its proposal in response to the RFP will reflect its reaction to the term sheet as well. The vendor's proposal should give a good indication of its opening position on contractual issues and, therefore, is a valuable input in preparation for contract negotiation.

Obviously the process of putting together a term sheet is good discipline. It forces your organization to think through the contractual issues associated with outsourcing and how you want to structure a relationship with a vendor. The development of a term sheet and the development of an RFP are interrelated; development of the two documents usually proceeds in parallel leading to the revising of one in light of the ideas and issues developed in the other.

Contract negotiation and contract provisions are taken up in the next two chapters. Review these for ideas on term sheet contents as it affects your outsourcing need. What follows is a brief and incomplete list of issues that might be taken up in a term sheet:

- Scope of the project and specifics on functions and costs not in the scope.
- Dates and activities not specified in the RFP.
- Expectations of vendors not specified in the RFP.
- Transition and implementation issues in moving the function or functions from your organization to the vendor's.
- Management and control of the client-vendor relationship, including expectations for management structures on both sides, joint committees, management reports, reviews, audit rights, confidentiality, and any other procedures necessary to support the contract and requirements.
- Specification of any baseline, service level, performance, or other activity issues not taken up in the RFP, and measures and measurement issues that relate to these.
- Pricing, invoicing, and payment issues, including incentives and penalties.
- Assumption of risk by the vendor, if this is desired in an outsourcing relationship. Risk-sharing mechanisms range from joint ventures to pricing and price incentives.
- Financial responsibilities other than those related to payment for services, as in transition and implementation of the outsourcing work, taxes, license renewals, and so on.
- Transfers of assets, leases, and licenses for all structures, hardware, and software that may be involved in the deal including ownership issues and renewal responsibilities.
- Intellectual property issues and nondisclosure issues.
- Issues relating to the term of the contract, renewal of the contract, the effective date of the contract, and termination provisions.
- Limitation of liability and warranties.

5.9.3 Request For Proposal

The team that does the analysis work should put together the RFP with the help of persons skilled in structuring requests for proposal and some guidance from legal counsel. If the ultimate users of the services to be outsourced were not part of the analysis team, they should be given the opportunity to provide input to the RFP. If you know up-front that you will be using a particular vendor, the vendor's people might also participate, but don't turn the job over to them.

Contents

The contents of the RFP will depend on the scope of the work to be outsourced and the underlying motives for outsourcing. Appendix C summarizes issues to be addressed in outsourcing RFPs. Appendix D presents an example Request For Proposal. The major issues are:

Introduction and Overview
Client Information
Services to be Provided
Performance and Change Control
Pricing
Employee Issues
Outsourcing Project Staff and Project Management
Expiration and Termination
Contract Terms
Vendor Information
Appendices and Other Terms and Conditions

Other RFP Process Issues

Vendors sometimes sell their services aggressively in ways that move around the RFP process to higher-level managers and to user managers. Alert higher-level and user-managers; ask them to redirect vendor communication to the proper channels. Add language to the RFP that requires all communication be through the person responsible for the outsourcing evaluation effort and the outsourcing evaluation team.

As the RFP takes shape, the team assembling it should also put together the criteria for evaluating vendor responses and the weights to be assigned to each criterion. These can be distributed as part of the RFP as additional information to vendors on what is most important to you. Don't wait until vendor proposals are received. Start the evaluation process on an unbiased basis by setting up criteria before considering vendors.

Include vendor culture and vendor size in the criteria. The issue of culture is addressed above. Vendor size may also be important. If your organization and the work you have to outsource is small relative to the vendor's organization and its operations, you may not get the attention you require.

Issue the RFP to the list of vendors developed as part of the RFI process.

Getting Information to and Responses from Vendors

Schedule a session to answer vendor questions. Be sure all vendors on the short list are invited. Not only will all vendors receive the same information by this method, but vendors will confront the competition and realized that they may have to better their offers. Set a deadline for receipt of vendor proposals so that the process can proceed in an orderly manner. Designate one person as the single point of contact for all communication with vendors to insure a consistent story from your side and to help prevent vendors going around the official communication and decision-making process.

Check References

Contract vendor references and collect their experiences. Determine to what extent their outsourcing requirements match yours. Size, volume, and complexity differences may largely invalidate their experience as an indication of what you can expect in a relationship with the same vendor.

Expand the reference list beyond those offered by the vendor. Ask organizations on the vendor reference list for other organizations that have experience with the vendor, including those known to have had unfavorable experiences. Make a real effort to find organizations whose experiences have not been so favorable.

Analyze Proposals

Look over vendor proposals and make any adjustments to the analysis that are necessary. For example, when comparing vendor costs to your own costs for a given service, be sure to include costs you retain (equipment, software, people, and so on) in order to support the service and add these to the vendor's estimate. Otherwise these "hidden costs" can turn a deal that looks favorable into a big surprise when it goes into operation.

The criteria developed for evaluation of proposals will set the stage for analysis. Since the information received from vendors is massive in an outsourcing deal of any size, it may make sense to look at the criteria and issues again and group issues into highest priority or "musts," secondary priority or "wants," and third priority or "nice to have." In the highest priority category, the inability of a vendor to meet an essential requirement may be immediate grounds for disqualification. If all vendors in the running can provide the essentials, move to the second priority group of issues and rate each vendor on each item, perhaps on a scale of one-to-five or one-to-ten. Multiply the ratings by the weights for each issue and sum them all for each vendor. The vendors with the best summary scores are preferred. If there is a large difference between vendors at this point, it probably isn't necessary to go to the third priority category of "nice to have" issues. But if it's close, use rankings on items in the third category and do the weighted sums to add additional information for the decision.

Consider the trade-offs carefully before deciding. For example, when the function or functions to be outsourced are mission-critical or support mission-critical business functions, extra care must be exercised to make certain the vendor selected can do the job. While it's human nature to want things at a bargain price, the best usually isn't available in the marketplace at the lowest price. If you want the best, most reliable, and expert service, expect to pay more.

Don't ignore the costs of bringing the outsourced work back inside your organization in both normal expiration of contract and abnormal termination of contract situations. Sometimes these costs are much higher if a function is outsourced in a particular way or to a particular vendor.

Recognize that the costs of managing the relationship with a vendor might be greatly reduced if the vendor is already doing outsourcing work of another kind for your organization. Some administrative functions can likely be shared between two outsourcing arrangements. The time and effort necessary to get to know the vendor's ways of working and to establish good relationships with the vendor may have been incurred already on another outsourcing project.

If the outsourced work is to be split between two or more vendors, the RFPs for the parts of the work must be coordinated and vendor proposals must be evaluated in tandem.

Vendor alliances are becoming more common. Alliances are two or more vendors with complementary specializations or strengths that contract to provide outsourcing services in tandem with each other. Vendors in alliances may submit a joint response to your RFP. This simplifies evaluation, but the response should clearly identify how the vendors coordinate to provide a service and who shoulders responsibility for each service.

Selection of Finalists and Due Diligence

Chose two top contenders from among the vendors who survived the cut in the phase above. Then, verify the vendor responses. With each of the finalists, hold a meeting in which lawyers are present and do due diligence on all vendor representations that have a real impact on the outcome of the deal. Due diligence efforts may also require on-site visits to the vendor premises, management assessments, background checks, reference checks, reviews, and the like.

Test and verify that vendor software or hardware can interface with and work smoothly with software and hardware that remain in your organization. Check all the compatibilities and capabilities necessary for success, including the ability of technology on both sides to interface smoothly and handle the volume of work required at peak times.

Rework any prior analyses as a result of changes uncovered in due diligence, including cost-benefit analysis, risk analysis, and the weighted scoring analyses of vendor proposals.

Once the list is paired down to a few finalists, Pete Mounts of HBOC advises clients to be "...as open as possible about the project to be outsourced, including budgets, goals, internal politics. In this manner, the vendor can truly propose a solution that takes into account all relevant information. Some buyers are hesitant to be up-front with their numbers for fear of vendors simply reworking those figures — along with a profit margin — in their bid proposal." At the same time he warns that, "A vendor that makes itself out to be something it's not is a danger. Avoid vendors that don't do their homework in really learning the organization's needs, goals, challenges, culture, and so forth. Other vendors to avoid are those that try to underbid the contract, use it as a "lead" to sell other products or services, or say they're negotiating a performance-based contract when what they really have in mind is selling bodies."

Chose a Vendor or Retain In-House

The analysis work and the controlled process for obtaining vendor responses should produce all the information necessary to make good decisions on whether to outsource or not and which vendors to involve in contract negotiations if the decision is made to proceed. If the data are on the line and don't clearly favor either outsourcing or insourcing, it's probably best not to outsource. If the analysis doesn't favor one vendor or another, factors that were left to the side because they were difficult to identify or quantify can be revisited and folded into the analysis for the additional insight they may provide.

Often it is advantageous to take two vendors into contract negotiations to generate continued competition and better offers. Vendors that tie or are very close in the RFP evaluation process can all be taken to the next stage of contract negotiations.

If good work has been done in analysis and development of a term sheet and RFP, there should be few surprises in contract negotiations. However, if loose ends exist, vendors can come up with deal breaking surprises in negotiations. Do the homework.

For DuPont, the whole RFP process took about a year. They issued the RFP to four vendors and gave them about 60 days to prepare their proposals. Approximately 60 days were spent evaluating the proposals followed by 90 days of due diligence, visiting other customers, and further evaluation of the proposals. During this process, one of the four dropped out. DuPont realized that to get the best services and the best chemical industry software applications, they would need to contract with two vendors. The complete analysis took about one year in a process that first determined which firms could best meet its needs and then determined which could most effectively take DuPont's know-how and market it outside the company in partnership with DuPont.

The key factors used to differentiate between vendors in the DuPont case were the vendor's flexibility, ability to deliver needed skills, worldwide delivery capability, and the vendor's commitment to continuing productivity improvements. Particularly critical were the human aspects — how people would be treated, development opportunities, and employee benefit provisions. They also placed a high value on the provider's willingness to work with DuPont as the leader/manager, to commit to reinvest in DuPont's infrastructure, and to provide opportunities for DuPont to learn from the relationship. In the end, DuPont concluded that no single vendor could do it all and decided to enter a partnership with both CSC and Andersen Consulting.

5.9.4 Fostering Competition Among Vendors

Having more than one qualified vendor at each stage is the most fundamental way to assure competition. Including vendors that aren't real candidates probably won't work. Vendors usually see through such tactics.

Give vendors knowledge of the competition. Vendors go head-to-head for business on a regular basis. If they know and respect the competition, they will act competitively and offer better deals.

Try to get vendors to improve their offers at every opportunity. At the due diligence stage, give each vendor an opportunity to improve its offer. Don't accept vague promises. Force the vendor to make it as specific and quantitative as possible. Sometimes extending the time for vendor response, with the clear expectation that this is to give the vendor time to improve the offer, works.

Declaring two winners at the end of the RFP evaluation process and proceeding to contract negotiations with both keeps competition going while negotiations proceed and may result in still better offers on the part of one or both final contestants. It's also possible to hit an impasse in contract negotiations with one vendor that causes you to fall back to a vendor that was a second choice in the RFP analysis.

Don't short circuit the competitive process by leaping for a vendor offer of "partnership." A vendor may make a major concession in exchange for an immediate favorable decision on your part and your commitment to a long-term arrangement that the vendor calls partnership. Partnerships only make sense under a limited set of circumstances. Know the rules, apply them to your situation, and don't dump the benefits of competition between vendors for vague promises of long term benefits.

While it's important to encourage competition, realize that the more RFPs you issue and the larger the number of vendors who respond, the longer the selection process will take. There are trade-offs.

5.10   MANAGING THE HUMAN RESOURCE ISSUES: AN INTERVIEW WITH GROVER WRAY

Grover Wray is the Director of Human Resources for Arthur Andersen's Contract Services Practice covering the outsourcing of accounting, internal audit, and tax. He has overall responsibility for human resource-related outsourcing issues, including transition activities, career path development, training, team building, and performance management activities. Grover has been personally involved in over 150 human resources transition contracts ranging from between 3 and 250 employees. He has extensive training and consulting experience in transition management, change management, total quality management, organization development, staff motivation, and performance management. Wray received his Masters Degree in Organizational Behavior from Brigham Young University.

What should a company expect of the outsourcer with respect to HR issues?
If you hear a potential provider tell you that "we'll deal with the HR issues after we get the work," it should be a red flag that the provider doesn't truly understand the HR implications of outsourcing. You should expect the provider to bring their HR team to the proposal process so that you and your HR team can ensure the people issues will be managed properly.

The general rule of thumb for HR involvement during the three principle phases of the outsourcing process (preparation, transition, and integration) is that during preparation it should be a 50/50 split between the amount of involvement from both HR teams. Each team has the responsibility to design and communicate a transition plan, analyze benefits, and personnel policies, and prepare for a short transition period. During the transition, 70 percent of the HR involvement comes from the outsourcer conducting interviews, making employment decisions, and orienting the employees. The company's 30 percent involvement is to ensure continued communication of severance plans and outplacement activities. In the integration phase the provider has 90 percent of the responsibility. The 10 percent activity from the company's HR team involves counseling employees as they make the transition to a new work environment.

When should Human Resources specialists be involved in the outsourcing process?
HR should be involved early and often in the outsourcing process. The common link to any outsourced IT function is the people. However, it is often the most overlooked area in the outsourcing decision process. Too often HR is considered after decisions on scope, pricing, and vendor selection.

If you are outsourcing your IT function, you should invite a member of the HR team to participate as early in the decision-making process as possible. Their role is to analyze the vendor's HR capability, assist in creating a communication plan for the affected employees and the company, and prepare the necessary policies and procedures that the company will follow during the transition of employees.

The company should also expect the provider to bring their HR resources to the table during the proposal process. The outsourcer should help the company understand how the outsourcer will manage the process during the transition. The company should ask the potential vendors during the proposal phase to:

1. Describe the employee selection process.
2. Describe benefits and personnel policies.
3. Describe corporate culture.
4. Explain any legal exposure as a result of past transitions.
5. Present your turnover statistics of outsourced employees.
6. Describe career development opportunities for employees.

When is the best time to communicate the outsourcing decision?
It is difficult to define the most ideal time to communicate a change like outsourcing. There are many factors that enter into a decision for the timing of communication. However, the principle reason for communication is to reduce the anxiety and uncertainty that accompany changes.

Often, when the outsourcing project is large enough, the company must involve several parties in the analysis of a decision to outsource. The more people involved with the decision, the greater the risk of rumors or misinformation. In these situations it is necessary to announce the change prior to the final outsourcing, and a communication plan should be defined so the employees receive regular communication throughout the process. As soon as management can identify a date when the final decision will be made, they should communicate it to the employees. This pattern of regular communication reduces the anxiety and uncertainty considerably.

If the project is small enough that the decision can be kept to a few decision makers, it is recommended to avoid making an announcement until the final decision is made. This delayed communication can work to the company's advantage as the length of the transition period can be minimized because the transition was planned in advance of the announcement. However, I caution that if you delay the announcement and you do not prepare for the transition, the employees will be upset. And they'll have good reason to be. They will expect that you had the time to work through the communication issues, and will want immediate answers.

What advice do you have about the transition period?
Keep the transition period as short as possible. Uncertainty about the future creates anxiety and increases legal risk. Be prepared to begin the transition immediately after the final decision has been communicated to the employees.

The most uncertain period of time is between the final announcement and the date when employees have accepted or rejected an offer of employment from the provider. Minimize this time and reduce the anxiety by communicating a defined transition plan to the employees. The transition plan should at least include dates for interviewing, communicating decisions, and a deadline for employees to respond to offers.

By eliminating as many unknowns as possible during this period, it increases the employees' feeling of control over the situation, and leaves less room for employees to react to rumors, sabotage operations, or suffer from declining morale.

Is there anything employees can do to prepare for the outsourcing decision and transition?
The employees should understand that they have as much to do with the successful outsourcing transition as the company and the provider. Their positive attitude can increase their chances of being employed by the outsourcing provider and increase their chances of success once inside the provider's organization.

Beyond a positive attitude, there are several skills the employee can develop to prepare himself or herself for this opportunity. The first is to learn to be "self-employed" — not in the literal sense, but in the attitudinal sense. Being "self-employed" means that employees understand that no matter who signs their paycheck, the company receiving the benefit of their worth is their "client," and the work they deliver must be high quality. "Self-employment" also means that they understand their core competency, and must take steps necessary to ensure they are continuing to deepen their core competency through training and other personal development activities.

The company can also assist in helping the employees prepare for the transition. The company should establish policies that don't increase employees' reliance on the company. For example, a culture of expected "lifetime employment" inhibits the company's and the employees' ability to change. Also, a policy statement at the time of outsourcing that the company will find jobs for employees who are not offered employment may inhibit employees from interviewing with the provider. This will make the transition for the provider more difficult and impact work because the provider can't hire the best people.

What about benefits (pension and medical) and personnel policies? How should the transition be handled?

Every company has different policies and benefits and there is no best answer about what policies and benefits should be. Instead, the company should determine if the policies and benefits are "outsourcing friendly." For example, this means that the outsourcer may recognize past service credit and allow the employees to carry forward their annual vacation accrual to the outsourcer as opposed to "starting over" in a new vacation plan. Allowing employees to waive waiting periods for participation in the outsourcer's plans is another example of "outsourcing friendly" benefits.

Family members can play an important role in how the employee feels about the change. Receiving support from family and friends can make the transition easier for the employee. Although policies and benefits are not the most important part of the decision process, the benefits and policies should be clearly, promptly, and openly communicated to increase the success of the transition. Because benefits and policies affect the employee and their family, it is important to realize that all of the issues related to the transition from one benefit plan to another be communicated clearly enough that the employee can answer the inevitable questions asked by family members.

What advice do you have for a company about a severance policy?

The company should consider the structure of the severance policy before a final announcement to the employees. Severance will be one of the first questions the employees will ask. The company should be prepared to answer the question as part of the outsourcing announcement. There are several options to evaluate:

1. Every employee receives a severance package regardless of whether or not offered a job from the outsourcing provider.
2. The employee must interview with the provider before receiving the severance package.
3. Only the employees who do not accept employment offers from the provider receive a severance package.
4. Employees who receive a comparable offer from the provider and reject the offer will receive a reduced severance package.

There is no universal answer to the severance question. However, the guideline the company follows should be based on past precedent. Has the company had similar transactions in the past and how was severance handled? If there are precedents, expectations have likely been established, and employees will assume that they will be treated the same as others.

What performance measures should a company use to measure the success of the transition process?
There are several measures that can be used. Some are easy to define and others are more intuitive. They include:

1. Number of employees offered employment with outsourcer.
2. Number of employees accepting offers from the outsourcer.
3. Length of transition period (announcement to employee acceptance or rejection of employment offer).
4. Lawsuits or complaints during the transition.
5. Retention of employees by outsourcer.
6. Effective communication throughout the company.
7. Degree of unusual concern or uncertainty expressed by the employees who are not directly impacted by the outsourcing decision.

When the company defines these performance measures in advance of the transition, it increases the chance of success because both parties are working toward common, clearly-defined performance measures. The company can also use these performance measures to help evaluate the performance of the outsourcing provider.

What about the change management issues? What advice do you have for a company in helping their employees manage the change?
There is an old axiom that says, "people don't resist change, they resist being changed." We have learned that the best way to manage change is to allow the employees to feel as much in control of the events surrounding the change as possible. Change becomes difficult to manage when information is not communicated in timely fashion and employees are left to wonder "what's next." Lacking any information about the uncertain future, and not wanting to be in a situation that is out of control, employees will attempt to gain control by creating their own ideas about what's happening and what the results will be from decisions that will be made about them. They gain this control by creating or listening to rumors and believing them to be facts. Some employees will leave the company as a result of their belief that they have taken control of the unknown situation. As a last resort, if things are completely out of control and they have been unsuccessful in seeking control, the employees may take legal action.

There is no reason for these feelings of helplessness to exist. Change can be managed. Before any announcement about outsourcing, pending or final, create a communication plan that includes who will communicate to key parties in the process, when they will communicate, and how they will communicate. If employees know that there is regular communication, every two weeks, for example, they feel more in control of the situation because they will be updated on the process, and be able to ask questions to validate or dispel rumors.

At the time the final decision is announced, it is important that a transition plan be clearly communicated. Employees will feel some control of the situation if they know the key dates of interviewing, employment decisions, and transition.

Another important aspect of the change management approach is to remember that other employees outside of the department being outsourced have a lot to do with how the employees being outsourced feel about the change. Do not just focus your communication efforts on those who are directly impacted. Help other employees who might have association with the department (e.g. their processes are integrated) understand how they will be impacted. They will always ask the question "am I next?" Don't let these employees become dissatisfied because you are not focusing your communication on them. They can influence the outsourced employees positively and the management can set the groundwork for a successful transition if these employees are outsourced in the future.

5.11 REFERENCES

Boehm, Barry W., "Software Risk Management: Principles and Practices, *IEEE Software*, (January 1991) 32–41.

Bowen, D. E, and Schneither, B., "Services Marketing and Management: Implications for Organizational Behavior," in L. L. Cummings and B. M. Staw (eds.), *Research in Organizational Behavior*, vol. 10, Greenwich, CT, JAI Press, 1988, 81–122.

Cronin, J. Joseph and Taylor, Steven A., "Measuring Service Quality: A Reexamination and Extension," *Journal of Marketing*, 56 (July 1992) 55–68.

Clemons, Eric K. and Weber, Bruce, "Strategic Information Technology Investments: Guidelines for Decision Making," *Journal of Management Information Systems*, (Fall 1990) 9–28.

Hiles, Andrew, *Service Level Agreements: Measuring Cost and Quality in Service Relationships*, Chapman & Hall, New York, 1993.

Mylott, Thomas R., *Computer Outsourcing: Managing the Transfer of Information Systems*, Englewood Cliffs, NJ, Prentice-Hall, 1995.

6

Contracts and Contract Negotiation

Nothing in this book is intended as legal advice. Get the help of lawyers and consultants knowledgeable in the area of outsourcing negotiations and contracts. The larger the outsourcing deal and the more critical the information services to be outsourced are to the smooth functioning of your organization, the more important is good legal advice. See Appendix A for advice on selecting consultants and lawyers to assist you with the outsourcing process.

Experience shows the importance of negotiating good contracts. In a study of 34 information systems outsourcing cases, Sanders, Gebelt, and Hu (1997) found that writing a "tight" contract was the single-most important factor in instances of outsourcing success.

Pete Mounts makes an important point:

> The contract must be a win-win for both the buyer and the vendor, especially when the contract specifies performance levels. The agreed-upon levels must be comprehensive enough to make solid business sense yet flexible enough to accommodate changes in the business without having to come back to the negotiating table. The contract represents a partnership from both sides. The buyer can't absolve itself of the responsibility entirely and instead must be committed to staying informed and staying involved.

This chapter discusses the limitations of contracts for retaining control of the outsourcing relationship, ways of addressing the limitations, and approaches to contracts for each type of outsourcing relationship. Preferred vendor relationships are also discussed. The chapter continues with material on contract considerations in project versus project work and on negotiation strategy.

The chapter concludes with an interview with David E. Kepler on some details of an outsourcing agreement between Dow Chemical and Andersen Consulting. This arrangement shows how service measurements and incentives can be blended to give direction to client and vendor activity and keep control of outsourcing.

6.1 LIMITATIONS OF CONTRACTS

A contract should accomplish the objectives of both client and vendor, be reasonably fair to both, and be clear enough to be understood by both sides and third parties (the courts). Your rights can be protected and disputes can be minimized if the contract is a good one.

While a good contract with an outsourcing vendor is critical, it must be recognized that contracts alone can't assure outsourcing success. The relationship with an outsourcing vendor starts with a contract but is more than a contract. It's important to understand the distinction so that the proper outsourcing relationship can be chosen and the best contract for that relationship type can be negotiated.

Two factors limit the effectiveness of contracts for controlling vendors: imperfect information and uncertainty.

6.1.1 Limitations Due to Imperfect Information

When work is delegated to another, there are two basic ways of controlling the worker. One is to monitor the worker's behavior by observing what the worker is doing. The other is to monitor what the worker produces, or his output. The same is true of controlling outsourcing vendors.

When a client contracts for vendor resources and manages those resources, behavioral monitoring may be more important than monitoring of output. For example, when contract programmers are hired from a vendor and incorporated in client development teams, it may be difficult at times to separate the work of vendor personnel from your personnel. Monitoring vendor personnel behavior may sometimes be the most practical method of control.

When a client hires a vendor to produce a product or service and the vendor manages its own resources, monitoring of output or results is usually more important than monitoring behavior. Output is directly related to the purpose of the outsourcing and is cheaper and easier to monitor than the vendor behavior involved in producing it.

Gathering accurate information for the purpose of controlling the vendor is often difficult and costly, and this is true in both behavior and output-based control situations. To constantly monitor vendor personnel is costly, and in moments when a worker is not monitored they may make errors or waste time. When trying to monitor a vendor's output, problems with the quality of vendor's work may be hidden from the client and may escape detection. The vendor may be unaware of the quality problems, or the vendor may be very well aware of them and may be opportunistically passing the work to the client knowing it is bad.

Information and measurement problems move outsourcing relationships away from market types and toward intermediate and partnership types. When measurable outputs cannot be completely specified in a contract, noncontractual, cooperative behavior helps assure that needs are met. When close monitoring is too costly, the client must depend on cooperation on the part of the vendor. Conversely, when behavior or output is easily observed and measured, more complete contracting can occur which moves the appropriate relationship more to the market side of the contracting spectrum.

6.1.2 Limitations Due to Uncertainty

Contracts can be structured to share benefits and risks between your organization and a vendor. The term "risk" is reserved for future conditions that can be anticipated but whose outcomes could go one of several ways. Risk-sharing provisions specify that the costs of unfavorable outcomes fall on both parties. For example, if costs rise, they are to be shared in some predetermined proportion between client and vendor.

The term "uncertainty" is reserved for future contingencies that can't be known at the time the contract is signed. These are more difficult to deal with in a sharing arrangement because most parties won't be willing to agree to sharing costs whose nature and magnitude are not at all predictable.

Unforeseen events in the future may also give the vendor an opening to behave opportunistically. For example, a new need may arise that is within the context of the outsourced function, and the need is one that could not be predicted at the time the contract was written. The vendor may want to levy large additional charges for serving the new need, knowing that your organization is captive to the relationship by the substantial costs of terminating the deal and moving the work in-house or to another vendor.

It's preferable to specify everything the vendor is to do up-front and impose iron-clad discipline on the vendor by putting requirements in a contract. On the other hand, it's advantageous to have flexibility so the work can be modified in response to uncertainty. The discipline versus flexibility conflict is inherent in outsourcing relationships. The best that can be done is to write a contract that addresses the contingencies that can be foreseen leaving the consequences of unpredictable environmental change to be handled through adjustment mechanisms that are outside the contract.

The degree to which a complete contract can be written varies significantly along the market-to-partnership outsourcing relationship continuum. Complete contracts can and should be written at the market end of the spectrum; all contingencies should be covered. Partnerships, on the other hand, are ongoing relationships intended to survive over long periods of time and multiple contracts. A single contract can't do it all, and many noncontractual devices will be necessary to assure continuity in partnerships as business and technology change. Intermediate outsourcing relationships lie between the market relationship and partnership extremes. Intermediate outsourcing relationships have some of the characteristics of market relationships and some of the characteristics of partnerships. In intermediate relationships, the contract addresses all the contingencies that can be foreseen, and the client and vendor depend on noncontractual mechanisms to address unforeseen events.

6.2 ADDRESSING THE LIMITATIONS

The information and uncertainty limitations of contracts outlined above can be addressed in both contractual and noncontractual ways. The contractual mechanisms attempt to provide for flexibility. The noncontractual methods put pressure on the vendor to perform by means of potential challenges to the vendor's reputation and potential action to terminate the contract.

Realize that these methods do not offer a complete and foolproof response to information and uncertainty problems in contracts. Even after taking the precautions outlined below, your organization will still be dependent to some degree on the good will of the vendor and a cooperative relationship to achieve outsourcing success.

6.2.1 Reputation

Reputation is a noncontractual control mechanism. When uncertainty is high, look for a vendor that has a reputation for working well and fairly with unforeseen contingencies. Contracting with a reputable vendor reduces the up-front costs of writing a contract; there is less concern with minutia on contingencies (although this doesn't displace the need for contract language on contingencies). Hiring a reputable vendor also reduces the risk of opportunism, and, thus, reduces the effort necessary to structure contractual and noncontractual mechanisms to control the vendor. Of course, more reputable vendors can often command higher fees.

Large outsourcing vendors typically undertake many kinds of outsourcing assignments, but they may not be as proficient and reputable in all of these. Be certain to investigate the reputation of potential vendors for the specific functions and services required.

In partnerships, it may be possible to scale up your involvement with the vendor over successive contracts. The initial contracting experiences are used to gauge the vendor's abilities and honesty. If performance is good, additional contracts are signed, and trust builds over successive contracts. An example of this evolution might be to transfer a subset of your work and your information systems personnel to the vendor in the first contract and gradually increase the work and personnel shift in subsequent contracts. Similarly, the first contracts might be for work that is less critical to business functioning and later contracts for more critical work.

6.2.2 Retaining the Ability to Bring the Work Back Inside

Retaining the capability to in-source again also helps control vendors. If vendors know you can readily in-source, they are less likely to try to take advantage of any loop holes. Slack resources, keeping some IT personnel, putting provisions in a contract that allow your organization to take back some of its original personnel when the contract ends are all ways to retain this capability.

Of course, this is can be an expensive remedy to information and uncertainty problems. Retaining resources buys a kind of insurance whose costs must be added to the other costs of outsourcing.

Realize, also, that contracts are more likely to fail under these circumstances. Retaining the capability to in-source can cause disagreements to more easily lead to termination of the contract. When there is less cost to termination of a contract, termination is more likely. For this reason, keeping an insourcing capability is a more likely tactic in intermediate relationships where the building of vendor trust is not such an important issue. It can be a counterproductive strategy in partnerships.

6.2.3 Contract Incentives Tied to Business Performance

The contract can give vendors incentives to do the right thing. The previous chapter outlines the possibility of setting requirements in terms of performance measures in your business and giving the vendor bonuses for meeting or exceeding the performance levels. Alternatively, the vendor might share in incremental revenue generated by its success in meeting your business objectives.

6.2.4   Circuit Breakers and Contract Renegotiation

Under conditions of high uncertainty, the contract can contain one or more circuit-breaker clauses that call for renegotiation of the contract when business and/or technological change exceeds some predetermined level. The previous chapter speaks to this issue as well.

6.2.5   Other Methods of Addressing Uncertainty in Contracts

Ang and Beath (1993) suggest other aspects of contracts that can help address problems of uncertainty. One is to give the client the kinds of power and authority a manager would exercise if overseeing work inside his or her own organization. Rather than anticipate every contingency, the contract reserves the client's right to react to contingencies as they arise or set up ways to react. For example:

- The contract might specify rights to change vendor personnel.
- The contract might specify the right to make price changes.
- The contract might specify price caps on what the vendor can charge for certain services.
- The contract can give certain persons or groups the authority to change the scope of the contract and renegotiate price and/or performance terms. These powers might be unilateral or they might require review and approval; they might result in changes in charges and/or duration of the work.
- The contract can reserve the right to audit work and/or output with follow-up recommendations and/or requirements for changes for improvement.

Second, incentives and punishments linked to particular behavior or outcomes is another approach to managing uncertainty and opportunism — incentives to reward good performance and punishments to discourage bad performance. Combined with the right to audit, incentives and punishments will also keep vendors more honest.

A third set of methods fall into the category of standard operating procedures. These include actions the vendor must take or aspects of the work or work product that the vendor must include. An example is progress reports and meetings where the contract requires the vendor to report regularly on work progress, including problems. Reviews fall into the same category, and reviews by the ultimate users or even expert third parties might be specified in the contract. Demonstration prototypes might be required to provide a foundation for review of the vendor's approach and work. All these provisions allow the client to react to contingencies as they arise and control the vendor's work in response.

Methods of resolving disagreements is a fourth category of contractual measures to deal with uncertainty and opportunism. When disagreements do arise, the aim is to resolve the dispute and complete the work without a breakdown in the relationship and premature termination of the contract. The contract should contain a dispute resolution process with escalation provisions. The successive steps might be:

- Discussions between operational level vendor and client managers responsible for overseeing the outsourcing work as a first stage.
- Moving to discussions at higher and higher levels of vendor and client management in the intermediate stages.
- Mediation by third-party experts in the information systems field in a late stage.
- Resort to the courts as the least desirable and last stage.

Need for contractual mechanisms to address uncertainty are least in market-type outsourcing relationships and greatest in partnerships. A discussion of contracting approaches in each relationship type follows.

6.3 MARKET RELATIONSHIPS AND CONTRACTS

Contracts based on market relationships are appropriate under the following conditions:

- No uncertainty. The outsourcing need can be clearly specified with no ambiguities. Everything is measurable. No changes in the internal or external environment will change requirements during the contract period. Vender performance can be clearly and unambiguously observed and measured.
- No asset specificity. The outsourcing does not require investments to build things, capabilities, or knowledge that are dependent on the relationship between your organization and the vendor.
- No need for repeat contracting. The contract stands alone. Its success doesn't depend on a relationship with the vendor in an earlier time and doesn't depend on a continuing relationship with the vendor after the contract ends.

These conditions are quite stringent and, for this reason, are not the norm in information systems outsourcing. The following discussion explains why.

6.3.1 Uncertainty

Work that will extend for more than a few months into the future will probably involve uncertainty, if for no other reason than prices and costs will change as a result of inflation. A host of other uncertainty factors arise around unknown future changes in the business and technology. When contracts can't specify all contingencies, true market relationships are not possible.

Uncertainty can arise on other accounts. Sometimes multiple outsourcing vendors are involved in doing work that is interdependent, or the primary outsourcing vendor needs to subcontract part of the work. Now success is dependent on more than one vendor and on the relationships between them. Market-type conditions do not hold here.

The work to be accomplished may depend on the availability and/or suitability of technology or some other resource from a third party. Again, market-type contracts will not work.

Because the future is inherently uncertain, outsourcing work that otherwise would qualify for a pure marketing-type contract can't be outsourced in a market relationship if the contracting period is long. To gain the advantages of market relationships, it's almost always necessary to keep contracting periods relatively short.

6.3.2 Asset Specificity

Questions to ask that will help clarify the existence of asset specificity are (Ang and Beath, 1993):

- Will the work result in physical assets or software that can only be fully functional and useful if the vendor is around to operate, support, or maintain them?
- Will giving the vendor a full understanding of your requirements involve a lot of time and effort (and thus, cost) on your part and/or the vendor's part?
- Will the work require a lot of time and effort (and thus, cost) to your organization in learning the vendor's methods or ways of doing things?

- Will the work require a lot of time and effort (and thus, cost) to the vendor's organization in learning your organization's methods or ways of doing things?
- Will the vendor's investment in knowledge of the client firm be transferable to work the vendor might do under a future contract?

"Yes" answers to any of these questions indicate the presence of assets specificity. The more time or effort or cost that is involved, the greater the degree of asset specificity.

The party that makes the investment specific to the relationship has an incentive to see that the relationship survives until the work is done. Typically, the other party is dependent on the investment made by the first party, and it also has a stake in seeing the contract through to the end.

Many kinds of outsourcing work involve the development of relationship specific knowledge. The work requires that the vendor learn your organization's systems or ways of working. You must develop an understanding of the vendor's methods. Pure market-type relationships don't apply in these cases.

6.3.3 Repeated Contracting

When a relatively short, market-type contract ends but the need persists, your organization may go back in the market and contract again for the same kind of work either with the same vendor or another vendor. So long as the nature of the relationship established with the vendor in the first period has no connection with the next contract, the relationship is a true market relationship. If, however, knowing the vendor and the vendor knowing your organization and its work gives an advantage to the same vendor in bidding for a second contract, then conditions for pure market-type relationships don't hold. One contract depends on the other. Investment has been made in knowledge or ways of doing things that are specific to the relationship between your organization and the vendor.

Nevertheless, if the asset specificity involved is low, some of the advantages of market relationships may still attach to the repeated and ongoing contracting between your organization and a specific vendor. Each time the contract is up for renewal, your organization lets the vendor know, directly or indirectly, that the work could be awarded to another vendor without too much difficulty. If the possibility is a real one, your repeat vendor will have to do good work and will still have to consider market forces and what other vendors have to offer as the succeeding contracts are negotiated.

When market-type or near-market-type conditions exist and the outsourcing need is ongoing, your organization may want to establish a preferred vendor program, a topic addressed later in this chapter.

6.3.4 Vendor Competition

In addition to the requirements for market relationships outlined above, it's also necessary to have multiple vendors actively competing for the outsourcing work. Competition disciplines the relationship. Vendors are motivated to do the work well because they can't hide behind ambiguous contract specifications, and they know if they fail to perform another vendor can easily take their place.

Vendors usually want their potential clients to think they are the only organization capable of doing the work. With the competition that now exists in most types of outsourcing, your need has to be very unique to avoid competition. A key part of preparation for the RFP is to identify capable vendors and notify them that they are in competition with other vendors. This is particularly true of market-type contracts, but fostering vendor competition is key to other types of contracting relationships, as well.

6.3.5 Contracts in Market Relationships

If your outsourcing need truly does meet the conditions of a market relationship, then:

- Define requirements completely.
- Make requirements measurable and observable in ways a third party (the judge and jury in a court) can understand.
- Get competent vendors to compete for the work and choose the best vendor.
- Negotiate a complete contract that gives the vendor no room for disagreement over terms.
- Include contract provisions that oblige the vendor to perform.
- Negotiate a good price.
- Sign and implement the contract, and monitor the vendor's performance.

The processes addressed in the previous chapter on requirements and the RFP are keys to success in developing the foundation for a good contract. Follow this up with a contract that gives protection against breach by the vendor, and you have done the best that can be done in a market-type relationship for outsourcing.

6.4 INTERMEDIATE RELATIONSHIPS AND CONTRACTS

Intermediate relationships occupy the middle of the relationship spectrum. One or more of the following difficulties arise:

- Not all requirements can be determined up-front, before the contract is developed and signed.
- Requirements are likely to change during the life of the contract, but in unforeseeable ways.
- The vendor has information your organization does not have about the quantity or quality of the work the vendor does. Not everything is measurable; not everything is observable. Sometimes measurement and/or observation could take place, but the cost of doing so is prohibitive. At other times the vendor does very specialized work — work whose quality no one in your organization is competent to oversee and judge. Under these circumstances the vendor could be opportunistic; for example, the vendor could cut some corners on quality assurance in a system the vendor builds as part of the outsourcing agreement. When measurement and observation problems exist, the vendor is in a position to take advantage of the situation.
- Your organization or the vendor invests in things or people or knowledge that is specific to the relationship with the vendor. If the relationship terminates prematurely, the investment can't be totally recovered. To bring in another vendor involves additional investment in time and effort.

Under any of these circumstances, it's best to take steps to help insure the relationship with the vendor survives until the work is completed while at the same time protecting against opportunistic behavior on the part of the vendor. The contract can't be a completely specified document. Specification and terms should be tight where it is possible to be tight, but other parts of the contract need to address the loose ends and how they will be handled.

In intermediate contracting situations, consider the value of each of the methods for addressing uncertainty and opportunism introduced earlier in this chapter. Comments follow on pricing mechanisms and contract termination provisions as they relate to controlling uncertainty in intermediate outsourcing relationships.

6.4.1 Pricing

Pricing mechanisms should correspond to underlying conditions and strategies in outsourcing relationships. Pricing options range from fixed compensation with no adjustment at one extreme to cost-plus profit margin pricing at the other. Between the extremes lie many variable cost schemes where compensation can be a mixture of fixed and variable elements, with or without partial payment before the work is completed, and with and without the existence of maxima.

Because the future is uncertain, contracts often contain provisions that allow vendor compensation to vary with inflation and that specify compensation for any extra work the vendor undertakes as a result of contingencies. Compensation can be at prearranged prices, at market prices, or at some percentage of market prices. Such contracts must also specify the index to be used for determining the magnitude of inflation and how market prices are to be determined.

Variable pricing arrangements are mechanisms for sharing risk between client and vendor. The structure of the deal can tilt the burden of risk toward one party or the other. Your organization will want the best deal it can get, and so will the vendor. The previous chapter dealt with analysis of business and technological futures. The better the understanding obtained by this analysis, the better the position of your organization in negotiating pricing arrangements with a vendor.

The price for vendor work might also be adjusted if the product of the outsourcing work is a system or some other capability that the client or the vendor could market to the rest of the world (perhaps after some modification). Now a market value attaches to the product of the work. Who owns the resulting product and/or how the commercial potential is to be shared involves issues that extend beyond the scope of this book, but it should be clear that the price of the outsourcing work might be adjusted as part of the negotiations.

As noted earlier in this chapter, vendor compensation can also be tied to business performance in your organization as a way of aligning vendor goals with the goals of your organization.

6.4.2 Expiration and Termination

Contracts usually have expiration and termination provisions that specify duties and responsibilities of client and vendor under normal expiration and premature termination of the contract. Termination provisions are another way to address uncertainty. If the worst happens and the relationship fails, termination provisions may help your organization recoup part of its investment.

Relatively new and untried vendors and vendors who are not in particularly good financial shape raise uncertainties that don't exist with more seasoned and financially secure vendors. Termination provisions might be worked around to guard against the greater risks that exist when dealing with weaker vendors. Warrantees, escrow accounts, bonds, and the like are issues here.

Other contract provisions can help guard against termination or situations that can lead to termination. For example, the contract might give your organization the right to simultaneously contract with a second vendor for the same, similar, or related services (Nuara, 1992). This can help keep vendors on their toes.

6.5 PARTNERSHIPS

When uncertainty is high, asset specificity is high, and there are gains to be had from repeated contracting; partnerships can be advantageous. These relationships work on the basis of mutual trust, not legal documents, although contracts will be written between client and vendor. The term "minisociety" is sometimes used to describe partnerships. Norms and values guide actions, as much as contracts.

Return to the marriage analogy of an earlier chapter. Marriage is a legal arrangement, but what makes marriages work at one level is mutual trust and sharing. When times are good, both partners enjoy the benefits. When times are bad, both partners share the losses. And both partners invest in mutually beneficial activities. One partner devotes time and effort to an activity the benefits of which are not captured entirely by that partner but also benefit the other partner. This is done on the expectation and trust that the other partner will reciprocate. In a good marriage the second partner does reciprocate by putting time and effort into a different activity that also benefits both. The ongoing sharing of gains and losses, the ongoing investment in efforts that benefit both partners, and the trust that the other will reciprocate helps hold the marriage together. A partner who indulges in self-gratifying activity with no benefits for the other partner puts the relationship in jeopardy and may cause it to ultimately fail.

The same mechanisms are at work in partnerships between client and outsourcing vendor. There are a succession of contracts, but the sharing arrangements and the mutually beneficial investments are the real glue that holds the relationship together. Continuity is obtained through expectations on the part of both client and vendor that mutually beneficial exchange will continue into the future through good performance of both parties at every point along the way.

Aspects of contracts that are consistent with partnerships include the following, although not all may be strictly necessary for success in partnership arrangements:

- Methods for revising the contract when unforeseen contingencies arise.
- Pricing methods that allow sharing of risks and gains.
- Profit sharing provisions, when the project will yield outside revenue.
- Commitment to an investment on the part of one party that it cannot recoup over the life of the contract. This commitment "ties its hands." It makes a sacrifice now in clear expectation that other, future contracts will be written that allow it to eventually benefit from the reciprocal investment of the other party.
- Dispute and disagreement resolution mechanisms.
- Incentives and punishments — but probably more emphasis on the former than the latter.
- Standard operating procedures and authority to change or renegotiate contract provisions. However, adjustments in work or provisions are as likely to take place through mutual discussion and agreement as through reference to contract provisions.

In partnerships, contracts are useful for confirming the commitment between client and vendor by setting out requirements aimed at achieving the next set of goals in the partnerships. They also serve a safety net function with termination provisions to handle the dissolution of the partnership should it fail. But the day-to-day functioning of the partnership does not depend in a central way on the contract.

Much of the legal scaffolding that supports intermediate contracting relationships is appropriate and can be found in contracts signed in partnerships. Major differences might be found in sharing arrangements (with more of these in partnerships than intermediate contracts) and "tying-of-hands" type commitments. The real difference is the heavy reliance on mechanisms outside legal documents to support partnerships.

Partnership arrangements with their patterns of reciprocal behavior are sometimes said to be self-enforcing. The relationship has longevity because the partners have an incentive to stay together to enjoy the future returns — whether inside one contracting period or over the life of several contracts. Problems can arise, however, if:

- The benefits of investments meant to be beneficial to the other party are hard to know or measure.
- The division of benefits from investments meant to be mutually beneficial are hard to know or measure.

Under either of these conditions, differences in perceptions and disagreements can arise over whether each partner is contributing as expected. Differences and disagreements can arise over fairness.

It follows that contractual commitments to investments meant to support trust and the continuing relationship should be ones that clearly benefit the other party and are easy to observe and measure. If the investment is meant to benefit both parties, clear observability and measurement of the relative benefits help allay suspicions.

6.6 PREFERRED VENDOR RELATIONSHIPS

Outsourcing needs that have characteristics most appropriate for relationships close to the market end of the outsourcing relationship spectrum can sometimes be structured as ongoing preferred vendor programs. If it's possible to institute a preferred vendor program, your organization could enjoy some of the benefits of both market and partnership relationships. Preferred vendor programs promote competition between vendors that reduces the costs of negotiating and policing the contract. They can also require vendors to make investments that benefit your organization over the life of several, successive contracts — the kind of investment that usually takes place only in partnerships.

Consider the possibility of establishing a preferred vendor program when the conditions favor a market-type relationship but the work is one for which there is a continuing need. The work might be part of ongoing processes or as the result of a succession of projects that require the same general kind of vendor services. Contract programming is a prime example; the work is more or less ongoing, although, related to different systems projects over time.

Normally, your organization could not expect much investment on the part of a vendor in your particular organization-specific ways of doing things because at the end of a contract you could hire another vendor in the next contracting period. However, a win-win or value creating deal can be structured if you require the vendor to make up-front investments in knowledge and/or capabilities that benefit your organization in return for putting the vendor in a pool of "preferred vendors" who thereby qualify to bid on work in the future. Vendors who don't make the up-front commitment don't qualify for future work. A select group of vendors is admitted to the pool, so competition still exists for future work. The benefit to your organization is vendor investment in knowledge and/or capabilities that are targeted to your organization and its needs. The gain for the vendor is greater access to and preferential treatment in competition for future work from your organization. Preferred vendor programs also have the positive effect of limiting opportunistic behavior.

Prequalify only the best vendors, according to aspects of vendors discussed in Chapter 5. Out of this group only admit to preferred vendor status those who make up-front investments that benefit your organization.

The plan can also be set up with grades or levels of preferred status. Investments of one sort admit vendors to the first status level that qualifies them for work of a certain kind, frequency, and/or duration. Additional investments of another sort qualify vendors for a higher preferred vendor status with access to other kinds of work, at greater frequencies, or for longer durations. The number of rungs on the preferred vendor status ladder can be many, depending on the amount of work you have to outsource and the ways in which you can segment it. Move vendors up the ladder over time as they make required investments and perform according to expectations. Remove vendors who don't do a good job.

6.7 PROJECT VERSUS PROCESS WORK IN CONTRACTS

Some outsourcing work is project in nature, while other work is process in nature. Project-type work is usually characterized by:

- Work that stems from a need that is unique, out of the ordinary, and not part of everyday functioning.
- Work that can be accomplished within a predetermined period of time with recognizable start and stop dates.
- Work that is important enough to demand focused management attention, as in larger, more complex, and organizationally important bodies of work.

Processes, on the other hand, have more of an ongoing, continuous nature. Both project and process work are commonly outsourced.

Where the contracting period is an issue, project work has clearer durations with associated start and end points. Process work often lacks such natural periodicity, and contracting periods are more arbitrary. The length of contracts for project-type work will usually be fixed by the length of time needed to complete the work. Process work, on the other hand, offers more flexibility. The best contracting period isn't always obvious in process work. Some aspects to be considered are:

- Uncertainty. The existence of uncertainty argues for shorter contracts. As changing circumstances require changes in outsourcing arrangements, shorter contracts allow new provisions to be written in the next contract without resort to mechanisms discussed above for midstream change in contracting relationships.

- Asset Specificity. When investment in things or knowledge is involved, the party making the investment will usually want a longer contract to provide more time to recoup the investment. The client will want a longer contract, if it has made the investment, the vendor, if it has made the investment.

- The costs of finding a vendor and negotiating a contract. The larger the set-up costs for a contract, the longer the parties to the contract will want the contract to last.

Vendors usually prefer longer contracts. They will present data on "norms" for contract lengths in various kinds of outsourcing deals, but you need not accept the norms. Contract length is a negotiable issue. Consider the factors discussed above and try to get a contract length that best suits the circumstances.

The nature of the outsourcing work in terms of project or process may affect the most desirable pricing arrangements. In a well-organized and understood single project where the requirements can be firmly established up-front, a fixed-price contract may work best. Clear specifications for what the vendor is to do can be written with the contract specifying a fixed price leaving little room for disputes. Time and material pricing schemes for this kind of project work would cause constant worry about unjustified charges. Disputes would be likely.

Process type work may be better compensated in a time and materials fashion. Here the exact amount of work to be done may be difficult to predict before the fact. In a fixed price contract, the vendor would be looking for ways to trim your demands to obtain its margins, and you would be looking to get as much out of the vendor as you can for the price you are paying. Conflict is likely.

Aspects of the contract other than pricing, depend on the underlying characteristics of the project work and how they align best with market, intermediate, or partnership arrangements in outsourcing.

6.8 CONTRACT NEGOTIATION

Negotiating power in outsourcing contracts relates to issues of relative dependence between client and vendor. Negotiating strategy should be conditioned by the kind of relationship that best suits the outsourcing situation and by bargaining power.

6.8.1 Relative Dependence and Bargaining Power

The bargaining power of a client relative to a vendor in outsourcing contract negotiations is a function of how dependent each is on the other. If organization A sees itself as being more dependent on organization B than organization B is on organization A, then organization A will feel that B has greater influence in contract negotiation. Conversely, if organization A thinks it is less dependent than B, it feels that it has greater influence in the negotiations (Anderson and Narus, 1990).

Relative dependence rests on the following factors (Heide and John, 1988):

- Dependence increases with both the size of the contract and the importance of the contract to the contracting party. Clients that outsource hundreds of millions of dollars worth of information systems operations are more dependent on their vendors than organizations that outsource a small amount of systems work. IT departments that outsource mission-critical systems are more dependent than those who outsource a routine, backoffice system. Similarly vendors' dependence increases with the size of the potential contract in absolute magnitude and in relation to the work they are doing and have done in the past.

- Dependence is higher in instances in which a party to a contract is dealing with the best vendor or the best client. "Best" to the vendor may mean the most visible, prestigious, influential, richest, or potentially long-lasting customer. "Best" to the client may mean the most reputable, the largest, the soundest, the least expensive, the most responsive, or the most technically advanced vendor. The organization that thinks it's negotiating with the best, will feel it has less influence in the contract negotiations than otherwise.

- Dependence on a vendor is higher when there are few other vendors offering the same service or skill set, or when there is little competition between vendors. And dependence of a vendor on a client is higher when there are few other clients looking for vendors. Concentration in either or both sides of the outsourcing market increases dependence because there are fewer alternatives.

- Finally, difficulty in replacing a potential contract partner increases dependence. The party to a contract that perceives much time, cost, and effort in finding and negotiating a contract with a replacement outsourcing partner is more dependent on the firm with which it is negotiating.

Of course, part of the game of negotiation is trying to make the other party think you feel less dependent on them than you are. But vendors have much experience in negotiating outsourcing contracts and know the basic strength of your organization's bargaining position. Skilled negotiators will be able to get a better deal than persons with less skill, but the range of maneuver is likely constrained by real differences in the relative dependence of client and vendor.

With the above factors shaping relative bargaining strength, a number of trade-offs come into play for a given outsourcing need that can increase the power of your organization in negotiations, but always at a cost:

- If the overall need can be split into separate components and outsourced separately to different vendors, the dependence on one vendor is reduced. The trade-off is the time, cost, and effort to negotiate multiple contracts and the effort involved in integrating vendor efforts.

- If mission critical systems have revenue potential, a contract might be written with a vendor that shares revenue, profit, and/or risk. The possible downside is retaining less revenue for your own organization.

- Hiring a smaller vendor rather than a larger vendor makes your organization more important to the vendor. But does the smaller vendor have the resources and the financial strength?

- Stepping down to vendors with lesser reputations will give your organization more clout in contract negotiations. The trade-off is the possibility of poor vendor performance and taking on a vendor who may try to take advantage of your organization.

- Increasing the number of vendors competing for your work is possible by scouring the available vendor pool. But this may bring in less desirable vendors. Having your own IT department make a bid for the work will increase the pool of competitors by one — although this may or may not be organizationally or politically feasible.

This points to the necessity of doing sound homework on potential vendors — their capabilities, reputations, business segments, volume of business, and desires to build up or retreat from certain business segments. Vendors will gather information on your organization, and they have the added advantage of negotiating outsourcing contracts frequently. To offset the information advantage they would otherwise have requires considerable work on your part.

Bargaining Power and Contract Provisions

If your organization is less dependent on the vendor than the vendor is on you, it is to your advantage to try to write a contract that slides more to the market end of the contracting spectrum. If vendor performance can't be observed, measured, and specified in the contract, it may at least be possible to write some contract provisions that give you greater midstream control over changes and other contract provisions that compensate you if the vendor fails to perform.

The converse is also true. If the vendor has greater bargaining power, you may be required to accept contract language that limits changes, compensates the vendor well for changes that are made, and puts minimal sanctions on poor performance. If you can't avoid outsourcing in such circumstances, the best that might be done is to slide the contract toward the partnership end of the contracting spectrum by putting in risk and gain sharing provisions that split the losses and gains and incent the vendor to act more like a partner. Good dispute resolution measures are also indispensable, including mediation by neutral third parties.

Don't go overboard with power. If a partnership is the preferable contracting relationship, don't try to pin the vendor to a lot of conditions that aren't partnerlike; this is a bad way to start a long-term relationship.

6.8.2   Vendor Standard Contracts

A vendor's standard contract is likely written to favor the vendor. Never sign a vendor's standard contract before close scrutiny and modification of the contract by a competent attorney. If you have a lot of bargaining power in contract negotiations, starting with the vendor's standard contract is probably a mistake. Start, instead, with your own term sheet outline of what you want in the contract. Let vendors know at the beginning of the RFP process that the procedure will not use vendor standard contracts. Many vendors are accustomed to starting with their standard contracts. Set expectations early.

6.8.3   Negotiation Strategy

Experts recommend that the parties in negotiation draw a clear distinction between their interests on the one hand, and the issues under negotiation and stands taken by the parties on the issues on the other. Interests are, after all, the bottom line in what your organization hopes to achieve by outsourcing. Interests, in turn, are shaped by factors addressed earlier, such as:

- Motive or motives for outsourcing and achievement of the benefits associated with each motive.

- Type of contract most appropriate to success for your organization, whether market or intermediate or relational.
- Contract term or length that best suits your organization.
- Contract provisions that help motivate and discipline the vendor's effort and protect against opportunistic behavior on the part of the vendor.

Once your interests are clear, you're in a position to consider trade-offs between interests inherent in issues and positions taken by both sides and the minimum acceptable position on each issue (Sebenius, 1992).

Negotiations often proceed from initial stands on issues by both sides to "log-rolling" in which the parties move toward an agreement by successive exchanges in position — one party giving up some ground on one issue in exchange for more favorable treatment by the other party on another issue.

Many tactics can be used to present one's position in a more favorable light or more forcibly. And, of course, the tactics available depend on your bargaining power. Some tactics to consider are:

- Staking out a position painted in the most favorable light such that further negotiation is ostensibly foreclosed. The most efficient, least cost, most conducive to enhanced reputation, the least risky, or most beneficial course is claimed and presented.

- Stalking horses, or proposals that stake out claims by a party that the party knows it can't get with the purpose of trading the claim away for some lesser claim. For example, the vendor might propose a strong clause on penalties and interest for late payment. The client rejects this, but agrees as a compromise to pay within fifteen days.

- Walking away from the table and actively looking to other vendors for better price, service, or quality.

Formulation of tactics is an art as much as a science. It's a game of guessing the most favorable outcomes that can be obtained with one set of tactics versus likely outcomes from others.

Tactics to be used are also conditioned by the desired outsourcing relationship. Consistently playing hardball in negotiations with a vendor to structure a partnership will likely backfire. Being a marshmallow in negotiations to structure a market contract will not achieve the desired result.

Win-Win and Win-Lose Strategies

Win-win strategies try to reach a mutually acceptable outcome for both client and vendor. Sebenius (1992) calls this "creating value," while win-lose strategies attempt to "claim value" when more for one party means less for the other.

To create value, or win-win, requires finding some gains from working together that would not be available in the absence of a contract. The basic sources of such gains are (Sebenius, 1992):

- Economies of scale. Achieving scale by undertaking activity that the parties could not do separately.
- Finding differences that create value, like differences in the ability to accept risk (maybe the vendor is better able to undertake a risky venture while the client has the capital to do it). Complementary technical abilities is another example.
- Creating shared interests like a vision of what is possible in the application of new technology with gains to be shared by both parties.

Partnerships have a foundation in win-win contracting strategies. Both sides must see long-term gain over a succession of contracts rooted in one of the factors outlined above.

Win-lose strategies, on the other hand, claim the value created by a relationship for one party or largely for one party. Tactics favored in these situations include:

- Strong, take-it-or-leave-it positions.
- Linking issues and/or interests to create leverage.
- Manipulating the perceptions of the other party in above-board or in misleading ways.
- Exploiting expectations of the other party.

The bases for negotiation seldom favor a single strategy — win-win or win-lose — and most often have elements of each. The challenge is to use value creating and value claiming strategies when they are appropriate. However, win-lose strategies are more confrontational by nature. If a party to a negotiation adopts this strategy on one issue, the other party may be tempted to retaliate with a win-lose strategy on the next issue. A downward spiral may result in which cooperation and win-win get crushed by successive rounds of win-lose gambits. Negotiations dominated entirely by value claiming win-lose strategies are not a good beginning for any outsourcing relationship, including market relationships.

A tit-for-tat strategy is often effective (Axelrod, 1984):

- Take a long run view of what can be accomplished in creating value.
- At the start, don't try to take advantage of the other party in negotiations. Remain cooperative.

- If the other party makes a move that creates value, follow up with a value-creating suggestion of your own. In other words, reciprocate.
- However, if the other party tries to take advantage of you, reciprocate with a move that claims value for yourself.

In other words, try to foster win-win by rewarding good behavior, but don't let the other party take advantage of you. Signal this by punishing bad behavior.

Fallback Positions

Think through a strategy on each important issue including one or more fallback positions. If you can't get all you want, what is an acceptable alternative, and an acceptable second alternative to the first alternative? For example, guaranteed performance by a vendor might be best. But for some difficult tasks the best that can be had might be "reasonable" or "best" efforts.

If negotiations with the selected vendor become extremely difficult, falling back to the second vendor might be wise. For this reason, don't cut all the competing vendors out before the contract is signed, sealed, and delivered.

It should go without saying, but never let the vendor begin work before the contract is negotiated and signed; your bargaining power is severely reduced if you do.

The Negotiating Team

Put together a team of negotiators that includes legal, financial, and technical people. When personnel issues are important, human resource people should also be part of the negotiating team.

As DuPont negotiated with CSC and Andersen Consulting, DuPont had six people on the negotiation team, and each of the two providers had about the same number on each of their teams. DuPont's team alternated with each provider — CSC on Monday, Andersen on Tuesday, and so on. DuPont also had two subteams which negotiated separately most of the time and together at other times. One subteam focused on the human resources, financial, and other business aspects of the contract, and the second subteam concentrated on the exhibits that contained the details about the services and the service levels. DuPont's team was chaired by its vice president of corporate iniatives. The negotiating team met frequently with the CIO and other key managers to obtain timely advice and assistance.

In its negotiations with IBM, the Riggs Bank negotiation team consisted of the CIO and legal counsel with help from the CFO, and Auditing Accountant, as necessary. During service level negotiations, the IT management team participated in the negotiations to bring their subject matter expertise to the table. When negotiations bogged down over the measurement of communications services,

Riggs brought in an outsourcing consultant to help. Jill Klein says, "We learned a valuable lesson from that and brought in the consultants from the outset when we later negotiated other outsourcing services." Klein contends that clients need outside counsel and other outside experts to help level the playing field. The vendors have far more experience with contract negotiations than the typical company considering outsourcing, in her view.

6.8.4 Other Aspects of Negotiation

Here are some other aspects to consider in negotiating with vendors:

- When entering negotiations, don't commit to a finish date for the process. This may put unwanted pressure on the negotiations later. DuPont made a commitment to its employees to have a contract by a certain date that put unnecessary and unrealistic pressure on its negotiating teams. The end date should have been announced after negotiations were well underway and with a better understanding of what was involved.

- Be certain vendor technical people are involved in negotiations, not just marketing people. Technical people know the constraints and limits of what the vendor can do; marketing people are marketing people.

- Get people with the power and authority to make decisions at the bargaining table, and make the vendor do the same. It's a waste of time to do otherwise.

- When negotiating with several vendors at the same time, set a deadline for best offers as a tactic for forcing best offers on the table.

- To foster competition between vendors, first do a term sheet. Use the RFP to gather vendor answers to questions of importance in deciding between vendors, then move two vendors to a final stage in which they have to answer the really hard questions. Go to negotiations with each vendor and perform due diligence to verify vendor answers on all critical term sheet issues.

- If one vendor is the choice from the start and serious negotiations take place with only that vendor, then create a financial model and service scenario that represents a good effort (perhaps one that exceeds actual performance) on the part of in-house IT department in performing the same functions. Then have the vendor bid against and negotiate against the model and scenario, even if internal IT isn't truly in the running. Good cost and service analyses of the type advocated in the previous chapter are the foundation for this approach.

- Keep a focus on the important issues in negotiations and get those out of the way first. Don't let the vendor dictate an agenda that gets lost in trivia, only to rush through the really important issues under time pressure later. Starting from the beginning of a proposed contract (yours or the vendor's) and working through it line-by-line is the antithesis of important issues first. State your agenda that leads with important issues, get agreement on the agenda, and follow it.
- If the important issues are also difficult issues to resolve, interleave the important-difficult issues with a few easier issues so that the negotiations are not perceived by either side as unrelenting conflict and hard going.
- If an impasse is reached on an issue, leave it to a later day but not to the last minute.
- Drafting the language of the contract should be a joint effort of both parties and should be controlled. Meet to confirm the exact language.
- Never rely on a vendor's oral statement of intentions. Get it in the contract.
- Be sure the contract is as complete as you want to make it before signing. Don't assume that details will be amicably worked out later.
- Do a side letter to state your interpretation of a contract provision, if you think there is some chance of disagreement even after careful drafting.
- Vendors may try to go directly to CEOs or CFOs to quickly negotiate and sign contracts. They can do this at the outset or in the middle of difficult negotiations claiming that the IT negotiating team is trying to sabotage the deal. This is dangerous and can lead to very unfavorable contracting terms. Warn senior executives of the danger. Report frequently on the progress of negotiations, and invite senior officers to visit the negotiating sessions whenever they like so that they can see that progress is being made.
- Vendor marketing tactics always involve creating good relationships with the people in your organization, and these relationships often stem from working together in the past on a previous contract. Vendors will try to get your people on their side. Be certain vendor efforts to entertain and ply your people with dinners, gifts, and junkets don't stand in the way of good judgment. The process for dealing with vendors outlined in the previous chapter is an antidote for this.

The difficult negotiating issues will vary from outsourcing situation to outsourcing situation, but aspects of a deal that involve pricing and personnel often head the list. In the Riggs Bank case it was human resource issues and charges for changes in usage of services that presented the greatest negotiating challenges.

It's best not to make a final commitment to outsourcing before contract negotiations are completed. Retaining the insourcing option gives you leverage in contract negotiations.

Keep this in mind as you communicate with your employees. A major downside to announcing an impending outsourcing deal is the impact the announcement can have on the negotiating stance of a vendor. A vendor might assume that telling your employees that contract negotiations are in progress is a clear signal that your organization is committed to outsourcing. Vendor bargaining positions can harden as a result. On the other hand it's difficult to keep negotiations secret, and there are real advantages to openness with your employees, as noted earlier. The best strategy might be to qualify communication with employees. Speak of outsourcing as a possibility, not a fact, until the contract is signed.

6.8.5 International Considerations

If the outsourcing deal will span more than one country, it may be best to negotiate a master contract and subsidiary contracts — one for each country in which the outsourcing arrangement will operate. The country-specific contracts should conform to the legal systems of those countries and address the country-specific issues involved.

When DuPont sourced with CSC and Andersen Consulting, its team negotiated more than forty contracts — a master contract and contracts for the United States, Canada, and each of 18 countries in Europe with each vendor.

6.9   DOW CHEMICAL AND ANDERSEN CONSULTING ALLIANCE: AN INTERVIEW WITH DAVID KEPLER

David E. Kepler is director of Global Information Systems with responsibility for Global Information Application. This includes Application Support Services, Information Technology Projects, Internal Consulting, and I/T Investment Planning.

Kepler joined Dow U.S.A. in 1975 in Information Systems at the Western Division in Pittsburg, California. After progressive positions in Information Systems in Western Division, U.S. Area Headquarters and Michigan Division, and Eastern Division, he was named manager of Computer Services for Dow Canada; he was named commercial director of Performance Products for Dow Canada in 1989. Kepler became director of Information Systems and Diamond System Project manager for the Pacific Area in 1991 and was named manager of Information Technology for Chemicals and Plastics in September 1993. In

July 1994, he was named director of Global Information Systems Services for Chemicals and Plastics. He was appointed to his current position in June 1995.

Kepler received a bachelor's degree in chemical engineering from the University of California at Berkeley.

What has been Dow's experience with outsourcing? Please describe briefly each of your outsourcing arrangements.
Dow has a defined strategy for outsourcing based on a set of criteria for selective outsourcing. Examples of activities we have outsourced to various vendors include:

Application Development.
Application Support.
Hardware Asset Management.
Workstations.
Data Network Management.
Help Desk.

You have a relationship with Andersen Consulting for applications. Does it include development and maintenance?
Yes.

What were the factors that led you to consider establishing that relationship?
The process for selection was based on our organizational and selective outsourcing strategies. This allowed us to set criteria to narrow the selection to a few suppliers.

Andersen Consulting was selected it was the most rapid and flexible in meeting our objectives and committing to our metrics.

What are the goals and objectives of the relationship for your company?
The objectives are to:

- Create the IT capability needed to enable Dow to achieve competitive advantage.
- Increase productivity of Dow's IT systems development and support in the next three years by at least 30 percent and decrease time to market by at least 40 percent.
- Form and manage an effective IT organization.
- Maximize Dow's "buy" strategy.

How do you manage the relationship?

The IT Investment Plan provides the discipline and framework to annually plan for development and support work. Historically, the supply of IS people available to work on projects has constrained the amount of development and support work that could be done. With the new annual planning process, our IS budget determines the amount of development and support work.

The Investment Plan is a Dow responsibility.

The Demand Plan is the detailed labor effort required by team type and month to deliver the Investment Plan.

Andersen sets the Supply Plan that identifies the number and size of teams by time period required to meet the Investment Plan. Staffing Agreements that specify Andersen Consulting staffing levels for the year are, in turn, based on the Supply Plan.

A Statement of Work (SOW) or Service Level Agreement (SLA) is the formal agreement between the Alliance and internal Dow Clients to deliver a project or support an application for a fixed-price within a defined time frame.

What are your performance metrics? How do you use them?
How do you encourage continuous improvement?

The Alliance objective is to increase productivity of Dow's IT systems development and support in the next three years ('97 – '99) by at least 30 percent. The 30 percent cumulative improvement in productivity is measured against the 1995 productivity baseline.

Output metrics are in function points. Function points (FPs) are an international standard measurement for determining units of functionality provided by an IT application.

The development and support productivity improvement goal is broken down into categories. Selected categories have a baseline and commitment in 1997; additional categories will be included in commitments for future years. Here's a table with the categories and associated measures; the 1996 baselines and the 1997 commitments are confidential.

Category	Measure
Application Support — corrective 'break/fix,' preventative and adaptive maintenance, as well as client and system support for production applications after the 90-day support period following the first site implementation. Does not include enhancement activities.	Alliance Cost $ per FP Supported

(continued)

Category	Measure
Development & Implementation I — all planning, design and development activities throughout initial implementation, which includes BS/PS, System Design, Detail Design, Construction, Product Testing, and first-site implementation including 90-day support period. * Includes new activities — additional testing, better requirements definitions, improved preparation for implementation.	Alliance Cost $ per FP Delivered
Implementations 2 — activities to support implementation(s) subsequent to the initial implementation (e.g., expansion to broader user groups, additional geographies). The 1995 baseline is based on a single data point; 1997 will be used to collect more data and refine the baseline.	Alliance Cost $ per FP per 1000 Users Implemented.
Individual Small Enhancements — small (less than 8 function points) enhancements made on an individual basis to stand-alone or nonintegrated systems.	Total Alliance Cost $ for Individual Small Enhancements
Premium Service — Resources/costs related to providing "premium service" (e.g., the IS Control Center) beyond the agreed definition of "break-fix" application support.	Alliance Cost $ per FP Supported for Premium Service
Alliance Consulting — Resources/costs involved in performing IT strategy, system architecture, opportunity analysis, and consulting activities. Non FP project activities (e.g., Service Program, Security Architecture, R/3 Strategy).	Total Alliance Cost $ for Alliance Consulting
ISS Consulting — ISS resources/costs involved in providing consulting services to the partner organization (e.g., account management, Opportunity Analysis).	Total Alliance Cost $ for ISS Consulting

In addition, there are metrics for value delivery, time to market, client satisfaction, and process and people capability.

Do your two companies share the risks and rewards? How?

Yes. Andersen Consulting is contractually committed to achieving productivity commitments. The Productivity True-up is factored into the Andersen Consulting fees.

Under the terms of this arrangement, Andersen Consulting is directly incented to maximize productivity. Likewise, Dow is equally incented to maximize productivity because the actual productivity achieved in a given year becomes the basis for future year commitment negotiations.

This win/win arrangement was emphasized during the earliest discussions between Dow and Andersen Consulting and demonstrates the shared leadership model which allows both companies to share mutually-agreed upon risks to gain maximum value.

How do you track productivity?

The information needed to track productivity measures should be a by-product of project/support arrangement and execution. Every project/support ID will be assigned to a productivity category. Function Point counts are standard deliverables and actual costs are accumulated. Monthly reporting of productivity results are produced from this data.

There are several other Alliance objectives that are measured and tracked in addition to the development and support productivity objectives. These measures are in place to ensure long term quality performance and may offset productivity improvements. Results in these areas will be factored into the annual Productivity Plan negotiations. The following table presents the objectives and associated measures.

Objective	Definition/Measure
Value Definition	All projects delivering greater than 50 function points will have a measurable, documented definition of value.
Value Delivery	Comparison of actual value delivered to Dow versus the value defined during Project Study. Target for '97 is to establish a valid baseline; cumulative improvement goals are 10% improvement in '98, and 20% in '99.
Time to Market	Achieve a 40% reduction in project duration (elapsed time) over '95 baseline by Dec. '99. The cumulative targets will be 10% in '97, 25% in '98, and 40% in '99.
Time to Zero Cash Flow	Decrease the time it takes to recoup the project investment by 20% over the baseline which will be established in '97. Cumulative improvement targets are 10% in '98 and 20% in '99.

(continued)

Objective	Definition/Measure
Process Capability	Obtain a Level 2.0 out of 5.0 on the industry standard Software Engineering Institute Capability Maturity Model (SEI CMM) by '97; Level 3.0 by '98.
People Capability	Achieve 25% improvement in world-class capability by Mar. '98 over the baseline which will be established in '97; reach the world class benchmark, as defined by Project Management Institute (PMI) industry benchmarks, by Mar. 2001.
Partner Satisfaction	Rank in the 2d quartile (top 51–75%) of all Real Decisions large companies in '97; rank in the 1st quartile (top 76–100%) in '98.
Long-Term Cost of Ownership	Ensure the long-term cost of ownership (LTCOO) of Dow's IT investment is optimized. LTCOO includes all costs associated with planning for IT investments, development and implementation, support, operations, and retirement. Target for '97 is to define this measure so that baseline data collection can begin in '98.

What lessons have you learned so far about a relationship of this nature?
Establishing operating principles and governance philosophy and measures are the key drivers in developing a partnership. A partnership should be entered into the same way you would enter into a joint venture, with a clear understanding of how to build a "Win/Win" relationship for both parties.

The division of responsibilities in the Alliance is clear. Dow focuses on managing the Investment Plan process, as well as project execution and issue resolution; Program Offices should also challenge/redirect projects or support with high costs and low FP units (The "What" and "When").

Andersen should focus on managing the processes used across the Alliance to maximize productivity and ensure successful delivery/service and the staffing necessary to execute the SOWs/SLAs. (The "Who" and "How").

Would you do anything differently based on what you have learned so far?
I would have placed more emphasis on the aspect of human change with both the employees and our clients.

What suggestions would you have for anyone considering a similar relationship?

Establishing operating principles and governance philosophy and measures are the key drivers to develop a partnership. A partnership should be entered into the same way you would enter into a joint venture, with a clear understanding of how to build a "Win/Win" relationship for both parties.

6.10 REFERENCES

Anderson, Erin and Barton Weitz, "Determinants of Continuity in Conventional Industrial Channel Dyads," *Marketing Science*, 8/4 (Fall 1989) 310–325.

Anderson, J. C. and Narus, J. A., "A Model of Distributor Firm and Manufacturer Firm Working Partnerships," *Journal of Marketing*, 54 (1990) 42–58.

Ang, Soon and Beath, Cynthia Mathis, "Hierarchical Elements in Software Contracts," *Journal of Organizational Computing*, 3/3 (1993) 329–361.

Axelrod, Robert, *The Evolution of Cooperation*, New York, Basic Book, 1984.

Heide, J. B. and John, G., "The Role of Dependence Balancing In Safeguarding Transaction-Specific Assets in Conventional Channels," *Journal of Marketing*, 52 (1988) 20–35.

Nuara, Leonard T. "Outsourcing Agreements," in Daniel T. Brooks, *14th Annual Computer Law Institute*, New York, Computer Law Institute, (August 1992) 411–474.

Saunders, Carol, Gelbelt, Mary, and Hu, Qing, "Achieving success in information systems outsourcing," *California Management Review*, 39/2 (Winter 1997) 63–75.

Sebenius, James K., "Negotiation Analysis: A Characterization and Review," *Management Science*, 38/1 (January 1992) 18–39.

7

Contract Provisions

The exact form and shape of a contract depends on what is being outsourced and the nature of the outsourcing relationship to be established. Therefore, not every issue in this chapter will be relevant. With the advice of your counsel, other issues not covered here will undoubtedly be discovered. See Appendix D for an example of an outsourcing contract.

The legal ramifications of doing a contract that specifies work in multiple countries, each with its own legal system, are obviously more complex than dealing with a single country. This chapter addresses some international outsourcing contract issues, but you will need the help of knowledgeable attorneys.

Sources you may want to consult for their extensive discussions of legal issues in outsourcing contracts include the books by Mylott (1995), by Halvey and Melby (1996), and by Brandon and Segelstein (1976). Reference services provide many of the details to be considered where hardware and software are concerned. You may want to consult Hoffman (1997) and Bernacchi, Frank, and Statland (1995) which are available in many law libraries.

The chapter concludes with a Richard Raysman interview on the essential aspects of outsourcing contracts.

7.1 REQUIREMENTS

It's hard to overemphasize the importance of writing a contract that is as complete as possible. When something is omitted from a list of requirements, as a matter of law it is not required. Assumptions don't count for much in legal circles.

If a good analysis was done in preparation for a Request For Proposal (RFP), most of what is needed with respect to service requirements in a contract is already in hand. Talking with vendors may surface a few additional ideas.

Business, organizational or technological change since the analysis may suggest other changes. But the work leading up to the RFP should have identified requirements fairly completely. Requirements are usually laid out in exhibits in the contract, and the RFP provides the starting point, outline, and the bulk of the content for the exhibits.

Requirements stated in observable and measurable terms are always better than requirements stated in less specific ways. Robert Rubin of Elf Atochem warns that contracts should embody a clear understanding of what is expected of each side and ways of measuring these values. Contracts are much more enforceable with measurable requirements. If attention was paid to these issues in preparation for the RFP, there should be no problem incorporating measurable criteria in the contract. Also include reporting requirements, and specify who pays for reporting.

Recall that one of the several ways of describing services is in terms of their importance to the functioning of your organization. These descriptions help establish vendor expectations and can be important if a dispute over performance ever goes to mediation, arbitration, or to the courts. Requirements can also be set in business terms and performance can be measured by business measures. When vendor performance and compensation are tied to the performance of your business, your objectives and vendor objectives may be more closely aligned.

7.1.1 Scheduled Work and Resources

When requirements involve time schedules, put these in the contract exhibits. The contract should then require that the vendor perform the service according to the schedule.

Schedules also apply to resources and services that must be available at particular times from the vendor to your organization and from your organization to the vendor. When your organization must make resources available to the vendor, for example data to be processed, the vendor may rightly insist that the contract contains provisions that require your organization to provide the data in a timely manner.

If your needs require flexibility in schedules or analysis of requirements indicates that schedules may change as a result of business or other influences, add a contract provision that allows your organization to modify the schedule for the service in question, perhaps on 30 days advance written notice to the vendor.

The contract can also contain provisions that state the priority of your work relative to the work the vendor performs for other customers. If your organization enjoys some leverage in vendor negotiations, according to the factors discussed in the previous chapter, such provisions may help assure service in times when the vendor struggles to meet all commitments.

Contract provisions can be added that specify certain resources, equipment, people, and so forth which are to be dedicated to servicing your organization, at certain times, or at all times.

7.1.2 Growth and Change

Every client is unique in the potential growth and change it may experience over the life of an outsourcing agreement, and contract provisions should provide the needed flexibility. For example, Riggs Bank outsourcing contract allowed change in provisions for any significant change in the bank's structure and book of business. The contract also allowed the bank to select another vendor to perform the work if the vendor was unable to meet the needs or accommodate changes in the business.

The analysis process should provide the basis for the contractual provisions on growth and change. See Chapter 5 on these issues. Allow flexibility for growth in services over time. For each service category, the contract can specify the basic amount of growth per year that can occur with no increase in vendor fees, and it can also specify the fee schedule for growth that exceeds the base amount.

If the analysis indicates that future business or technological change can substantially revise the requirements in an outsourcing relationship, it is wise to consider the possibility of circuit breaker contract provisions that allow renegotiation of some areas in the contract or even a complete renegotiation of the contract. To avoid disputes over what constitutes substantial change, the circuit breaker can be tripped by a contract provision that specifies divergence of some measure of your organization's business or some measure of technology from a predetermined amount or from some predetermined growth or rate of change.

Change Processes

The contract should specify a change notification process — who can propose changes, when changes can be proposed, to whom changes are proposed, what approvals are necessary, and when change requires renegotiation of any aspect of the contract, including charges.

If your organization is subject to mandated changes by governments or other regulatory bodies, be certain the contract speaks to the related issues of notification to the vendor, determination of requirements, the schedule for making changes or how they will be determined, and the pricing or payment for the additional work or how it will be determined.

7.1.3 Additional Work

Situations may arise that require the vendor to do additional work not specified in the original agreement. The contract should contain provisions for additional work addressing issues like:

- Identification of additional work or kinds of additional work. If the vendor identifies the additional work, the contract can specify how client outsourcing managers are to be notified.

- Authorization to do additional work. Additional work should only be done after written authorization by client outsourcing managers.

- The basis and rates for payment for additional work, depending on its type. When the nature of additional work cannot be anticipated, the contract should specify methods for negotiating charges.

- Maxima on the payment that will be made for additional work units of a particular type.

7.1.4 Upgrades and Change of Character Clauses

The vendor may want to change hardware and software involved in providing services to your organization during the life of the contract. The vendor's motives can be many, but usually these changes reduce vendor costs. Such changes may benefit your organization — the hardware is faster, the software has greater functionality. But sometimes a change can require that you change aspects of hardware, software, or data inside your organization to be compatible with the new vendor technology presenting your organization with an unforeseen cost.

It's reasonable that the vendor have some flexibility, but watch out for so-called "change of character" clauses in contracts. These might specify the vendor can increase its charges if it provides new equipment or software that enhances performance and/or functionality. These are slippery issues that often lead to disputes. Such changes often decrease vendor costs, in which case higher charges are hardly reasonable.

Scrutinize change of character clauses carefully. Negotiate contract provisions that put in place advance notice by the vendor, fact finding rights on the part of your organization, and negotiation of any issue that involves changes in charges. Clearly defining services also helps. The contract can refer to vendor-initiated changes in service as a new service, not an extension or refinement of an existing service. The new service cannot be delivered and charged to you without your agreement. Another tactic for avoiding increased charges from change of character issues is to base charges on delivery of functions, not platforms. Then, the contract can provide that charges are based on a rate per unit for that function times the number of functional units delivered. If the vendor changes hardware or software, it would have to show an increase in functionality to claim additional charges.

7.1.5 Vendor Accountability

Be certain the vendor is fully accountable for all the specified requirements. Vendors may work terms around to providing a certain percentage of the required service within a given time limit. If you agree to this, set a time limit by which all work must be completed.

Guarantees and Warranties

Vendors may want to duck guarantees that the services will be delivered and warranties that they will make it happen. If guarantees can't be negotiated, requirements put in clearly defined, measurable terms help immensely. If blanket warranty terms cannot be negotiated, the warranties issue might be addressed through warranties for the most essential services.

7.1.6 Vendor People and Communication

The contract can specify the number, type, qualifications, position, and even names of persons on the vendor side who will provide and manage the outsourcing work. You can gain some control over the quality of vendor people by requiring that new vendor people receive your approval after reviewing resumes and interviewing candidates.

Communication between vendor project management staff and the persons in your organization responsible for overseeing the vendor's work is important and should be specified in the contract. Make one manager on the client side and one manager on the vendor side primarily responsible for the outsourcing arrangement. On smaller projects the contract can specify that all official communication be channeled through these managers. Larger projects might be divided by functions with persons responsible for management and communication on both client and vendor sides for each function. Regular meetings, meetings at milestones, and meetings for other purposes can be included in the contract's terms.

7.1.7 Other Requirements-Related Issues

In selective outsourcing, the RFP and the contract should address the interface issues between the function being outsourced and functions retained in-house.

Recall that the analysis leading up to the RFP should specify the information, communication, and reports the vendor must make and at what frequency reports are to be made to keep your organization informed on what is being done and how it is being done and on problems, when they arise. Don't forget provisions that lay out reporting requirements for causes of problems and demonstration of improved performance over time if these are important to your outsourcing objectives.

In international outsourcing, it's important to carefully specify where services are to be delivered and how the requirements vary between locations. Even large vendors have gaps in their ability to serve every part of the world. They often rely on subcontractors where they lack a local presence. The contract should anticipate this and specify that requirements must be met whether the work is subcontracted or not.

Requirements Not Met

The contract can levy penalties for requirements not met. Failure to meet requirements can also be addressed by giving the client power to require vendor changes in staffing quality and/or numbers to insure requirements fulfillment going forward.

In its outsourcing contract with IBM, Riggs Bank used penalties and a red light, amber light, green light notation. If the vendor developed a pattern of poor delivery (successive red lights for any particular service), the vendor could be penalized. The penalty provisions were attached to services that the bank determined were of central importance.

Security

Standard nondisclosure provisions should be a part of all outsourcing contracts. These are particularly important when vendors have access to competitively sensitive systems and/or data and are vital when the outsourcing deal involves partnerships.

Disaster Recovery

Backup and disaster recovery are issues to be addressed as part of the requirements in the contract. These should be addressed for every service whose performance can be affected by backup and recovery issues.

When outsourcing work is distributed to multiple sites, the minimal level of acceptable service and the time schedule for recovery from disasters might vary from site to site, and these need to be spelled out. Interconnected international sites have their own special requirements and related issues when problems arise in provision of services. Think through disaster recovery issues as they affect international sites, and put in requirements for disaster recovery that bring back service in an order that makes sense against the requirements of the outsourced function.

Overlooked Requirements

Lawyers can suggest contractual language to help include accidentally overlooked requirements. However, accidents shouldn't happen if the analysis is done properly. It's much safer to do good analysis work than rely on contract provisions like these.

Hours of work

Don't forget to include contract clauses that set out the times of the day when your organization does business and the requirement that vendor personnel be present and services be provided during those hours. Also specify holidays. If overtime will sometimes be required, make provision for this as well.

Overhead Cost Issues

Be certain to specify in the contract whether the client or the vendor has tax and insurance obligations. If travel is involved back and forth between client and vendor, the division of travel costs should also be specified. If hardware leases, hardware maintenance agreements, or software licenses are transferred to the vendor, the contract should specify how the fees for these will be handled and what mark-up for overhead the vendor should receive.

7.2 SYSTEMS DEVELOPMENT WORK

When the vendor will develop systems as part of outsourcing, not only should you specify system scope and requirements, you can also specify:

- That prototypes or other intermediate results will be presented and on what schedule.
- What testing and testing environments will be used.
- Methods and processes for acceptance testing and criteria for acceptance at every testing stage. Vendors don't like vague criteria because they want to know what the target is and when they are done. They also want acceptance decisions within reasonable periods of time, for the same reason.

- General aspects of what is required in documentation and training.
- Responsibilities for site preparation — yours and the vendor's.
- Implementation. Site preparation and cut-over criteria, schedules, and responsibilities should be specified.
- And any other aspects of milestones that will give the project greater definition and give you, the client, greater control over vendor output and behavior.

7.2.1 Requirements and Incentives

The contract can be quite specific about requirements for vendor systems development methodologies and the extent to which they need to be compatible with your own.

Project requirements often change in midstream. The contract must address change and change control. This is difficult to do, since the exact nature of future changes can't be known at the time the contract is negotiated. However, a mechanism should be established under the contract, perhaps a committee of client and vendor representatives, that will hammer out what is to be done with requests for changes as they occur.

Incentives can be written into the contract. Periodic payments can be contingent on meeting milestones and acceptance tests at milestones. Rewards can be offered for being on time or early.

7.2.2 Resources

The vendor may want to adjust schedules and require additional payment for changes, but large vendors with large staffs and many concurrent projects should be able to absorb a certain amount of change by juggling resources. The contract could include provision for some change without adjustments in schedule or cost and a threshold above which adjustments to schedule and cost will be negotiated. Since changes are more disruptive the later in a project they are made, the vendor may want a cutoff date or project stage after which no further changes will be entertained.

It may be advantageous to write contract provisions that require the vendor to utilize staff at a certain level of qualifications for aspects of the development work.

If equipment and/or software is to be purchased, leased, or licensed as part of the system, the contract should specify responsibilities for this and any criteria, consultation, or review that should govern selection and acquisition.

7.2.3 Conversions and Maintenance

All activities and costs of conversion should be anticipated, and the contract should specify responsibilities.

The contract can also address maintenance issues and the extent to which the vendor will be responsible for and involved in maintenance. Fees for maintenance can be part of the contract, negotiated later, or renegotiate at periodic intervals.

7.2.4 Other Issues

The contract can also provide a means for your organization to take the work in-house or to another vendor if progress is unacceptable or work is not of sufficient quality. If satisfactory progress is a very large concern, say in a mammoth project, consider breaking the project into phases and outsourcing the phases separately so that satisfactory performance on one part is a condition for getting a contract to do the next phase.

Also, consult with attorneys on property rights, warranties, and indemnities. The contract should specify who owns what while the system is under development and after the system is completed and delivered. If the vendor has an ownership interest in the resulting system, the contract should also address ownership of changes due to maintenance and enhancement. Warranty clauses on system performance, valid leases and licenses, performance of subcontractors, and performance of the system are all standard boiler-plate issues. Indemnities for things subcontractors do and say, and claims others may make for rights violated, personal injuries, and all other concerns should also be included in the contract.

If the system has the potential to give your organization some competitive edge, you may want contract provisions that prevent the vendor from selling the same or similar system to a competitor or using the system for a competitor.

If the system developed under the contract has the potential to become a package that is marketed by the vendor to other organizations or could be used by the vendor to do processing for other clients, you might want a percentage of the revenue.

7.3 PRICES, FEES, AND PAYMENT

7.3.1 Pricing Alternatives

The contract will usually contain a fees section for the services described in each exhibit. Pricing arrangements can vary between two extremes:

- Fixed-price agreements where the specified work is to be done at one, agreed upon contractual price.
- Time and materials or unit price agreements where the contract specifies how much the vendor is to be paid for each labor hour, CPU hour, unit of disk space, or other unit of work that is done or usage that is required.

Variations on these two basic schemes are many. There can be a fixed price for service up to some level with additions for volumes above the basic level. The same idea works, but in reverse, for a drop in the fee when usage falls below some level. Unit pricing can include volume discount schemes. Unit pricing may also specify some fixed amount or percentage amount the vendor is to receive as profit — so-called cost plus pricing agreements.

The basic motivation that underlies outsourcing may dictate a preference for one kind of pricing or another. If outsourcing is being undertaken to save costs or make costs more predictable, fixed-pricing may be particularly attractive. But pure fixed-price schemes involve an element of risk. If your usage of a service is below the levels predicted in the analysis prior to outsourcing, your organization will be paying more on a per unit basis than anticipated. On the other hand, if your usage exceeds expectations and the contract specifies a flat fee for the provision of a service no matter what the usage, then vendor margins are squeezed and may even go negative. Vendors are usually careful to define maximum service units in fixed pricing with additional charges for units above the maximum. If the vendor will enter a fixed-price contract without restriction on units of service, it means the vendor anticipates substantial economies of scale or other sources of falling costs, like steady improvements in hardware price-performance, over the life of the contract.

Pure unit price agreements can preserve flexibility, if that is the goal. Your organization can spend more or spend less, depending on how many units of the service are ordered from the vendor. However, the element of control may be illusory. The need for services may be driven by factors not entirely under your control. The vendor may want some minimum level of services written into the contract to assure that overheads and the set-up costs that result from asset specificity are recovered over the life of the contract.

It's common to price some aspects of the work covered by a contract using pricing more to the fixed side and other parts with pricing more to the unit-cost side so that the overall contract is a mixture of pricing schemes. Think through the pricing that best meets the goals of your organization during the preparation of the RFP. Put information on desired pricing in the RFP or term sheet so that vendor expectations are set from the beginning. Vendors will have their preferred ways of pricing work of different kinds, but to get your work they may be willing to bend or compromise. Understanding how vendors make their money in various kinds of work is a prerequisite to negotiation. Understanding what the vendor can accept in terms of pricing is also a prerequisite to effective negotiation.

Sometimes it is possible to negotiate a contract that guarantees the same pricing as for other customers the vendor serves in one or more categories of service. This wouldn't be advisable if you have sufficient bargaining power to get better pricing than other customers, but it would be an advantage to clients that are in a position of dependency relative to the vendor.

The vendor will want to pass through charges it receives from third parties, like network and telecommunications companies and perhaps for travel, training, and certain supplies. Be certain the services and prices are verifiable and reasonable and that a vendor with multiple clients can't charge you for services provided other clients. The contract also needs to anticipate growth in pass-throughs.

Avoid loose ends on pricing in contracts. For example, if the contract provides for additional services, be certain to include the pricing for additional services and specify that payment is to be made only upon written request and authorization and with proper documentation of the work done. If contingencies are part of the pricing scheme, the contract should specify these and stipulate that nothing will be paid above the contingencies. Specify how taxes and changes in taxes will be handled. When pricing is based on volumes, be sure that all volumes have agreed upon measures and methods of measurement. Measures should also be ones that can be readily produced by the vendor and audited by your organization.

7.3.2 Allowing for Growth and Change

Contract provisions can allow for a certain amount of growth per year with no change in vendor charges, as was mentioned earlier in this chapter. Many vendors are willing to write such contracts. The contract should specify what measures will be used to track growth, such as hours, number of people, CPU usage, storage, and so forth. The contract also specifies a base service charge that includes all specified requirements with allowance for certain growth factors per year with no additional charges. If growth exceeds the prespecified growth rate, excess charges apply. The excess charge rates should also be specified, perhaps a certain percentage increase in base charges for every percentage increase in growth above the stipulated growth rate.

When future growth is hard to predict, this approach to pricing may have advantages if the vendor is willing to negotiate a lower base rate than would otherwise apply. On the other hand, your organization may value predictable costs from outsourcing, in which case these flexible arrangements may not be satisfactory to you.

Complexity of change is another issue to address. The contract may allow for a certain annual increase in the number of CPU units or storage space, but the really important aspects of growth may not be captured by these measures and may be much more qualitative. What happens if the technology changes and you move from mainframes to client-server? What happens if new technology is installed that isn't measured by the yardsticks in the contract? Is the new technology covered under the provisions for change in the contract, or can the vendor levy excess charges? Differences of opinion between client and vendor can become quite heated over issues like these. It might be more straightforward to have a base charge and negotiate charges for changes as they occur.

Allowing for Fluctuations in Demand

Chapter 5 addresses the issue of defining service levels in normal and peak periods with the possibility of degrading service levels in some tasks so that resources can be thrown into the more critical jobs. If the contract allows for this, don't forget to get the price break the vendor may be able to offer as a result of spreading its resources more evenly over time.

Mergers and Acquisitions

If your organization grows through mergers or acquisitions while the outsourcing contract is in force, considerable growth may occur in the services you require of the vendor. Be sure the contract specifies the charging arrangements that will apply in cases like these so the vendor can't claim excess charges for the additional work. If the added work simply increases the volume of what is being done and not its character, the vendor may realize some economies of scale with an overall lowering of per unit costs. The excess charge rate certainly shouldn't apply in cases like these. On the other hand, if the vendor must engage in a substantial conversion effort as the result of a merger or acquisition, this is another issue that might be addressed through contract provisions or contract renegotiation.

Chargeback

Ultimately information services are consumed by and the costs are paid by the organization. Chargeback of vendor costs to ultimate users of services provided in an outsourcing deal makes good sense in terms of connecting costs and use, hopefully in ways users can understand. If users can see the connection between what they're getting and what they're paying, they will be wiser consumers of information services. When chargeback is in place and excess charges can be claimed by the vendor, the ultimate users will decide how much service to purchase at those prices.

Vendors generally have good, efficient systems for chargeback-type accounting. Theirs may be superior to yours, and it might be to the advantage of your organization to adopt the vendor's. If you retain your system, costs will be incurred to make it interface with the vendor's system, and the contract should specify how the costs will be divided between client and vendor.

7.3.3 Setting Prices

It is probably wise not to stray too far from market prices. Your organization or the vendor's may find it harder to live under a contract, particularly a longer term contract, when compensation varies substantially from the rest of the world. Market prices are the standard for market-type contracting relationships. Market prices can also serve as a marker or standard for work done under intermediate and partnership contracts, as well. On the other hand, prices may diverge from market prices when negotiations lead one party to give a break to the other in exchange for a favor provided in another part of the negotiations.

If it is difficult to find market prices that are relevant to the service being priced, consultants may have ideas on relevant price data. Or, use internal information systems costs as a starting point for price negotiations.

Recognize that prices aren't the same in all parts of the nation or the world and are not the same in every industry. Taxes also vary. It may be part of the vendor's strategy to make money by doing your work in a lower wage, lower tax part of the nation, or the world. On the other hand, vendors may claim high costs because of their location. Certainly if the work is large enough, the vendor can move it and take advantage of whatever economies are to be derived from location.

Don't overlook the opportunity to get discounts when work with vendors extends over longer periods of time or more than one contract, as it will in partnerships.

Adding and dropping work is facilitated when services are priced separately in contracts and the pricing of one service doesn't depend on the pricing of another.

7.3.4 Incentives and Sharing

Price incentives can be part of any contracting relationship from market to partnership. Since vendors are in the game to make money, it may be possible to get better or faster work — even lower cost work or additional revenue — by offering vendors incentives. A contract can specify a fixed or unit price for work to be done but offer the vendor more in total or per unit if the work is above some standard, saves costs, or increases revenue.

To solidly align vendor goals with the direction of your organization, vendor incentives can be tied to requirements stated in terms of your organization's business objectives.

To give incentives for better performance at the level of individual services, set service requirements at two levels with differential pricing — a minimum level that is compensated at one price and a higher level of service that is rewarded with greater compensation. Also consider linking incentives to business related issues so that the vendor gets a bonus when its performance boosts some indicator of business value.

To give incentives for meeting your organization's business objectives, set service requirements in measurable business performance terms with a sliding scale bonus for performance above a predetermined level in some time period. The threshold might move up over time to encourage continuous improvement.

Share savings by guaranteeing the vendor a certain amount as a fixed price to cover the cost of performing work but split any savings that the vendor is able to produce. The vendor's share might increase as the magnitude of savings the vendor is able to generate increases.

Vendor work that underlies revenue generation can be incented by sharing additional revenue on the basis for some formula. Be certain the vendor is required to document improvements.

Incentives are most common in contracting relationships that lie toward the partnership end of the contracting spectrum. Here incentives can play a role in making the relationship positive for both parties. In repeated contracting situations, it is often the case that more incentives are built into successive contracts over time. The partners get comfortable with and develop deeper trust in each other leading the way to more sharing arrangements. Chapter 10 takes up these issues in greater depth.

7.3.5 Price Changes Over the Life of the Contract

In the real world, prices change over time, and business relationships that don't provide for price changes will generally be less stable than relationships that allow for adjustments. Ways to handle price changes include changing prices in response to changes in some price index or passing through of properly documented vendor cost increases to your organization.

Be careful using the consumer price index or other broad index to adjust prices. In information systems, as in other industries, prices of different inputs don't change in unison, and they don't necessarily track the consumer price index or any of its major components. Labor costs generally rise; hardware costs generally fall. Rates of change vary over time. Consulting firms maintain price indexes for various kinds of information systems inputs. Choose the appropriate indices for the work covered under the contract. If the aim in outsourcing is to reduce costs, try to negotiate a price that tracks an index but is lower than the industry price for the same service. If excellent or superior service or the introduction of new technology is an aim of outsourcing, it might be best to negotiate a price that tracks the index but gives the vendor a somewhat higher price than the industry standard to reflect the better service differential. Again, pricing services separately aides in finding appropriate indices to apply.

Hardware costs have steadily declined over time and can be expected to do so into the foreseeable future. Vendors might be willing to share hardware cost savings by adjusting the prices charged over the life of the contract. On the other hand, a standard vendor tactic is to charge a fixed price or unit rate that is low initially relative to the cost of the same services performed inside your organization and keep that rate throughout the life of the contract with the anticipation that technological change will cause its costs to fall in the future allowing the vendor to make its margins.

Since there are economies of scale in some kinds of information services and diseconomies of scale in others, prices might be allowed to change over the life of a contract to reflect changes in volume. This can be a particularly valuable pricing strategy when future service volumes are difficult to predict at the outset. Pricing can be established so that certain rates are paid for service volumes within a given range. If volumes increase (or decrease) beyond the first range to a second, then another set of higher (or lower) prices will apply. Or the parties can agree to renegotiate prices at that point, perhaps with contractual limits on the range within which the new prices will be set. Additional volume ranges can be set beyond the first range, each with its corresponding prices or range of prices. Such contract provisions allow for flexibility, but also preserve some level of predictability.

When the outsourcing deal spans international boundaries, the contract should specify how exchange rates and changes in exchange rates will be handled. Most contracts will have some provision for billing or price adjustment based on the exchange rates that rule at the time of billing or payment. Alternatively, an average of the relevant exchange rates over some period of time might be used. However it's done, it's probably unrealistic to expect the vendor to completely bear the risk of exchange rate fluctuations.

7.3.6 Invoicing and Payment

Outsourcing contracts require very clear understandings on invoicing and payment terms and conditions. The vendor may have standard methods for invoicing and have expectations of how payment will be handled. These may or may not correspond to the ways your organization is accustomed to receiving invoices and making payments. The differences need to be clarified, and the invoicing and payment methods that will govern your contract need to be specified. Issues to be resolved include:

- How the vendor will document the services rendered.
- Payment before or after the vendor renders the service.
- Invoicing and payment on a monthly cycle or some other and any financing fees that the vendor expects to collect in longer billing cycles.
- Late payments and any penalties or financing charges associated with late payments.
- Disagreements over invoices. The contract should probably allow your organization to set aside payment for any services that you don't think you received or were not up to standard. Then some mechanism needs to be specified that will allow these disagreements to be resolved, starting perhaps with informal discussions between client and vendor but escalating eventually to third-party arbitration.

When the outsourcing deal spans international boundaries, the contract should specify details of billing and payment where these will occur in more than one country.

7.3.7 Pricing Systems Development Work

If the requirements for the system to be developed are quite certain and not subject to much change, it's probably best to negotiate a fixed-price contract. At the opposite extreme, when the requirements are fuzzy and/or likely to change substantially a time-and-materials approach can be taken. Between these two extremes, the vendor might agree to put a certain amount of hours into the project with further negotiation over charges when the requirements of the project become more clearly defined. Another approach is a fixed-price, up-front commitment with a sharing of additional costs when the full dimensions of the system become apparent.

7.4 TRANSFERRING RESOURCES TO THE VENDOR

When resources are to be transferred to the vendor as part of the outsourcing deal, aspects of these transfers must be specified in the contract.

7.4.1 Human Resources

When transferring employees to a vendor, the human resources department should check to see what laws may apply to severance in the states or countries where the transferred employees work. Sometimes advance notification and other measures are required. Employment laws dealing with minorities might also affect transfers. Your organization may have severance agreements with some of its own employees that state what constitutes severance and the obligations of severance. Confidentiality issues should be considered. Is there any confidential information on your employees that shouldn't be shared with the vendor? Will the vendor want the transferred employees to sign a confidentiality agreement?

When personnel are transferred, the contract should specify:

- Which employees.
- Any screening that the vendor will do on employees to be transferred — reference, drug, credit, or other background checking.
- Length of time employees have to consider the offer of employment from the vendor.
- Who offers employment if the vendor has subcontractors.
- When employees will start work with the vendor and when they will first be paid, if payrolls aren't in sync between client and vendor. Provision may also be made for employees on vacation or leave at the time of the transfer.
- Employees working hours.

- Where employees will work. If there is an advantage in having the people who do the work remain on your premises, this should be specified.
- Positions transferred employees will occupy in the vendor firm.
- Initial salaries and benefits, including bonuses, to be given the transferred employees by the vendor. When benefits are being transferred as part of the deal, consult knowledgeable attorneys on the rules that must be observed in such transfers.
- How outstanding claims against benefits by transferred employees will be handled, like health-care benefits claims.
- Pension, saving, and medical plan transfers, if any. How the vendor will assume responsibilities, if relevant. How the vendor will treat service credit when these benefits depend on years of service.
- Accrued vacation days, if these are to be transferred.
- Period of time transferred employees are to be guaranteed employment with the vendor.
- Period of time during which the vendor cannot terminate a transferred employee except for cause.
- Any efforts the vendor must make to help find jobs for transferred employees if they are released after the period of guaranteed employment.
- Some employees may decide not to transfer and may seek other employment, in which case the contract should state that the vendor bears the expense of finding replacements.
- Rights, if any, to rehire transferred employees at the end of the contract or upon premature termination of the contract.
- If the number being transferred is large, the contract may state that the vendor will put one of its own human resource people in your firm to help employees with the transition.

It's standard procedure to include a provision that prohibits the vendor from raiding and hiring anyone you want to retain in your organization.

Consult attorneys about contract language to handle situations that may be in violation of state or federal laws, work related injury, and any claims by employees against either party. The vendor may want a provision stating there are no existing claims against your organization by employees to be transferred. If there are claims the vendor will want to know the nature of these.

When international transfer of employees will occur, the foreign laws that apply and the needs of transferred employees must be researched so that the contract can address these issues, responsibilities, and specify who bears the costs.

If the vendor will use subcontractors and your employees will be transferred to a subcontractor, the contract needs to spell out subcontractor requirements.

7.4.2 Hardware

When hardware is transferred to the vendor and the hardware is leased and/or is on maintenance agreements, the leases and agreements must be transferred to the vendor. The analysis phase of the outsourcing process should produce an inventory of the hardware to be transferred. Lease agreements for the hardware in question must be checked for the provisions that govern transfer, and these must be followed. Maintenance agreements usually provide for transfer upon the proper notification.

The outsourcing contract should contain an inventory of the hardware to be transferred and provisions for dates of transfer and maintenance. If the hardware is to be physically moved, the contract should specify these details and who bears responsibility and cost. If the hardware is to remain on your organization's premises, this needs to be specified.

The requirements portions of the contract should specify how the vendor will utilize the hardware. Requirements can also specify the process for resolution of hardware problems and can specify that replacement parts and technical people be close by and available. The pricing sections of the contract should specify what hardware-related costs the two parties will bear; if the vendor takes the hardware, the vendor bears the related costs in most cases. The new technology portions of the contract will specify when or under what conditions hardware will be upgraded or replaced. Hardware related disaster and disaster recovery provisions should enter the contract, but these can probably best be addressed in the requirements portions of the document.

If the useful life of the hardware exceeds the term of the contract, the contract needs to specify who gets the hardware at the end and on what terms.

If the contract terminates prematurely, it may be important to your organization to have the use of the hardware again. The contract needs to specify rights under termination and any related compensation or methods to determine rights and compensation.

7.4.3 Software and Software Licenses

If the operation of ongoing systems is transferred to the vendor, the vendor will typically use the software that is in place for that purpose.

If software is developed and owned by your organization, there is no license problem, but you may want a contract provision that prohibits the vendor from disclosing anything about your software to third parties or using the software for any purpose other than meeting the needs of your organization. The contract might also specify the rights of the two parties at expiration of the contract or its premature termination. In both cases, your organization will probably want to retain full rights to the software and prohibit its use or disclosure by the vendor.

If the software is licensed from a third-party software vendor, there are potential problems that must be resolved. Most software licenses are tightly written to protect the intellectual property rights of the software vendor — this includes nondisclosure. Riggs Bank found a way around vendor objections to transferring software licenses by keeping the license in its own name. Situations vary, and you will need the help of counsel that knows software licensing issues and, perhaps, your financial people and auditors, as well.

The analysis phase of the outsourcing process should look into software licenses and determine their impact on the economics and feasibility of out-sourcing. If the analysis found a way through and around the obstacles, and the contract negotiation hammered out the details with the outsourcing vendor, then the contract simply records the fact that certain software and/or software licenses are to be transferred to the vendor, the schedule for transfer, and the schedule for start-up and ongoing operation by the outsourcing vendor. If your organization has been making modifications to vendor software and future mod-ifications are anticipated, the contract should specify the outsourcing vendor's responsibilities in this regard.

The software vendor might agree that your organization retain the primary license but that the outsourcing vendor be allowed to use the software. This can have advantages in the event the contract terminates prematurely so that your organization retains the right to use the software. It also gives your organization more control if the software vendor should go out of business.

If the software is owned by your organization, the contract can also con-tain provisions for maintenance and enhancement of the software, nondisclo-sure provisions, and rights to the software on expiration or termination of the contract. The contract may specify that the outsourcing vendor can only process your organization's data using the transferred software.

7.4.4 A Phased Transfer of Resources

Outsourcing may involve a phased transfer of resources to an outsourcing ven-dor. It is often impractical, particularly in larger or more complex outsourcing deals, to stop an in-house information systems function at the close of business today and have the vendor take it up tomorrow. A more gradual transition is often necessary to allow for the movement of resources.

The analysis leading up to the RFP should anticipate the need for a phased approach and alert vendors who bid on the work. Negotiations with vendors should determine how the phasing will proceed. The vendor has experienced many transfers and probably has a preferred or standard approach.

Nevertheless, what is agreed upon in the contract should also fit the constraints of your organization. Completion of some piece of work or a project, consideration for employees who might have to move to another city as a result of the transfer, and a host of other factors can affect a timetable for transfer.

In addition to specifying what resources are to be transferred, the contract should also set out the schedules for transfer, the dates on which resources will be in place and functioning, who will manage the transfer, and who will bear each and every cost involved in a transfer.

Despite advance planning, it may not be possible to anticipate all the issues and problems that can arise in a transfer. It is advisable to set up a committee with representatives of client and vendor firms to address and resolve issues and problems as they arise in the transfer of resources.

7.5 CONVERSIONS

When outsourcing involves conversion of systems from yours to a vendor's equipment and/or software, much advance planning is necessary, and the contract should address conversion tasks. The planning includes a full understanding of the resources, methods, and operations involved in both your organization and the vendor's organization. With this understanding, the transition process can be planned in sufficient detail to define all the steps or tasks and the order in which they must be accomplished. The plan should also define what constitutes successful task completion at each step.

The contract should contain provisions that define the conversion, the tasks entailed, and the responsibilities associated with it including:

- Conversion tasks and task order.
- Roles and responsibilities on both sides.
- Responsibility for costs in all conversion activities.
- Critical dates in the conversion.
- How and when data will be transferred and converted, if relevant.
- The method and schedule for cut-over from operation of systems from your organization to the vendor's.
- Backup and recovery issues in the conversion.

Systems involved in day-to-day functioning might best be converted in a parallel fashion with proof of successful conversion and operation in the vendor's organization before pulling the plug in your organization. The conversion might also be accomplished in stages, particularly for systems that operate in dispersed geographical locations.

7.6 PROVISIONS RELATING TO MANAGEMENT OF THE OUTSOURCING RELATIONSHIP

Chapters 8 and 9 are devoted to the management of outsourcing relationships. This chapter takes up aspects of contracts that establish the framework and lay the foundation for good management of outsourcing relationships.

7.6.1 Communication and Management

The contract should put in place a management structure for the outsourcing relationship. The structure can be quite simple in smaller outsourcing deals and in many market-type contracting relationships. It will be more complex in bigger deals and in intermediate and partnership relationships.

At the simple end of the spectrum, the contract specifies contact or liaison persons in both the client and vendor organizations whose duty it is to coordinate and manage the outsourcing relationship. It's best to have backups or alternates for the times when the contact persons are traveling, on vacation, sick, busy with other work, or otherwise not available. The contract can name backups.

In larger outsourcing deals, primary managers or executives are named for both client and vendor with a team of people in both client and vendor organizations to help manage the outsourcing work and relationship. The teams, organized into councils or committees, can have specialized roles that relate to technology, operations, review, and any other useful division.

Outsourcing contracts often mention specific persons who will be primary managers and specific persons who will staff committees or councils on both client and vendor sides with a procedure for notification and approval of any changes in these persons on either side. This protects your organization against shuffling of vendor personnel and the substitution of persons more difficult to work with in place of persons who work harmoniously with your organization.

Regular meetings and reviews should be specified in the contract. You might want to specify who will attend the meetings, where these meetings and review sessions will take place, as well as their frequency. There can be an advantage to holding meetings on your premises. Specifying the vendor people who must attend and/or positions of vendor personnel adds assurance of having access to the right people at the right level in the vendor organization.

The contract can also require that either party separately or both parties jointly set up procedures to be followed that will help govern the outsourcing work and the relationship. Some of these procedures will follow from various requirements in the term sheet and RFP. Others might already be in place in the vendor organization. Additional procedures might be created in the start-up phase of the outsourcing relationship. In the latter case the contract will have language stating whose duty it is to write up new procedures and that these require approval of the other side before use.

Don't forget the planning elements involved in all good management. The contract can specify the plans to be produced by the vendor, their scope, their schedule, or when they will be produced and how they will be reviewed.

Audits might also be specified, including their scope and frequency. Your auditors may want and need regular access or when-needed access to the people, processes, equipment, work or work products, and data that a vendor is using for your outsourced function or functions. Your audit people may want to bring in their own audit software. If audit rights are required, the contract should specify all requirements and rights and outline the responsibilities on the vendor side. Check with your auditing department, and get their input to the requirements.

The previous chapter addressed the issue of audits as a way of controlling vendors. The contract can specify that your own auditors or inspectors or third-party auditors or inspectors will have access to certain machines, software, and data on the vendor's premises, and have the cooperation of the vendor, at regular intervals or at the request of your organization, for various purposes. The contract should specify who will bear the cost; usually the client pays the auditors or inspectors and the vendor bears the cost of providing access. The contract should also specify the vendor's obligation to fix things that are discovered to be wrong as a result of an audit or inspection and bear the cost of fixing them.

In international outsourcing agreements, additional provisions might govern management arrangements across all the locations involved in the arrangement. It may be desirable to specify local managers or liaison people on both client and vendor side in all the locations involved in the deal to get good communication and control.

7.6.2 Penalties or Sanctions

Contracts can have penalties, including cash penalties, for failure to meet contractual obligations in any category of service. Obviously, vendors prefer to avoid penalties in contracts, and are particularly resistant to cash penalties. They generally favor penalties that involve issuing credits against future payments to compensate for work that isn't up to par or provisions that allow you to delay payment until a disagreement is settled.

Penalties are very effective motivators. Get them in the contract if you have the bargaining power to do so. Cash penalties are usually better than other types, since vendor outsourcing managers are judged on financial performance, and cash penalties are likely to get the attention of their superiors.

You can also investigate offset provisions that give you the power to determine when the vendor's work doesn't meet standards and also give you a credit against future payments. Offset language must be coupled with other contract provisions that allow withholding payment, otherwise withholding payment can be a breach of contract.

It may be unrealistic to attach penalties to every service level requirement in a contract, but aim for penalties on the services most important to your business.

Be certain penalties are tightly tied to measurable service performance so that the penalty is unambiguously defined in terms of service levels and its amount defined by measurable criteria.

7.6.3 Dispute Resolution

In market-type relationships, the vendor should be expected to perform with little or no deviation from the contractual agreement. Contract provisions should dictate performance and the vendor should be held to it.

In intermediate contracting, there is uncertainty; not all contingencies can be predicted at the time the contract is signed; and there are real losses to one or both parties if the relationship terminates before the work is done. Contracts to establish intermediate relationships will need careful definition of mechanisms for dispute resolution to keep the contract in force and prevent termination until the work is done.

In partnerships, the parties anticipate multiple contracts stretching into the indefinite future. The management and control of partnerships involves many extra-contractual mechanisms based on commitments, trust, and sharing that are taken up in Chapter 10. But contracts underlying partnerships should still have robust dispute resolution mechanisms as one of the basic frameworks for promoting continuity in the relationship.

Escalation

Good dispute resolution provisions should specify an escalation procedure. The hope and expectation is that disputes can be resolved in ways that are inexpensive and that do not produce distrust and antagonism. But if first efforts fail, the contract should specify what happens next.

The criteria for escalation should be clearly spelled out. The contract might specify several levels of problems — say, critical and noncritical — and speak to the number of incidents of nonperformance or the severity of problems that will escalate procedures to the next level.

The least expensive, least antagonistic method is informal resolution of disputes between managers of the outsourcing agreement on client and vendor sides. Contracts cannot specify informal mechanisms; these are established as part of a working relationship.

The contract picks up where informal mechanisms fail. At the first level of escalation the contract can specify that disputes originating on either side of the relationship should be put in writing to both the client and vendor management.

If meetings between client and vendor outsourcing managers fail to resolve the dispute, the contract can specify that the issue is put to the governing councils or committees of the outsourcing relationship. In smaller, less complex outsourcing relationships such committees or councils may not exist, and this rung of the escalation ladder is skipped.

If the dispute cannot be resolved within the management structure of the outsourcing arrangement, the next level of escalation can be a meeting or hearing before the senior management in client and vendor organizations.

If the dispute is not resolved at the senior management level, the contract can specify escalation to nonbinding mediation and then binding arbitration. Provisions can specify how mediators and arbitrators are to be named, the limits on mediator and arbitrator authority, and the duty of both client and vendor to abide by the decisions handed down in binding arbitration. Arbitration clauses should also have provisions for discovery and the duration of discovery so that the facts can be determined in a timely fashion. Provisions for confidentiality in arbitration should also be addressed.

The dispute resolution provisions in the contract will also set out the duties of the parties to respond to a notice of dispute and requests for information to help resolve the dispute.

Time limits are normally set for each rung on the escalation ladder. If time-sensitive and critical-to-business success services are provided by the vendor under the contract, these should be specified and time limits for resolution might be set in hours at each stage of escalation. For less time-sensitive issues, contracts can also set a maximum number of days for resolution at any stage on the escalation ladder to discourage stalling by either party. To avoid being pushed by the contract when the parties want a more leisurely pace, the contract could specify that these limits be extended if both parties agree to do so. On the other hand, don't make intervals in the dispute resolution process too long and encounter problems of disputes that drag on and on.

To foster continued good relations in the wake of a dispute, the contract can specify that arbitrators won't award damages and that both sides agree not to begin a lawsuit against the other until the dispute escalation process has gone as far as it can go and has exhausted all possibilities for agreement.

In international outsourcing, dispute resolution procedures should probably specify site specific mechanisms with eventual escalation to the managers that control the agreement worldwide. It's almost always better and more efficient to first try to handle disputes locally.

7.7 TERMINATION

The contract needs to guard against the unfavorable consequences from premature ending of the relationship. Of course, your willingness to see the arrangement end in divorce depends on the relative costs of (a) limping along in the present outsourcing relationship and trying to patch things up, versus (b) taking the information systems functions back inside your organization, or (c) finding another vendor, getting a satisfactory contract with that vendor, and making the transition to the second vendor. If the best alternative is divorce, then the contract should help your organization survive it.

The contract should preserve the rights of both parties. If the relationship does end, it is in the interests of both client and vendor to have a smooth transition, even though the dispute may continue and not be resolved in the courts until some later date. The contract should require that the vendor continue to do your work during the transition and that the vendor cooperate in specific ways to make the transition successful from your perspective. In return the vendor expects to be paid for the work it does without prejudice to its legal position in the dispute.

Typical termination clauses contain provisions for notification of the other party and the right of the other party to fix the problem to avoid termination. The time allowed to fix a problem or problems should not be overly generous, especially when your organization depends on vendor services for good business functioning.

The contract should specify how termination is initiated and how the process will proceed. If the process calls for steps in a termination procedure, don't make the intervals between steps too long. Services levels can suffer and costs can mount in a termination that drags on and on.

The transition from vendor to insourcing is a lot easier if the equipment, people and other resources are on your premises. No move is needed in cases like these. Keeping resources under your own roof is insurance against termination.

7.7.1 Termination Possibilities

Good contracts will include standard termination language which preserves the right of your organization to terminate:

- For convenience with advance notice of a certain number of days.
- With cause if the vendor fails to perform.
- Under circumstances in which the vendor organization changes dramatically as in a merger, a purchase of the vendor by another company, or a move out of the line of business that is involved in services to your organization.
- If your organization is acquired or merged or spins off businesses.
- If the vendor gets into financial trouble or fails financially.

Providing for termination on convenience essentially gives your organization the right to take the outsourced functions back. Nonperformance clauses usually state the right to terminate after a certain period of nonperformance. Of course, other contractual provisions specify what adequate performance is.

If the vendor moves away from the business segment that is involved in supporting your organization, you may want the option to terminate and find another vendor more committed to the area of outsourcing you require, with the people, resources, and active involvement in staying up with the field that is essential for good service. How to measure commitment to a particular business segment is another issue; perhaps the contract can say something about the amount of business the vendor does in this area of outsourcing, the number of customers, the active marketing for new customers, and the like.

The vendor will want language that allows termination if your organization fails to pay or goes out of business.

7.7.2 Termination Provisions

Think through all the processes and resources necessary to bring the outsourced functions or functions back inside your organization or to transfer them to another vendor. Preserve your organization's ownership of and access to critical resources for this transition.

The contract should guarantee your right to your own data and all the ancillary aspects of data, like log files and access to or ownership of the media on which it is stored. Insure that you can move the data to another site and continue processing. Since a vendor won't want you to take fixed-disk storage devices, the contract should specify backup to tape or removable disks at regular intervals so that a current copy of the data is always available. Also, guarantee your access to these media through appropriate contract provisions. Access to documentation and program code should be protected, particularly when the vendor uses new software or develops new code.

If the outsourcing vendor processes data from other clients that are similar to yours, avoid situations in which your data are mixed with data from other clients and can't easily be disentangled. Specify in the contract that your data will always be available as an integral whole, on demand or within a reasonable period of time.

Transfer of people, hardware, software, licenses, leases, buildings and other facilities, documentation, technical information, and all other aspects of information services necessary to successfully operate again in-house or with another vendor need to be anticipated in the termination provisions. You might include provisions that allow you to take back certain key people originally transferred to the vendor. If conversions are necessary to move services in-house or to another vendor, the contract should anticipate these.

Specify that the vendor must assist in a transfer of the outsourced functions in the event of termination. In its contract with IBM, Riggs Bank requires assistance from the vendor in making a transition should the arrangement terminate. Include language that requires the vendor to help with migration, conversions, transfers, and training. The vendor should also provide information vital to handling the function in-house or with another vendor. If the vendor engages subcontractors or licenses software from third parties, you may need access to and information from them as well.

The contract should specify a time period of sufficient length to make the transition. Be realistic about the time and effort needed here. Taking it back may be a lot more time-consuming and expensive than you think at first.

Provisions for termination also specify who owes what. Usually you must pay the vendor for services performed but not yet paid. The vendor will probably require a termination or buyout fee based on the time remaining in the contract. Some vendors may try to set termination fees unrealistically high to discourage your organization from terminating. Carefully negotiate the termination fee arrangements making sure you are not being overcharged. Don't allow the vendor to include any of its up-front marketing or analysis costs leading up to the deal. You shouldn't have to pay the full termination fee if the vendor has performed poorly or misbehaved, and contract language should state this.

Because technology changes over the life of a contract, it may not be possible to specify the exact inventory of equipment to be transferred on termination and its value, but the contract can refer to the technology necessary to support an outsourced function and formulas for determining its value.

It is unlikely that a vendor will agree to a contract provision that allows the client to withhold payment during a dispute, particularly if the vendor keeps doing the client's work. However, the vendor might agree to some reduced payment during the period of dispute with full compensation later or payment after resolution or termination, and perhaps some financing charges on balances paid late. Escrow accounts are another mechanism for withholding payment while still guaranteeing ultimate payment to the vendor. Negotiate standard contract rates for vendor services during termination so that the vendor can't take advantage of you.

In international outsourcing, research the data transfer issues involved in the laws of the countries involved and make sure the contract makes it possible to retrieve data from a foreign location if the need arises. The contract needs to specify what happens at each site affected by termination. If fees are involved, the contract should say where and in what currency.

7.8 OTHER ISSUES

A host of other issues can be addressed in outsourcing contracts. A collection of these follow.

7.8.1 Transition Costs

Be certain the transition costs mentioned in Chapter 5 are addressed in the contract so that it's clear which party bears these. Usually it is the vendor.

7.8.2 Multiple Vendors

If you outsource to more than one vendor and the functions outsourced have interfacing components, each contract must specify how the vendors will work in concert. If the contracts are not negotiated simultaneously, some renegotiation of existing outsourcing contracts may be necessary to specify the interface between vendors.

Contracts with two or more vendors in a vendor alliance present the same issues where the interface between vendors is concerned. Alliances are meant to exploit the specialized resources and capabilities of each of the vendor firms. The allied vendors will have worked together in the past which gives you greater assurance that they will work successfully together in the future. Nevertheless, be certain that the contracts clearly specify the functions and responsibilities of each party.

7.8.3 Subcontractors

Outsourcing vendors often subcontract work. It may be best that they subcontract, as in situations in which your organization requires services in a geographical location where the vendor has no presence or for skills that the vendor needs to supplement. In other instances, subcontracting may not be so desirable and may put control of services one more organizational level from your own organization.

A contract can specify when, where, and under what circumstances subcontractors can be used. It should state that requirements are always in force, no matter who does the work, and that the vendor is responsible for the performance of any work subcontracted.

Be sure the contract preserves all your rights when work is subcontracted, including the issues addressed in premature contract termination above.

If your organization gets involved in selecting subcontractors, the outsourcing vendor will probably insist that you take some responsibility or share responsibility for subcontractor performance. Be careful in drafting contract provisions so that you don't shoulder responsibility that should be the vendor's.

7.8.4 Confidentiality

Get standard language in the contract on confidentiality. Your organization may want data and information held from the public, the vendors' employees, or both. If the vendor is entrusted with your customers' data, consider confidentiality issues for these data as well. Contracts can contain "need to know" provisions whereby the vendor limits data access to only those employees who must have access to perform their jobs adequately. It also guarantees return of all data and information to you or its distruction when the contract expires or terminates prematurely.

Also, consider whether confidentiality is required for your operating procedures and techniques and for systems configurations. The contract can state that the vendor can't divulge these to others or replicate your procedures or techniques in the environments of other clients.

If competitively sensitive systems and/or data are involved, the confidentiality issue is paramount. Be sure good lawyers who know contract law and language on these issues are involved. Consider also the possibility of incentives. If it makes sense to make a vendor a partner, the vendor who shares returns from a competitive system has a powerful motivation to preserve confidentiality.

7.8.5 Security

When security is an important issue, you may want contract language that prescribes how the vendor must organize and function to control security. For example, the contract might specify that certain equipment be dedicated to your outsourced function so that the work of other vendor clients is not mixed with your own. The contract could also specify security measures on vendor networks.

7.8.6 Outsourcing to Introduce New Technology

When new technology is brought into your organization, two stage projects are a possible approach — one project to do the initial analysis and design and another stage that is negotiated after completion of the first to undertake construction and implementation. The operation of existing systems might also be outsourced to the vendor, with cut-over of existing systems to new systems in the second stage of the project.

Contracts in cases like these can be quite specific about terms and cost in the first stage, but less so in the second stage. However, the contract might put time limits on both stages. It might put a cap on outsourcing expenditure in the second stage. And the contract should still be specific about meeting your organization's business information needs during both stages.

7.8.7 Expiration of the Contract

Contracts should specify what will happen at expiration. It may be your intention to renegotiate and renew the contract with the same vendor, but for a variety of reasons your organization may decide to insource at the end of the contract or outsource again with a different vendor. The contract needs to anticipate a transfer of the work in-house or to another vendor. All the transfer issues raised earlier in this chapter under termination need to be addressed where normal expiration of the contract is concerned.

Also think through the resource situation at the end of a contract. Who should own what, including rights to software and other products built during the contract period? How should personnel be allocated? Should either party have the right to hire people from the other organization at the conclusion of the contract? Do you want to take back personnel who were transferred to the vendor?

7.8.8 Other Contract Details

Contracts typically address a variety of other issues that are more or less standard, such as:

- Warranties, in which parties affirm they are eligible to contract, have undertaken the prior actions necessary to contract, and will abide by the contract.

- Often the warranties are blunted by disclaimers and other contractual language that limits what one or the other party will do. Avoid the mistake of warranting performance by one party when it takes the cooperation of both parties to do the work. Don't let disclaimers completely void warranties or indemnities. Lawyers may spend a lot of time and effort on issues like these. Be sure your counsel looks after your interests in these matters.

- The vendor should be responsible for correcting errors of its making without additional charges.

- Liability for errors in data may or may not be assumed by the vendor. If this is important, specify it in the contract. Some vendors carry errors and omissions insurance. The vendor may want your organization to pay the premium or the increment in premium that results.

- Negligence on the part of the vendor should be part of standard liability clauses. Any limitations of liability should pertain to both client and vendor.

- Client data should remain the property of the client, and the vendor should not retain client data when the contract expires or is terminated.

- Force Majeure, or Act of God, provisions excuse the vendor from performance when impacted by natural disasters. This provision should place a time limit on the period for which the vendor is excused, and it should not conflict with disaster recovery requirements in the contract.

- Terms for renewal of the contract usually include some advance notice prior to the expiration date. Normally renewal is not automatic but only occurs on positive action by both parties.

- Expiration dates and schedules are set, and expiration procedures specify exactly who does what for whom, and who pays the costs associated with winding down the arrangement including transfers of hardware, software, data, and personnel. If your organization anticipates taking back the outsourced function at the end of the contract, these provisions are very important for a smooth transition.

7.9 EXPOSURE TO RISK

When contract terms start coming into focus, you may want to do an analysis of the extent to which your organization is exposed to risk. First, have technical people and users carefully review the contract exhibits defining services to be certain they are correct and complete. Then, conduct a risk analysis. Brandon and Segelstein (1976) suggest several approaches.

One is a top-down, maximum exposure analysis in which you evaluate the costs to your organization if the vendor defaults completely at the most critical moment in the life of the contract. For a systems development project, this might be at the beginning of the implementation period, after months or even years of effort, when the vendor figuratively throws up its hands and says the system can't be made to work. For a data center project, it might be at a moment after all equipment, software, and data have been put in the vendor's hands and your personnel have been transferred to the vendor organization. For other contracts, it might be the entire duration of the contract that limits flexibility in what your organization can do when environmental or technological circumstances change. Whatever the most critical moment might be for the outsourcing work under consideration, make an estimate of the cost to your organization of a total contract failure, which can include:

- Payments to the vendor that can't be recovered.
- Legal expenses involved.
- Benefits forgone — as in revenue not realized or work or service that could have been done or provided if the outsourced function was done in-house or by another vendor.
- Wasted training costs or other costs incurred by your organization in anticipation of the vendor delivering.
- Finding, negotiating with, contracting with, and transferring work to a new vendor.
- The costs of taking the function back inside your organization by recovering or buying and installing new equipment, recovering and/or reinstalling software, recovering data, and taking back personnel or hiring new personnel and training costs of new people.

The magnitude of the risk may surprise you. The question then is how can the number be reduced by adjusting contract terms or through risk management over the life of the relationship? If fiddling with the contract or risk management doesn't change much, it's necessary to return to more fundamental issues of changing the scope of what is outsourced or returning to a reconsideration of the feasibility of outsourcing.

Another approach to exposure analysis is bottom-up from individual contract clauses to risk exposure. Take contract provisions and divide them into four categories — those that are critical, significant, minor, and of no significant impact to the success of the contract. Brandon and Segelstein suggest a weighting approach that takes the number of contract clauses in the first three categories, assigns relative weights to a clause in a category, multiplies the number of clauses by weight per clause in each category, and seeing what percent of total weights across all categories are accounted for by each category. The weights should reflect a notion of the relative risk of the categories "critical," "significant," and "minor." Critical clauses get more weight per clause than significant clauses. Significant clauses get more weight per clause than minor clauses. The division of total points between categories indicates where most of the risk lies.

With this knowledge, review the individual clauses in the category or categories that present the most potential risk for ways to tighten or revise them, or consider additional contract provisions or new contract approaches to reduce risk, if the risk is excessive.

It is recommended that persons not previously involved in negotiating the contract undertake this kind of rating analysis. A fresh prospective can uncover issues overlooked by those bending over the provisions on a day-to-day basis. The analysis should be done by lawyers who have good experience with information systems contracts and the ways in which they can go wrong, perhaps with the help of IT managers or technical people who know the ways in which information systems efforts can go wrong.

When Riggs Bank outsourced to IBM, it evaluated the risk in broader terms, as well. It had to ensure that the outsourcing contract did not prevent the bank from being sold in the future, or from growing through acquisitions. Contract provisions were added and outside assessments were developed to make certain there were no problems. Riggs was also concerned about the impact on its local job market and the bad publicity that might result from moving jobs to the vendor's location.

7.10   CONCLUDING REMARKS

As detailed contract terms are negotiated, don't lose sight of the basics. Keep coming back to the overall goals for outsourcing and the ways to insure that the contract meets your organization's needs. For example, vendors may argue for different pricing at different geographical locations based on differences in their costs. But this can throw great confusion into your organization if costs are charged out giving managers in one location a break that managers in other locations don't receive. Be sure the contract lines up with the objectives and incentives in your organization. As another example, don't get mesmerized by financing and the amount of money the organization will save as a result of outsourcing and lose sight of the fact that the savings can be jeopardized by excess charge provisions in the contract.

Even if outsourcing is politically motivated by a strong desire to get rid of the IT department, negotiating a bad contract is a very undesirable side effect of the haste to wash your hands of IT.

Review the cost-benefit-risk analysis of the outsourcing deal once again before signing the contract. The analysis may change in light of insights gained during contract negotiations and the contract terms that can be negotiated. Estimates of benefits, costs, and risks can all be changed. Does it still make sense to outsource? If so, sign the contract. If not, don't outsource.

The above discussion does not begin to exhaust the issue of contract provisions. Consultation with competent attorneys and consultants is a necessity in these matters.

7.11 OUTSOURCING CONTRACT ISSUES: AN INTERVIEW WITH RICHARD RAYSMAN

Richard Raysman is a partner with the New York City firm of Brown Raysman Millstein Felder & Steiner LLP with offices in Los Angeles, Hartford, and Newark. He is author of the treatises *Multimedia Law: Forms and Analysis* and *Computer Law: Drafting and Negotiating Forms and Agreements* published by the Law Journal Seminars-Press, and he writes a monthly column on computer law for the *New York Law Journal*. Mr. Raysman is also past Chair of the Business Law Section, the largest section of the New York State Bar Association, and past Chair of its Finance Committee. Prior to practicing law, he was a systems engineer with IBM Corporation. He is a graduate of M.I.T. and Brooklyn Law School.

How many years have you and your firm been involved with outsourcing?
The firm of Brown Raysman was formed in 1979. Since its inception, the firm has been involved with information technology transactions. I am a graduate of M.I.T. and worked for IBM Corporation for six years prior to practicing law and many other members of my firm have such technical experience. Because of our information technology experience, we have been involved with outsourcing

since the early 80s. In the early days of outsourcing, outsourcing was sometimes referred to as a service bureau operation. Our outsourcing clients include major money-center banks, New York based investment banks, insurance companies, and major New York hospitals. On the vendor side, we also represent large consulting firms and international telecommunications companies that use our firm to structure and negotiate their agreements.

What are the key components of a good outsourcing contract for both parties?

From the perspective of both parties, the key components of a good outsourcing contract are a well-defined statement of work and a precise and understandable pricing schedule.

From the vendor's perspective, what are some of the key contract issues which are the most critical?

From the vendor's perspective, a key contract issue is the limitation of liability. A vendor must negotiate this clause carefully and with precision so that in the event disaster strikes, the vendor can disengage without being put out of business. Another key element for a vendor is a precisely drafted statement of work. If the statement of work is ambiguous, many future related services could be considered "in scope" which may not have been intended by the vendor at time of contract.

From the buyer's perspective, what are some of the most critical contract issues?

From the buyer's perspective, a critical issue is the pricing schedule. The pricing schedule should precisely define what the buyer thinks it is getting in the way of services. An imprecise pricing schedule may cause future services to be considered as new or additional services with separate pricing. Another key element for the buyer is the level of individual talent from which will be assigned to the buyer. The buyer wants to be certain that it receives the best talent the vendor has available. If employees are to be transferred from the buyer to the vendor, a critical element is the human resource schedule. The buyer wants to be certain that its employees are properly treated and receive pension and other benefits commensurate with the buyer's standard practices.

What are the advantages and disadvantages of different cost structures to consider?

Some cost structures give an annual fee for a defined level of service. Other cost structures itemize the fees depending upon the services provided. If the parties feel that it is difficult to specifically determine a mix of services during the term, an overall annual fee may be the best way to structure the arrangement. However, if the parties anticipate that the level of services will increase or decrease dramatically during the term based upon specific additions and deletions of services, a fee schedule tied to specific services may be the best way to proceed.

How can the parties prepare for unforeseen business changes?
Generally, in an outsourcing agreement, the parties will address the issue of acquisitions or divestitures of the customer. Usually, dramatic increases or decreases in volume of services will permit one or the other party to revisit the pricing and level of services in the agreement. Additionally, most outsourcing agreements will contain a termination for convenience clause. Under the termination for convenience arrangement, for a fixed predetermined fee to be paid by the buyer to the vendor, the buyer can terminate the outsourcing agreement without either side claiming a default. This clause is particularly handy in the event the buyer is acquired during the term of the agreement.

What are the most important points for both parties to remember about negotiating and implementing a sound outsourcing contract?
The most important point for both parties to focus on is having a detailed yet amicable negotiation process. The parties should discuss as many key issues as possible prior to signing the agreement and have the schedules reflect those discussions with precision. Hasty negotiations and ambiguous schedules can often cause major headaches for both the vendor and the buyer.

Are there any guidelines for deciding what services to include in an outsourcing agreement?
Guidelines are generally included in the services defined in the statement of work. The representatives of a buyer should include the business personnel who are expert in the services being outsourced to review the services definitions in the statement of work. Most attorneys and consultants practicing in the outsourcing area have their own list of guidelines and there are also several published books on the subject.

Do you have any suggestions for ways to reduce risks in the negotiation of an outsourcing agreement?
Yes. There are several. I will list and comment on each issue which should be addressed in an outsourcing agreement.
   Definition of the relationship and statement of goals and objectives. Depending on the scope of the outsourcing arrangement, the customer typically outsources most, if not all, of a particular set of functions (e.g., information technology

functions). The vendor often wants to be the exclusive provider of the outsourced functions. In such circumstances, the customer will lose control over the outsourced functions, and will want protections which recognize the loss of customer's control and balance it with the vendor's commitment to support the customer's business through competitiveness, cost cutting, and market expansion. Other objectives may include the recognition of changing technologies and the need for strategic technology planning, and for the conversion to the vendor's services to be implemented with minimal disruption to the customer's business.

Definition of services and deliverables to be provided, services excluded, and service levels. The outsourcing agreement should contain detailed descriptions of the services to be performed. If not properly addressed, disputes will arise as to whether a particular request is outside the scope of the basic services and subject to additional fees. Also, the outsourcing agreement should include service levels which detail the various functions the vendor will perform, the performance standards required for each function, performance milestones which require a specific time frame for performance, and the staffing requirements of the vendor's personnel to perform the various tasks.

If the outsourcing contemplates a conversion to the vendor's system or method of doing business, the outsourcing agreement should also contain a mechanism for changing the service levels postconversion and agreement on the costs of conversion.

To the extent that the vendor will deliver work product to the customer, the customer should have an opportunity to acceptance test each deliverable. This is particularly important if the deliverables are computer software.

Term of the agreement. The outsourcing agreement should indicate a specific term, which can be renewed. The vendor will typically want to have the agreement renew automatically for a specified period at the end of the initial term. The customer will typically want to have the option to renew on notice to the vendor based on the same pricing structure, but not an automatic renewal. It is usually the customer's preference to have the option of evaluating the vendor's performance and "lock" the pricing for any renewal period.

The people issues, including staffing requirements, employees to be offered employment with the vendor, and the employee transition plan. If the customer in an outsourcing relationship wants any control over the personnel who will perform the outsourced functions, the outsourcing agreement should specify such control rights. This includes a designation of whether the services will be provided at the customer's site, whether the customer will have the right to approve or disapprove of vendor personnel, and the number and types of personnel (by training and/or title) who will perform certain tasks. With regard to key personnel, the outsourcing agreement should indicate the names of such personnel, a minimum time frame that such personnel will provide services for the customer, and how the vendor will maintain succession plans for such key personnel, and restrictions on the reassignment of such personnel, particularly to customer's competitors.

A typical outsourcing relationship is different from a facilities management agreement or a processing services agreement because the employees of the customer who perform the outsourced functions are initially transferred to the vendor. The particulars surrounding the offers of employment including salaries, benefits, and guarantee of employment of such personnel should be clearly specified.

The outsourcing agreement should also include a plan or the procedures for the creation and implementation of a plan for transition of the customer's employees to the vendor's control, which indicates the respective responsibilities of the parties and the allocation of costs related to the transfer. Finally, the outsourcing agreement should allocate the risks of lawsuits arising out of the transfer of the customer's employees, including appropriate indemnities and responsibilities of the parties. This is important because, like the outsourced functions, the customer will have little control over the manner in which the vendor treats the transferred personnel.

Vendor use of the customer's facilities and the customer's owned/leased equipment. In many instances, the vendor will perform the outsourced services from the same customer location as such services were performed by the customer prior to the outsourcing arrangement. This is usually the case during an initial "start-up" period, until converted to a vendor system or service to be performed from a vendor location.

Unless the outsourcing agreement contemplates the sale of such customer facilities to the vendor, the agreement should include details of the terms on which the vendor will be able to use the customer facilities. The agreement should also specify any changes which will be required to the customer's facilities for the vendor to perform the outsourced functions, and specify which party will be responsible for such changes, including the cost of such changes.

Once the outsourced functions are transferred to the vendor, the customer typically provides some means for the vendor to use the customer's equipment to provide the outsourced functions. With regard to equipment which the customer owns and will have no use for after the effective date of the outsourcing agreement, the customer may want to sell the equipment to the vendor, rather than leasing the equipment to the vendor. From the customer's perspective, this will allow the customer to remove the equipment from its financial books and transfer the responsibility for maintenance of the equipment and risk of loss to the vendor.

If possible/practical, there should be a complete inventory of all equipment that will be sold to the vendor prior to negotiation of the outsourcing agreement and a determination of the "value" of such equipment. Although the customer will want to sell the equipment for the depreciated value, the vendor may only want to pay the market value. The prior inventory of the equipment will permit the parties to negotiate the purchase of some or all of the customer's equipment as part of the overall contract negotiation, rather than trying to negotiate afterwards, when the negotiation leverage of the parties may have changed.

Depending on the type of equipment to be sold to the vendor, there may be certain environmental issues which will have to be addressed. An example of the type of equipment which could involve environmental issues is the sale of a back-up electric generator for computer equipment, for which the parties may have to allocate responsibility for fuel leakage and cleanup.

Certain equipment which the customer used to perform the services to be outsourced may be leased rather than owned by the customer. Depending on the terms of the lease agreements, the customer may want to terminate the leases or assign them to the vendor. The leases may also have purchase options which the customer may want to exercise and then sell the equipment to the vendor. If the vendor requires the use of certain leased equipment and the customer is unable to assign the lease or purchase the equipment under the lease, then the customer may want to grant the vendor the right to use the leased equipment and have the vendor reimburse the customer for the ongoing lease payments.

Customer owned and not-owned intellectual property and vendor intellectual property. If the services to be outsourced include data processing services, the vendor usually will need to use customer's intellectual property, including computer software. The customer typically owns some of the software and licenses software from third parties. Each of these types of software need to be addressed separately in the agreement.

With respect to customer owned software, the customer may grant a limited license to the vendor to use such software in order to provide services to the customer. The license should limit the vendor's right to use the software solely on behalf of the customer, and only for the term of the outsourcing agreement or until conversion to an agreed upon vendor system. The license should also address other concerns which arise in a standard software license transaction, such as the vendor's confidentiality obligations with regard to the customer's software.

When the customer needs to have the vendor use software owned by a third party, other issues will need to be addressed. The third-party software is typically licensed by the customer from various third parties under license agreements each containing different terms and conditions, including restrictions as to scope of use, right of use, confidentiality, and the right to transfer or assign. All third-party software which the customer desires to permit the vendor to use should be identified together with the license agreements for such software.

Sometimes license agreements require a single license fee payment for a perpetual license, while others may require several payments. Still other licenses are term licenses rather than perpetual licenses, where the license is for a fixed term (e.g., one year) and the license must be renewed periodically.

Depending on the terms of the third-party license agreements, the customer may want to assign the licenses to the vendor. Some license agreements require the consent of the vendor to assign the license, and the outsourcing agreement should address which party will be responsible for any fees required to assign the license.

However, in some instances the customer may want to retain the license and to permit the vendor the right to use the software. In such circumstances, the license agreements for all such software should be reviewed to determine whether the permitted scope of use under those agreements allows the vendor, as a third party, to use the software. Some licensors, for confidentiality concerns, have strict policies restricting third parties, including outsourcers, from having access to their software without permission and the payment of an access fee. The outsourcing agreement should clearly address which party is responsible for obtaining the consents of third-party licensors, for paying any access fees, and for resolution if the third-party licensor will not consent to the requested use by the vendor.

In many instances, the vendor has intellectual property which the vendor will use to perform the outsourcing services (and which software may have been the basis for choosing the vendor to perform the outsourcing services). Once converted to the vendor's software, the customer may find that it is "locked" into using that computer software system, even after termination of the outsourcing agreement. If the customer terminates the outsourcing relationship before the end of the term based on circumstances such as a breach by the vendor, the customer may want to use the vendor's computer software to continue processing. For this purpose, the outsourcing agreement should contain a license permitting the customer to use the vendor's software. The license should also address substantive license terms such as the fee, if any, for the license, the scope of the customer's use of the software, and the vendor's responsibilities to the customer for maintenance and updates.

Additionally, the vendor may be the subject of a bankruptcy proceeding during the term of the outsourcing relationship. In such instance, the customer will need the right to use the vendor's computer software to continue processing. The customer may want to have the vendor place the source code of the vendor software in escrow to ensure that the code is available to the customer, if necessary.

Assignment of third-party services to the vendor, responsibilities for cost of third-party services, and vendor rights with respect to replacing a third party. The customer may have contracts in place with third parties for the provision of services which relate to the functions being outsourced. Some third-party services may include services related to the customer facilities which the vendor will use, such as maintenance services. Other third-party services may relate to the customer equipment or software which will be transferred to the vendor by purchase or assignment of leases, such as maintenance agreements. From the customer's perspective, it is preferable for the vendor to have full responsibility for the customer's obligations under such third-party service agreements, including payment.

One method to accomplish the transfer of the third-party service agreements is to assign the agreements to the vendor. The same issues discussed above with respect to assignment of third-party licenses and consents to transfer also apply to assignment of third-party service agreements.

In some circumstances, the vendor will want to replace the third-party services with its own services or the services of another third-party provider of such services. To address this vendor concern, the outsourcing agreement may permit such replacement subject to certain conditions. In such instances, the agreement should address which party will be responsible for costs incurred by customer due to the termination of third party service agreements.

Responsibilities of each party with respect to ongoing projects at the time of execution. The customer may have projects ongoing within the functions to be outsourced to the vendor. Such projects should be specified in the outsourcing agreement with sufficient detail and procedures to ensure that the vendor will continue the projects with proper staffing, and that the vendor will meet the scheduled completion dates for the projects. The outsourcing agreement should also state the additional fees, if any, which will be charged for vendor's services for the ongoing projects.

Responsibilities for management of the outsourcing relationship. The outsourcing agreement should set forth the respective responsibilities of the parties to manage the relationship.

Particular individuals should be named as the principal liaisons between the parties who will be responsible for the day-to-day contact between the parties. For management of the relationship, the parties should meet regularly and have written status reports of the progress of projects and problem resolution. For planning issues, the parties should create a steering committee to discuss changes to the services to meet the customer's needs and to address incorporation of technological advances in the vendor's services.

Customer data and confidentiality. With regard to confidentiality obligations, the vendor in the outsourcing relationship should be treated as an independent consultant who is likely to learn confidential information regarding the customer, its business and financial information and data, marketing information, customer lists, and customer's intellectual property, including computer software.

Performance goals and continuous improvement. The outsourcing agreement should include performance goals for the vendor to attain during the term of the outsourcing agreement in order to help customer meet its business goals.

In order to provide the vendor an incentive to meet or surpass the performance goals, the outsourcing agreement can include monetary bonuses if the vendor exceeds the performance goals, and a charge to the vendor if the performance goals are not met.

The performance goals should be specifically defined so that there is an objective method in which to measure the vendor's performance under the agreement.

Conversion from customer's to vendor's procedures in providing the services. During the term of an outsourcing relationship, the vendor typically will want to convert some or all of the outsourced functions to the vendor's method of providing such functions.

To the extent that the conversion will require modifications to the software or procedures used to perform the outsourced functions, such modifications should have the customer's approval using an agreed upon testing process.

Once conversion is complete, the vendor should remain responsible for compliance with all legal and regulatory changes applicable to the outsourced functions. The charges, if any, to the customer for such compliance services should be clearly stated in the outsourcing agreement either by inclusion in the base charge or by specifying the charges applicable for such services.

Training provided by the vendor to the customer. The outsourcing agreement should specify what training services the vendor will provide to the customer, and the charges for the training services. If the customer has any specific training service needs such as for the training to be provided at customer's site or during certain hours, these needs should be stated in the outsourcing agreement to avoid additional charges.

Fee Structure. Depending on the functions to be outsourced, the fee structure is typically based on (i) a fixed fee for a particular time frame (typically as a percentage reduction in customer's cost of performing the outsourced functions); (ii) a time-based fee, based on the time the vendor's personnel spend performing the outsourcing services; or (iii) a volume-based fee based upon the types and volumes of particular transactions processed. The outsourcing agreement should also specify the expenses each party will be responsible for, and which expenses will be reimbursed by the other party.

Specific milestones should be identified, and the payments to the vendor should be linked to successful completion of such milestones in a timely manner.

If the customer disputes amounts charged by the vendor, the outsourcing agreement should include a procedure which will allow the services to continue while the parties resolve the dispute according to an agreed upon dispute resolution process.

Liability limitations, warranties, disclaimer of warranties, and indemnities. From the customer's perspective, the limitation of the vendor's liability should have some relation to the customer's potential monetary exposure if the agreement is materially breached by the vendor. The customer should consider its potential liability to its clients in determining an acceptable limitation of the vendor's liability. To cover any shortfall in liability, the customer should consider obtaining errors and omissions insurance.

The outsourcing agreement should also include warranties from the vendor regarding the quality of the vendor's services and the vendor's personnel.

Also, since under the outsourcing relationship the customer may have transferred its resources to perform the outsourced functions to the vendor, including its employees, software, and equipment, the customer may need the right upon termination of the outsourcing agreement to offer employment to the vendor's employees who perform services for the customer and/or reacquire the equipment and software the vendor uses to provide the services.

Sharing of resources. The vendor may want to provide computer-related services to its other customers using the same computer resources that the vendor will use to provide the outsourced functions to the customer. The customer may want to preclude such activity for confidentiality purposes.

The outsourcing agreement should also state what rights the customer has to use the computer resources itself, and what rights the clients of customer will have to access the vendor's computer resources (i.e., remote inquiry access).

Audit of sites, services, and the relationship; correction of audit deficiencies; access to audit reports. By the very nature of the outsourcing relationship, the customer will have little control over the manner in which the services are provided, and will have to rely on the vendor for information regarding the internal operations of the vendor. The outsourcing agreement should include the right for the customer to perform an on-site operational audit of the vendor's facilities where the services are provided on behalf of the customer.

The customer may also require the right to perform a financial audit regarding the fees charged to the customer for the outsourcing services.

The customer should also have access to vendor's audit reports which relate to the services provided to the customer.

Other key issues: Dispute resolution process; rights of vendor to assign the agreement; insurance requirements; restrictions on hiring other party's employees; taxes; disaster recovery; emergency backup and force majeure should all be addressed in the agreement.

Termination for cause, convenience, insolvency, and other reasons. If the outsourcing agreement terminates, the customer will not be able to immediately switch vendors or perform the outsourced functions itself. Therefore, the parties need to provide for a transition period after termination, during which the vendor will continue to provide services to allow for an orderly transition to a new vendor.

7.12 REFERENCES

Bernacchi, Richard L, Frank, Peter B., and Statland, Norman, *Bernacchi on Computer Law: A Guide to the Legal and Manufacturing Aspects of Computer Technology*, New York, Little, Brown and Company, 1995 (2 volumes).

Brandon, Dick, H. and Segelstein, Sidney, *Data Processing Contracts: Structure, Contents, and Negotiation*, New York, Van Nostrand Reinhold Company, 1976.

Halvey, John K., and Melby, Barbara Murphy, *Information Technology Outsourcing Transactions: Process, Strategies, and Contracts*, New York, John Wiley & Sons, Inc., 1996.

Hoffmann, Paul S. *The Software Legal Book*, Croton-on-Hudson, NY, Shafer Books, Inc., 1997 (2 volumes).

Mylott, Thomas R., *Computer Outsourcing: Managing the Transfer of Information Systems*, Englewood Cliffs, NJ, Prentice Hall, 1995.

Nuara, Leonard T. "Outsourcing Agreements," in Daniel T. Brooks, *14th Annual Computer Law Institute*, New York, Computer Law Institute, (August 1992) 411–474.

8

The Transition to Outsourcing

Previous chapters have addressed many issues related to transition including personnel, equipment, software, and conversions. This chapter touches briefly on some of these but is mainly concerned with execution of transition plans and with setting up management structures. The chapter also addresses the beginnings of conflict resolution processes.

Personnel issues can be serious impediments to a smooth transition to outsourcing. In the interview that concludes this chapter, Edward A. Pisacreta addresses the legal issues that must be addressed in conforming to the laws that govern employee transfers.

The chapters on negotiation of contracts and contract terms and provisions have counseled for inclusion of transition issues in contracts before outsourcing arrangements begin. But loose ends are common, and it is not always possible to anticipate all the issues that may arise in a transition to outsourcing. It follows that additional planning activity may accompany the transition.

The vendor's business involves a continual stream of new outsourcing deals. Transitions, like many other aspects of outsourcing, are something the vendor does every day. It's in the vendor's best interests to see that transitions go smoothly and that the new outsourcing relationship starts on a high note. Rely on vendor experience and motivation to provide your organization with information and advice in planning that will help make the transition to outsourcing successful.

8.1 INTEGRATION AS THE KEY TO MANAGEMENT IN OUTSOURCING

It is a mistake to think of outsourcing as getting rid of something, of sending work outside the boundaries of the organization, so that no one need think about and worry about it again. Instead, think of outsourcing as adding additional specialized units that must be integrated with units that remain inside your organization.

An important pillar of outsourcing success is integration. Specialists are required to handle the complexity of modern organizations. Specializations are by nature differentiated, and specialists often work in their own specialized organizational units. It's common practice to divide IT departments into applications, operational, and technical units. Vendors perform specialized tasks and are differentiated from client organizations, not only by the fact that client and vendor are separate organizations, but also by the fact that vendors have their own specialists in their own organizational units. To have success, the combined efforts of the specialists in your organization and the specialists in the vendor organization must be tightly integrated in coordinated actions that lead to good outcomes. (Lawrence and Lorsch, 1969)

Aspects of integration include (Stuckenbruck, 1988):

- Planning for integration.
- Getting started on the right foot.
- Developing a plan for integrated work and schedule.
- Developing integrated management control.
- Managing conflict.
- Removing road blocks.
- Setting priorities.
- Establishing communication.

The three previous chapters outline the efforts necessary to set up a vendor relationship and some of the details necessary for successful integration. Now in the start-up phase of the outsourcing relationship these plans are put in motion and other integrative actions are taken. Getting started on the right foot involves:

- Selling outsourcing to your organization and getting buy-in from the people who are necessary to make it succeed. If people inside your IT organization were skeptical of outsourcing but now must work with vendor people, if some users were uncertain that outsourcing is a good idea, these doubts must be minimized and good faith cooperation and effort put in its place. Explain the advantages, stress the importance of their role, pledge and follow through on any needed training and support, win their trust, and get their cooperation.

- Setting up management structures including conflict resolution mechanisms.
- Putting people who will undertake and direct the integration effort in place, including the outsourcing managers in both client and vendor organizations.
- Establishing good working relationships between client and vendor management characterized by negotiaton and cooperation.
- Setting up procedures that direct work and management.
- Establishing communication mechanisms.

The transition should foster a working relationship of cooperation and teamwork. Pete Mounts of HBOC says, "Once the vendor has been selected and the project is under way, both the organization and the vendor should regard themselves as working for the same team, even to the point that the organization consider the highest-ranking outsourcing representative as a member of its senior staff. In 95 percent of HBOC's outsourcing contracts, our outsourcing director is a titled member of the health-care organization and as such, participates in the organization's regular meetings."

8.2 PLAN AND SCHEDULE

A plan for the transition should have been shaped through activities in the analysis phase and subsequent dealings with vendors in the RFP process and contract negotiation. If no real planning has occurred up to this point or if the plan is incomplete, the first step should be meetings with the vendor or vendors to establish a plan.

Large outsourcing deals will typically involve several phases through which the transition to outsourcing will move. Different dimensions of phasing might be employed:

- Functional. The transition might proceed by function, moving primary functions to the vendor before other functions that depend on them. For example, in a total outsourcing arrangement, networks and data centers might precede application development and user support.

- Geographical. In an outsourcing deal that involves multiple locations, one or a small group of locations might be transferred to the vendor first with other locations following in some staged fashion. The first experiences with transfer can serve as pilots that guide and improve the smooth transfer of the followers.

8.2.1 Multiple Vendors

Outsourcing sometimes involves multiple vendors whose activities must be coordinated. The transition to outsourcing is particularly challenging under these circumstances. A coordinated plan that involves all parties is essential, and the broad outlines of this effort should be included in the contracts with all vendors.

It is often a good idea to set up a transition management and oversight board or committee for transitions involving multiple vendors. The managers responsible for the outsourcing deal in each vendor organization and your own outsourcing manager or managers serve on the board or committee. Technical people and user representatives might also have a presence when technical expertise and/or user-service issues are critical to a good transition. The board or committee's responsibilities include:

- Planning any elements of the transition not included in the contract.
- Modifying any elements of the plan that need change in light of circumstances as they evolve.
- Executing the plan by seeing that necessary resources are applied in a timely and coordinated way — both internal to each client and vendor organization and between client and vendors.
- Receiving any change requests relative to the transition that arises from client or vendor sides, analyzing and determining the feasibility of changes, incorporating changes in the plan if they are appropriate, and recommending any addendums to contract provisions or agreements that might arise from changes.
- Resolving disputes that occur from activities in the transition and serving as the first phase in any dispute escalation procedure when disputes cannot be resolved at this level.

When new-to-the-market technology is involved in an outsourcing deal, the possibility for problems between vendors is magnified substantially. The need for a board or committee to coordinate activity between vendors is particularly acute in these circumstances.

8.2.2 People Issues

Most of the personnel issues are addressed below under communication and transfer of resources. At this point it's sufficient to add a reminder to include personnel issues in the plan and schedule. Schedule issues include:

- Dates on which your IT personnel will be told their fate in terms of retention in your organization, transfer to the vendor, or termination.
- The dates on which the vendor will make formal offers of employment to the persons who will transfer.
- The dates by which personnel must respond to the vendor's offer.
- The point in time when formal transfer from your employment and payroll to the vendor's employment and payroll will take place.

8.3 MANAGEMENT STRUCTURE AND RELATED MANAGEMENT ISSUES

The contract should specify management arrangements. Earlier chapters mentioned that appropriate management structures for outsourcing deals can run a gamut from quite simple arrangements for smaller deals to very elaborate structures for large and complex deals.

8.3.1 Interfaces

Managers typically expend a good deal of effort in managing interfaces. Interfaces are of several kinds (Stuckenbruck, 1988):

- Organizational interfaces or interfaces between organizational units. This is a preoccupation of managers inside your organization when working in an organizational project or process. In outsourcing, these issues are expanded to management of interfaces with the vendor and its various functions as organizational units.
- Personal interfaces or relationships between people. Managers often find personal relationships easier to manage when people report to them. Managing relationships with people or between people in other functions is more difficult. Relationships with vendor people and managers, working in a different organization, may present still more challenges.

- System interfaces or the relationships between subsystems. These may be physical interfaces, for example the way your data relates to the vendor's equipment and software in the vendor's data center. Or the interface may link two functions through performance, where the output of one subsystem is the input of another. An example is the development of information systems by your application development people to be run in the vendor's data center.

- Organizational interfaces or the interface between two entirely different organizations with different management, different culture, and different ways of working.

Managing in an outsourcing relationship often involves three or four interfaces simultaneously. Two completely different organizations are involved with different goals. Different units in the two organizations are involved. Different people owing allegiance to different organizations are involved. And different subsystems are involved — your subsystem(s) and the vendor's subsystem(s).

Managing outsourcing also involves relationships with user managers whose functions are affected by the services provided under outsourcing and with senior management inside your organization.

Issues of relative power carry over into management of outsourcing arrangements. If your organization is more dependent on the vendor than the vendor is on your organization, the power balance tips toward the vendor. Expect to be on something of an upward slope in getting from the vendor what you want and when you want it. If the power balance tilts your way, the opposite can be true.

In its relationship with CSC and Andersen Consulting, DuPont sees great advantage to the vendors in being associated with the world class IT functionality in DuPont. The vendors have the opportunity to learn from DuPont and leverage this knowledge in their relationship with DuPont and with other customers.

When the client does not have the upper hand with a vendor, the task is made much easier by contract provisions that hold the vendor accountable on any number of requirements and procedural issues. Also recall that the vendor usually wants repeat business from your organization and has a reputation to defend.

A power disadvantage can be offset to some extent and a power advantage enhanced by several factors (Stuckenbruck, 1988):

- Levels of management. The vendor will pay more attention to you if you can involve managers higher in their organizational structure. Try to get higher-level managers in the vendor organization interested or directly responsible for your outsourcing work. It's best to have the attention of the vendor's senior management, as well. Even if your outsourcing work is small relative to all the work in the vendor organization, approach vendor senior management and make them aware that you exist so that they have more than a passing interest.

- Physical distance. Try to locate vendor outsourcing managers close to your outsourcing managers. The same set of offices (even if not occupied continuously by managers on the two sides) is best. The same building is second best. The same city is third best. Different cities and different continents are at the bottom. The section on communication later in this chapter explains why.

- Time devoted to the outsourcing arrangement. Try to get vendor management to spend time on your outsourcing deal. The issue of regular meetings and reviews is addressed below.

- Personal relationships. Establish good personal relationships between managers on client and vendor sides. With closeness comes more attention and more concern for your issues.

8.3.2 Management Structure

To bridge the gap between client and vendor across the interfaces discussed above requires effort to integrate the activities of your organization and those of the vendor organization. The need to integrate increases when (Morris, 1988):

- The nature of the work requires close coordination.
- The business and/or technology environment is complex or changing.
- Your organization is changing rapidly, requiring revisions in the outsourced services and service levels.
- Your organization is complex, making it harder for the vendor to provide adequate service to each and every part.

Integration

Management theory sets out three types of interdependencies involved in integration and three appropriate, matching mechanisms to achieve integration:

- Pooled interdependence is appropriate for simple situations that don't require a lot of integration effort. This type of integration can be accomplished by people on both sides obeying rules or sticking to established standards.

- Sequential interdependence requires that activities on both sides of the interface be scheduled in order to mesh properly. Here activities are coordinated by means of schedules.

- Reciprocal interdependence is the most complex and requires that representatives from both sides interact regularly to identify the need for and set in motion actions that bring about mutual adjustment in the work being done across the interface between organizations. The communication required to accomplish this can be done through managers in liaison positions, committees, councils, and task forces.

Outsourcing will typically involve all three, but in different proportions depending on the nature of what is outsourced. Recall the market-type, intermediate-type and partnership-type outsourcing relationships introduced and discussed in earlier chapters. In market relationships all the issues involved can be anticipated and addressed through contract provisions. In this simplest of all outsourcing relationships, rules and standards (pooled interdependence), and schedules (sequential interdependence) can be negotiated and agreed upon in contractual terms. The outsourcing arrangement can go forward with a minimum of day-to-day liaison or management oversight effort. Often two managers, one from the vendor side and one from your organization, can do the coordination necessary to make the outsourcing deal work.

Intermediate and partnership type outsourcing relationships are ones in which it's impossible to anticipate all future circumstances that will affect the outsourcing deal. Here all three integrating mechanisms will come into play — rules, standards, and schedules for the simple interfaces that are possible to anticipate and specify in advance and liaison activities between the two organizations to handle changes and make adjustments.

Partnerships demand the most complex and costly integration efforts. Rules, standards, and schedules are still important, are incorporated in contracts and provide the foundation for the interface, but much effort must also be put into monitoring to detect changes that need to be made and into liaison to adjust rules, standards, and schedules in response. Client and vendor organizations mesh tightly and organizational boundaries blur. In its partnership arrangement with CSC and Andersen Consulting, DuPont set up teams to oversee technical, finance (chargeback and billing), contract administration and oversight of the relationship with its vendors, but purposely left many of the details of management structure to be decided and put in place as the relationships develop and the needs become clearer. See Chapter 10 for more detail on integration in partnerships.

Structure

The organizational structure should reflect the nature of the outsourced services. When multiple functions are outsourced, a functional structure often makes the most sense with managers in both client and vendor firms responsible for each function. For example, a large outsourcing deal that involves data center, networks, and user support might have managers on both sides responsible in each of these functions. A few managers in each organization oversee the whole of the outsourcing deal.

A business-technical split is another axis along which to organize. One set of client and vendor managers address support of the client's business, another group deals with underlying technical issues. The two groups can report to a top manager, or, alternatively, the business group can be made paramount.

If multiple and widely separated locations are served in the outsourcing deal, it may be best to have client and vendor persons responsible for overseeing the services at each location, or at least at major locations, so that communication is enhanced and feedback and response are more immediate. These could be persons with part-time, rather than full-time, management responsibility.

Large outsourcing deals, including total outsourcing, will most likely require a hierarchy of managers. A two-level hierarchy might consist of a top-level executive committee or board to make high-level plans with the vendor, monitor progress, keep the relationship on track, and resolve major differences. The second level below the board might consist of two committees. One oversees day-to-day operations. The other is a management committee that monitors the delivery of services by the vendor, analyses, and approves requests for changes in services, and resolves differences with the vendor.

Management of a Portfolio of Outsourcing Deals

If your organization does a lot of outsourcing, the management of one particular deal with a vendor should be part of a larger team of managers concerned with all the outsourcing going on in your organization. It is important to coordinate activities across the various outsourcing arrangements. Managers of each outsourcing deal sit on a superordinate outsourcing council or board that plays a major role in planning future outsourcing initiatives and has responsibility for seeing that the outsourcing strategy supports the overall business strategy now and in the future. The superordinate outsourcing council also has the responsibility for understanding directions in new technology (through their own efforts or combination with a technology assessment capability elsewhere in the IT department) and making sure that current and future outsourcing deals are in line with the organization's overall technology plan and direction.

8.3.3 People

If the contract doesn't specify persons who will take up management responsibility, these people should be identified as the outsourcing arrangement starts up. The outsourcing evaluation and negotiating team is well versed in the details of the outsourcing arrangement and has established relationships with people in the vendor's organization; these people are the best candidates for managers of the outsourcing arrangement from your side. Try to begin the outsourcing arrangement with people you already know, respect, and trust on the vendor side. Make your wishes known. Make requests for persons to fill the vendor management team. Consider rejecting a vendor nominee if you're not comfortable with the vendor's choice. The vendor wants to get started on a good footing as well.

It is also a good idea to specify backups or alternates on both client and vendor sides should the primary contacts not be available.

Don't allow the vendor to change its managers without the approval of your organization. You want vendor people with whom you can comfortably work. If the contract doesn't specify the involvement and approval of both sides in management changes, get this adopted as a procedure to follow as the outsourcing relationship starts up.

In the Riggs Bank — IBM deal, the bank has a dedicated manager and a team with the appropriate skills to oversee the vendor. The vendor has a project executive offsite, a project manager on site, and a data center manger on site. An executive council of top bank officers and senior vendor executives meets quarterly to review the status of the relationship. Furthermore, the bank interviews and approves all of the vendor's management appointments. Both the CIO and the vendor manager conducts the interviews.

As you appoint managers for the outsourcing arrangement, don't forget the users of information systems services in the business functions of your organization. Robert Rubin, CIO of Elf Atochem, appointed a director of its legacy systems outsourcing project whose sole job it is to work with its internal business people who are serviced by the vendor. The vendor's project manager interfaces with this director.

Management Skills

The skills required of the persons in charge of the outsourcing relationship from the client side are not the same skills involved in managing the typical IT department (Lacity and Hirschheim, 1995):

- The outsourcing manager must manage the contract with the vendor; the IT manager's focus is on managing people.

- The outsourcing manager is heavily involved in getting the agreed upon services from the vendor which is the customer demand side of services, while the IT manager is concerned with the people, equipment, and systems on the supply side of information services.

- When the need for outsourcing services exceeds the contracted levels and excess charges are to be levied, the outsourcing manager is involved in managing both the cost and benefits sides of the services in question. An IT manager leaves benefit considerations largely to customers or users and spends a lot of time managing the cost side of providing information services.

- The outsourcing manager is responsible for monitoring vendor performance and trying to balance the cost of monitoring against the benefits that monitoring brings. The IT manager will certainly monitor his or her own department's performance, but the ultimate arbiters are the customers or users.

In other words, the perspective and skill set needed by outsourcing managers is somewhat different than the perspective and skill set for IT managers. Yet it's common to put the IT director in the position of managing a total outsourcing deal or lesser IT managers in charge of managing selective outsourcing deals. Managers put in charge of outsourcing arrangements need to review their skill set and refurbish it as needed. Necessary skills include:

- Operations oversight or abilities in monitoring requirements, approving changes, and handling disputes.

- Technical oversight or abilities in planning technology architectures and setting standards.

- Financial oversight or abilities in monitoring costs and paying bills.

- Contract administration or abilities in negotiation to adjust the client-vendor relationship in response to changing conditions.

Cinda Hallman of DuPont identifies strong communication skills—openness, being good listeners, and effective speakers — as important for success. Outsourcing managers must be good team players with a genuine win-win attitude. They must be good at developing the "what" and be content to let the providers handle the "how." They must be comfortable and effective in identifying business opportunities and cutting edge solutions. They must be good at identifying the business requirements, establishing the metrics, broadly monitoring while permitting the partners to provide day-to-day services, and working with the providers to improve productivity and performance. They should show respect and an eagerness to learn from the providers while ensuring that DuPont is receiving value for the price it is paying.

Foster Good Working Relationships Between People

Check the matchup of people who will work with each other across the client-vendor interface to see that personalities will mesh in harmonious ways. Sometimes personalities and ways of working stand in the way of good relationships. Make adjustments in the outsourcing management team or suggest to the vendor that it make changes, as needed.

Take steps to develop good working relationships between personnel at the same level in client and vendor organizations. Schedule outside-of-work meals, golf rounds, social events, and the like between people on both sides to nurture the beginnings of good personal relationships.

8.3.4 Procedures

As mentioned in earlier chapters, contract provisions can specify procedures that will be followed over the life of the outsourcing deal. These are activated in the transition phase. The vendor will have other procedures that are standard in its operations. Your own organization will have procedures that impact the function or functions being outsourced. Smooth startup requires that these procedures be communicated in both directions, that procedures be adjusted to mesh properly, that training occurs, and that people involved in outsourcing work and coordination begin using the procedures and their underlying standards in the work they do.

New procedures may have to be created. These might be done by either client or vendor or jointly, depending on whose sphere of influence is involved. Where new procedures influence the workings of the outsourcing arrangement, they should be reviewed by management on both sides.

Information Flow and Documentation

Regardless of the management structure adopted, designate one focal point for receipt and distribution of information from the vendor. If the deal is a large one, a point of contract might be designated for each of the major functions in the arrangement. A focal point assures that vital information is passed to the right persons that helps your organization manage the outsourcing relationship. Document the flow of information, including information passed in all meetings, so that questions and statements of problems can be matched with vendor responses.

Vendor Access

You may want to restrict vendor access to certain places and certain times consistent with the needs of the outsourcing relationship and the way your organization works. The moment vendors sign one contract they start thinking about the next, and their marketing people may roam your hallways if they are not checked.

Changes and Change Control

Few outsourcing relationships exist without changes of some sort during the course of the relationship. Client and vendor need to establish ways of addressing and controlling change. Large changes may require amendment of the contract, but many smaller changes can often be made within the framework of an existing contract. Changes can be very challenging when they involve more than one vendor. The parties need to develop policies and processes for accepting or rejecting change and for implementing changes.

8.3.5 Meetings, Reviews and Audits

The strong communication necessary for effective outsourcing starts with regular meetings and reviews involving managers on both sides. The meeting and review schedule may be specified in the contract. If it wasn't, a schedule should be established early in the transition phase. Be sure the relevant people from the vendor side are obligated to attend these periodic meetings or reviews and have authority to make decisions. Don't be frustrated by trying to work with vendor personnel who do not have authority to address the issues you bring to the table.

Audits are an important way of maintaining control over vendors and insuring the quality of vendor work. The previous chapter on contract provisions speaks to this issue. Now, in startup, the audit procedures are put into action. It's best if the contract specified audit frequency and/or the conditions under which audits occur. If these are not identified in the contract, you should establish vendor expectations on audits with respect to the areas to be audited, conditions, and frequency.

8.3.6 Communication With Stakeholders

Managers of the outsourcing arrangement are at the hub of communications with vendor management, but also with senior managers in your organization, with user managers dependent on the services outsourcing provides, and with information systems personnel in your organization who must interface with vendor personnel. Each of these groups have their own concerns, and sometimes their goals are in conflict. Conflict can exist between senior managers and users, for example senior managers may focus on cutting costs, while user managers want better service. IT personnel may want responsiveness from vendor personnel that vendor personnel do not feel compelled to provide. Ignoring communication with and between these groups is a big mistake. If senior managers and user managers are dissatisfied with the outsourcing arrangement as it is implemented and as it progresses, outsourcing won't be viewed as a success in your organization, no matter what IT managers and vendor managers think.

Consider the stakeholders in the outsourcing deal, and act in the startup phase to establish good communication. Make introductions; hold preliminary meetings; set up procedures for communication where they don't exist; anticipate the need for outsourcing project management to foster and manage communication.

Users should have been involved in the analysis, RFP, and contract negotiation processes, but they will still have many issues and questions. Identify a member of the information systems outsourcing management group who will receive and resolve user issues. The need for this role continues throughout the life of the outsourcing arrangement.

Communication of information on the outsourcing deal to the outside world is best done through your public relations people or senior management.

8.4 PERSONNEL ISSUES

Personnel issues may be the most difficult to manage in a transition to outsourcing.

8.4.1 Communication

Honest communication with employees is usually the best policy. It's hard to hide the fact that outsourcing is in the works, particularly large outsourcing deals. The atmosphere of rumor and recrimination that accompanies outsourcing shrouded in mystery results in morale problems and often turnover problems that can be reduced if employees receive timely and accurate information.

Acceptance also depends on the perception that management is acting in good faith. Good faith efforts are addressed in more detail below. Be sure to communicate these.

As talks and negotiations are progressing with vendors, communicate at least the broad outlines or scope of the possible outsourcing arrangement. If scope changes, pass this along. While part of the analysis exercise is to draw up lists of personnel to keep, transfer, and let go, don't pass along this information until contracting is complete. Lists can change in the negotiating process, and you don't want people expecting one thing only to have plans abruptly reversed.

Once the contract is signed, it's only fair to quickly inform employees of the details of the outsourcing deal relevant to them, including who stays and who goes, reallocations, provisions for transfer of benefits, and other human resource issues. Basic human decency forbids notice of a person's fate by anything other than one-on-one communication. E-mail is too impersonal; use a phone call or, better, a face-to-face meeting.

Think through a schedule of information releases to employees and the methods of communication that will be used:

- Status briefings with opportunities for questions might be used throughout the RFP and contract negotiation process. Briefings might follow significant forward (or backward) steps in the outsourcing process. This can be supplemented with memos and electronic mail.

- A major announcement and briefing should follow contract signing at which time the details of the contract as it affects employees is distributed and discussed. Immediately precede this with private communication to each employee affected through retention, transfer, or layoffs informing them of their status under the contract.

- Subsequent meetings with IT managers, human resource specialists, and vendor personnel should follow. Some will be general purpose briefing and question answering gatherings. Others will address specific aspects of the outsourcing arrangement and transition to outsourcing, such as sessions on benefits, sessions on relocation, sessions on vendor employment benefits and policies, sessions on training, and introductions to vendor personnel.

- If unions and collective bargaining arrangements are involved, there will be meetings with union people, as well.

- More briefings, meetings, memos, e-mails and individual face-to-face communication will take place throughout the transition, as needed. Personnel who stay in your organization will need to meet with and start relationships with the vendor personnel with whom they will work.

DuPont communicated with its employees frequently using local, regional, and global town meetings, e-mail notes, printed materials, small group question and answer meetings, videoconferences, and every other means available. They prepared and distributed briefing packages for managers in every region to use for presentations to employees. They kept business unit and IT managers involved at every step. DuPont also used a hotline and an e-mail facility to respond to employee questions and an intranet Web site that was frequently updated with the latest information.

Honesty, good communication, and incentives are keys to success, as described by Jill Klein who helped lead the Riggs Bank outsourcing effort: "I met regularly with employees in small groups and maintained an open door to all employees. We never made any promises. We offered incentive bonuses for employees to stay during the transition. Although the vendor had the right to deny offers to any employee, only one employee out of 70 was unemployed at the end of the process. Today many of the same employees work for the vendor and support the bank. I am also very pleased that some of the employees have advanced to key positions with the vendor and have enjoyed advancement opportunities we never could have offered within the bank."

8.4.2 Managing Reactions to Outsourcing

As soon as the mention of outsourcing gets out, some of the people in your IT organization will start looking for alternative employment (Mylott, 1995). Often these employees are ones with a strong professional attachment to your industry; they don't identify with working in an outsourcing firm. And because they are often good, they may readily find other jobs if they try. Another subset will welcome transfer to a vendor and may shift loyalties before they are actually on the vendor employment roles. A third subset will feel they are stuck and resist change, criticizing the idea of outsourcing at every opportunity.

An important part of the planning for outsourcing is to identify the persons in your organization who will be affected by outsourcing and to decide what you want their role to be during the transition to outsourcing and after outsourcing is in place. Planning also identifies people who will be terminated. Now, in the transition, it's time to keep or move these people, as desired.

Incentives are the major weapon in your arsenal for keeping people you want in your organization, either permanently or while the transition to outsourcing occurs. Layout a career path under the new regime and be prepared to offer more salary and benefits, if that is what is necessary.

The vendor must also be prepared to offer strong incentives to the persons you want to transfer to the vendor side. Identify these people in contract negotiations, and get vendor commitment to transferring them and retaining them. Schedule talks between these people and vendor managers early in the communication process.

A good part of the resistance to any change is fear of the unknown. The communication strategy is to make things known and calm fears. As soon as the idea of outsourcing is broached with your employees, assurances should be made to the extent that assurances can be made. Some steps that can be taken to calm fears are:

- Assurances that your people will get accurate information on late breaking developments in the outsourcing process as they occur.
- Information on the vendor or vendors as soon as it is clear which vendors will prevail. Provide vendor literature; have vendor representatives speak to your people.
- Research and communicate advantages that may exist in vendor employment, such as the opportunity to focus on specific types of work, opportunities for training and advancement.
- Face-to-face meetings between vendor management and the key personnel you want to transfer to the vendor.
- Training and professional development activities offered in the vendor organization.
- Details of guaranteed periods of employment and other benefits negotiated with the vendor.
- Details of relocation and outplacement services to be made available.
- Details on the community and living environment of locations to which your personnel will be transferred, including community services, schools, housing markets, and the like.

Don't promise anything that you know can't be done. Carry through on the promises and deliver the support and services promised. When employees can see a way through the transition and can become reasonably comfortable with their lot on the other side, the complaints and disruption will subside considerably. Be prepared, plan, and work hard to accomplish this.

Because of the advance planning and effort put into handling the human relations side of its outsourcing deal, DuPont experienced few problems. A high percentage of its employees identified for transfer chose to take the vendor offers. DuPont attributes its success in large part to the good compensation and benefits packages offered to transferring employees and the IT career opportunities available with its two partners. DuPont used human resource consultants to help it and the vendors with the HR issues. That yielded attractive opportunities for transferring employees.

8.4.3 Employees Retained

The concerns of employees differ depending on whether they are retained, transferred, or terminated, and the management of each of these groups needs to reflect the differences. Retained employees are often upset when co-workers leave and are unsettled about changes in responsibilities that may come their way. They may distrust management, feeling that performance has little relationship to job security. After the general announcement that outsourcing is going forward, hold face-to-face meetings to discuss concerns and individual situations. Open the door to drop-in sessions to discuss concerns as they arise. (Laribee and Michaels-Barr, 1994)

Some of the employees who are retained in your organization will take up new responsibilities as work is shifted to the outsourcing vendor. Don't forget to take the steps that all such transitions require in terms of briefings, training, encouragement, and support.

The change in responsibilities can be particularly dramatic in total outsourcing arrangements. The roles of people retained tend to shift from managers and deliverers of information services to interface-with-the-vendor roles and consultants to users. This is a big shift in job responsibilities and requires new skills acquired through considerable preparation and ongoing support.

8.4.4 Employees Who Will Be Transferred

Try to retain the good will of employees who will be transferred to the vendor and whose services are seen as important to continuity and quality of the outsourcing arrangement. They will feel the pain of leaving co-workers and venturing off to a new company, perhaps a new city. Sell them on the advantages of making the transition and staying with their work. This is made easier, of course, if the deal has attractive aspects for them. Employment with a vendor usually offers a career path in an organization devoted entirely to information technology. To many employees this aspect of vendor employment may be more attractive than continued employment in your organization, particularly if your IT department is a cost center and viewed as a utility. (Laribee and Michaels-Barr, 1994)

Arrange meetings with vendor managers as soon as possible to provide information and reassurance from the vendor side. Vendors will lay out career paths and training opportunities that may be quite attractive to many of those who will be transferred.

Transferring employees across international boundaries involves much advance work and preparation:

- Work permits may be required in foreign countries.
- Pay and benefit scales may have to be adjusted to account for foreign country differences.
- Moving expenses need to be addressed.

- Employees need to be informed of the personal tax implications of foreign employment.
- Cultural and language training may be involved.

The contract should specify who bears the responsibility and costs of these tasks. Usually it is the vendor, but if the job falls on your organization, human resource people and the outsourcing management team need to start work on international transfers as soon as the contract is signed.

8.4.5 Employees Who Will Be Terminated

Employees who will be terminated need to know that outsourcing is done for valid organizational reasons. They will also want to know the criteria for termination and that these criteria are fair and fairly applied. They should receive outplacement services and ample notice before layoff occurs.

When large numbers are affected, the services of an outplacement firm might be cost-effective. For smaller numbers the effort might be organized with the existing resources of the IT and human resources departments. In addition to counseling and help with resumes, job searches, and office resources such as phones, your organization might extend benefits after termination and while a job search is still proceeding to help employees make the transition.

The contract negotiation might also involve the vendor in offering outplacement services, in which case implementation of the transition plan will see that your organization and the vendor organization follow the agreement in providing these services.

8.5 RESOURCE TRANSFER AND CHANGE OF LOCATION

Most outsourcing arrangements involve the transfer of resources of one kind or another.

8.5.1 Change of Location

The transition to outsourcing is much easier if the vendor is to take over your facilities as part of the outsourcing arrangement rather than moving operations to the vendor's place of business. Obviously there is less planning and much less disruption if the vendor simply takes over facilities that were previously yours. A move of operations, on the other hand, usually involves a data conversion and a move of equipment and people to another location.

The contract will specify what is to go to the vendor. How the move will take place may not be spelled out. Planning for moves should be one of the first tasks in a transition to outsourcing, and it must, of course, be done with the help and agreement of all vendors involved. Think through what must be done:

- Start with and work from the idea of continuity in services throughout the course of a move. What must be done to assure continuity?

- Should a move be phased, or an immediate transfer with shutdown in one location on one day and startup in another location on the next, or should operations be run in parallel for a time at several sites?

- What system and data conversion activities, if any, must be performed?

- What site preparation activities are necessary, including utilities and their location?

- How should personnel moves be coordinated to support service continuity?

- How and when should people be oriented, trained, and put into service at the new site?

- How will moves of equipment and any other physical objects be scheduled and accomplished?

- Of all the responsibilities identified in a move, which are the responsibility of the client and which will the vendor undertake? Who will pay, if this is not specified in the contract?

The transition to outsourcing implements the staffing plan. If some details of staffing and staff locations were left out of the planning and contracting process, these must be addressed as part of the transition. The vendor's bid is based on assumptions of staff and staff location. If your needs and desires don't correspond to the vendor's assumptions, the potential for disagreement exists and the vendor may not be willing to meet your requests without extra charges or some renegotiation of the contract.

Moves are part of modern corporate life, and many organizations have a lot of experience with relocation of facilities. You might get the facilities management people in your organization to help fill in the details of the physical aspects of a plan.

8.5.2 Location and Communication with the Vendor

Location of vendor personnel can be a very important issue, particularly when coordination with users or coordination with your own in-house IT people is critical for smooth provision of services. Several dimensions of location affect the ability to communication with, work with, and manage a vendor.

The magnitude of the distance separating you and the vendor is one dimension. Communication is easiest and best for people located in the same suite of offices. It is a bit more difficult for people in the same building on different floors. It is harder still for persons in different buildings, but on the same campus. The difficulty and cost increase progressively for persons in different locations in the same city, in the same area of the country, in different regions of the country, and in different countries. If vendor people are located on different continents in widely differing time zones, the problems can be particularly severe.

Another dimension is the quality of communication with a vendor in terms of the communication media used. Media theory speaks of richness of communication. Richness refers to the extent to which a communication medium conveys information and the emotion or feeling that accompanies it. Different media are inherently better or worse at conveying information in all its possible richness. The continuum of media with respect to richness might be arrayed as follows, from richest to least rich:

- The richest medium is face-to-face communication. Here simultaneous two-way communication, expression, body language, tone of voice, and gestures add a lot to the message and convey much more than words alone.
- Video conferencing communicates much visual information, as well as verbal information, and still allows for interaction. It is the next richest medium.
- Phone conversations retain the verbal clues, but not the visual.
- Written communications — e-mail, memos, and letters — are the least rich. What is conveyed is limited to words only and is not simultaneous.

Of course, the dimensions of distance and media richness are directly related. When your people and the vendor's people are co-located, face-to-face communication will naturally and easily take place in the work setting. Opportunities for breakfast, lunch-time, and after-work contact will abound. The means for quality communication will be readily available.

When separated by distance, your people and the vendor's people will rely more on phone and written communication. Face-to-face meetings will take place, but less frequently. Either the quality of communication will be lower, because less of it is face-to-face, or the cost of getting together for face-to-face meetings will be higher — most likely both.

Of course there is a cost to relocating people so that they are in close proximity, and this has to be balanced against the costs of more difficult and expensive communication if they are apart. The vendor's lower costs may be based on its location in an inexpensive, low-wage state, region, or country. To insist that vendor people be with your people may negate fundamental aspects of the relationship that make it attractive to outsource. When relocation costs do not destroy the advantages of the outsourcing arrangement, it's better to have vendor people, particularly the interface people, together with your people.

If some of your people are transferred to the vendor as part of the outsourcing deal, it may be possible and appropriate to negotiate an arrangement that leaves a portion of them in place, in your working environment, so that distance is not a disadvantage to communication.

8.5.3 Hardware, Software, and Data

The deal struck with a vendor should specify issues of ownership, licenses, maintenance, and other issues associated with transferring hardware and software. It should also address data transfer and data rights and control.

Execution of the transfer plan carries out the contract provisions. As noted above under change of location issues, the schedule for hardware and software transfer and data movement and conversion must be coordinated with other transition activities.

8.5.4 Conversions

Some issues to address in conversions include:

- Conversion tasks and task order.
- Roles and responsibilities on both sides.
- Responsibility for costs in all conversion activities.
- Critical dates in the conversion.
- How and when data will be transferred and converted.

- The method and schedule for cut-over from operation of systems in your organization to the vendor's. Parallel operation of both the vendor's and your systems might be best in the case of conversion of mission-critical systems to vendor software. Pilots might be good for systems moved to the vendor's facilities in multiple locations.
- Backup and recovery issues in the conversion.

The outsourcing analysis, RFP process, and contract negotiations should have established requirements, investigated vendor capabilities, and established that the vendor will be successful in handling the application in its environment. What remains to be done is to plan and then carry out the steps necessary to move and convert data and to switch to systems operation in the vendor's place of business. Both sides should be involved in planning the steps and laying out a schedule for the conversion, and the vendor should provide any information necessary to make a smooth and successful transition.

When conversions involve a switch to vendor application software, the vendor's software won't be identical to the old software in your organization. The interfaces will differ; the functionality may vary. Because your business processes must interface with the vendor system, it may be necessary to redesign some of your business processes and train users in the new ways of doing things. Hopefully your analysis team anticipated these needs and factored them into the effort and cost associated with outsourcing.

8.6 CONFLICT AND DISPUTE RESOLUTION

Conflict is inherent in outsourcing relationships between client and vendor organizations and their people. The two organizations have different goals relative to an outsourcing deal: the client wants excellent and always responsive service at a low price; the vendor wants profits that can be increased through charging more or skimping on service. The people on client and vendor sides report to different managers in different organizations and have no natural allegiance to each other across the line that separates the two firms.

Conflict is contained and managed through several mechanisms. The contract defines the service the vendor is to provide and what will be paid for the service, and the contract binds the client and vendor to its terms. Good contracts provide the basis for good and reasonably harmonious outsourcing deals, and bad contracts are almost certainly an invitation to conflict and trouble. Conflict is also contained through good and harmonious working relationships between the people at the interface between client and vendor firms. Finally, when conflict does surface, it is managed through formal and informal dispute resolution mechanisms that prevent the conflict from escalating and threatening the overall outsourcing relationship.

A good conflict management process has the following attributes (Ertel, 1991):

- It has ways of clarifying the parties' basic interests rather than stated positions. Positions can have underlying elements of fear, anger, and retribution for previously perceived wrongs. The idea is to get away from emotion and get to the bedrock of fundamental interests. Sometimes positions are in conflict when fundamental interests are not. One or both parties may be reluctant to divulge interests for fear this will give the other side too much leverage in the dispute. But a good dispute resolution process takes the risk out of being honest about interests.

- It builds or sustains a good working relationship between the parties by first seeing that the work for which the relationship was established continues, and second by trying to foster and move toward the kind of relationship both parties desire. In other words, in the short run the dispute resolution mechanism should not terminate the relationship but should instead offer ways to move forward and reach agreement.

- It surfaces and invents good ways to resolve differences, preferably by win-win or create value for both parties resolutions to disagreements rather than win-lose solutions.

- It should be seen as fair by both sides.

- It is better than resolution by litigation in one or more of the following ways: being less expensive, more harmonious and supportive to a continuing relationship, and more private than a public court battle.

- It fosters good communication rather than hiding of information.

- It leads to good solutions to which both parties can commit.

Contracts usually set out the basics for resolving disputes in terms of the:

- Persons or groups in client and vendor management who are responsible for identifying, investigating, and resolving disputes.

- Escalation procedures that take the dispute to higher levels of outsourcing management and then to senior management in client and vendor organizations, if disputes cannot be resolved at lower levels.

- End points in the escalation process that can be arbitration, mediation, minicourts, or some combination of these.

From the characteristics of good dispute resolution above, one can see that there is much more to dispute resolution than can be specified in a contract. Contracts only begin to set the framework for cooperative dispute resolution and conflict management. The bulk of the work must be done through the relationship established between client and vendor people and the manner in which they handle disputes as disputes arise.

In the startup phase, management of the outsourcing arrangement from the client and vendor sides should review contract provisions on dispute resolution and then launch a discussion of how they would prefer to approach disputes when they arise. The central part of these discussions is how to resolve disputes in ways that achieve the characteristics of good methods.

Talking about approaches to disputes at the outset has several advantages. First, it allows both sides to say what they would prefer to do and how they would prefer to do it. Second, if there are differences in approach, these can be discussed and a more unified approach can be agreed upon. Third, and most important, it is the first step in the establishment of a cooperative attitude toward disputes and a step away from an adversarial attitude. It sets expectations on both sides that can lead toward cooperation and away from confrontation.

Exactly how a dispute is resolved depends on the dispute. The steps are to (Ertel, 1991):

- First, identify the causes of the conflict.
- Then, find alternative approaches to resolving the conflict.
- Finally, take action.

The facts and circumstances of an actual dispute shape the alternatives and the action that follows.

Think through a strategy for handling the first situations that have potential for disputes. With all the emphasis on establishing a good relationship with the vendor, clients sometimes let the first vendor transgressions go without expecting much. This can be a mistake. Your approach to the first problems sends signals to vendors on your expectations of service and service performance. A cooperative attitude toward disputes is not the same as being a doormat. If vendor performance is not adequate and in line with the contract and you don't call the vendor on it, the vendor will assume you are largely satisfied. Insist that the vendor uphold the contract and perform as required. Remember that good dispute resolution starts with a clear understanding of and communication of your interests.

8.7 EMPLOYMENT LAW AND OUTSOURCING: AN INTERVIEW WITH EDWARD A. PISACRETA

Edward A. Pisacreta is a partner in the New York City office of Brown Raysman Millstein Felder & Steiner LLP, a seventy lawyer firm with offices in New York, California, New Jersey, and Connecticut. Mr. Pisacreta concentrates in the area of computer law and related intellectual property issues. He has extensive experience in drafting and negotiating a wide range of agreements in the data processing and information services areas. He has also been involved in numerous outsourcing transactions, representing both the outsourcing vendor and the recipient of outsourced services for a variety of services and industries. Mr. Pisacreta has lectured in the area of computer law and intellectual property. He is a graduate of Fordham University (Bachelor of Arts and Juris Doctor) and Temple University (Master of Arts) and prior to practicing law was a management consultant with Ernst & Whinney (now Ernst & Young) in the information systems area. Mr. Pisacreta is a member of the American Bar Association's Sections of Business Law and Science and Technology, the New York State Bar Association, and the Association of the Bar of the City of New York, and is Editor in Chief of the Computer Law Strategist.

How can the outsourcing parties avoid a discrimination claim?
The law allows an employer to exercise business judgment in employment decisions, except that state and federal statutes forbid the employer from discriminating against certain protected groups. There are antidiscrimination statutes for:

(1) Age, sex, race, national origin, and disability.
(2) Bankruptcy protection, veterans, and "whistle blowers."
(3) State specific (e.g. sexual preference and "outside" activities such as hobbies and potential affiliation).

Employment decisions should be made on an as objective a basis as feasible and should be carefully documented so that the business justification for personnel decisions is preserved. Courts and juries give great weight to documents written prior to the lawsuit. Documents connected with an outsourcing transition will be discoverable, including informal notes. Off-the-record discussions will become part of the record as a result of the legal process.

An outsourcing context creates a heightened concern about discrimination and therefore requires closer scrutiny.

What about defining the group of employees affected?

The business basis for the transaction is the first and most determinative criterion for defining the group of employees who will be affected by the outsourcing. Questions that should be considered to increase the chances of successfully defending a discrimination claim are:

(1) What is the function that is being outsourced and which employees currently provide that function at the company considering outsourcing?
(2) Have the business reasons for defining the group been well articulated and documented and have they been logically and consistently applied in carving out the group of affected employees?

What are some potential discrimination claims?

One potential claim is one based on the demographic statistics of the affected employees as a group (e.g., dismissal of a group of older employees who are close to retirement age). Under the Employee Retirement Income Security Act (ERISA), it is improper to terminate an employee simply to prevent vesting of pension rights.

A second potential claim is "Disparate treatment" i.e., a claim based on an individual's claim that he or she was treated differently, and unfairly, based on age, sex, disability, and so forth. A company should adopt neutral rules when defining an affected group.

Discrimination claims may arise when subjective decisions are made in arriving at exceptions to neutral rules. An employer may be able to defeat a discrimination claim by articulating a legitimate business reason for the employment decisions. A decision not documented in advance might be construed as an after-the-fact attempt to hide a discriminatory motive.

Both the vendor and the company should be concerned with how the group of affected employees is defined for a number of reasons:

(1) Indemnity or risk-sharing in the outsourcing contract.
(2) An improper definition of group may increase the likelihood that the vendor will face discrimination claims.
(3) An outsourcing company may seek to retain some favored employees from the affected group and the vendor agrees to allow the outsourcing company to carve these people out of the group.
(4) An arrangement can give rise to a claim of disparate treatment.

What are some guidelines for remaining candidates and making or not making employment offers?

There are two types of transactions.

> (1) Transactions that do not give the vendor a right to select. This arrangement is beneficial to the customer because it diminishes the likelihood of suits against it for wrongful termination. This arrangement obligates the vendor to hire employees that it might later dismiss with all of the attendant risks of liability for wrongful termination.
>
> (2) Transactions that give the vendor a right to select.

The key point here is whether the position is redundant either because the outsourcing company did not staff efficiently or because the vendor's staffing structure renders the position duplicative or unnecessary. The analysis is objective and does not turn on the qualifications or performance of the particular potential employee. This analysis should be defensible if it is well-reasoned and well-documented.

What if a position is redundant, yet vendor considers one of employees in this position sufficiently valuable to hire into a newly-created position?

A terminated employee may argue that redundancy is a fabrication or a pretext for a discriminatory motive. The vendor's best defense against a claim is a record that documents the fact of the redundancy, and the concrete business reasons for making an exception for the favored employee.

The decision to offer or not offer employment should be based on due diligence as to the person's qualifications and performance. The vendor could be charged with "negligent hiring" if no inquiry is made into the candidate's background and the employee later acts improperly. The vendor should formalize the due diligence process so that it is documented and defensible in the event of discrimination or other claims. The vendor may consider obtaining a representation from the customer company that it knows of no reason to suspect the employees of violent or other dangerous propensities.

What about job applications?

Falsified information on the job application may preclude or limit damages in a wrongful termination or discrimination claim. The application should also not include any discriminatory questions.

How should interviews be conducted?

Interviews should be conducted on a professional basis with avoidance of illegal practices, or comments that suggest improper bias. Reviews should be obtained from peers or supervisors at the outsourcing company. The vendor should inquire sufficiently into the circumstances of negative reviews — to discern if the reviewer is speaking out of bias. The vendor's actual observation of the workers could be significant in discerning patterns of discrimination. The vendor should obtain concrete information to avoid relying on conclusory evaluations.

How should personnel records be handled?
Access to personnel records could give rise to discrimination claims.

States have various privacy laws that restrict an employer's ability to collect, maintain, use, or disclose information about an employee that is unnecessary or overboard.

How about administering tests?
If it is the vendor's normal practice to administer a test as a selection or qualification criterion, the test should be administered in the outsourcing context as well, because one of the criteria for determining whether a test is legitimate is that it be required of all applicants in similar circumstances. The test should be related to successful performance on the job, and be administered in a nondiscriminatory manner. "Honesty" tests have been widely upheld as legitimate, however, they may lead to invasion of privacy claims. Polygraphs and other mechanical lie detectors have been essentially prohibited in the vast majority of employment contexts.

How can the outsourcing parties prevent claims for severance?
The customer company might pay severance to its affected employees, including those who are subsequently employed by the vendor. The vendor may prefer that the employees not have the option of taking severance pay instead of accepting the vendor's employment offer. A severance policy is generally an "employee welfare benefit plan" not a "pension" plan. The outsourcing company is allowed a degree of flexibility to set or change its severance policy. The outsourcing company is obligated to honor the severance policy in place at the time of outsourcing. Determining whether a policy requires the outsourcing company to pay severance depends on the language of the policy and the past history of interpretations.

Absent an explicit outsourcing provision, the company may decide that severance is not warranted under a fair reading of the policy as a whole. When outsourcing does not require an interruption in employment, the outsourcing company may be able to credibly argue that severance is not warranted.

How can the parties best defend employee claims of denial of benefits?
The key question here is does the policy expressly give the company discretion to interpret the plan? A policy without reservation for discretion will be viewed de

novo and the court will likely adopt a stricter view of the company's obligations. Some courts, have upheld denials of severance where the employee would receive a "windfall" if uninterrupted paychecks were supplemented with severance.

Other jurisdictions have upheld there is no "windfall" where factors such as the loss of credit for past services under the new employer's severance policies, or minor differences in benefits packages, diminish the comparability of the new position.

Policies should be amended to specifically address outsourcing. Amendments must be done in accordance with the terms of the plan. Publication of the amendment to the employees should be in advance of the transaction.

What are the notice requirements?
Advance notice of a transaction to outsourced employees may be required to accommodate provisions that exist in the company's policies, or satisfy obligations under state and federal laws. The Workers Adjustment and Retraining Notification Act (the WARN Act) requires 60 days notice before a plant closing or mass layoff. The Act only applies if the company employs 100 or more full-time employees, or 100 or more employees who in the aggregate work at least 4,000 hours per week exclusive of overtime. The Act notice provision will be triggered if a company temporarily or permanently closes one or more employment sites, including facilities or operating units within a site if (i) the shut down results in a loss of 50 or more full-time employees during a 30 day period or (ii) in the event of a mass layoff which is defined by the act to be a reduction in the workforce that involves, at a single site and within any 30-day period, 50 or more employees (provided those affected constitute at least a third of the full-time workforce at the site). A mass layoff is also defined as a reduction that affects 500 or more full-time employees, regardless of what percentage of the workforce they constitute.

What about the timing and substance of employment offers?
With respect to timing, the period of time between the announcement of the transaction and the extending of job offers should be as short as possible. Employee resignations are likely to increase if the announcement is made but the decision as to the individual employees' future has not yet been determined. The timing of the announcement depends in large part on how the due diligence is to be accomplished.

Scheduled periodic updates of negotiations should be given to avoid rumors or speculation in order to minimize the number of resignations due to the employees' uncertainty. Oral communications are often misunderstood; therefore, some critical announcements should be made in writing.

As for substance, written letters of employment should be carefully drafted to avoid implying a contract of employment.

With some exceptions, the law generally provides that the terms of the employment are "at will," that is, employer and the employee are free to terminate the relationship at any time and for any reason, except as prohibited under various statutes relating to certain forms of discrimination.

The employment relationship will no longer be "at will" if the parties agree to restrict the ability to terminate the relationship. An offer of employment should make clear that the employment will be at will unless something else is intended. Although many states require that a contract for a term be in writing, employees may still look to a range of documents to reflect an agreement to be bound.

Is the vendor bound by the terms of the outsourced employee's contract?
The vendor is not free from all liability to the employee under all circumstances. The new arrangement should be clear from the onset so that the customer company, the employee, and the vendor are each fully aware of the nature of the arrangement. Employees should be provided with adequate resources from both parties to answer questions concerning benefits, and so forth. If the employee does not accept the vendor's offer of employment, many policies will treat the employee as having voluntarily terminated employment. The employee may claim that the new job is not comparable, therefore termination is not "voluntary." The contract should specify that the customer company remains the employer until the effective date of the transfer.

What about employment guarantees?
The vendor may agree to hire the outsourced employees for a guaranteed term. The contract should specify the length of the guaranty; exceptions to the guaranty (e.g., termination for cause); vendor's right to relocate the employee or change his or her job functions; and the terms should be explained to the employee in writing.

What are some of the issues after implementation of the outsourcing contract?
Several issues arise when the outsourcing company maintains some level of control over the affected employees or, conversely, where the outsourced employees remain on site. The employer-employee relationship may become one of an independent contractor. Courts apply the "right of control" test to make the determination. The more detailed the supervision and the stricter the enforcement standards, the greater the likelihood of an employer-employee relationship.

If customer company's worker is an independent contractor, the vendor may not have to adhere to the contractual requirements as it does for other employees.

The vendor may be able to structure the new worker's employment to create independent contractor status and alleviate the vendor from various responsibilities. The vendor may be liable for "constructive termination." The vendor may also be liable for wrongs committed by third parties against its employees.

8.8. REFERENCES

Ertel, Danny, "How to Design a Conflict Management Procedure That Fits Your Dispute," *Sloan Management Review*, (Summer 1991) 29–42.

Lacity, Mary C. and Hirschheim, Rudy, *Beyond the Information Systems Outsourcing Bandwagon: The Insourcing Response*, New York, John Wiley & Sons, 1995.

Laribee, Janet E. and Michaels-Barr, Lisa, "Dealing with Personnel Concerns in Outsourcing, *Journal of Systems Management*, (January 1994) 6–12.

Lawrence, Paul R. and Lorsch, Jay W., *Organization and Environment: Managing Differentiation and Integration*, Harvard University, Division of Research, Graduate School of Business Administration, Boston, 1969.

Morris, Peter W. G., "Managing Project Interfaces — Key Points for Project Success," in David I. Cleland and William R. King (eds), *Project Management Handbook*, 2d ed, New York, Van Nostrand Reinhold, 1988, 16–55.

Stuckenbruck, Linn C., "Integration: The Essential Function of Project Management," in David I. Cleland and William R. King (eds), *Project Management Handbook*, 2d ed, New York, Van Nostrand Reinhold, 1988, 56–81.

9

Managing the Ongoing Outsourcing Relationship

This chapter begins with general approaches to managing the outsourcing vendor and issues of managing users, senior managers, and IT personnel involved in the outsourcing relationship. It returns briefly to the issue of risk management that was introduced earlier in the book, then proceeds with discussions of monitoring and control of vendors. Sections on managing project-type outsourcing work and on dispute resolution are next, and an interview with Michael Corbett concludes the chapter. Corbett is founder of the Outsourcing Institute, and in his interview he outlines important considerations in making an outsourcing relationship work successfully.

Robert Rubin, Vice President and CIO of Elf Atochem, notes that the risks in outsourcing arrangements are substantial and must be managed, "If outsourcing is not managed properly, control of a company's information stream is put at risk with very little short-term recourse. Without careful planning, it may be very difficult to remove the outsourcer because the knowledge of how your own information systems operate is lost. A further risk is that costs will escalate because user service requests are not managed. It is essential that significant client management time be expended on the ongoing relationship. Outsourcing requires more, not less, high-level attention in order to be successful."

Jill Klein points to the important element of responsibility that underlies monitoring and control: "The CIO still owns the function and has the same responsibilities as any CIO. Just because you have outsourced the performance of the functions to a vendor, the CIO is not relieved of the responsibility. The CIO must have an elite team to keep an eye on the vendor performance and an eye on the future. It is essential to understand change orders and stay focused on the relationship. The CIO can now be a real CIO by keeping an eye on the business value of IT and not get bogged down with running the day-to-day operations."

9.1 GENERAL DIMENSIONS OF MANAGING THE OUTSOURCING RELATIONSHIP

Managing the relationship is a mixture of discipline and compassion or discipline and cooperation. It's parallel to "tough love" in relationships between persons. As such it reflects the inherently conflictory nature of depending on another organization to provide services through outsourcing. On the one hand, the client wants absolute adherence to the contractual obligations the vendor has made, or a tough, disciplined relationship. On the other hand, in most instances of outsourcing, the contract isn't complete and doesn't specify all the aspects of service the client needs from the vendor as the contracting period progresses and the environment changes. Because the client will likely need service not specified in the contract, the client wants a cooperative, understanding relationship with the vendor — one in which the vendor will respond favorably to requests for changes and "extras," perhaps in return for favors to the vendor granted by the client. Furthermore, differences will inevitably arise in an outsourcing relationship, and cooperation is a firmer foundation on which to resolve disputes than antagonism and retaliation.

9.1.1 Types of Outsourcing Relationships and Outsourcing Management

The required mix of discipline and cooperation varies with the nature of the contracting relationship. The idea of a continuum of contracting relationships between client and vendor was introduced in Chapter 4 and has reappeared frequently in subsequent chapters. It's useful here for sorting out the approach to managing ongoing outsourcing relationships. To recap:

- Market-type relationships with vendors are ones in which the outsourcing requirements can be completely specified up-front and included in a contract; no changes inside the organization or the environment will require changes in requirements over the life of the contract; there is no great advantage to doing a subsequent deal with the same vendor if the service need is a continuing one; and if the deal should fall apart in the middle of the contracting period, no great losses would be suffered in bringing the work back in-house or finding and contracting with another vendor.

- Intermediate-type relationships with vendors are ones in which it's not possible to write a complete contract that anticipates all changes that may occur during the life of the contract. Furthermore, a breakdown of the relationship in the middle of the contract will result in considerable losses to client or vendor or both because of investments made in undertaking the outsourcing work that can't be recouped when moving to another vendor or taking the work back inside.

- Partnerships with vendors are ones in which — like intermediate contracting — complete contracts are not possible. Unanticipated changes in needs will require a change in what the vendor does; there is considerable investment by one or both parties in investments that are specific to the relationship. In addition there is an ongoing need for the services involved in outsourcing, and there is a considerable advantage in recontracting with the same vendor for these services because getting to know the vendor and the vendor getting to know the client organization improves service and lowers the cost of contracting in the next contract period.

At the market relationship end of the contracting spectrum discipline is all-important and the need for cooperation is much less. At the opposite end of the spectrum, in partnerships, cooperation is paramount if the relationship is to last and successfully carry over from one contract to the next, and discipline — while still necessary — is less important when viewed over multiple contracts. In intermediate contracting, discipline is important, but changes come along that need the vendor's cooperation. The relationship must be harmonious enough to survive to the end of the contracting period or real losses are incurred by one or both parties as the consequence of a deal gone wrong.

Monitoring and Control

Where discipline is required, it is very important to hold the vendor to its obligations at the outset and be consistent in this purpose. Nothing will cause a relationship to slip faster than looking the other way when a vendor fails to perform. This is an invitation to the vendor to try another small transgression, then another, then another. A vendor is more likely to be on its best behavior when it has a very clear understanding of what constitutes good behavior. The contract provides the foundation or the rules of behavior.

The fundamental methods for keeping a vendor in line are monitoring and control. Monitoring is used to see that the vendor is doing what the vendor should. Control is used to get the vendor back on track if monitoring indicates the vendor is deviating from agreed upon performance. The contract is the foundation for monitoring and control activity in outsourcing relationships. At one level, outsourcing management is contract management.

The monitoring-control-planning cycle is a familiar one to project managers and is very relevant to managing outsourcing:

- The goals and objectives of outsourcing determine what is to be measured and the standards or criteria that must be met.
- Monitoring is the process of observing, gathering data, and analyzing the results against the standards and criteria that have been established.
- When monitoring indicates things aren't going right, controls are implemented to correct the way work is done and get services back on track.
- And planning more fundamentally resets the way the work is done if minor corrections don't fix the problem. This can include revising the goals of outsourcing, changing the scope of the outsourcing work, and changing the nature of the relationship with a vendor.

Monitoring and control issues are addressed later in this chapter.

9.1.2 Managing Other Stakeholders — Users, Senior Managers, and IT Personnel

The vendor is the first and most obvious focus in managing outsourcing, but attention must also be paid to users of vendor services, senior managers, and IT people in your organization. The ultimate consumers of services provided by outsourcing vendors are users or customers. Unless they are satisfied with the outsourcing arrangement, it can't be called a success. If senior managers are involved in the initiation of outsourcing, if they champion the outsourcing effort, or if they have concerns for how well outsourcing supports the organization's business, then they have a vital interest in how the outsourcing deal is progressing as well. Finally, the IT people in your organization who manage the outsourcing arrangement and interface with services provided by the outsourcing vendor have a stake in the success of outsourcing.

Outsourcing is a success if it's viewed as a success in the eyes of the various stakeholders. Their views and their concerns are important. Setting their expectations, monitoring their views, and responding to their issues and concerns are vital aspects of outsourcing management.

9.1.3 Risk Management

Risk management in outsourcing begins in the analysis stage of the outsourcing process (see Chapter 5) with analyses of things that can threaten the success of the outsourcing initiative. The RFP and contract try to anticipate and nullify the threats. When risk can't be avoided but can be anticipated, the contract assigns the risk to client or vendor or provides a sharing mechanism. Risk management continues as the outsourcing arrangement operates by:

- Monitoring those factors previously identified as posing a potential threat to the success of the outsourcing effort.
- Managing those risks assigned to your firm in the contract by prevention or reduction or correction.
- Continuing to look for and assess new, not previously recognized threats that may offset the positive outcomes of outsourcing.

Environmental changes are major sources of risk in outsourcing. All the other internal workings of the vendor relationship may go well, but the deal can still be quite unsatisfactory because what the contract calls for is no longer what the organization needs.

9.2 MONITORING

Monitoring can be viewed as proceeding on several levels. First, and most obvious, it is necessary to monitor the vendor's behavior or work output. Second, it's essential to monitor the ultimate users of outsourcing services to see that they are satisfied with the results of outsourcing. Third, monitor senior management for their reactions to outsourcing. Fourth, monitor the IT people who remain in your organization to see that they are performing properly in their interface and management roles relative to the vendor or vendors. Finally, monitor developments in the business and technological environment.

9.2.1 Monitoring the Vendor

The goals of outsourcing drive monitoring at the highest level. Monitoring should provide the information necessary to determine that the objectives of outsourcing are being met. A review of the possible objectives of outsourcing in Chapter 3 shows that the goals can be quite diverse, and there can be several goals that drive a single outsourcing deal. So, the first rule of monitoring is consider all the goals to be met in your outsourcing project and devise measures and methods of monitoring to see that they are achieved.

The second rule is to direct monitoring to the issues identified in the first step. Are the requirements being met? Is service timely? Are the costs in line? These are the drivers of most monitoring regimes.

The Contract As the Framework for Monitoring

The basis for monitoring is already established if good analysis work was done on requirements and schedule preparatory to issuing the RFP and if the requirements and schedule issues were included in contract negotiations and found their way to exhibits in the contract. Monitoring the vendor should start from and be based on the agreements that have been made. Chapter 5 stresses the great advantage in specifying quantitative measures of all service requirements and characteristics, when possible, and it urges that the reporting requirements for each and every service be specified and included in the contract. With these beginnings, the monitoring task is fairly straightforward.

If a monitoring framework was not established in the contract, there is much preliminary work to do in getting this in place. And, there is the additional problem of getting the vendor to agree to what will be monitored and how it will be monitored after the contract has been signed. Clearly your organization will be in a much less favorable position to check up on the vendor if the preliminary work of Chapters 5 and 6 were not done or were not done well.

There is also an informal side of monitoring in outsourcing arrangements that needs to be undertaken. This has to do as much with atmosphere that surrounds the arrangement and the mood of the people involved in it as anything else. Much less formal data gathering methods will be used here. Informal information is gathered by walking around, visits, and in conversations with stakeholders.

Organizing to Manage Monitoring

Either in prior planning on the part of your organization's outsourcing managers or through procedures set up as the outsourcing deal starts, it must be decided in your outsourcing management group:

- Who will check to see that monitoring data is collected in a timely and accurate way.
- Who will gather the monitoring data.
- How the data will be analyzed and by whom.
- How variances or discrepancies will be detected, flagged, and addressed.

Outsourcing project management teams are usually small. Monitoring and data responsibilities should be assigned, but there should also be ample opportunity to share data and analyze the situation in less formal ways.

At regular intervals an assessment of the success of the outsourcing effort should be made. This should start in the outsourcing project management team but ultimately be expanded to senior IT managers, users, and senior organizational managers in a succession of steps after the necessary data and analysis is compiled at lower levels.

In project type work done by a vendor, the broader assessments should logically fall at points in time that correspond to milestones in the project. In process type work done by a vendor, the reviews should be at regularly scheduled intervals and also on an as-needed basis when problems or opportunities arise in the outsourcing arrangement.

Vendor Analyses of Vendor Work

Vendors are often anxious to demonstrate that they are performing well and doing what is required. Many vendors have their own methods for measuring, analyzing, and reporting the work they do. Don't discourage this effort, but don't let vendor data substitute for or supplant your own monitoring efforts.

Vendors are often honest and well-intentioned in these endeavors. But what they measure, how they measure it, how they analyze the data, how they interpret their own data, and how they report the data may not be what you need to determine what is going on in the outsourcing work.

9.2.2 Monitoring Users, Senior Managers, and IT People

Inform user managers and senior managers of the status of outsourcing projects and get their reactions as the project progresses.

Senior Managers

The role of senior management in the ongoing management of an outsourcing deal depends on how large and significant the project is for the organization as a whole and how involved senior managers were at the outset in terms of being motivators or champions of outsourcing. The greater the significance to the organization and the greater the initial involvement of senior managers, the greater is the need to keep them informed and monitor their reactions to what is happening. In very high profile outsourcing projects, invite the senior managers concerned to the most important reviews that are held with users and vendors.

At a minimum, consider regular written status reports to the relevant senior managers with invitations for comments and questions. Clarification and follow-up are especially important if senior managers express concerns about services or progress. When vendor projects are in trouble, senior managers should be invited to reviews so that they can ask questions, collect information first hand, and provide direct input.

User Managers

If vendors are doing process type outsourcing work that supplies services directly to users, develop a monitoring scheme that includes regular monitoring and data submission by and from users. Let users contribute to developing measures and methods of analysis; they typically have more insight into the quality of services where these are delivered to them on a day-to-day basis and users are often in the best position to gauge service effectiveness. Conduct periodic reviews of vendor performance with user managers. Then, communicate user reactions to vendors as part of reviews of vendor performance.

Much information systems project work doesn't produce definitive outputs until the project is complete or nearly completed. Monitor project work done by a vendor as you would project work done by your own IT department. Reviews can be scheduled at the end of particularly important work tasks, and should be scheduled at project milestones. When users interact with vendor people, as in the analysis phase or testing phase of a project, be sure to get user reactions to the project and vendor performance at those junctures. Managing project work is addressed in more detail later in this chapter.

IT People

Since outsourcing often changes the roles of the IT people who remain in your organization from providers of services to monitors of vendor service provision, ongoing monitoring of IT people in their new roles is a good idea. The previous chapter spoke of the need to move IT people into their new roles with training and support, where necessary. Now in the operational phase of the outsourcing project, outsourcing management should keep tabs on the management team making sure the monitoring and control functions assigned to team members are being carried out. Other IT personnel may be working in functions that interface with or use the vendor services provided, as in vendor supplied network services. Monitor the satisfaction and concerns of these IT people for indicators of vendor performance.

9.2.3 Audits

Earlier chapters suggest audits as a method of checking up on the vendor. Audits are also a way of checking up on what the vendor reports. Audits are open to use in any kind of contracting situation for any kind of work. Process work generally produces a continual stream of outputs, and much useful information can be obtained from these. Progress, quality, and cost are more obscure in project work, until the project is completed. For these reasons, audits may be more useful in projects, but shouldn't be ruled out in process work, particularly when behind the scenes capabilities are not transparent, as in disaster, back-up, and recovery capabilities.

9.2.4 Risk Management and Monitoring the Environment

Monitor the outsourcing environment to manage the risks of outsourcing. This is a more vital concern in intermediate and partnership type outsourcing than it is market relationships.

- The environment is monitored for signs that the underlying assumptions of the outsourcing deal are no longer true.
- If changes in basic circumstances are foreseen, analyze their impact on the service needs of the organization.
- If the need for services indicates the assumptions on which the outsourcing deal is built are changed, determine how vendor services must be changed to meet the new circumstances.
- Then determine whether these changes are within the bounds of the present contract or not.
- If they are, realign what the vendor does with the changed needs if the cost of change is less than the additional benefits of change.
- If not, estimate the costs of renegotiating the contract (which may include termination charges in the old contract) and operating under a new contract and compare these to the magnitude of the benefits that can be gained by making the change.

If vendor services need to be adjusted, but the adjustment is not within the terms of the contract, the vendor can put you in an uncomfortable bargaining position knowing that you need to make the change and need its consent to do so. This is where cooperation enters.

The business side of environmental change might be most effectively monitored by your planning department or by the managers otherwise charged with tracking the environment. IT management and outsourcing project management can benefit from their observations. Users of the services provided by vendors will also have views on environmental change and how it affects what the vendor delivers.

Information technology monitoring is something that is probably best done by the IT department, and may already be a well-established, ongoing process in your organization. If it is not, and technological change can work changes in your needs and the outsourcing relationship, a technology monitoring function should be set up, even if it is only an additional responsibility added to one or more persons' job descriptions.

Of course consulting help is available. Large amounts of money are spent on information technology assessment each year. There are consulting firms that specialize in these services.

9.2.5 Cost-Effectiveness in Monitoring

Collecting and analyzing data have a cost that is part of the cost of outsourcing management. There are corresponding benefits to monitoring in terms of meeting the goals of the outsourcing initiative and containing risk. Finding the right amount of monitoring effort that balances benefits and costs at the margin is the issue in cost-effectiveness.

The nature of and the size and complexity of the outsourcing deal obviously have a strong influence on the amount of effort to put into monitoring. Several additional considerations follow.

One consideration is the risk your organization is faced with and is willing to bear. Greater time, effort, and money should be put into monitoring if the outsourced functions are critical to good business performance.

Another consideration is the reliability of the vendor. If the vendor is known to be reliable and trustworthy, less can be spent on monitoring. If the vendor is new, unknown, or of dubious reputation, put more emphasis on monitoring.

A third consideration is the type of relationship established with the vendor. In market type relationships, vendors are more likely to perform reliably because there is little or no room to deviate from contractual obligations or potential for disagreement over performance. The legal sword hangs over their head for nonperformance. This is not an invitation to neglect monitoring in market-type relationships, but merely to acknowledge that less effort may be necessary. Intermediate and partnership type relationships pose more unknowns and more uncertainty and more opportunity for vendor opportunism. Typically, more effort must be put into monitoring in these situations.

Furthermore, the cost-effective quantity of monitoring may vary over the life of an outsourcing deal. It may be a good strategy to monitor rigorously at the outset of an outsourcing arrangement in order to send clear signals to the vendor on standards and expectations. This stance might be relaxed later when it's clear the vendor has the message and is in compliance with your standards and expectations.

9.3 CONTROL

Where monitoring indicates an aspect of the outsourcing arrangement that is not meeting the standards and criteria established to assure project success, outsourcing management needs to bring the project back in line through control activities. Control is usually approached by:

- First, discovering the nature of the problem that causes performance to deviate from the desired standards.
- Second, investigating and coming to conclusions about the underlying cause of the problem.
- Third, thinking through possible solutions to the problem and choosing the best one.
- Finally, implementing the solution that brings the process back in line with desired standards.

The obvious difference in control activities in an outsourcing context, compared to control within the walls of your own organization, is the need to exercise control across the interface with another organization. At one level this makes your problem easier because it's the vendor organization that has to investigate the problem, find a solution, and implement it. All you have to do is point out the fact that a problem exists. But at another level the problem is more difficult because you don't have direct control over how the vendor investigates and analyzes the problem or how the vendor attempts to solve the problem. You may also lack control over the time in which the problem is resolved.

9.3.1 The Contract as the Basis of Control and Its Limitations

Contract provisions on standards to be met and vendor commitment to these are the obvious starting points for control.

Having stressed the importance of the contract, it should also be apparent that contracts won't solve every control issue. There can be disagreements over measurement and what the data show (although careful construction of quantitative measures of performance will minimize disagreements). Contracts can't realistically speak to the details of how particular problems are resolved. Vendors can use methods and go for quick fixes that wouldn't pass muster in your own organization; they can utilize resources that you see as inferior; they can make changes that don't squarely address the goals of the project; and they can stall problem solving or only resolve part of the problem while maintaining that everything is now back in line. In other words, there can be real and honest differences or real and somewhat dishonest differences of opinion between your managers and vendor managers over how the vendor controls problems.

Furthermore, in devising control systems in your own organization, you would probably want to put control activity close to where the work is being done. Decentralizing control is best because problems are caught by the people doing the work, who can correct it immediately, and who will hopefully avoid the problem in the future. The control system exercised through a vendor moves detection of problems and resolution of problems outside your organization with consequent delay and the potential for misunderstanding and miscommunication.

Simply sticking to the letter of the law laid down in a contract may still not give the kind of performance needed. Like unions that sometimes put pressure on management by working to the rules as a way of actually slowing down work rather than expediting it, a vendor that works strictly to the rules laid down in a contract may not give the service required.

Other situations will arise that involve problems with performance not addressed by the contract. Control is much more difficult in these circumstances because any actions you ask of the vendor will probably increase the vendor's costs and may well be resisted by the vendor for this reason. Furthermore, you are dependent on the vendor, the vendor knows it, and the vendor might be tempted to take advantage of the situation. Certainly the vendor holds the upper hand in bargaining over these issues if the contract is ambiguous or doesn't address the issue at hand.

When viewed over time, a contract cannot always address the need for change, particularly in nonmarket type contracts and contracts that last for longer periods. Whenever changing needs and changing circumstances move requirements a bit beyond what the contract stipulates, you are in uncharted territory where controlling the vendor is concerned.

So control of vendor work through contracts alone has inherent limitations and costs. Many of these are not encountered with work in your organization or are not as severe when the work is done inside the boundaries of your organization.

Therefore, for all but pure market-type relationships, control rests on two pillars — the contract and a good working relationship with the vendor, also known as cooperation.

9.3.2 Balance in Controls

There are issues of cost-effectiveness and balance in control systems:

- Control activity always involves a cost to your organization, or the vendor organization, or both.
- Control should not be exercised for the sake of control but should be clearly aimed at achieving the objectives of the project.
- Controls have short-run effects and long-run effects and these need to be sorted out.
- Control efforts almost always have diminishing returns so that each additional increment of control effort yields less and less in the way of improvements.

When control is exercised through a vendor, add the issue of balance in the relationship with the vendor. Going easy on the vendor in the short run may lead the vendor to slack off in the long run. Putting a lot of pressure on the vendor to perform in the short run, where the vendor sees its performance as already meeting the terms of the agreement, can lead to a hardened vendor stance on other issues over which client and vendor disagree in the future.

9.4 MOTIVATING THE VENDOR AND COOPERATION

A control system should motivate the vendor to do the right thing (provide excellent service to your organization within the costs and conditions set out in the outsourcing agreement). Three fundamental motivational levers are available:

- The vendor actively shares your goals and strives for them.
- The vendor does the right thing to avoid sanctions.
- The vendor does the right thing because you force the vendor to do so through recourse to the courts.

Again, some will argue that vendors never have the same motivation as clients. Clients want good service at a fair price; vendors want profits. The two are in fundamental opposition at one level. But, at other levels, the choice of an appropriate vendor and a good structuring of the relationship with the vendor can help bring vendor goals in alignment with client goals. The client understands that the vendor is an ongoing business concern in a service industry with a reputation to make and defend and the need to make a profit. The vendor understands the client's outsourcing goals and how these relate to its business.

9.4.1 Motivating the Vendor

The motivation issues in this section apply to all types of vendor relationships — market, intermediate, and partnership. However, sanctions are not appropriate for ongoing, successful partnerships (although they may be employed in partnerships that are falling apart).

The best vendor motivation comes from bringing the vendor's goals into alignment with the goals of your organization through incentives and tying outsourcing service requirements to the performance of your organization at the level of business functioning and success. Requirements statements can specify how each requirement fits in your organization's business context and how fulfillment of each requirement supports organizational business goals and functions. Give the vendor an understanding of the business reasons and rationale for the requirement, as well as the letter and law of the requirement itself. With this understanding the vendor has the factual basis for making a connection between your business goals and its outsourcing services.

Additional steps that can be taken toward structuring a good relationship with a vendor and motivating the vendor to do the right thing are:

- Establishing good personal relationships with vendor managers — ones in which they know you are depending on them and have faith in them and are confident in their ability to deliver the goods.

- Letting the vendor firm know that it can expect future work and may even be made a preferred candidate for future work contingent on doing good work on the current outsourcing deal (the implication being that there will be no future work if current work is not good).

- Letting the vendor firm know the ways in which you can spread the word of its good work and your willingness to do so (the implication being that you will spread the word of its bad work if the vendor does not perform).

Positive motivation on the part of the vendor is preferable to negative motivation or the threat of punishment. But punishment has its place in motivation schemes. Contracts should contain consequences for nonperformance, and if necessary, the vendor should be reminded of these. If the contract omits sanctions there is little you can do except threaten to sully a vendor's reputation and deny the vendor future business with your organization.

As a last resort the vendor is forced to perform, by taking the vendor to court. This is the least desirable motivational tool and is to be exercised only after all other approaches fail. The reasons are fairly obvious. Litigation is costly; litigation is usually lengthy (during which time services to your organization presumably suffer); litigation will probably irreparably damage the relationship with the vendor making it very difficult if not impossible to get back to a good working relationship. Litigation is the last resort.

9.4.2 Cooperation in Intermediate and Partnership Contracts

In intermediate and partnership type contracts, much more cooperation on the part of the vendor is needed than in market contracts, because adjustments will be necessary that couldn't be foreseen at the time the contract was negotiated. When your needs change and the contract doesn't cover the change, you are dependent on the vendor to adjust. The vendor could take an opportunity like this, which creates a substantial bargaining advantage for it, to make you pay more for the change than is otherwise reasonable or delay the change or not make the change at all. The vendor has you at a substantial disadvantage.

On the other hand circumstances will arise in which the vendor's environment changes and it will need adjustments from you.

The fact that both parties will need changes from time-to-time sets the stage for cooperation, but doesn't guarantee it. If one party needs a favor and doesn't get the favor, it may be motivated to retaliate when the second party comes later with a request. Cooperative acts lead to more cooperative acts. Uncooperative acts can lead to a spiral of reprisals.

Obviously you need to build a cooperative relationship with the vendor in intermediate and partnership-type contracting situations, but you don't want to be taken advantage of by a vendor. A vendor might cooperate in a succession of instances, but extract an increasingly high price from you in terms of reciprocal acts on your part. The vendor fears that you might play the same game.

Furthermore, one side will typically have more information about a need and the circumstances that surround it than the other side. The same is true of the costs of meeting needs. The side with more information on some issue might hide part of it or misrepresent it to inflate the value or diminish the cost of some proposed action. Disagreements can arise over what information means, even when it is presented openly and honestly.

Total honesty and open sharing of information on both sides seems the best policy for a client and vendor both motivated to cooperate without playing opportunistic games. But how do you know the vendor is honest when it says it is honest. And how does the vendor know you're telling the truth?

As an outsourcing arrangement progresses, both sides will be involved in an interrelated strategy of trying to figure out what the other side intends by what it is doing and how to respond. No techniques can be prescribed that guarantee cooperation, but certain approaches have more promise of success than others.

First and most obviously, unrelenting negative and uncooperative behavior on either side will doom all chances of working together to make adjustments in a cooperative way. The parties have only the contract and the courts to fall back on.

Second, the tit-for-tat strategy from Chapter 6 often works. Presume cooperation on the part of the vendor and reward cooperative acts by the vendor with cooperative acts on your part. But if the vendor fails to cooperate, then retaliate. Cooperation follows cooperation, and retaliation follows noncooperation.

Third, the tit-for-tat strategy can be fine-tuned a bit by clearly communicating your promises of cooperation contingent on the vendors' cooperation and your threats of retaliation if the vendor does not cooperate. In other words, clearly communicate your strategy and intentions so there is no guessing on the part of the vendor about your strategy. Knowing the other's strategy (if it is believable) cuts down the second-guessing and games that otherwise can be played (Scott, 1987).

Another variation is not to retaliate immediately when retaliation is called for. Delay it or implement it gradually, giving the other side an opportunity to make amends for noncooperative behavior. But don't delay retaliation consistently; to do so undermines the vendor's belief in your strategy. An extension of the leniency approach is to teach by example and forgive a transgression (once?) in the hopes of teaching a lesson.

Cooperation is fundamental to partnerships, and the next chapter addresses these issues. A cooperative relationship is also conducive to good dispute resolution, which is the topic of the next section.

9.5 DISPUTES AND DISPUTE RESOLUTION

A contract with clear provisions and requirements is a powerful force for avoiding disputes. Monitoring, which effectively spots potential problems before they happen or catches them while they are still small and can easily be handled, is another. Still others are:

- A good working relationship with the vendor characterized by cooperation.
- Good personal relationships between outsourcing managers in client and vendor firms free of personal antagonisms.

- Good control and accountability in the outsourcing relationship.
- Adequate time and resources — in other words an outsourcing deal that is realistic from both sides. For example, the vendor's price is realistic for the work to be accomplished.

Despite attempts to ward it off, a certain amount of conflict is to be expected. Except for the simplest and most straightforward marketing type relationships, there can be conflict for many reasons, including the following:

- Unexpected contingencies not addressed in the contract will arise.
- One or both parties will leave something out of the contract by mistake or omission.
- Things will go wrong if they can go wrong (Murphy's Law).
- One party will make assumptions not shared by the other party.
- Vendors (and even clients) will be opportunistic at times.

9.5.1 Approaches to Dispute Resolution

Basic approaches to resolving conflict include persuasion, bargaining, resort to third parties, and problem solving (Dant and Schul, 1992).

In persuasion, one side tries to get the other party to adopt its goals or a subset of its goals, or it promotes a move to common goals. Maintaining quality standards might be an example in which the client tries to convince the vendor that their disagreement over quality in the development of a system has long-run consequences for the vendor, since the two parties have also contracted to have the vendor maintain the system.

Bargaining occurs when the game truly is zero sum. When one side wins, the other side loses. Bargaining situations tend to be resolved through power or the domination of one party over the other or by sharing rules. In sharing, the parties might split the difference in some ratio in each dispute or engage in sequential sharing where one party gets the gains in this dispute and the other party gets the gains in the next dispute.

Third-party solutions involve going to mediation, arbitration, minicourts, or real courts. The contract should have an escalation provision with an end point in some alternative dispute resolution process involving a third party. Mediation or arbitration or minicourt processes are vastly preferable to going to the courts where the lawyers will get rich and the dirty laundry will be hung out for the world to see. As mentioned above, outsourcing relationships don't tend to go well in the wake of a court battle.

Problem solving occurs when there is potential for creating value for both parties in a dispute; the game is not zero sum. The discussion of dispute resolution mechanisms in the previous chapter outlines the general process to be followed.

9.5.2 Dispute Resolution Mechanism Considerations

Disputes differ and the nature of the conflict underlying a dispute varies from case to case. There is no one mechanism or formula that works to resolve all disputes. Instead creativity and a willingness to come to a resolution must be used to find a way. Here are some considerations:

- Be sure full information is exchanged in both directions. It's an obvious, but easy, mistake to assume the other side knows what you know. Full communication in both directions is a first step.

- It's better to confront the vendor over some variance or difference rather than hide it. If the vendor misstep was one of commission rather than omission, averting the eyes or turning the other cheek invites further misbehavior. If the misstep was an oversight, the vendor will usually want to be informed. Either way it's best to confront the appropriate person in the vendor organization, raise the issue, and resolve it.

- If the contract contains penalty provisions for poor vendor work, it may be better to apply them rather than agree to accept a vendor credit against future work. A negative cash item as a result of poor performance is more likely to get the attention of higher level vendor managers and is more likely to lead to better vendor work in the future.

- Try to resolve routine issues at the lowest rung of the escalation process. This often saves time and resources and it helps preserve a cooperative relationship between client and vendor people. Nothing breaks down cooperation quicker than disputes that can't be worked out and have to be referred on to others for resolution. Regardless of how the difference is ultimately resolved, the people on both sides who first engaged each other in the dispute will tend to see winners and losers and be a lot more wary of the other party in the future. DuPont tries to settle disputes at the lowest possible level with its vendors, CSC and Andersen Consulting. Riggs Bank in its outsourcing deal with IBM tries to resolve all disputes at the CIO-project executive level or lower. Only when this fails are disputes taken to an executive council consisting of bank officers and vendor senior executives.

- On the other hand, very important problems with vendor performance that seriously disrupt your business should be referred to vendor senior management very rapidly. Reserve this action for the truly important problems.

- Linking two issues or linking two disputes sometimes helps resolve both. For example, disputes often occur in outsourcing over which services are in the contract and which are not (with the vendor wanting extra charges for services it views as not covered contractually). Good analysis of needs and contractual specification of these services would prevent these disputes. But if they occur, it might be possible to reach agreement by conceding on one in exchange for the other side conceding on another.

- When a performance issue arises look for ways to resolve it that will redesign a process so that the problem can't reoccur in the future.

- Speed in the solution of a dispute is often of great concern to the client, but of less concern to the vendor. This asymmetry can work against the client in a resolution giving the vendor some power it otherwise would not have. This might be nullified by delays in payment on the client's part or slow down in resolution of other things of interest to the vendor. Again, linking issues might help resolve both.

- The focus should be on interests, not positions, but sometimes one party or the other will get stuck in a position from which it's hard to back away without losing face. Money issues are often of this type and too easily become a zero sum game from the perspective of one side or the other. Avoid putting specific money proposals on the table immediately; rather frame proposals in more general terms. To find possible solutions, try widening the framework to include outcomes that contain more than money (like changes in future expectations and performance).

- Be watchful of managers on either side who are developing personal antagonisms toward the opposite side as a result of disputes. Allowing personal issues to enter adds an unnecessary complication. Get a more neutral third party to represent you in communication with the vendor over hotly contested issues, if necessary. Urge vendor senior management to change interface personnel if emotions seem to blind the vendor managers who interact with you in a dispute.

- Watch out for padding of proposals on either side with demands whose real purpose is to up the ante with the hope of winning a concession or bigger concession from the other side. Raising the stakes is a game that usually leads away from solutions, not towards them. Look for ways to create solutions rather than fortify positions.

- Document the poor service that is the source of your side of the dispute. Good documentation will be necessary if the dispute is escalated to higher levels.

- Treat the other side with respect. It's easier to accept an offer if it's made sincerely and with deference than with contempt.

- Train your outsourcing managers and IT personnel who interface with the vendor in the rudiments of dispute resolution. Instruct them to report disagreements with the vendor to the outsourcing project management team immediately. Give help and support in resolving disputes quickly and at the lowest operational or management level possible.

- The vendor probably has a lot more experience with litigation of outsourcing disputes than you do and knows the costs of litigation (financial and to the relationship) better than you. Don't assume you are on level ground here, and get good experienced-in-outsourcing counsel if you do move in the direction of litigation.

9.5.3 Managing Dispute Resolution Over Time

Dispute resolution has a temporal component. As the outsourcing relationship progresses, persons resolving the current dispute will look back to how previous disputes were resolved. Patterns will evolve:

- There may be a pattern in the persons involved in dispute resolution. Perhaps two people, one on the vendor side and one on the client side, have a good personal relationship and are particularly adept at resolving disputes.

- There may be a pattern in the source of the underlying conflict. Perhaps one or a few systems functions or one or a few contract requirements spark most of the conflict and some adjustment needs to be made in the agreement to prevent future conflict. Identify and fix the underlying problem so that disputes don't continue over this issue.

- There may be a pattern in who pays the costs of resolving a dispute. Perhaps issues are resolved by splitting the difference or taking turns so that the client absorbs the extra cost first, then the vendor, then the client, and so on.

On the other hand, bad patterns may develop in disputes. For example, personal relationships may sour across the line between client and vendor as one dispute follows another. One side or the other may move more quickly to escalation. A progression toward hardened positions and unwillingness to compromise may develop.

Try to sidetrack, correct, or reverse the bad patterns. Look for good patterns and use them to avoid future disputes or improve the way in which disputes are resolved. Since it's not always possible to create a win-win solution to a dispute, develop patterns that allow fair sharing of costs in disputes over time, like splitting the difference or taking turns.

Having said the good and appropriate things to do in conflict and dispute resolution, it has to be recognized that conflict and disputes have their gritty realities and dark undersides. One involves vendor opportunism and a consistent pattern of disputes that reveal a vendor strategy that tries to take advantage of the client. Good faith may be lacking. There is little to do except use the disciplinary powers at your disposal in terms of the contract and its sanctions, doing damage to the vendor's reputation, and the refusal to enter another contract with the same vendor. Termination of the contract is a last resort and is addressed in the last chapter.

Another reality is the use of power in disputes. As mentioned before, either the client or the vendor can have more power in an outsourcing relationship than the other. Power can be used in disputes to get one's way, and outsourcing disputes are no exceptions.

Use of power to force a resolution that is win-lose or very imbalanced has a cost. The cost is the increased wariness and decreased lack of trust experienced by the losing side. The fallout may be a greater willingness to escalate the conflict the next time, a greater willingness to go to the courts, a greater willingness to terminate the contract, and a great reluctance to enter into a contract with the same party in the future. In market-type contracting relationships the future costs may not be burdensome. In partnerships these costs, if they continue, will wreck the relationship. The next chapter on partnerships addresses these concerns in more detail.

9.6 MANAGING PROJECT TYPE OUTSOURCING WORK

Project type outsourcing work should be managed with project-type methods. Systems development work or any other project type work is amenable to these methods.

The extent to which information systems development work is complete is notoriously difficult to judge. The report that "we're 90 percent done" repeated week after week is a syndrome familiar to many software development organizations. When you hand over total responsibility for development of a system to a vendor, regular status reporting is a must if you are to have any idea of where a project stands.

A schedule for the project should have been set as part of the contracting process. The contract should specify a review process and intermediate deliverables. If the contract does not, this is the first order of business as the arrangement starts up. Get some firm commitments from the vendor on schedule.

9.6.1 Reviews

The vendor should be managed, as all good projects are managed, by frequent checks on progress relative to the schedule. Several levels of review are necessary:

- The first is weekly or bi-weekly status checks in which the vendor reports on progress and problems.
- The second is milestone or major events — like the end of each major phase of the project.
- The third is sign-off or acceptance on the part of your organization of vendor intermediate products and the final system.

The personnel who should be present in reviews varies with the nature of the review and the stage of the project:

- Regular weekly or bi-weekly reviews should be attended by the vendor manager responsible for the project and vendor personnel involved in key tasks in progress. People attending from your organization should include the person with overall responsibility for managing the outsourcing project. For larger projects, your managers responsible for overseeing vendor work from the applications side and/or the technical side may also be present, depending on the nature of the work at the time. A user representative or representatives should also attend when what the vendor has to report concerns the requirements of the system.
- Milestone event reviews are bigger meetings attended by all managers concerned with the project from both client and vendor sides. Application and technical experts should also attend, as should user representatives. For really big projects and/or those with particular business significance, you should invite the senior managers who champion the project to participate in the milestone review.

- Sign-off and acceptance reviews are attended by the highest level managers that have an interest in the project from the client and vendor sides. This should include the senior managers of the project from both client and vendor organizations and user managers and the senior manager champion of the project if the project is a significant one.

Although higher level managers won't attend the lowest level review meetings, keep them informed in writing on progress and problems so that they develop a familiarity with the project as it unfolds.

The active participation of representatives and/or managers at higher levels in higher level reviews is necessary for two reasons. First, it keeps the important players informed and up-to-date on progress and problems. Avoiding surprises and setting expectations is the outcome of their involvement. When systems are developed in your own organization, management of expectations is critical to gaining acceptance and development of understanding. Since formal communication with the vendor takes place largely through the review process, reviews are the mechanism for getting buy-in and setting and resetting expectations when a project is outsourced.

Second, when schedule slips or budgets are overspent, as they sometimes do in projects, you need the active involvement of managers who can make the tough trade-offs and decisions on how to move forward. If the higher level managers who must make these decisions are out of the loop and don't know what has been happening in the project, you have a steep hill to climb in bringing them up to speed and getting their understanding and acceptance of the need for trade-offs.

9.6.2 Problems

Look for variances in what the vendor is doing against the project plan. This can't be accomplished without adequate information from the vendor. Again, the contract should specify what the vendor brings to reviews in the way of information. If these requirements are absent in the contract, work out an up-front agreement with the vendor as the project starts on how reviews will be conducted, including the information to be presented.

You can supplement the formally presented vendor information with your own independent observations on what the vendor is doing and how things are going. This is more easily done if vendor people are working at your site. If you must travel to the vendor to observe, this avenue may not be open to you, unless you have allowed for this in the contract. Even if access to the vendor's people at work is limited, your own users and application and technical people are in contact on issues as they arise. Use these opportunities to gather information on how things are going from the vendor side. Set up a system to gather information from your own people. Bring up any possible problems that may exist at the next regular review meeting.

Warning signs of problems are the same signals that fly when projects start to degrade in your own organization. These include issues like:

- Vendor staff assignment delays or problems in assigning persons with the proper skills.
- Schedules that slip.
- Signs that the vendor is spending more on the project that it anticipated, perhaps evidenced by attempts to limit changes that seem to be within scope or to impose excess charges that don't seem warranted.
- Difficulties with interfaces between the project system and other existing systems with which it must work.
- Difficulties in keeping up with routine tasks, like documentation.
- Problems getting new technology to work or problems with getting one technology to work together with another technology.
- Major problems at any of the test stages.

Taking Steps to Correct Problems

Nip problems in the bud. Address them as they arise. Taking the attitude that problems are the vendor's for the vendor to resolve is a big mistake. It does your organization little good if the system is ultimately late or the budget balloons in ways that necessitate the vendor coming back to you for more money or system quality is compromised.

Reviews should identify problems, and each review should conclude with agreement on action items to be taken up by either client or vendor and a schedule for their accomplishment. When issues need clarification or problems surface, be certain that steps are identified to rectify the situation and responsibilities are assigned. Put action items in writing and have them signed or initialed by client and vendor managers.

9.6.3 Change Control

If change control procedures were not outlined in the contract, get agreement on these early on, as the project starts. The contract should allow for some change, as change in projects is inevitable. When requirements can't be completely known in advance, expect a lot of change and allow for more of it in the contract.

Changes usually arise from users, but changes also come from IT application or technical people who realize as the project progresses that its scope did not sufficiently address various factors in the system's environment.

The change control process is usually one in which client project management submits written requests for changes to vendor project management. The vendor won't normally accept changes without review. When changes are within the scope of the contract, vendor approval should be routine.

Larger changes and changes that are outside the scope of the contract should be reviewed by a joint client-vendor change control committee. The committee's function and responsibilities are several:

- The committee serves the same filtering function as change control procedures when undertaken inside your own organization. It determines which of the legitimate changes submitted to it should be done, which should not be done (perhaps because they don't contribute sufficiently to project benefit or would delay project schedule unduly), and which should be delayed to a later date (including a date after project implementation).

- The joint committee reviews changes that are outside original project scope as a first step to deciding whether the scope should be changed and the contract renegotiated. Out-of-scope changes might arise from government regulations promulgated while the project is in process, or from unforeseen changes in the competitive environment, or from simple oversight in the original scope definition and feasibility study. The change control committee determines that the change is out of scope and passes its findings on to higher project management and ultimately to the upper managers in charge of the project in both client and vendor organizations. Out-of-scope changes accepted by both sides will normally require renegotiation of the contract and additional compensation to the vendor.

- The committee surfaces disagreements between client and vendor on change requests that fall inside the scope of the project from the client's view but outside the scope of the project where the vendor is concerned. If the project requirements were defined with some rigor as part of the RFP and contract negotiation process, these disputes shouldn't arise or shouldn't arise very often. When they do, the facts of the case can be documented by the change review committee and passed on to the dispute resolution mechanisms set up for this purpose.

When the change control committee finds a change that should be done, it also judges and passes on the technical feasibility of the change. If the vendor is compensated by some variable pricing mechanism, the change control committee also makes a determination of the costs associated with the change so that these are mutually agreed upon, documented, and authorized.

9.7 MANAGING THE OUTSOURCING RELATIONSHIP: AN INTERVIEW WITH MICHAEL F. CORBETT

Michael F. Corbett is president of Michael F. Corbett & Associates, Ltd. Mr. Corbett has been recognized as an expert witness on outsourcing by the President of the United States and has advised senior executives from the world's largest organizations, such as, GlaxoWellcome, NASD, Mercedes-Benz, and Pacific Enterprises. He has been referred to by *Fortune* as "the nation's leading authority on outsourcing," and has been featured on CNBC's Technology Edge, CIO and CFO Magazines, Investor's *Business Daily*, and *The Wall Street Journal*.

Mr. Corbett's work at IBM in the late 1980s helped lead to the creation of ISSC — today the largest provider of outsourcing services in the world. In 1993, he cofounded The Outsourcing Institute, recognized as the leading professional association for networking on the topic of outsourcing. In 1996, Mr. Corbett formed his current company, a strategic outsourcing consultancy providing training, advisory services, and information products for managers and executives.

Mr. Corbett has lectured to thousands of executives around the world and his writings include numerous articles, reports, and studies, as well as three major management briefs on outsourcing published in *Fortune* Magazine from 1994 through 1996.

How has your interest in outsourcing developed over time?

I actually began work on outsourcing in the late 1980s while with IBM. I was asked to put together a strategy to expand IBM's software services business. As that strategy unfolded, it became clear that there was an enormous opportunity to leverage the company's expertise and resources to play a more direct role in designing, setting up, and operating corporatewide systems for IBM's largest customers. IBM's landmark contract in 1989 with KODAK was the direct outgrowth of this thinking — and one of the first highly visible outsourcing deals.

From 1989 through 1993, I continued to study and report this trend for Frost & Sullivan, then a New York-based market research firm. In 1993, I cofounded The Outsourcing Institute, the first professional association dedicated to the topic. Most recently I've formed a training, consulting, and market research firm, Michael F. Corbett & Associates, which is dedicated to advancing outsourcing as a management discipline.

What is managing the outsourcing relationship? Why is it important?
When I talk about managing the outsourcing relationship, I'm referring to the entire set of people, processes, tools, and systems that are needed to make the relationship work. It is important because it is everything the company needs to do to make certain that the value is realized from the contract. It's all the things that companies do today to manage internal activities — just refocused and recrafted for success in this new outsourced world.

On the surface, this seems very simple and straightforward. Is it really a problem and, if so, why is it a problem?
It is a problem and the reason is that until recently, outsourcing was viewed primarily as a transaction, a contract to be signed, results to be booked in the business. Management of the relationship was an afterthought. And this is a real problem. The work of outsourcing only begins when the contract is signed. To be successful, the relationship must be managed from the first to the last day of the contract. Without ongoing management, the relationship will fail.

The problem is a result of flawed thinking on the part of the managers involved. The first problem is that managers often confuse outsourcing with abdicating. Successful management of outsourcing contracts requires the same energy, enthusiasm, and professionalism found in good management anywhere. The second issue is that managers often fail to realize that outsourcing contracts require a very different style of management. They demand new thinking, new skills, new approaches, new techniques, and new measures of success. The fundamentals of good management don't change but the way these fundamentals are executed change a great deal.

At the same time, managing outsourcing relationships is not rocket science. It is simply the systematic application of sound management principals — establishing goals, monitoring performance, taking corrective action, creating an environment that fosters continuous improvement and peak performance. The way this is done is what changes.

How about an example of this?
Sure. Within any well-run company, management systems define how day-to-day operations are monitored, how exceptions are identified, and how corrective actions get initiated and followed through. These systems define who's responsible for what, what represents doing a good job, and the resources and tools available to get the job done. These same things have to happen when a company outsources. What is different is that it is probably the provider's systems that now have to identify the exceptions and it is probably their people who have to initiate the corrective action. Then, resources from both companies may

be required to fix a problem and managers from both companies may need to follow through to make sure a fix holds and that the problem isn't repeated. As you can already tell, outsourcing produces a more complex environment. A much larger pool of resources is available, but this also demands communications, coordination, and sense of shared risk and reward. This is not easy to do in companies that have always operated as self-sufficient, vertically integrated businesses.

Why is managing the relationship so important?

It is simply a question of ensuring maximum value from an organization's investments and world-class services for its customers. Once a company outsources, the new relationship becomes a critical company asset — a critical resource in which the organization has invested. World-class service for the customer can now only be achieved if the intended services are delivered by the provider — in the way they were intended. In effect, the outsourcing service provider becomes as integral to the business's success as were the previous in-house resources.

These simple facts mean that it is only through the management of the relationship that the intended value can be realized. The contract provides a framework for dispute resolution. It adds protection in the most extreme eventualities. But the contract does not, in and of itself, create value for the company or services for its customers. People do, and it is person-to-person management of the relationship that makes the right things happen at the right time. Nothing else. I would go so far as to say, outsourcing is relationship management, pure and simple.

When does this management process begin?

Technically, the management of the relationship can't begin until there is a relationship. So, it starts, technically, when the contract is signed. But, the foundation upon which successful management is built is laid well before then. It begins when the company contemplating outsourcing begins to communicate with potential providers about what it is looking for and how it intends to create a management system to ensure success. This is at least as early as the request for proposal, but should be sooner.

The stage for successful management is set at the very beginning. In the way the requirements are defined. The way the goals and how they will be measured are described. The way the vendor is chosen. The way the contract is written. The way people are selected, in both companies, to manage the contract. The systems that are built to support their activities. The role played by senior management in both companies. The way continuous improvement is defined and expected. In effect, the management actually begins on day one.

Let me give you one example of this, and it is something I know we'll get back to later. I believe that one of the most important parts of the foundation for managing the contract is its pricing formulation. After all, think about it; the way the provider is compensated says volumes about how the customer intends to measure the value of the services received and this goes a long way in defining how the relationship is managed. And, there are a wide range of pricing formulations being tried — some which work well and some which, in my opinion, cause ongoing relationship management problems.

At the one end is pricing based strictly on some unit of work — people, hours, items, computer seconds — multiplied by an agreed to rate per unit. In effect, the customer is paying a specified rate for every unit of input they receive. Now, what happens to this relationship over time? Well, let's look at the motivations of the parties. If no other considerations are worked into the compensation formula, then the provider is motivated over time to maximize profit by driving down their internal cost per unit and driving up the number of units the customer utilizes. The customer's motivation, if anything, is exactly the opposite. The customer wants to see continuous reduction in the cost per unit and continuous improvement in throughput, i.e., in their ability to get more work done with less units of input. The customer and the provider have created a relationship where their interests diverge from day one. Everything else being equal, it will become increasingly difficult to manage this relationship as time goes by as the differences in the parties interests become increasingly apparent. Things may look good at first, but over time a rift will almost always develop and all the good management applied may not be able to overcome the flawed foundation upon which the relationship was built.

On the other hand, let's look at a contract based upon a pricing formulation that focused not on inputs, but on outputs, upon the business value actually realized by the customer through the use of the provider's services. There are lots of examples of this. Duke University Medical Center and Baxter International share 50/50 in cost savings the hospital realizes from Baxter's services. They also share 50/50 in covering any cost overruns. In other words, both parties have to be successful for either to realize their anticipated returns. It is much easier in this environment for the two parties to successfully manage the relationship — the pricing formulation has ensured that their interests continue in locked step as the years go by.

Are there approaches, best practices if you like, that are common among successful companies and their management teams?
Absolutely. When I've looked at companies that are particularly successful in managing their outsourcing contracts, I find seven characteristics. To me, these seven best practices represent the state-of-the-art in managing outsourcing relationships. Companies that apply these practices will be successful, those that do not, do so at their own peril.

1. **Objective Performance Criteria Are Negotiated, Measured, and Reviewed**

   Successful outsourcing relationships focus on results not resources. To be meaningful, these results must be objective, that is measurable in quantifiable terms, and must be compared against preestablished criteria. It is only through comparison to objective performance criteria that the customer knows that they are receiving the anticipated benefits and that the vendor knows that they are meeting their customer's expectations.

   The specific performance criteria will differ depending upon the type of services being provided, the customer requirements, and the level of service the customer is prepared to pay for. Properly defined performance criteria for an outsourcing engagement do, however, have the following characteristics:

   - Objective, quantifiable, and collectible at a reasonable cost.
   - Service quantities, costs, and quality as well as customer satisfaction with the services, business value (not just technical measures of the process itself), and continuous improvement are included.
   - Benchmark service requirements against other organizations and providers.

2. **Formal Relationship Management Structure**

   A formal, typically multilevel, relationship management structure exists linking the customer and their vendor. The outsourcing relationship requires its own management structure to replace the previous internal management systems. This new structure typically takes the form of joint management teams. The team, or teams in the case of larger contracts, have responsibility for day-to-day, tactical, and strategic aspects of the relationship. Each team has a clearly defined responsibility, agenda, frequency of meetings, and relationship to the other teams.

   Identification, resolution and rapid escalation of issues is a key responsibility of each team. Problems are not permitted to fester and the goal of all team members is to ensure the success of the relationship through the correction of problems as quickly as possible.

3. **Performance-based Pricing**

   Performance-based pricing ensures that the provider is continuously incented to meet or exceed the stated performance criteria. When performance exceeds the criteria then bonuses apply, when it falls short, there are penalties that impact the provider's profitability.

Similarly, these incentives are translated into performance measures for the individuals on both the vendor and customer side of the relationship. Translating overall performance-based risks and rewards into individual measures maintains the proper focus up and down both organizations.

4. **Internal Training and Communications on Business Goals and Relationship Management**

The individuals responsible for managing the outsourcing relationship for the customer receive specific training on how to do this job. This includes a compete understanding of the business goals of the contract, the specific performance criteria agreed to, and their individual roles, responsibilities, authority, and reporting structure.

Furthermore, this same information is communicated to the larger end-user community. In this way, the entire organization understands what is intended and why, how problems will be identified and resolved, what their communication channels are, what's expected of them, etc. Training and communications are also used to reduce any resentment or resistance that may be present in the customer organization.

5. **Vendor Training on Customer's Business Environment and Goals**

The fifth best practice is training for the vendor's personnel on the customer's business environment and goals. Although the vendor personnel are experts in their field, they require specific, ongoing training on the client's business and its goals. In this way, they develop the needed sensitivity to the issues driving their client's needs and how their services relate to them.

6. **Cultural Normalization**

The culture of an organization reflects its value system, what is and what isn't important. It also establishes norms of behavior and defines the implicit contract between people and to the organization itself. As such, it is a powerful factor in establishing how individuals perform their jobs and how they respond to various situations. The fact that both organizations have, and will continue to have, their own culture is recognized. At the same time, cultural differences are actively identified and bridged.

There are a number of techniques for doing this: informal meetings and social events; education on company heritage and history; rotation of employees between the companies; participation of employees in "internal" meetings of the other firm; participation in the partner's internal improvement programs, such as quality teams; jointly sponsored recognition events, et cetera.

7. Ongoing Exchange of Knowledge and Expertise

The ongoing, free exchange of knowledge and expertise between the companies is a trademark of successful outsourcing engagements. Each partner has their own specialties which when shared, contribute to both the success of the relationship and the success of the partner. Training programs, on-the-job experiences, access to experts, techniques and procedures are all ways this is accomplished. Participation in task forces and improvement teams is another frequently used technique.

Source: Michael F. Corbett & Associates, Ltd.

Can you give some examples of companies that are applying these best practices and how they are working?

Yes, but, I can't say that I've seen all seven fully executed anywhere. I have seen all of them, and frequently more than one, applied in the more successful outsourcing relationships.

Most companies define performance criteria as part of their contract. Some actually collect and report actual performance. And fewer yet, take proactive corrective action and drive toward continual improvement. One powerful example of doing this very well can be found at Duke University Medical Center where logistics for its surgical supplies are now handled by Baxter. The cornerstone of their relationship is specific, continually improving cost targets for the operation, targets that the companies are jointly monitoring and toward which they are working.

McDonnell Douglas established, in advance of signing the contract, a three-tier management structure. It is an excellent example of the second of the seven best practices. At McDonnell Douglas, day-to-day, contract and strategic teams were formed with specific responsibilities, meeting frequencies and escalation paths. That structure proved central to the company's management approach for its $3 billion information technology outsourcing contract.

Performance-based pricing is, in my opinion, key. And these payments should be tied as closely as possible to the results achieved, not just the effort expended. For example, Wisconsin Electric has multiple outsourcing contracts — seven at last count — and for each their director of outsourcing has identified exact criteria to be used in evaluating the providers' performance with quarterly payment adjustments based on those criteria.

Elf Atochem used a very detailed contracting process primarily as a tool for providing internal managers with a mechanism for managing the outsourcing vendor. They wrote the contract in such a way that the responsible managers could fill in the blanks. It showed how to manage the vendor and established performance criteria. There are 15 to 20 performance criteria. They cover such things as how quickly changes are made to systems, the availability of systems, and how quickly problem resolutions are obtained.

All of the leading providers provide ongoing training for their personnel on the customer's business, goals, and objectives. This helps ensure the proper ongoing awareness of what means success to the customer.

Kodak has chosen to manage its outsourcing contracts through its corporate quality program. This helps infuse their quality culture into their outsourcing providers.

Finally, a good example of ongoing exchange of information and expertise between the companies can be found at medical manufacturer Puritan Bennett. The company that did the design work for their next-generation respiratory ventilator also shared with them their design process, helping Puritan learn how to do "fast track" product development. This is an excellent example of the type of ongoing exchange that really helps to ensure a successful relationship.

How about the managers themselves? How do you find, or make, managers that can excel in this environment?

Successful management of outsourcing relationships requires a new breed of managers — or, at least, managers who have developed some new skills.

In 1994 I did a study for The Outsourcing Institute where we surveyed a number of executives to understand how the way they spent their time and the skills that were most critical changed with outsourcing. These were all executives who had managed a function, outsourced, and then managed in the environment. One thing is they were successful in making the transition, which means these are skills that can be learned. I think that the most important characteristics is, in fact, the willingness to change.

If managers who have been successful in managing internal company resources, people, and processes are then asked to achieve the same, or better, results by managing through an outsourcing service provider, they have to not only be willing, but to really want to make the change. And, the change is significant. It's hard not to micro-manage. It requires a new way of thinking. It's difficult sometimes to share success as well as blame, to recognize that both parties have to succeed. It is interesting how deeply our traditional view of outsiders as "work-for-hire contractors" runs. These concepts are ingrained in the thinking of most American managers. And, even if the manager makes the shift, they also have to get their boss and their customers thinking and behaving the same way, or the change won't hold for long.

So, what special skills are required?

In the same study I mentioned a moment ago, we found that the skills that became most important after outsourcing were what I would call general management skills — as opposed to the traditional operational and technical management skills. By the way, these operational and technical management skills were probably the skills that the individual manager had relied on up until outsourcing. This only reinforces how significant a transformation we're talking about.

The first of these general management skills that became increasingly important after outsourcing was negotiation skills. With outsourcing, a manager becomes more a broker, facilitator, and integrator of resources. This is in contrast to the more traditional role of the manager as a planner and director of how the work gets done. Because of this, negotiation skills become central to the manager's — and the outsourcing contract's — success.

We're not just talking about the negotiation that takes place between the manager and the outsourcing service provider at the time the contract is being "negotiated." We're also talking about the negotiation that takes place between the manager and the ultimate customer he or she is trying to serve. We're talking about the ongoing negotiation that takes place each and every day of the contract. Negotiation that continually keeps the services provided in line with the services needed. Negotiation isn't a one-time event that concludes with the contract signing. Negotiation is actually at the heart and soul of outsourcing.

The second skill that jumped up in importance is communications. Outsourcing managers aren't doers anymore, they are communicators. They are the people who create the bridge between the organization's needs and the provider's services. They spend an enormous amount of time communicating with everyone — up and down the line — who has a stake in what is happening and why. Communications is the essence of an emerging model of the manager as a broker and facilitator of needed services.

The third was business skills. The ability to help identify and interpret the business requirements and translate these requirements into services. Strategic, managerial, and tactical thinking is required. Today's problems need to be solved — through the service provider — and tomorrow's needs need to be identified.

The final skills that became more important with outsourcing were financial skills. Traditionally, managers operate within the parameters of an operating budget for current operations. When managers plan outsourcing relationships they often need to completely recast the existing budget to capture all of the costs associated with the services provided. Next they need to evaluate the financial implications of the service provider's proposal. Since outsourcing contracts are typically multiyear, return-on-investment has to be used to understand the total financial payouts and when they occur. The financials have to be monitored and tuned on an ongoing basis. Frequently, there is a level of financial involvement that is new, is at a higher plane than most managers have needed in the past.

Negotiation, communications, business, and financial skills are the skills that are demanded of successful relationship managers.

Was there also a change in how the managers spent their time?
Yes. The amount of time managers spent in operational management activities dropped in half — from 14 percent to 7 percent. The amount of time spent doing resource planning almost fell in half — from 10 percent to 6 percent.

Where did this time go? Exactly where you might expect it to. Strategic and business planning time increased by almost a third — from 20 percent to 26 percent — and outside relationship management time went from 7 percent to 16 percent. All of this is absolutely consistent with the notion of the manager going from a controller of resources to a planner, facilitator, and integrator of solutions.

How many people do you need to manage an outsourcing contract and, if more than one, what are the different roles of the team members?
There will be a lot of people involved on a part-time or periodic basis — executives, end users, specialized staffers. But on a full-time basis I've seen it range from one person or less on small contracts up to tens of people for very large, complex, high-dollar relationships. It also depends on how the contract is structured. For example, the more end-result-oriented the contract is, the more you can rely upon the provider to worry about how the results are achieved, while your company can focus on understanding and communicating its needs. This generally translates into a smaller management team overseeing the relationship. On the other hand, where smaller, more niche-oriented providers have been selected and the customer has maintained much of the integration role, then more staff will likely be required to manage the relationship. Of course, there are other advantages the customer is looking for and so they feel this trade-of is worthwhile.

As for the team members and their responsibilities, there are a few areas of expertise you'll need. First, there needs to be an experienced manager with overall, ultimate responsibility for managing the relationship and ensuring that everything is working properly. Typically, this will be a seasoned manager with the right general management skills. Next, if the services are provided an a distributed basis, then there will probably be local liaisons who report to this overall relationship manager in at least a dotted line relationship. Third, there is a need for retaining expertise in the particular functional area that was outsourced — administration, logistics, manufacturing, technology, finance, or the like. The customer needs to make certain that they continue to have the expertise needed to understand how to translate their business needs into clear, complete, and measurable requirements to be addressed by the service provider. You don't want to give up the expertise needed to understand how excellence at the operational level can be translated into competitive advantage at the business level.

Finally, there is the negotiation, communication, and business skill needed to actually oversee the contract. Collect and review actual performance, review and approve changes in services and scope, monitor end-user satisfaction and drive continuous improvement in all aspects of the relationship — these are some of the skills needed here. And, of course, financial skills are also needed. So, these are the key areas on which members of the oversight team will be focused.

One study found that you require one person for every $20 million dollars of annual contract value for contracts from $5 to $100 million dollars. For contracts over $100 million of annual value, some economies of scale begin to take effect and the number of full-time people involved in managing the relationship will be from six to ten or more.

What's the role of senior management?

Senior management must stay involved. On important relationships, senior management, from both companies must get together on a planned, regular basis to review the health of the relationship and its future direction. There are decisions to make and resources to be committed that only senior management can step up to.

For example, only senior management can assess the ongoing strategy of the provider to determine if the direction and resource investments are consistent with where the customer needs the provider to be going. And only senior management in the provider company can make the necessary commitments of resources and overall company direction. Certain issues that are clearly outside the scope of things considered when the contract was crafted may need senior management involvement.

There is also the issue of ongoing communications within the company. Senior management plays the critical role in making certain that the reasons for and results from outsourcing are communicated across the company. Leadership comes from the top.

Where do end users and other employees fit in?

The end users are the ultimate customers of the outsourcing services being provided, so they play an important role. As customer, they should be an integral part of the feedback process and the process for identifying future needs. In effect, the manager of the outsourcing relationship is the broker and integrator of the services needed by these end users. So, they play a critical, ongoing role.

One way that this should be accomplished is through ongoing surveys of the end user's satisfaction with the services provided. Formal customer satisfaction survey techniques work well here in conjunction with less formal, but sometimes equally valuable, meetings and roundtables. This process may be managed by the provider with results reported by the relationship manager, or both. Also, if the contract is properly structured then you would expect to see incentives and penalties tied to the results achieved and continuous improvement targets or benchmarks against best-in-class industry standards.

As for other employees, who may not be direct customers for the services being provided, communications is still very important. Newsletters, e-mail, intranets, meetings, and other techniques should be used to continually demonstrate the benefits being realized through the services of the outsourcing provider with very candid acknowledgments of problems and what's being done to fix them.

Are there training and tools available to help with all this?
Initial and ongoing training for the people responsible for managing the outsourcing contract is the single most important investment the company can make to help ensure success. This training has to look at both developing the right attitude and the right skills. We've talked a lot about both.

In fact, this where I'm focusing most of my time right now. I believe that the debate is over and that outsourcing is now accepted as a powerful management tool for transforming organizations and driving continuous improvement. The real challenge going forward is whether or not we can train America's managers to be successful in an outsourced world. If we can, then the benefits will continue to be expanded. If we can't, then organizations may well start sliding back into the traditional vertically-integrated approach which would be a real shame for them and for their customers.

As for tools, that is an area where I believe there is a lot of work yet to be done. I've seen some great tools developed by individual organizations, but I've yet to see the types of tools that organizations will need going forward. There are, however, some people working in this area, and I suspect we'll see some products coming to market soon.

Sometimes we learn more from our failures than from our successes. Can you share some of the problems you've seen?
Generally, I would say that problem relationships seldom result in a complete breakdown. What we hear more about is a general sense that the managers and executives involved just don't feel that they are getting as much out of the relationship as they think they should. It's more a realization after a period of time that the value, the real opportunity for synergy between the organizations, just isn't materializing. I'm also hearing of a number of cases where the outsourcing contract is being switched from a large international provider to a smaller local provider.

Both of these scenarios develop from the same cause. And that is, if you view outsourcing as an event as opposed to a process, less-than-needed attention gets paid to the ongoing management. Managing outsourcing relationships — like any good management — is hard work. It requires constant attention. It requires an expectation of continuous improvement and a proactive approach toward achieving it.

Finally, both partners play an equal role here. Providers can't let themselves fall into the trap of viewing outsourcing just in terms of the transaction — the sale. If they put all their energy into winning the business, then drop into maintenance mode until the contract comes up for renewal, they'll probably get a rude awakening. Providers have to make certain that they are managing the relationship with the thought in mind that they have to win that business every single day. If they don't, then someone else will take that business away.

The whole point is, I believe, to bring best-in-world services to the table each and every day. Anything less is simply not acceptable, nor in the best interest of either party.

As far as specific examples, that's hard to do without embarrassing those involved. Let it suffice to say that if an organization manages against the seven best practices we talked about earlier, they will be successful in both the short and long term. Where these things aren't happening management has failed to recognize that the relationship is critical and its value will be underrealized.

Do incentives play an important role in achieving the types of behaviors you've been talking about?
Incentives are very important. There's an old saying that what you measure you achieve. Even more, it's what you reward that you achieve.

Just as managers have always had incentives tied to achievement in the traditional model, they now need incentives tied to success in the outsourcing relationship. In one way, we're really not talking about anything new — if the incentives have always been tied to the results achieved. In that case, it is just the way those results have to be achieved that have changed. This is also the preferable approach.

How important is the provider to making the right things happen?
It almost goes without saying that the provider, and especially the account manager assigned to you, is a full partner in making the relationship work.

In fact, you should reserve the right to approve the key people assigned to you as a customer. If problems develop in the relationship, requesting a new account manager is often a first step in bringing focus and some new thinking to the problems.

It goes beyond the account manager, however. Day-to-day activities will require the involvement of many people from both your company and the providers. Managing the health of the overall relationship takes senior management from both companies. So, in the end, it takes a total commitment, on the part of both companies, to make the relationship work.

What if there's a problem and the provider won't respond, regardless of what you try to do?
If the provider won't work with you, that says about all that needs to be said about how they value the long-term relationship. Savvy providers are in this business for the long haul. They realize that their future success is based on ongoing relationships with the right customers. Because of that, I have yet to see a provider simply refuse to respond to issues raised by their customers.

If this does happen, one thing to think about is why won't the provider respond. What are the internal issues that the provider may be having trouble overcoming? What might you be able to do to help? Or, maybe it's an individual problem. Perhaps there's a problem with the account manager who has been assigned to you. Sometimes this person has to be changed as a first step toward making progress. (The contract should always give you the right to request that this person be changed.) Another question to ask might be, are other customers of this provider having the same problems? Go find out. If they are, then a pattern may be developing. If they are not, then what's different? This insight may be very helpful.

Finally, if all else fails then termination of the contract should be considered. The contract itself should define what recourse is available to you. A well structured outsourcing contract should be like a prenuptial. It should define in detail what happens if the relationship is terminated as it defines how the relationship was created and operated. The steps to be taken, the rights and obligations of each party should be well defined. If they aren't, then you're into uncharted territory. Proceed with care and have a plan for all of the scenarios that may develop.

Are there right and wrong ways to end an outsourcing contract?
It's important to think about what happens when outsourcing contracts end. Seldom does the company bring the operation back in-house. It is far more likely that the company will transition from one provider to another or remain with the same vendor. The most critical issue, then, is to ensure that all of the needed intellectual and physical resources are transitioned effectively between the providers. Continuity of services and protection of investments already made are the key issues in this situation.

It's important to keep in mind that how this transition is handled will also set the tone for the new relationship. So it should be done quickly, professionally, and with an eye toward the future.

What do you see on the horizon? What is the future of outsourcing?
First of all, outsourcing is here to stay. It is not just a fad. In fact, I dare say that it will be as natural to the next generation of managers as computers have become to our children. I suspect that these new managers will wonder how, if not why, organizations ever tried to operate with everything in-house. They will see managing outsourcing contracts as just a natural part of what it means to be a manager.

In the mean time, most organizations will need to do some specific things.

The most important is to make specific organizational changes to make the concepts of core competencies and strategic outsourcing a reality. Each core competency should have a specific executive named who has personal responsibility to make certain that the competency is being invested in and continually advanced. Most other activities should be structured as service centers, again, with specific managers responsible for driving the optimal sourcing decision for those activities.

Next, as outsourcing becomes increasingly more important, it needs to be treated as a critical business skill. If outsourcing is central to a company's success, then it needs to be supported. I recommend that companies look at creating an Outsourcing Center of Excellence to drive this point home. (The mission and responsibilities of this center are documented in the sidebar.)

Outsourcing Center of Excellence

Mission

The mission of the Outsourcing Center of Excellence is to develop and manage an overall, comprehensive process for improving the success of the organization's outsourcing efforts. The function measures its success in terms of the organization's achievement of the business value expected from its strategic outsourcing initiatives — typically quantified in terms of the shareholder value factors of revenue, cost, and asset management.

Responsibilities

1. Develop corporatewide outsourcing policies and promote their reflection in the company's long-term strategies and short-term plans.
2. Develop and promote best practices in the corporation's outsourcing process across the strategic, transactional, and management phases.
3. Promote senior management's proactive involvement in outsourcing as a critical corporate activity.

4. Develop and execute education and communications programs for executives and managers on corporate outsourcing policies and industry best practices.
5. Develop and recommend organizational changes to ensure optimum investment in corporate core competencies.
6. Develop and recommend organizational changes to ensure optimal sourcing decisions for noncore business activities.
7. Collect, disseminate, and ensure regular reviews of organizational measurements and continuous improvement goals in outsourcing.
8. Develop and recommend organizational reward and recognition programs for achievement of corporate goals through outsourcing.
9. Develop and recommend education and communication programs for the company's outsourcing service providers.

I believe that outsourcing will become as natural as any other aspect of the organization. But it will take some time and the development and refinement of a number of new skills for us to get there. Ultimately, an organization's success in managing outsourcing relationships will be a major determinant of its business success.

9.8 REFERENCES

Dant, Rajiv P., and Schul, Patrick L., "Conflict Resolution Processes in Contractual Channels of Distribution," *Journal of Marketing*, 56 (January 1992), 38–54.

Ertel, Danny, "How to Design a Conflict Management Procedure That Fits Your Dispute," *Sloan Management Review,* (Summer 1991), 29–42.

Fisher, R., and Ury, W., *Getting to Yes*, Harmondsworth, UK, Penguin Books, 1983.

Scott, Robert E., "Conflict and Cooperation in Long-Term Contracts," *California Law Review*, 75/6 (December 1987) 2005–2053.

10

Partnerships

"Partnership" as used in this book refers to an outsourcing relationship between a client and vendor, not to a joint company or partnership form of business or a partnership arrangement between two or more vendors. The idea of partnership and how to choose between a market, intermediate, and partnership relationship with a vendor was introduced in Chapter 4. This chapter begins with a brief review of the conditions necessary for partnership. The chapter continues with explanations of how partnerships work and how they can be built and sustained.

10.1 WHY PARTNERSHIPS?

Several factors favor partnership. One is the inability to write complete contracts. Uncertainty or unanticipated changes in needs will require a change in what the vendor does, but these changes can't be predicted at the time the contract is negotiated. A series of short contracts, competitively led to the best vendor bidder, might seem to be a solution. Then contracts could be adjusted through time to reflect the changed circumstances. But vendors aren't on a level playing field in sequential bidding. The vendor who gets the first contract gains valuable knowledge about the client organization, its needs, and how best to meet them. This vendor has an advantage in bidding for the next contract and each succeeding contract. One vendor tends to dominate and can take advantage of this position by raising its prices, or reducing the quality of its services, or both. When the conditions underlying outsourcing favor repeated contracting with the same vendor, partnerships are necessary to curb opportunism.

Second, there is considerable investment by one or both parties in assets that are specific to the relationship. If the arrangement falls apart this investment is lost. Partnerships have continuity mechanisms that protect such investments and promote further investments.

Finally, when the needs met through outsourcing are ongoing and best met through a long-term relationship with a vendor and repeated contracts, a partnership provides the mechanisms for sustaining such long-term relationships.

A very small subset of all outsourcing deals actually work effectively as partnerships because the costs are high. The proper cost-benefit-risk mix for partnership doesn't occur frequently. Considerable effort has to be put into developing a close relationship and maintaining it. The risks of partnership are usually high because one or both parties make investments that are worth substantially less if the partnership does not survive. It follows that the benefits of partnership must be substantial to make partnerships worthwhile. This limits most information systems partnerships to arrangements that have a large impact on the organization through direct revenue production, market share enhancement, or dramatically decreased costs of some major categories of information systems services.

The gains might arise from leveraging a core competency of one or both partners or by bringing together resources from both firms in a way that is unique. Then each party has a great interest in the other's success because without the partner's participation and success, neither succeeds. Chapter 2 gives the example of Caterpillar and Andersen Consulting's partnership to develop and operate a highly automated spare parts ordering and distribution system. Each firm brought resources and capabilities to this deal that complemented the other. Neither could do this on its own.

Don't "partner" with a vendor simply because the vendor urges that you do so. Determine whether both sides have capabilities or resources that when put together produce a real and substantial bottom-line impact. The benefits have to be substantial, and the benefits that justify a partnership are those that you could not achieve if the work is performed within the boundaries of your own organization.

In its partnership alliance with CSC and Andersen Consulting, DuPont aims to increase its growth and shareholder value as bottom-line benefits. It hopes that the partnership will allow it to better respond to the changing business environment with flexibility and speed, to gain access to new technologies and skills, to continuously improve productivity, to maintain the ability to lead, manage, and renew, and to increase operational reliability. At the same time it is intent on keeping control of its information systems destiny by retaining leadership of the IT functions that serve its business, even when these are provided by vendors. DuPont wants to renew its infrastructure, maintain low unit costs, maintain a unified global infrastructure, and continue fair treatment of its current and former employees.

10.2 HOW PARTNERSHIPS WORK

Why are information systems partnerships relatively new? Part of the answer seems to lie in the changing business environment of the 1980s and 1990s (see Chapter 2). As global competition increased and consumer markets became more specialized, long production runs of standardized products in vertically integrated firms was replaced by flexible production of customized products in downsized, flatter companies or in networks of organizations. Services saw similar differentiation and emphasis on rapid response to market changes. Partnerships, coalitions, and alliances are all forms of cooperation between firms that allow rapid response, a lowering of costs, and sharing of scarce know-how (Powell, 1990).

Walter Powell (1990) identifies the bases for partnership relations:

- Reciprocal, mutually supportive actions so that both gain over time.
- Trust that the other partner will take positive actions and refrain from opportunistic actions.
- A long-term perspective and the willingness to give and take, resolving differences as they arise and sharing gains, risks, and losses.
- Reputation as the most significant sign of reliability and a reduced need for monitoring. The desire for continued participation in the gains of the partnership limits opportunism.
- Performance monitoring that occurs more through a peer review process than explicit measures.
- Mutual consent instead of formal rules and procedures.
- A meshing of processes in the two organizations and a blurring of the line between them.

Contracts are not in this list because a contract is not adequate to sustain a relationship over a long period of time in an uncertain business environment. While a contract should be written between the two parties in a partnership, it acts more as a starting point for cooperation and as a safety net in case the relationship falls apart. The real basis of a partnership rests elsewhere.

10.2.1 Essential Aspects of Partnership

Partnerships have long- and short-term aspects. The long-term aspect is the joint goals of the partnership and the things that underlie long-term cooperation. The short-term aspects are the day-to-day actions that move the partnership toward the long-term goals. In market and intermediate relationships the rules of the game are fairly fixed and both parties ultimately depend on a contract and the courts to guarantee the actions of the other. In contrast, partnerships are characterized by a series of contracts with no clear end point and a collection of ways to operate on a day-to-day basis that promote the long-term goals. According to Henderson (1990) what sustains the long-term aspect of partnership, or what he calls "partnership in context" involves:

- Mutual gains, or the belief on the part of both partners that working together will bring benefits that can't be achieved individually, whether these are increased revenues, product or process improvements, or risk sharing.

- Commitment to the partnership through shared goals, incentives that reinforce the goals, and the existence of contracts. Contracts are important, not so much for enforcing behavior because of the complexity of joint work, but more as a symbol of commitment and a means of defining joint goals.

- A predisposition to partner based on (a) managerial belief that competition demands close working relationships with other organizations, and (b) trust that the other firm will do the right thing and not take advantage of the situation. Trust, in turn, is based on a demonstrated record of mutually beneficial behavior on the part of the other firm and good relationships between individuals at the interface between the organizations in the partnership.

DuPont sees its partnership relationship with CSC and Andersen Consulting as being mutually beneficial. The vendors bring much skill and experience to DuPont, but the relationship with DuPont also benefits the vendors. DuPont brings a world-class IT function, strong IT skills, and the quality reputation of the entire DuPont Company. The learning that occurs as a result of doing work for DuPont will also help the vendors deliver superior service to other customers. All of these offer considerable value to the vendors.

To the above list one can add trust as an essential factor in partnerships. Trust has two dimensions (Doney and Cannon, 1997). One is the credibility of the partner's promises and actions. The other dimension is the belief that the partner is truly interested in your welfare. Partnership requires mutual trust; the vendor must also find you credible and find you to be genuinely interested in its welfare. Trust has the following long-term benefits in partnerships:

- High levels of trust allow the partners to focus on long-term objectives and not worry so much about day-to-day issues that would otherwise consume them.

- Trust works to suppress opportunism and increase cooperation.
- Trust allows the partners to make themselves vulnerable and take risks, such as investments that cannot be recovered if the partnership fails.
- Trust reduces conflict.

The day-in-and-day-out factors that make partnerships work (what Henderson calls "partnership in action") are:

- Shared knowledge of the general business environment, culture, and work processes of the other firm in the partnership.
- Mutual dependence on distinctive competencies and resources. Here one or both firms have an ability or resource the other does not. The success of A becomes dependent on the abilities or resources of B, producing dependency on the part of A. But A changes the way it works, which further leverages B's advantage and gives gains to B that B would not otherwise have. Thus, B becomes dependent on A. The dependency runs in both directions.
- Organizational linkage in processes, information, and social or personal relations.

Because an environment of intense competition fosters partnerships, organizations not in highly competitive environments — like monopolies, government agencies, and not-for-profits — may have less need for partnerships.

Because the goals of client and vendor firms must be closely aligned, partnerships are less likely to succeed between a client firm and an alliance of several vendor firms than between a client and a single vendor. In an alliance, one vendor is likely to have less commitment to a partnership than the other(s) making it less willing to invest and act in mutually beneficial ways. Developing satisfactory ways to share gains, costs, and risks is also more difficult when three or more parties are involved.

10.2.2 Critical Success Factors

Based on the above understanding of partnership, it follows that to partner successfully two firms need the following:

- Complementary strengths.
- Ways of combining their strengths and working together.
- A joint vision, a shared purpose, and a common strategy.
- Senior management commitment to making it happen.

If the partnership is to operate successfully, the two firms will need to work together in ways that produce:

- Substantial gains.
- Successful sharing of the gains.
- Mutual dependency.
- Cooperation.
- Webs of linkages.
- Trust.
- Robust ways of handling differences or disputes.

Both partners have to change to maximize the gains from working together. Both have to adjust what they do at the boundaries of their organizations to most effectively link to and take advantage of the capabilities of the other. This mutual accommodation has two sides. It increases joint gains, which must be equitably shared if each is to be satisfied with the relationship, and it makes each dependent on the other. (Rackham, Friedman, and Ruff, 1996)

Changing the way a firm works involves an investment. The investment at the boundaries of two firms is specific to the way the *other* firm works; it can't be recouped if the partnership falls apart. Dependency is deepened by these asset specific investments.

To further increase joint gains and trust in a partnership, firms can make investments that primarily benefit the other partner. These are the ultimate indicators of commitment to the partnership. The academics who study partnership refer to these as "pledges" or "tying of hands" type commitments, and they are frequently observed in partnership arrangements.

Rackham, Friedman and Ruff use the term "intimacy" to characterize the linkage between partner firms. Success in accommodating to the other firm's way of working cannot be done without an intimate understanding of the other firm. The understanding is gained through extraordinarily good access to and good relationships with the people in the other firm. Both sides are willing to share their information and knowledge and make suggestions for incorporating their ways of working into the processes of their partner to the mutual benefit of both.

Information informs the cooperative process or what Rackham, Friedman and Ruff call "information with value." For example, when one firm considers making an investment, it might first consult with the other firm to see if it's possible to invest in a way that will be mutually beneficial to both partners. Provision of unbiased information is another example, as in situations where a vendor might admit that for some need it is not the best source to fill a need and direct its partner to another vendor.

The boundaries of the two firms often blur in this process for several reasons. First, the sharing usually involves information that is considered confidential and proprietary. Second, the sharing can't be effectively done without spending large amounts of time together in each other's workplaces. And finally, sharing is often most effective when the partner's people actually work in your firm so that they can help in the integration of the ways in which the two organizations work, and vice versa.

Trust is obviously central to working partnerships. No firm makes investments with such risk and allows knowledge of and entry into its operations by the people of another organization with such intimacy unless it trusts the other firm.

Conflict resolution is also key. Disputes are inevitable, but the partners must find ways to peacefully resolve disputes and keep long-term goals foremost.

10.3 HOW TO BUILD PARTNERSHIPS

Partnerships can't be built overnight; it takes time. A personal relationship between a man and a woman begins with a first meeting or date and progresses through time to closer and more intimate relations and perhaps to marriage. Similarly a client-vendor partnership usually begins with intermediate outsourcing experiences that introduce the two firms to each other, builds some personal relationships across the interface between the two organizations, and provides the basis to move toward partnering, if it is advantageous to do so.

Some romances are faster than others. It takes time to get to know the other person and decide that a close relationship is desired, but some couples accomplish this in a matter of days or weeks, others in months or years. Once a client and vendor have a relationship, partnerships can develop quickly and directly, or slowly and gradually.

10.3.1 The Quicker Route to Partnerships

Rackham, Friedman and Ruff lay out a way to develop partnerships more quickly between a client and vendor, but they stress that this process still takes time and can't be done overnight. Some key factors from the client firm perspective are:

- Prior knowledge of and experience with the vendor is usually necessary to know that the vendor is the right one in terms of capability and that the vendor has a culture that matches the client organization.
- Good personal contacts between the client and vendor organizations.

- The potential for substantial benefit from partnering with the vendor firm.
- A shared vision of the benefit on the part of managers at a high enough level in both client and vendor firms to champion and have authority in these matters.
- A win-win approach on both sides, and a willingness on both sides to make partnership happen in a time frame that makes sense to both.

A good match between the resources in client and vendor firms is obviously a must. This is more likely to be the case if the vendor has experience in your industry.

The size of the benefits often depend on the size of transaction volumes or other measures of business activity. If the potential margin per transaction is high but the volume of transactions is low, the overall gains may be too small to support the high costs of partnership.

Culture and values are important. Values that don't align will wreck a partnership. Both firms should be driven by the same imperative, for example, excellence, or low cost, or the desire to push the envelope in some direction. Where less important or secondary values are concerned, neither firm should have values that deviate too far from the values of the other.

Partnership means win-win. A client or vendor that plays "win-lose" games is not a candidate for partnership.

Both client and vendor should have similar expectations of the time frame in which the partnership can be built and the benefits realized. If this matter is much more urgent for one than the other, expectations differ and the chance for success is greatly reduced.

Developing a Vision

The process of developing a vision of partnership is initiated by higher level managers in client and vendor firms. Small teams are formed in both organizations that work together to analyze the potential of a partnership and develop a vision or position statement on partnership.

Team members on both sides should be excited about the possibility of partnership and have the skills to sell it to others in their organization. Members should be at the same managerial level in client and vendor organizations and have the power in their respective organizations to make it happen.

The teams from client and vendor come together in a joint team that gathers the relevant business and technical information, analyzes the potential, and creates a short vision statement. The vision has to clearly demonstrate the benefits. The action plan sets out the steps necessary to make the partnership happen.

If the teams have trouble coming to terms or anticipate trouble, they might hire an outside facilitator who knows both firms and the business area. The facilitator helps move the teams to resolution.

The vision must be believable and compelling, and it must be sold. Partnerships can't be forced. Many people in both client and vendor firms must believe in the concept to make it work day to day. The teams make the contacts in their respective organizations to sell others on the idea.

The initial vision and action plan are not the last. As the two sides work together, the vision grows and the action plan evolves as the goals become clearer. The idea is to get started with a direction that is fundamentally sound and to modify and elaborate the goals and plan as time goes on.

Getting Started

The plan should target initial activities between client and vendor that can quickly benefit both sides. This will demonstrate the advantages to doubters and help to establish good relationships between people in the two organizations.

Governance measures and procedures should be put in place at the outset that establish expectations of how processes work, how interorganizational relationships are established and go forward, and how differences are to be handled.

Measurement and the ability to document the benefits of partnership are important to cementing the relationship and moving forward in both organizations. The partnership team or a successor joint team of client and vendor personnel should develop measures and put data collection and analysis procedures in place. Measures should focus on the magnitude of the benefits and the division of benefits and costs. Fairness and the demonstration of fairness is important to long-term success.

Partnerships must find ways to resolve conflicts amicably. Cooperative aspects of conflict resolution are explored in the previous chapter. Their application in partnerships is critical.

Once the partnership is started, its success and survival are dependent on the steady application of mutually beneficial behavior on both sides and growing trust. Processes that accomplish this include attraction, communication, bargaining, power and its exercise, expectations, and norms development. The next section of this chapter explains the role of these in the context of gradual routes to partnership. These factors are also essential to the more direct route to partnership, once the partnership is agreed upon and started.

10.3.2 The More Gradual Route to Partnerships

Klepper (1996) proposed a model of gradual partnership development. The model has four phases or stages — awareness, exploration, expansion, and commitment. See Figure 10-1.

In the beginning or awareness stage, client and vendor already know each other, either through previous outsourcing experience or by reputation. Now persons in one or both organizations see advantage in a closer relationship with the other firm.

In exchange, or the second stage, client and vendor do business together, and through a succession of contracts they become increasingly interdependent. They purposefully move along the contracting continuum from intermediate toward partnership, contract by contract, without trying to proceed quickly to pure partnership in one move.

In the commitment phase, client and vendor enter full partnership. Getting to commitment is a journey. In looking back over the experience, the exact moment of commitment may be not be a watershed event at a point in time but rather a transition that takes place over several successive contracts.

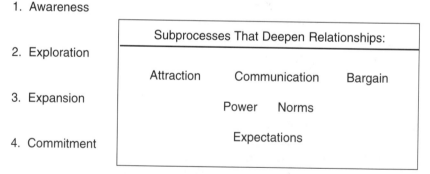

Stages:

1. Awareness

2. Exploration

3. Expansion

4. Commitment

Subprocesses That Deepen Relationships:

Attraction   Communication   Bargain

Power   Norms

Expectations

Figure 10-1: A Model of Partnership Development.

Adapted from "Developing Buyer-Seller Relationships" by Dwyer, F. R., Schurr, P. H., and Oh, S., *Journal of Marketing,*1987 by permission of the publisher.

Throughout these stages six factors work to deepen the relationship and move it toward partnership. They are attraction, communication, bargaining, power and its exercise, expectations, and norms development.

Attraction is the positive outcome or rewards from a relationship. Relationships that can exploit the unique combination of resources that the two parties bring to a deal produce benefits that are attractive. Vendors that do high quality work within time and budget constraints offer higher direct rewards than vendors who do not. Vendors whose personnel work easily and cooperatively with personnel of the client firm offer higher direct rewards than vendors who do not.

The characteristics of the vendor are also aspects of attraction in that they are predictors of benefits to the client in the future. These characteristics include vendor objectives, beliefs, values, culture, capabilities, financial viability, managerial capabilities, and status or reputation. Vendors that share the client's objectives, beliefs, and values are more attractive. Vendors with service capabilities complementary to the client's are more attractive. Vendors with good management capabilities are more likely to have consistent, good performance and are more attractive. Vendors that have good reputations in the information systems field and are financially viable are more attractive.

Managers in both client and vendor firms can take steps to increase attraction. Either party can make investments that change its capabilities and make it a better fit to the other's needs. The client can award contracts to the vendor that build mutual experience and a base for business that can be a foundation for a future partnership. Many possibilities exist to increase attractiveness on both sides.

Communication consists of the day-to-day exchange of information; it is also the open revelation of needs and resources related to the future of the relationship. Vendors who are willing to openly discuss their directions for the future, their capabilities, their strengths and weaknesses and who expect to receive like information from the client are acting to deepen the relationship. Opportunities to demonstrate openness and increase communication are always available in outsourcing relationships. Managers on both sides can pursue these to move the relationship toward partnership.

Bargaining takes place in contract negotiations, in the daily working out of client-vendor work processes, and in dispute resolution. Vendors with whom the client more easily and successfully bargains in all these contexts are better potential partners than vendors who are difficult. Action on both client and vendor sides to bargain honestly and fairly with a win-win objective can deepen trust and enhance the chances of partnership.

Power exists in a relationship if one party is dependent on the other for valued resources, and this power is enhanced if there are limited alternative sources available to the party with less power. Exercise of power where partnership is concerned can be classified as "just" or "unjust." It is unjust if the party with power uses its power for its benefit, without the second party's consent or understanding. It is a just use of power if both parties jointly benefit from or if the second party is adequately compensated for the exercise of the first party's power.

When power exits, the way in which it is exercised is of fundamental importance to the movement of the relationship toward or away from partnering. Relationships in which power is used to provide joint benefits will flourish and grow; relationships in which power is applied unjustly will wither and die. Client and vendor managers have ample opportunity to use power justly. The more powerful side in an incipient partnership has the greater responsibility to prove it can and will use power for the joint benefit of the two parties.

Expectations of the behavior of the other party that are fulfilled increase trust and deepen the relationship. Expectations that are disappointed move the relationship in the opposite direction. Contracts set expectations, but partnerships are built on expectations fulfilled that exceed contract terms. Much of the mutually beneficial investment behavior in partnerships and relationships that build to partnerships are based on an expectations-trust spiral. One party makes investments and takes actions that are beneficial to the other party in expectation that the second party will reciprocate. The second party does reciprocate leading the first party to make further investments of this kind. Expectations that are fulfilled build trust, and trust allows more investment.

Norms are standards for behavior that are shared. Norms set limits on acceptable behavior and curb deviant behavior (Heide and John, 1992). In an outsourcing context where client and vendor share confidential information and make investments that benefit the other party, norms act to prohibit the opportunistic behavior of the other party. An example of one essential norm for partnering is the following: If one firm shares information with its partner or makes an investment that benefits the partner, then by the standards of behavior that define the relationship, the second firm will not take advantage of the first firm's action.

In addition to information sharing and investments, a norm that requires the parties to adjust their relationship in mutually beneficial ways when the environment changes is usually a fundamental underpinning of partnership. When the environment changes in ways that would harm one party if the relationship is not adjusted, client and vendor find a way to adjust that builds trust rather than diminishes it. For example, suppose part of the current contract calls for the vendor to support and maintain the desktop computers in the client's organization. A new generation of equipment or software replaces the old, and the client has a business need to switch to the new technology. The contract was written for the old technology and did not anticipate the new. Client and vendor find a win-win way to move to the new technology in a situation that might have allowed the vendor to stall or prevent the introduction of the new technology if the contract was observed to the letter. This is an example of behavior in line with a norm of adjustment to changes in the environment that aid both parties.

By the time client and vendor reach partnership by the gradual approach, most of the norms necessary to support partnership will be in place. Norms will grow out of the shared experience of moving to partnership that sets the rules of the game.

Throughout these processes trust grows (Doney and Cannon, 1997). Trust grows because each partner is better able to predict the other's actions which demonstrate sincere interest in the other partner's welfare. Trust grows because the capability and capacity of the other party to deliver on its promises is revealed and confirmed. And trust grows because the underlying motives of the other partner are at least partially revealed and act to confirm its credibility and interest in its partner's welfare.

While client and vendor might arrive at partnership without ever openly striving for this goal, more likely the relationship gradually deepens and at some point managers on both sides seize the potential and take more aggressive steps, of the kind outlined in the previous section, to create the vision and the action plan.

The extent to which the gradual approach can be accelerated depends on circumstances. If the underlying conditions for gains are favorable, the process might proceed more rapidly. If one side leads aggressively with behavior that makes it more attractive and demonstrates its commitment and fairness, partnership may develop more rapidly.

Nothing is inevitable about the gradual approach, or the more direct approach for that matter. Things can and do go wrong — everything from changing business conditions that cause the potential gains to evaporate, or changed priorities on the part of either side, or roadblocks in terms of expectations that are dashed. To guard against the losses that can arise in these circumstances, be sure the contractual side of the relationship with the vendor is sound in every contract you make.

10.3.3 Unilateral Commitments

A powerful mechanism by which either side can demonstrate its allegiance to partnership and the building of partnership is through unilateral commitments. Unilateral commitments are of several types. One party can show it is serious about partnership by making a commitment that reduces its own returns if the partnership doesn't progress or fails. An example is contracting for resources necessary to support the partnership in its next phase *before* the two partners have moved to the next phase. This is like posting a bond; one partner commits to a sacrifice that occurs only if the partnership does not continue and in this way helps to assure that it will continue (Gulati, Khanna, and Nohria, 1994).

Another type of a unilateral commitment is to make an irreversible offer that is beneficial to the other partner and let the partner choose to accept the offer or not. An example is a vendor firm that offers the resumes of all its systems people inviting the client to choose those it deems most suitable for some task.

Another form of unilateral commitment is a pledge of exclusivity. The vendor promises the client not to do a particular kind of work for any other client, or the client promises the vendor it will not hire any other vendor to do a certain kind of work.

10.4 CONTRACTS IN PARTNERSHIPS

While contracts are the bedrock of market and intermediate relationships, contracts play a different role in partnerships. One view is that contracts are unnecessary in partnerships. Instead of producing a 2,500 page contract, partners should be able to move forward with a contract of a few pages since the process is fundamentally based on trust, not legalities. It is true that a contract alone can never be the basis for a true partnership. No contract can be written that will adequately anticipate all the changes that partnerships must endure. It simply isn't possible to set out and enforce mutual trust and fairness in a legal document. Desire and the commitment to partnership has to come from sources other than a contract.

To the contrary, a good contract, or more accurately a succession of good contracts, is essential to a good partnership. Contracts in the context of partnership serve two functions. Contracts allow both partners to set expectations of the other and to commit to short-term goals. Contracts also provide a safety net in case the partnership fails.

The shared goals of partnership are long-term aims. Viewed against the many potential years of partnership, contracts are short-term instruments. Therefore, the two parties can't contract to achieve the long-term goals, but they can contract to attain intermediate steps or intermediate goals on the way to achieving long-term goals. Each and every time a new contract is negotiated between client and vendor in a partnership, the two sides should return to the issue of ultimate goals and the intermediate steps that can be put in the contract as part of the process of moving toward the long-term goals.

The contract should also provide a safety net in case the partnership fails during the contract period. The premature termination of contract issues addressed in Chapter 7 should be included in contracts that underlie partnerships. Doing so is not a signal to the vendor that you expect the partnership to fail. Rather it is a signal to the vendor that your organization is free to commit to a long-term relationship because some of the risks have been addressed. An analogy might be buying burglary protection for your home so that you experience the pleasures of a vacation undiminished by worry and concern.

10.4.1 Contract Negotiation

The power, bargaining, expectations, and norm development issues addressed above in developing partnerships come into play in negotiating contracts.

If there is an imbalance in power between client and vendor, contract negotiations are an ideal opportunity to demonstrate fairness and the willingness to share gains, to share losses, and to share risks without regard to relative bargaining power. If the balance of power is on the side of your organization, you need not give everything away. Rather demonstrate that you will not take nearly as much as you could have.

Contracts can embody some of the expectations that build partnership through requirements specifications. As the partners negotiate the next contract, the expectations embodied in requirements can be increased. In this way the parties make a legal commitment to the rising expectations that are fundamental to the partnership. Some norms can also find their way into contracts and commit the parties to standards of behavior.

10.4.2 Contract Provisions

Chapter 6 sets out aspects of contracts that help to support partnerships. To recap some of these, the contract might provide:

- Clearly defined and measurable benefits and the methods for sharing these.
- Formulas for sharing costs.
- Methods for revising the contract when unforeseen contingencies arise.
- Pricing methods that allow sharing of risks and gains.
- Profit-sharing provisions, when the project will yield outside revenue.
- Dispute and disagreement resolution mechanisms.
- Incentives and punishments, with more emphasis on the former than the latter.
- Standard operating procedures.

These set a framework in which the partnership operates during a contract period. The actual working out of sharing, the actual method by which revision takes place, the way disputes are handled, and the way in which procedures are set may be much more flexible, consultative, and responsive to conditions as they arise than the contract can provide. The contract is a reference point and a fallback should the partners find consultations difficult. It helps prevent the beginnings of a downward spiral that undermines the trust and cooperation that have developed up to this point.

Termination

The contract should address the following termination issues:

- The time granted your organization to take back the outsourced functions.
- Means for retrieving your organization's data and other resources.
- Continued service provision by the vendor until the transition to in-house processing or outsourcing with another vendor is complete.
- Means to assure the confidentiality of your organization's data and processes after the partnership is terminated.
- Payment to the vendor during a transition and termination fees.

Since partnerships involve the creation of assets, the contract needs to specify whose these will be or how they will be divided on termination and what compensation, if any, goes to the parties on this division. If a revenue generating business is created on the basis of partnership, the contract must specify what happens to the business if the partners go their separate ways.

Information sharing in partnerships is often extensive, and the termination provisions should protect competitive and confidential information as well.

10.5 MANAGING THE PARTNERING RELATIONSHIP

Once partnerships are up and running, a number of factors contribute to deepening and strengthening of partnership relations.

10.5.1 Mutual Influence

Mutual influence is the ability of each organization in a working relationship to affect the key policies and decisions of the other (Nelson and Cooprider, 1996). Mutual influence is necessary in partnerships, otherwise tasks in the two organizations that need to be tightly integrated can become decoupled, leading to outcomes that do not meet expectations.

A plethora of integrating activities are the mechanisms for building and sustaining mutual influence in partnerships.

10.5.2 Integration

Kanter (1996) identifies five levels in integration:

- Strategic integration brought about by the top managers in both firms who set long-term goals and directions of travel.
- Tactical integration architected by middle managers who develop plans for and carry out projects and joint activities, find ways to better link the firms, and transfer knowledge.
- Operational integration that provides ways to carry out the ongoing work of the partnership with access to information and resources across organizational boundaries.
- Interpersonal integration or the good personal ties and rapport across firm boundaries that lead to sharing of information, technology, and resources.
- Cultural integration or the ability to assume something of a common identity and bridge any remaining differences.

The strategic level of partnership arrangements is created through relationships between senior managers. The top managers who put the partnership together have the vision of what the partnership is to be. The daily workings of partnership go on between persons further down in the two organizations. Integration of the two firms is necessary to make it happen. This job can't be delegated. The managers who initiated the partnership have to lead the effort to make the vision an operational reality (Niederkofler, 1991).

Education is one way to integrate the partners at a tactical and operational level. Education of your personnel can be directed to the culture and processes of the partner organization and to the skills necessary to make best use of the capabilities offered by the other firm. Education also begins the process of sharing information and knowledge between the two organizations.

New and strengthened management skills may be necessary to handle the complexity that integration with a partner creates (Kanter, 1989). Authority and reporting relationships may be much more ambiguous than they were before the partnership. Diplomacy, consensus building, consultative skills, and the ability to motivate people in another organization become very important abilities.

Both partners should appoint tactical, midmanagement level liaison persons to oversee the integration activities in the partnership and be the primary points of communication. Good liaison people are keys to success. It's best if they already have an understanding of the other firm based on previous experience. Educational efforts should focus on filling gaps. Some interface people will be from your organization's IT department and others should be from the functional areas of your business impacted by the partnership.

Cross-functional teams can be established across organizational boundaries to do tactical planning, perform tactical oversight, increase information sharing, create linkages between the operations of the partners, and further social relationships (Henderson, 1990).

Joint planning translates the strategic vision of the partnership into short run tactical goals and steps for achieving them. Joint planning also addresses operational issues and problems as they arise. Representatives from the cross-functional, cross-organizational teams are key members of the planning group or groups. Senior managers should sponsor and oversee the planning process to assure that it aligns with the strategic objectives of the partnership.

Persons in operational roles in both firms must adopt partnership ethics and norms, develop the trust that underlies partnership, and embrace the partnership enthusiastically. It's unrealistic to expect each and every employee on both client and vendor sides to have the same commitment, but a critical mass is necessary.

To forge good personal relationships, cultural differences that stand in the way of cooperation must be bridged. Information sharing must be fostered. A transfer of knowledge on how each organization works precedes understanding and action. The goal is to mesh the processes of the two organizations to produce gains through joint operations.

The communication issues addressed in a previous chapter, particularly the co-location of people at the interface of the two organizations, should be a priority.

In addition to the communication channels opened up through the types of integration addressed above, managers, liaison people, and teams should address information needs and design other communication mechanisms, as necessary, to further the partnership (Niederkofler, 1991). Exchanging personnel can be a valuable communication enhancing move, especially when the partnership needs tight integration at the process level.

Finally, measures of partnership performance can be developed as part of the planning process. The data for these can be collected by the teams and used in the planning process to control the operations of the partnership.

Close and careful monitoring should accompany the beginning stages of partnerships to see that integration is going smoothly. Problems that arise can be short run or long run in nature. Long-run problems are ones that persist throughout the life of the partnership if they are not addressed at fundamental levels. For example, some problems may be the result of a cultural difference, say, in the way communication is handled in the two organizations. Simply fixing one instance of miscommunication may not fix the underlying problem. A long term, more permanent solution should be sought, which in this case might be the implementation of procedures that direct how future communication is to be handled. Top management support and intervention may be needed to make fundamental changes.

10.5.3 Monitoring, Controls, and Cooperation

Monitoring and control, a topic addressed in the previous chapter, take on a different meaning in partnerships.

Monitoring

Because the operations of client and vendor are meshed in ways that blur the line between the two firms, vendor processes and outputs are not the only or necessarily the most important subject of monitoring, rather it is the joint effort and outputs that count.

Much of the monitoring in partnerships goes on along the boundaries between the two firms. More of the monitoring will be peer-review in nature; less will be boss-subordinate type monitoring.

Monitoring in partnerships also differs in that the daily, quarterly, and yearly results of partnership must be judged in two dimensions — their contribution to current functioning and their contribution to the successful long-term aims of the partnership.

Setting measurable targets, short run and long run, is a good idea in partnerships. Then monitoring can take place against these targets to demonstrate that the gains are real, the progress is tangible, and that fairness prevails in the distribution of benefits, costs, and risk. Some of the requirements and related monitoring will involve expectations, norms, and goals not stated explicitly in a contract.

As is true of all monitoring systems, information collected should be free of bias and business based. Monitoring should also pay attention to developments that have future business potential and look for ways in which the partnership might be adjusted to work more effectively or be redirected to generate still more gains.

Control

Control actions also differ. Control should be much more diffused and decentralized in partnerships than it is in market and intermediate outsourcing relationships. Individuals at operational level on both sides of the partnership should be aware of opportunities for information sharing, further integration of operations, fine tuning of operations in support of partnership goals (both short term and long term), and corrective action if processes are deviating from expectations or norms. Decentralized control and cooperative that control cross-organizational boundaries are characteristic of controls in partnerships.

Cooperation

Cooperation is the essence of partnership. Cooperation is the force that sustains partnership and moves it forward. It follows that cooperation must be much deeper and characterize the relationship to a much greater extent than in other outsourcing relationships.

10.5.4. Dispute Resolution

When partnerships are first announced and launched, there is a reservoir of good will that often carries a relationship for some time. But eventually this well goes dry and the realities of working with another firm bear down. Conflict can't be avoided in partnerships. Since close working relationships are necessary to achieve the benefits of partnership, differences between the two organizations in culture, structure, and procedures can cause real friction. Liaison people and cross-functional, cross-organizational teams should all work to address differences and the problems that spring from them.

The level of integration and cooperation demanded of successful partnerships require decentralized dispute resolution to a degree not found in market and intermediate outsourcing relationships. If the partnership is working well, problems should be identified and resolved at the team level. Rarely will disputes escalate to higher levels of management. When conflict is persistent, the planning process needs to address its source or sources and control the underlying causes.

This does not obviate the need for formal dispute resolution mechanisms. The escalation procedures addressed in earlier chapters are still necessary when issues cannot be resolved at lower levels.

Disputes that surface repeatedly may indicate fundamental problems at a strategic, rather than an operational level in a partnership. The monitoring effort should be attuned to these kinds of disputes, and higher level managers should be involved in their resolution. Fundamental problems often arise from inflexible and hard-to-change structural and cultural differences between organizations. In some cases, strategy may have to change to accommodate such differences.

10.6 CHANGE, ADJUSTMENT, AND TERMINATION

Adjustment in partnership strategy and objectives is to be expected over time. Often the vision is not complete at the outset, and adjustment will occur as the picture becomes clearer. Other adjustments become necessary as a result of the misalignments that were ignored at startup or differences that develop as partnerships progress. Problems arise if the two firms have different levels of commitment to the partnership with one firm making it a much more central concern than the other. Differences in management philosophy and resistance in one or both organizations to outsiders and their ideas and ways of working is another potential problem. Implementation problems, such as inappropriate persons in liaison roles, can plague partnerships. Problems also occur when either party fails to abide by the partnership building and strengthening activities of attraction, communication, bargaining, just exercise of power, expectations, and norms development. Misuse of power by withholding of vital information is an example. Adjustments in strategy are to be expected. Partnerships that cannot adjust will not be stable.

Partnerships can also cause friction inside your own organization. Power relationships between or within functions may be upset when internal processes integrate with vendor processes. Persons who were of lower status and less central to business success may rise in influence and others may be effectively demoted. Persons in interface roles with the partner gain power; others may lose power. These frictions must be resolved if effective integration is to take place with the vendor.

Changes in business conditions and strategy may dictate adjustment in the terms of partnership. For example, business changes may require much faster service on a partner's part or investment that the partner would not otherwise make.

Because a changing environment may stress a partnership, periodic reassessments of the strategic and operational structure of the partnership should be made. Open information flow and proactive monitoring and control activity by liaison people and teams is valuable for this purpose.

Fundamental changes are likely to require redistribution of benefits, costs, and risk in the partnership. The sharing formulas and norms that evolved through a courtship between partners or were hammered out in negotiations to establish the partnership must be revisited. A contract may have to be renegotiated or the next contract changed to reflect the revised distributions. Procedures that are distributive in effect should be redesigned if necessary.

The greatest threat to successful partnerships is changed business circumstances that diminish the gains to be had from the partnership relative to gains to be had elsewhere. Even in a fairly placid business environment some realignment of strategic objectives is necessary and to be expected. With more radical business change, realigning the strategic goals of the partnership may be necessary to allow its survival. Now one partner may be in a stronger bargaining position than the other, and realignment may cause a substantial redistribution of gains, costs, or risks. The bottom line for both firms is how and to what extent the partnership benefits them. When the benefits of partnership no longer cover the costs or the risks become unbearable, it is time to leave.

The next chapter treats termination issues in outsourcing relationships. One aspect of termination can have a particularly insidious impact on partnerships, and that is the end game that can occur in a contractual relationship that both players know will not be renewed. Once it is clear that there will be no contract after the current one, the self-regulating factors that act to hold partnerships together evaporate. The long-term goals are gone. The discipline of wanting another contract is gone. Even fears of a damaged reputation from misbehaving may be reduced because the reputation that matters most — the esteem in which your partner holds you — has diminished in importance.

It can end amicably, but if the partnership collapses in bitterness, one or both partners may take whatever advantage they can of the situation. It is a field day for opportunism. Since both parties have likely made substantial investments that are worth less when the contract ends, they can play games over distribution of those assets and greatly affect the stream of benefits from the assets over the remaining life of the contract.

The contract underlying the partnership is like a prenuptial agreement in that it doesn't establish much of the framework for the day-to-day functioning of the partnership. But now that the partnership is unraveling the prenuptial agreement comes into force. The legally binding duties of both parties set out in the contract is of great value for assuring that service needs are still met and for protecting the assets that the two firms have created under the terms of the partnership. At the termination of a partnership, the contract serves the safety net function mentioned above.

10.7 REFERENCES

Doney, Patricia M. and Cannon, Joseph P., "An Examination of the Nature of Trust in Buyer-Seller Relationships," *Journal of Marketing*, 61/2 (April 1997) 35–51.

Dwyer, F. R., Schurr, P. H., and Oh, S., "Developing Buyer-Seller Relationships," *Journal of Marketing*, 51 (1987) 11–27.

Heide, Jan B. and John, George, "Do Norms Matter in Marketing Relationships?" *Journal of Marketing*, 56 (April 1992) 32–44.

Gulati, Ranjay, Khanna, Tarun, and Nohria, Nitin, "Unilateral Commitments and the Importance of Process in Alliances," *Sloan Management Review* (Spring 1994), 61–69.

Henderson, John C., "Plugging into Strategic Partnerships: The Critical IS Connection," *Sloan Management Review*, 31/3 (Spring 1990), 7–18.

Kanter, Rosebeth Moss, "Becoming PALs: Pooling, Allying and Linking Across Companies," *The Academy of Management EXECUTIVE*, 3/3 (1989,) 183–193.

Kanter, Rosebeth Moss, "Collaborative Advantage: The Art of Alliances," *Harvard Business Review* (July–August 1994), 96–108.

Klepper, Robert, "Management of Partnering Development in I/S Outsourcing," *Journal of Information Technology*, 10/4 (1995), 249–258.

Nelson, Kay M. and Cooprider, Jay G., "The Contribution of Shared Knowledge to IS Group Performance," *MIS Quarterly,* 20/4 (December 1996), 409–429.

Niederkofler, Martin, "The Evolution of Strategic Alliances: Opportunities for Managerial Influence," *Journal of Business Venturing*, 6 (1991), 237–257.

Powell, Walter W., "Hybrid Organizational Arrangements: New Form or Transitional Development?" *California Management Review*, 30/1 (1990), 67–87.

Powell, Walter W., "Neither Market Nor Hierarchy: Network Forms of Organization," *Research in Organizational Behavior*, 12 (1990), 295–336.

Rackham, Neil, Lawrence Friedman, and Richard Ruff, *Getting Partnering Right: How Market Leaders Are Creating Long-Term Competitive Advantage*, New York, McGraw–Hill, 1996.

Scott, Robert E., "Conflict and Cooperation in Long-Term-Contracts," *California Law Review*, 75/6 (December 1987), 2005–2053.

11

Contract Expiration and Termination

Outsourcing deals end in several possible ways. In the more favorable scenarios the work is complete, the contract expires, and both parties go their separate ways. In another good ending, the contract expires but the work continues, so client and vendor negotiate a new contract and continue the relationship. In the not-so-good endings, client and vendor have a bad relationship, the work ends, the contract ends, and they go their separate ways, or the contract ends but the work continues, and the client searches for a new vendor and contracts with another outsourcing firm. In the worst case scenario, the relationship is so bad the contract is terminated before it expires.

Contracts can also be terminated when the underlying assumptions of the contract are no longer valid so that it is better to be out of the relationship than in it. An example is a fundamental change in technology that your organization needs and an inflexible contract based on now outdated technology. It may be best to terminate a contract of this sort rather than be denied the benefits of the new technology. On the other hand, the vendor may be willing to renegotiate the contract rather than terminate the relationship altogether. The chapter ends with considerations in renegotiation of contracts.

11.1 ENDGAMES

One problem haunts relationships, good and bad, where both parties know the work will be finished at the end of the contracting period and no follow-on contract will be written. This is the problem of opportunistic endgames in which a party having power over some aspect of the relationship takes advantage of that power and engages in opportunistic behavior. For example, the vendor skimps on service as the contract is about to end.

If both sides have the power and the ability to cause damage to the other, the endgame can be complicated with opportunistic sorties by both sides and threats and counterthreats. These games can become very complex and, once started, hard to end.

Self enforcing aspects of contracts may help where this kind of opportunism is concerned. The vendor has a reputation to uphold. If your big, visible, influential organization signals the vendor your expectation of continued good performance, the vendor may be persuaded to curb opportunism. A veiled reference to the consequences if it doesn't, may help as well. A smaller, less consequential organization may not be able to use this weapon effectively. A measured retaliation to vendor misbehavior with a clear statement of the reasons for the move and/or the threat of future punitive moves if vendor opportunism persists might be effective in preventing or ending vendor opportunism.

The contract may offer other mechanisms for deterring vendor opportunism. If the contract has significant penalty provisions for poor performance, these can be a powerful deterrent to a vendor that would play games with service delivery and quality, and it's another reason why the contract should have good, measurable requirements. The ability to withhold payment is always a powerful weapon.

Despite the safeguards, endgames can be vicious. For this reason it is important to have a plan for termination. Think of the worst case scenario as something akin to recovery from a major natural disaster.

11.2 CONTRACT EXPIRATION

When a contract expires, the contract can usually be renewed with the vendor, or the work can be directed to a new vendor, or the work can be brought in-house. The contract provides the first level of planning for expiration in all these cases. It contains provisions for transfer of resources and work at the time the contract expires.

11.2.1 Contract Expiration with Renewal or a Switch to Another Vendor

Don't let contract expiration arrive unexpectedly. Planning should begin well in advance of the expiration date. Is there now a competitive or core competencies aspect to information systems work that wasn't present when the current contract was signed? If so, it may not be a good idea to outsource this function or functions again. Ask whether there is a change in the basic objectives of outsourcing or changes in the scope of what is to be outsourced in the next contract.

Whether the decision is to outsource the work to the same or another vendor, go back to the issues of Chapters 5, 6, and 7 in analyzing needs, finding a vendor, negotiating, and implementing a new contract.

If basic objectives and scope remain the same and the work should still be outsourced to one vendor, it is possible to reuse much of the analysis done for the current contract. As a consequence, the analysis can go much faster. But carefully consider how business and technology have changed over the contract period, and analyze what is coming over the horizon in both business and technology. Revise requirements in the light of these changes. Also rework the RFP as it relates to the relationship with a vendor in areas like incentives, monitoring, control, dispute resolution, and other aspects of the management of the outsourcing deal. In other words, review the outsourcing experience and benefit from it in preparing for and negotiating a new contract.

If the work will be divided among several vendors in the next round of contracting, redo the analysis work with an eye to creating clean divisions between functions that will be outsourced to different vendors. Then, develop separate term sheets and RFPs for each type of work.

In market contracting situations, recontracting with the same vendor offers no substantial benefits. Put the contract out to bid again and generate competition. Decide whether to stick with the previous vendor list or to widen the pool of vendors who might compete for the new contract.

In intermediate-type contracting situations, the vendor on the current contract will likely have an advantage over others in competition for the next contract. Intermediate contracting means that some relationship specific knowledge or assets were developed as the vendor did the work. The current vendor has this knowledge or has invested in these assets and is more attractive on this account. Of course, other factors also come into play, not the least of which are vendor fees and commitment to service quality. Despite the built-in advantage of your current vendor, look for others if the chances of a better deal are possible. But realize that you may have to invest again in transfer of knowledge to a new vendor and include these costs in the cost analysis as you choose between vendors.

Even though the current vendor has the inside track in the bidding for a new contract, and knows it, you might negotiate a new contract at more favorable terms if you can foster some believable competition by other vendors.

In partnership arrangements, contracts play a different role, as the previous chapter points out. Successive contracts can be used to continually raise the expectations of performance by both sides. Contracts also serve a safety net function that acts to dissolve the partnership in an orderly way if it does fail.

If the new contract does go to a new vendor, transfer issues come into play. The current contract should contain provisions for transfer upon expiration and address issues of ownership of assets and transfer of data, hardware, software, and people. Put together a planning team that includes your people and the new vendor's people to set the steps and schedule for the transition.

In moving work to another vendor, think about the advantages of doing this in phases or stages. The work being done by the current vendor may be separable in various ways. It may be advantageous to split it and move some to a new vendor before others, if the contract provisions allow this or if some sort of bridging arrangement can be made with the current vendor.

11.2.2 Insourcing Again

Bringing the work back in-house requires good planning and execution. Resources must be assembled and put into place to make this happen. It will be a lot easier if people who have been doing the work on the vendor side are transferred to your organization. Perhaps these are some of the same people transferred to the vendor when the function in question was originally outsourced. Equipment and software must often be acquired or transferred from the vendor. Data must be transferred, and probably converted.

Think of insourcing as something like the beginning of an outsourcing arrangement in terms of the issues that must be addressed and the structures that must be put in place.

Most organizations know well before the current contract ends that they want to insource at the end of the contract period. Much preliminary work can be accomplished before the contract ends to smooth the transition:

- Additional managerial staff can be put in place, as needed.
- Sites and office space can be obtained and prepared.
- Equipment and software can be secured and installed.
- Personnel hiring processes can begin.

The advantages of keeping a core management staff in the IT function of your organization throughout the outsourcing period now pays off. These managers know the organization and its information systems needs. They have kept up with technology and how technology can address the needs of the organization. They are the cadre who plan and lead the transition to insourcing. And they are the managers who direct the information systems function once the function is back inside your organizational walls.

11.3 CONTRACT TERMINATION

Planning for termination begins with contract negotiations and the inclusion of good termination provisions in the contract. See Chapters 6 and 7 on this issue. Even with a sound contract, termination has real and substantial costs. The benefits and costs must be carefully weighed before moving to terminate for convenience or cause. Some of the costs are:

- Legal and court fees.
- Termination or buyout fees due the vendor under the contract.
- The costs of finding and negotiating a contract with another vendor and transferring the outsourced functions to the new vendor, or the costs of bringing the outsourced function or functions back inside your organization.

If the contract does not have the strong termination provisions discussed in Chapter 7, you may face large costs. Services can be disrupted if the vendor stops doing your work in the middle of termination proceedings. Also add the costs of transferring the outsourced function to another vendor or moving it in-house, perhaps without help from the current vendor. Transition without the help of the vendor (or with the vendor's active resistance to a transfer effort) can be very chaotic and costly — so costly that termination is not a real possibility.

Expect most vendors to fight termination under most circumstances, unless termination fees are tilted heavily in their favor. Vendors often structure contracts in ways that produce most of their margins on the backend of the contracting period. Unless it is late in the contracting period, they will want the contract to continue so that they capture those margins.

If the vendor is large and you are small, the legal battle can be a very expensive and may be worth it only if some larger issue is at stake, like preserving your organization's reputation.

Get the best legal representation possible. Go into litigation with well-documented instances of vendor nonperformance. Different states have different statutes of limitations that govern the period between a breach of contract and the application to the courts for remedy of the breach, and judges and juries assume that you won't delay in going to the courts if the harm is at all serious (Mylott, 1995). The termination decision and legal proceedings should be made and initiated without delay.

Form a team to do the analysis before any final decision is made on termination. Analyze the costs and benefits. Use scenario analysis for best, most likely, and worst cases. Many costs will depend on how long the transfer takes. Don't assume cost relationships are linear; the longer the termination takes or the more difficult or contentious it is, the more costs may skyrocket. User managers should be fully informed and made part of the decision process. Their analysis of the business costs of various options may be crucial to the decision.

Carefully consider how services will be provided if the current contract is terminated. Is your organization really able to in-source again; are other vendors with the appropriate infrastructure, skills, and slack resources available to take up your work? Can the transition from the current vendor to in-house or alternative vendor services be undertaken smoothly, or are there unique aspects of the way the current vendor does your work that would make transition difficult? Do the vendor's people have knowledge or skills not available in-house or with another vendor? Are your users prepared to suffer some periods of disruption in services?

The work already done by a vendor may have little salvage value. For example, the vendor whose people learned your systems in order to do maintenance on them have knowledge transferred to them that can't be retained if the relationship is ended. These are sunk costs over which you have no control. The decision should be made on the basis of future costs and benefits of termination, including the costs of moving to a new vendor or back in-house, not the costs of the past.

One of the traps in coming to grips with termination issues is the tendency of managers to justify their original decision to contract with the bad vendor. They will often want to stick with the vendor in hopes the situation will improve. If analysis of termination is left to them, they might do biased analyses of data to avoid confronting a failure. The antidote is to get people who were not involved or responsible for the original decision to do the analysis and make the call on termination.

If the decision is made to proceed with termination, plan it carefully. Get the necessary legal staff and support. Put together a team with the necessary information systems business and technical people and with representatives from the user community. If the contract limits the vendor's cooperation to a certain time period after termination is set in motion, planning is constrained by this window.

When should the vendor know you are thinking of termination? It depends on circumstances, the most important of which may be how much the vendor wants your business. If the vendor wants the business, the prospect of contract termination might have a very salutary effect and bring the vendor around and even prevent termination. Let the vendor know the moment you're thinking of termination in this case. If the vendor doesn't care about your business, then a signal of possible or planned termination could be an invitation to even poorer service. Hide the fact that you're terminating until the planning is finished and the lawyers are ready to swing into action.

The move to terminate against a vendor who wants your business has an even greater prospect of changing the vendor's behavior for the better when your organization already has resources or some of the resources necessary to insource or when you openly move to solicit the interest of other vendors for the same work.

Don't initiate a law suit to terminate as a tactic to scare the vendor into good behavior when you're not serious about carrying through with the legal action (Mylott, 1995). The vendor may not be scared, may see through the bluff, and may take up the challenge.

Carefully plan the process by which services delivered under the current contract will be transferred to another vendor or brought in-house. The same issues addressed above under handling transfers of work at contract expiration come into play in instances of contract termination.

If poor service from the current vendor is costing a lot in terms of business functioning, it may be worth starting the process of transfer to another vendor or bringing the function in-house before the contract with the current vendor is actually terminated. The vendor probably won't let go of the resources and processing used to produce the services, but the outsourced function can be duplicated in-house or with another vendor. This strategy runs a risk; you may duplicate the service and then find that it is not possible to terminate. If the contract allows termination for cause but not termination at will, the courts may not agree that the contract has been breached.

11.4 **CONTRACT RENEGOTIATION**

Faced with a contract that is no longer tolerable and with considerable costs of termination, it may be wise to investigate the possibility of renegotiating the contract. Unless termination fees are heavily in the vendor's favor, the vendor may face net termination costs of its own. The vendor may also be anxious to keep your business.

It may be best to put renegotiation in the hands of persons who were not central to managing the current, troubled contract. Enmities often develop between client and vendor outsourcing managers through the round of disputes that precede renegotiation. At the same time the negotiators should have outsourcing experience and insight. The problems that caused the current contract to fail shouldn't be replaced by a new set of problems in a succeeding contract. Consultants may be of assistance here. Legal counsel should also be involved.

Renegotiation might be seen as an opportunity to completely rethink and reshape outsourcing starting with its objectives and scope. However, your vendor might not be prepared for a total rework of the outsourcing arrangement, unless there are obvious vendor benefits. Time is another constraint. If renegotiation is to be successful, it needs to be done in a timely manner, or the opportunity may slip away as conflict escalates and your senior managers and users lose patience.

Normally renegotiation will focus on the underlying circumstances and needs that caused problems. Develop your own analysis of the underlying problems. Go back and quickly restructure requirements and the cost-benefit-risk analysis in light of the revised circumstances. Develop a term sheet document (see Chapter 5) in preparation for negotiations that defines the issues and your organization's negotiating position on each issue and provision that should appear in a new contract. Follow the guides to contract negotiation found in Chapter 6.

Even though renegotiation of the contract is your objective, don't assume it will be successful. Prepare for termination if renegotiation fails.

11.5 REFERENCES

Mylott, Thomas R., *Computer Outsourcing: Managing the Transfer of Information Systems*, Englewood Cliffs, NJ, Prentice Hall, 1995.

A

Outsourcing Consultants

An outsourcing evaluation and negotiation requires technical, legal, management, negotiation, and outsourcing expertise. Your company probably has internal technical and managerial expertise that can be assigned to the outsourcing team, but you may not have in-house outsourcing and negotiating experience. Outsourcing vendors, on the other hand, have negotiated and implemented scores of outsourcing agreements. You can "level the playing field" by using outside experts. The right consultants and lawyers can greatly ease the struggle for both parties in an outsourcing transaction.

A.1 ADVANTAGES AND DISADVANTAGES

The advantages of using a competent outsourcing consultant are several. In addition to leveling the playing field, a consultant can help overcome the biases of internal staff and can untangle problems. A consultant can put concentrated effort into the outsourcing project; whereas your employees, with other jobs to perform, may face conflicts of time and commitment between their work and the project.

The advantages should be weighed against the disadvantages. One obvious disadvantage is cost. Consultants can be expensive. Formulate expectations and objectives with corresponding budgets. Cost overruns result from the failure to control a consultant. It is important to communicate a clear picture of what the consultant is expected to deliver.

A second potential disadvantage is finding the wrong consultant among many choices. The quality varies widely. Anyone can become a consultant. It is not a licensed profession, and, in some instances, consulting has become the last resort of the downsized executive. This could be a plus if the consultant is an IT

329

manager with outsourcing experience. But, there are also those who oversell their capabilities.

A third disadvantage is the danger of relying too heavily on a consultant. Consultants cannot do everything and cannot replace good business decision making on the part of people in your organization. Don't delegate responsibility for outsourcing decision making or management to consultants. The responsibility is yours. Don't let the consultant own the outsourcing evaluation or contracting processes; keep the consultant in an advisory position.

A.2 FINDING THE RIGHT CONSULTANT

The available consultants and lawyers and the growing number of outsourcing "experts" have varying levels of experience and proficiency. It is important, therefore, to conduct a search to find an individual consultant or consulting firm that meets your needs. Leads can be generated from:

- Referrals from other companies. Contact a peer in a company that has announced an outsourcing contract. Inquire if the company used one or more consultants, ask for his or her name and phone number and how the client felt about the consultant's contributions, skills, and other factors.

- Research trade journals and other information sources, including the Sourcing Interest Group and the Outsourcing Institute.

- The authors of this book, who know many highly qualified outsourcing consultants.

A big consulting firm, like a supermarket, offers you more to pick from. There is more breadth and depth of experience, know-how, and special talent among its members. And they can draw on each other's specialties and expertise. On the debit side, big firms tend to be more expensive; they have scheduling problems, so they can't always put preferred people on certain jobs (and tend to save their best people for the bigger jobs with the bigger clients); and consequently, your assignment may be given to a junior member of the firm.

The advantages of a small firm, by and large, are these: Their senior members are generally available (in a 10-man firm, for instance, all the consultants are senior members); small businessmen tend to feel more comfortable with small consulting firms, a point that shouldn't be disregarded as trivial; and the small firms tend to offer a more personalized service. What's more, being a small business itself, the small consulting firm tends to establish greater rapport with the small client, and frequently has greater insight into the small company's problems.

After researching potential consultants and compiling a list of several, evaluate the consultants based on the tasks to be performed in the outsourcing process. You may need the consultant's assistance and expertise to perform a strategic analysis of what should be outsourced, define requirements, prepare an RFP, negotiate a sound contract, select the appropriate vendor, plan for and make the transition to outsourcing operations, or manage the relationship over the term of the contract.

Few consultants would be appropriate for the entire process, as the skills and experiences of consultants vary considerably. For example, the skills required to help with the strategic analysis of your company are different from the technical expertise required to make a successful transition, define service levels, or manage the relationship. Similarly, the negotiation of the contract calls for both strategic and technical thinking.

Factors to consider in an evaluation include cost, responsiveness, outsourcing experience in your industry and in general, a good reputation as an outsourcing consultant, general knowledge, experience in your company, technical experience with systems, strong communications skills including creative thinking, listening, and talking without use of too much computer jargon. Strong analytical abilities such as problem definition, solutions identification, and research of relevant facts are also important skills. Deal only with consultants who are independent of all vendors. Avoid conflict of interest situations.

Other things that are important to look for when interviewing and screening a potential consultant follow:

- Is the consultant a good listener? That's one of the most important personal qualifications a consultant needs.
- If there is more than one representative from the same firm, do they seem to have rapport? In many long assignments away from home, consulting teams are thrown together for days at a time. If they don't work well together, you do not want them.
- Does the consultant make knowledgeable references to your company, product, industry that reflect either pertinent experience, or enough professionalism to have done some homework?
- What sort of questions does the consultant ask? Are they probing? Do they lead anywhere? Does she make any initial, intelligent recommendations?

Also be alert to warning signs of potential trouble that may flash as you talk with and evaluate consultants:

- Beware of any consultant who refuses to provide a list of references. Some may say, "All our work is highly confidential," but the practice is to provide names, and a consultant who doesn't should be scratched off your list.

- Anyone who points to jobs like yours and glibly reassures you to "stop worrying, all these problems are alike," ought to be avoided.

- If a consultant's fee is out of line, for example, three others ask for $10,000–$20,000, and he wants $1,000 — be wary. He may not be a charlatan, but chances are he either misunderstands the problem or is going to sell you a gimmick.

- Solutions that just don't seem to fit your situation.

- Fads and gimmicks. Undue reliance on charts, diagrams, and the like should make you wary.

- A consultant who makes promises before he has had a chance to understand your company should be avoided.

- Don't be swayed by gross claims and hyperbole. Nobody's track record is perfect — if it were, you couldn't afford the person.

- Does he refer to past assignments in detail that should be confidential? If he talks about his other clients, he'll talk about you.

- Be suspicious if the consultant is willing to offer you a bundle of free services — such as a week or two spent in your place, at no charge to you. Since any consultant is largely selling time, it isn't feasible to give time away and still render a service. The consultant will make up the cost somehow.

Protocol says that you should tell each consultant how many others you're interviewing. Many consultants will simply not come in at all if they know they're competing against several others. They feel you're still at the "hunting and fishing" stage rather than at the decision-making stage.

Serious consideration requires narrowing the field down to a manageable number of alternatives before you interview in depth because the process will be time-consuming. The process, then, usually takes the following path:

- Have each candidate come into your office for a day of discussing the problem and looking around. (Depending on the size of the project, many will ask for another date on which they can come back, spend more time, and talk to more of the people involved; some will even ask for three visits.)

- Get a list of references of former clients. (If the list isn't forthcoming, ask for it.) Check out the references and ask each referent if they know of other organizations that have used the consultant. Check these out, as well.

- Request a proposal or "letter of understanding" outlining the consultant's perception of the problem, her methods of solution, the time involved, and the cost.

- Select the best consultant for your need and sign an agreement or contract.

There can be great advantage to acquiring outside expertise to help you create a sound win-win contract and a win-win relationship with a vendor.

B

Outsourcing Examples

This appendix lists a few of the thousands of commercial information systems outsourcing agreements made in recent years and discusses some examples of outsourcing contracts.

Table B-1. Outsourcing Examples

Company	Outsourcer	Industry
British Aerospace	CSC	Aerospace
Hughes Aircraft	CSC	Aerospace
McDonnell Douglas	IBM	Aerospace
General Dynamics	CSC	Aerospace
America West	EDS	Airline
Continental	EDS	Airline
Delta	AT&T	Airline
US Air	Bell Atlantic	Airline
J. P. Morgan	CSC and Multiple Vendors	Banking/Finance
National Westminster	EDS	Banking/Finance
Riggs National Bank	IBM	Banking/Finance
Swiss Bank/Warburgs	Perot Systems	Banking/Finance
Proctor & Gamble	IBM	Consumer Goods
Chrysler	IBM	Automotive
Ford of Europe	CSC	Automotive

Company	Outsourcer	Industry
General Motors	EDS	Automotive
Jaguar Cars	CSC	Automotive
Saab	EDS	Automotive
United Technologies	Genix	Automotive
Europcar	Perot Systems	Automobile Rentals
Hertz	IBM	Automobile Rentals
ABN AMRO Bank	MCI-SHL System House	Banking/Finance
American Express Bank	EDS	Banking/Finance
Chase Manhattan	FISERV British Telecom IBM	Banking/Finance
Continental Bank	IBM	Banking/Finance
First Fidelity Bancorp	IBM	Banking/Finance
First American Bankshares	Perot	Banking/Financial Services
Kaiser Permanente	IBM	Health/Pharmaceutical
United Healthcare Corporation	CSC	Health/Pharmaceutical
Dow Chemical	Andersen, Digital and others	Chemicals
DuPont	Andersen Consulting and CSC	Chemicals
Kodak	Digital, IBM, Entex, Northern Telecom	Manufacturing
Polaroid	CSC	Manufacturing
Xerox	EDS	Manufacturing
Moore Corp.	EDS	Paper/Print Management
Scott Paper	CSC	Paper
British Petroleum	Multiple vendors	Petroleum
Exxon	Multiple vendors	Petroleum
Time-Life	EDS	Publishing
Kash n' Karry	GSI	Retail
Kooperativa Forbundet	EDS	Retail
Riser Foods		Retail

Company	Outsourcer	Industry
Southland Corporation	EDS/NCR/Canmax Retail	Retail
Supermarkets General	IBM	Retail
Thrifty Drug	IBM	Retail
Tom Thumb	IBM	Retail
United Retail Group	IBM	Retail
VONS Cos.	SHL	Retail
Southern New England	CSC	Telephone
Sun Microsystems	CSC	Technology
Tandem Computers	EDS	Technology
Southern Pacific	IBM	Transportation
US Travel	EDS	Travel
Commonwealth Edison		Utilities
East Midlands Electric (UK)	Perot Systems	Utilities
IES Utilities	EDS	Utilities
Nashville Electric	Seltman, Cobb & Bryant	Utilities
PECO Energy Co.	IBM	Utilities
Public Service Co. of Colorado	IBM	Utilities
San Diego Gas & Electric	CSC	Utilities
Southeastern Electric Board (UK)	Andersen	Utilities
Texas Instruments United Illuminating	CSC	Utilities
Washington Water Power	EDS	Utilities

Kodak, General Dynamics, McDonnell Douglas, J.P. Morgan, and Xerox are examples of major U.S. companies that outsourced most, if not all, of their information technology services. Referred to as full or total outsourcing, these contracts are usually in excess of a billion dollars with contract periods of up to ten years. Other examples, not as well known but still interesting, are discussed below to illustrate the range of possible outsourcing arrangements.

The Canadian Museum of Nature chose Digital Equipment Corporation to assume responsibility for the Museum's existing information technology and to create new vehicles for transforming the Museum's holdings into consumable products. Some of the first projects include: a national, multimedia collection repository for disseminating information on the Museum's resources throughout Canada and worldwide; an information clearinghouse on biodiversity; nature-related video-on-demand products; an Internet home page; and guided tours of the Museum.

An interesting example of the many datacenter outsourcing contracts signed in recent years is Camino Healthcare in Mountain View, CA. After looking at several outsourcing firms to take over its datacenter, Camino Healthcare chose IBM. IBM offered projected savings of $5 million over a five-year contract.

CSC and Sun Microsystems signed a three-year, $27-million agreement to move Sun Microsystems to a client/server environment. CSC now runs Sun's worldwide operations, handling orders, inventory inquiries, and messages between manufacturing and distribution.

General Electric Company's Aircraft Engines division selected Digital Equipment Corporation to take over management, operations, administration and technical support of the division's distributed computer systems at 13 locations across the United States. These were not just computers bought from Digital Equipment, they included systems from multiple vendors, peripherals (like printers and disks), and software.

Desktop Systems include personal computers and the local area networks that connect them. Activities outsourced here include procurement, installation, network hookups, operations, and help desks. Some companies choose outsourcing providers to help manage large projects, others for day-to-day operations. Florida Power and Light recently outsourced the replacement of over 8,000 old-style computer terminals with PCs. Microsoft, the leading software developer for PCs and local area networks, chose to outsource day-to-day operations to Digital Equipment Corporation.

Elf Atochem, a Philadelphia-based chemicals manufacturer, needed to free up internal resources so it could focus on its migration to a client-server architecture. To accomplish this, ELF decided to outsource the maintenance and support of its multiplatform legacy systems. Elf chose Keane, Inc., the Boston-based software services firm.

The National Association of Securities Dealers (NASD) which operates the Nasdaq Stock Market and regulates the industry wanted to free its staff from working on legacy systems and permit them to work on new technology projects. NASD signed an agreement with an offshore company, Tata Consulting Services, to perform legacy systems maintenance with TCS staff co-located with NASD employees in Rockville, Maryland and located in TCS facilities in Bombay. NASD estimates that the less costly labor rates save the company $3 to $4 million annually.

C

Request For Proposal (RFP) Outline

Once you have decided that outsourcing is a viable alternative, you need to make an inquiry from potential vendors. A Request For Proposal (RFP) is how you make the inquiry. An RFP is also useful in that it forces you to analyze your current operations and to specify your requirements. By sending the same RFP to all prospective vendors, you will be receiving vendor proposals that permit you to compare each vendor's proposal to the others and assess how well each vendor can fulfill your requirements. With an RFP, you make it clear to the vendors that you are aware of your own operations and that you intend to fairly, but competitively, investigate your outsourcing options.

The specific details of the RFP will vary depending on the services to be outsourced and whether you are contemplating total or selective outsourcing, but the general content is similar.

It is important that the RFP be complete in that it specifies what you expect the vendors to respond to in the proposal. If not requested in the RFP, the vendors are less likely to provide the information. The topics included in the typical RFP are as follows:

1. INTRODUCTION AND OVERVIEW

- Overview of the RFP. Provide a general description of what functions are to be considered for outsourcing.

- Objectives of the RFP. Specify the goals and objectives of outsourcing such as cash infusion, cost reduction, improved performance, reducing risk, sharing risks, gaining access to new technologies, maintaining legacy systems, obtaining new resources, gaining access to special skills, implementing a variable cost approach, and so on.

- Scope of the Proposal. Make it clear that the proposal must be comprehensive and reflect the vendor's best bid and note which if any of the services the vendor is not bidding. If the vendor is planning to subcontract any of the services or partner with another vendor, the RFP should specify that the proposal make note of this and fully describe the role of the services to be provided by the other party.

- Key Dates in the Proposal Process. Outline the dates for each of the major steps in the process–RFP release, proposal due date, proposal evaluation, negotiations, decision, and so forth.

- Proposed dates for outsourcing startup, implementation, expiration and renewal.

- How to Respond to the Proposal. In addition to the date and time of day that the proposal must be submitted, describe how to respond — on paper and/or on disk, number of copies, are faxes permitted, name and address of person to whom the proposal must be delivered, if the proposal must be in a sealed envelope.

- Format of the Proposal. Specify exactly the format expected for the proposal so that the evaluation and comparison of proposals will be easier.

- Contracts for Each Area Covered in the RFP. Specify the person or persons in your company the vendor may contact for additional information or clarification. It is advisable that only one person be the initial contact for all vendors and that the questions and answers be provided to all vendors. Make it clear how communications should be handled (by phone, mail only, etc.).

- Vendor Presentations. Include a provision requiring or giving you the option to require the vendor to make a presentation at your site.

- Firm Offer. Make it clear that all offers are firm for a specified period such as 90–180 days.

- Confidentiality. Include a detailed confidentiality provision and require the vendor to sign it before distributing the RFP.

- Ownership. Specify in the RFP that you own all your data and the vendor must return it upon request. You may also want to specify that you own the proposals and have the right to use anything contained in the proposal.

- Vendor Costs and Expenses. State that the vendor is required to cover its own costs incurred prior to signing the outsourcing contract.

- Rights and Obligations. Note that you are under no obligation to make an agreement with any vendor and that you reserve the right to negotiate with other vendors.

2. CLIENT INFORMATION

- Provide information about your business, its size, location, customers, products, and other general information.
- Describe the services you are evaluating for outsourcing. Provide a more detailed appendix for each service, if necessary, to fully describe the service as to type of systems, locations, users, and other information.
- Explain where you plan to be or desire to be in 2, 5, and 10 years. (If you do not have a strategic business plan and associated technology plan, it may be useful to brainstorm the future with a group of business and technology leaders within your company.)
- Specify your short and long-term IT goals. You may be in the process of consolidating data centers and you want that completed before the vendor takes over, or you may intend to fully migrate to a client/server environment in three years. It is important for the vendor to know these IT goals, even if these are only loosely related to the company goals and objectives of outsourcing specified elsewhere in the RFP.

3. SERVICES TO BE PROVIDED

- Describe existing services and the services the vendor will be asked to provide. List all locations effected in the organization. Describe platforms and environments that will affect services and what your organization will do to support vendor services. The description must be sufficiently detailed so that the vendors can understand your operations. State service requirements in measurable terms.
- Expectations of future improvements in productivity and quality of information services involved in the outsourcing deal and request for information on the vendor's programs and capabilities for meeting these requirements.
- Provide statistics on your current operations such as hardware, software, and communications configurations, number of users, size of data storage, frequency of reports generation, and the like.
- Describe a typical day's processing cycle.
- Ask the vendor for a description of its plan for assuming responsibility for your IT functions.

- Layout vendor reporting requirements.
- Expectations of future improvements in productivity and quality of information services involved in the outsourcing deal and request for information on the vendor's programs and capabilities for meeting these requirements.
- Expectations of knowledge and skill transfer from vendor to client, if skill transfer is one of the motives for outsourcing.

4. PERFORMANCE AND CHANGE CONTROL

- Describe current service level measurements (if available). Specify service levels that the vendor will be required to meet.
- Require the vendor to indicate how liquidated damages will be applied in the event that the vendor does not achieve service level commitments.
- Require the vendor to perform a root cause analysis for any service failures.
- Describe reporting requirements with respect to service level.
- Describe benchmarking procedures and how the vendor will implement customer satisfaction surveys.
- Ask the vendor to describe how changes will be controlled.
- Transition of the information systems function or functions to the vendor with requirements for timing and responsibilities for costs.

5. PRICING

- Include your budget for the services to be considered.
- Ask the vendor to provide its best base-case figures and clearly specify what is included and what is not.
- Ask the vendor to provide separate pricing for functions/projects. Explain how changes in volume affect the price, and how growth is built into this price.
- How will adjustments be handled? What are the customer's requirements?
- Describe mechanisms the vendor will use to increase/decrease services. Rates should be provided on an hourly, weekly, and monthly basis.

- How will additional services be priced?
- State that significant changes in business requirements should trigger renegotiation or changes to pricing structure.
- How will inflation adjustments be handled?
- What currency will payments be made in? Who bears the currency risk?
- How will unanticipated decreases in technology cost be handled? The customer and the vendor should share in unanticipated savings.
- Who will be responsible for service taxes?
- How will new/divested entities be handled?
- Describe desired timing for invoice and payment. In addition, describe invoice detail.

6. EMPLOYEE ISSUES

- State how many of your employees will receive offers by the vendor. Clearly specify any desired employment terms.
- Requirements for positions and benefits offered employees who will be transferred to the vendor firm. All benefits should be addressed, even minor ones.
- Transfer of years of service in your organization to the vendor organization for employees to be transferred.
- Ask for a copy of any employment agreement that transferred employees will be asked to sign.
- Ask the vendor to describe how employees will be transitioned.

7. PROJECT STAFF AND PROJECT MANAGEMENT

- Project Executive. You should require the vendor to provide the name and qualifications of the initial project executive. You should be provided the opportunity to meet and interview the candidate. You should also reserve approval rights over all project executive appointments. The vendor should also be prohibited from "churning" project executives (e.g., specify minimum duration of appointment).

- Key Employees. There should be a requirement that the vendor provide the name and qualifications of any employees that are key other than the project executive. This usually includes the project executive's direct reports as well as employees key to certain projects. You should be provided the opportunity to meet and interview the candidates and reserve approval rights over all key employee appointments. The vendor should also be prohibited from "churning" key employees (e.g., specify minimum duration of appointment).

- Management structure for the outsourcing relationship, including governance and communication structures, planning requirements, and key personnel roles.

8.   EXPIRATION AND TERMINATION

- Specify processes, procedures, and time schedules for normal expiration of the contract and its renegotiation, if applicable.

- Specify circumstances that may trigger termination for convenience, cause, failure to perform, for change of control, and specify assistance the vendor will provide upon termination.

9.   CONTRACT TERMS

- Who will own what rights to intellectual property?

- Who will obtain third-party consents, and who will bear the costs of obtaining these?

- Insurance requirements.

- Confidentiality requirements.

- Security requirements.

- Guarantee and warranty issues.

- Limitations and conditions on the use of subcontractors, if any.

10. VENDOR INFORMATION

- References. Client lists and references to clients in similar companies for similar outsourced functions.
- Vendor objectives and financial condition, if these data were not collected as part of the RFI process.
- Questions related to vendor competency (if not obtained in the RFI process) can be included. These might address knowledge, experience and resources related to the area of outsourcing required, technology employed, personnel, personnel turnover, security, backup and recovery capabilities, and experience. They might also include how the vendor is organized and its procedures and methodologies.

11. APPENDICES

Attach a complete description of the services being considered for outsourcing, technology plans, business plans, and anything that can help clarify and explain what you want the vendors to know.

12. OTHER TERMS AND CONDITIONS

- Consider other terms and conditions that may apply and attach these to the RFP.

D

Sample Request For Proposal

To illustrate what a Request For Proposal (RFP) might include, this Appendix contains an actual RFP except that the name of the company has been changed to the ABC Company and certain information has been excluded such as Section 1.6 which describes the company background.

SELECTIVE OUTSOURCING FOR THE SOFTWARE MAINTENANCE OF ABC's CORPORATE LEGACY APPLICATIONS
Request For Proposal December 30, 1996

TABLE OF CONTENTS

SECTION 1. INTRODUCTION AND PURPOSE

1.1 Introduction

The ABC invites responses from suitably qualified providers of application support services (hereafter referred to as "Vendor/s") to propose a contractual arrangement for the *technical design, programming, testing, and documentation involved in the maintenance and enhancement of Corporate Legacy Applications as described in this document.*

The due date for receipt of proposals responding to the RFP is
ABC's Corporate Legacy Applications will continue to be run on site in ABC's Data Center located in New Orleans, LA. **The ABC will not consider a Vendor proposal to outsource the Data Center, Communications Network, or any other services not specifically described in this RFP.**

This Request for Proposal (RFP) is not an offer by the ABC, but an invitation for Vendor response. No ABC contractual obligation whatsoever shall arise from the RFP process unless and until a formal contract is executed by duly authorized officers of the ABC and the Vendor. The ABC reserves the right to accept or reject any and all proposals, to revise the RFP, to request one or more resubmissions or clarifications from one or more Vendors, or to cancel the process entirely. No Vendor is obligated to respond or to continue to respond to the RFP. Additionally, the ABC reserves the right to alter specifications during the RFP process, and (without reissuance of the RFP) following the selection of the Vendor. Each party shall be entirely responsible for its own costs and expenses which are incurred while participating in the RFP and contract negotiation processes.

This document contains information confidential and proprietary to ABC. Disclosure of receipt of this RFP or any part of the information contained herein to parties not directly involved in providing the services requested could result in the disqualification of or legal action against the Vendor.

1.2 Structure of the RFP

The RFP is divided into three *overview* Sections that provide essential information regarding the requested services. In addition, three Appendices provide important *details* about the specified services, and include strict requirements for the format and content of proposal responses. *Vendors must adhere to the response format* (see *Appendix C - Proposal Preparation Instructions) in order to be considered a valid candidate during the proposal evaluation process.*

As additional background about the ABC, a brochure entitled *ABCs - An Introduction* has been included. Note that the brochure does *not* contain any RFP-related requirements or specifications; it is merely helpful background material about the ABC.

By way of a brief overview, the RFP is structured as follows: *Section 1* describes ABC's approach to the outsourcing effort. It contains the terms and conditions of the RFP, and defines the ABC. This Section also spells out ABC's purpose, scope, and objectives in outsourcing specific application-related tasks and includes the projected schedule for this project.

Section 2 describes ABC's current legacy application environment.

Section 3 identifies the information and organization required in the Vendor's proposal.

Appendix A - Candidate Application Maintenance Activities for Outsourcing provides the Vendor with those legacy software maintenance activities targeted for outsourcing and their current environments.

Appendix B - Descriptions of ABC Corporate Legacy Applications lists the candidate applications, each accompanied with a brief writeup identifying its purpose, users, hardware and software environment, the number of programs included, and the schedule of its planned retirement.

Appendix C - Proposal Preparation Instructions details the format and content of the Vendor's proposal sections and subsections as required by the ABC.

Enclosure - The brochure, ABC — *Information Brochure,* introduces the reader to an overview of ABC's mission, relationships, and activities.

1.3 Terms and Conditions

The ABC directs the Vendor's attention to the following terms and conditions which underlie this RFP/Proposal effort and which provide a statement of understanding between the parties. These terms and conditions are in addition to the confidentiality legend noted above in *Section 1.1*:

1.3.1 Date of Bid Expiration

Due to the nature of the evaluation process, and approval and procurement activities that may occur, proposals must be valid for a minimum of 120 days. Responses must clearly state the length of the bid and its explicit expiration date.

1.3.2 Bidder Indication of Authorization to Bid

Responses submitted by a Vendor to this RFP represent a firm offer to contract on the terms and conditions described in the Vendor's response. The proposal must be signed by an official authorized to commit the bidder to the terms and conditions of the proposal. Vendor must clearly identify the full title and authorization of the designated official and provide a statement of bid commitment with the accompanying signature of the official.

1.3.3 Proposal Ownership

The proposal and all supporting documentation submitted by the Vendor shall become the property of the ABC unless the Vendor specifically requests, in writing, that the proposal and documentation be returned or destroyed.

1.3.4 Receipt of Proposals

The ABC will not accept fax transmitted proposals. Proposals submitted after the stated deadline will not be accepted. Vendors are encouraged to submit their proposals as far in advance of the stated deadline as possible due to potential delays in mailing.

1.3.5 Bid Pricing Information

By submitting a signed bid, the Vendor certifies that:

The Vendor has arrived at the prices in its bid without agreement with any other bidder of this RFP for the purpose of restricting competition.

The prices in the bid have not been disclosed and will not be disclosed to any other bidder of this RFP.

No attempt by the Vendor to induce any other bidder to submit or not submit a bid for restricting competition has occurred.

1.3.6 Bidder Status

Each Vendor must indicate whether or not they are under investigation or have been prosecuted by any local, state, or federal agency or authority in connection with any improper business practices. Each Vendor must indicate whether or not they have any actual or potential conflict of interest related to contracting for services with the ABC.

1.3.7 Vendor Utilization of Know-How and Personnel for Competitors.

The ABC will request a clause that prohibits the Vendor from using any information or know-how gained in this contract for another _____ anywhere in the world for a period of three years from the date of the contract.

1.3.8   Intellectual Property Rights

The ABC expects to own all intellectual property rights to all software and/or systems created by the Vendor under this contract.

1.3.9   Security

The Vendor's proposal must include a plan to safeguard the confidentiality of ABC's legacy applications and data.

1.3.10   Solicitation of Employees

ABC will request a clause that states the parties agree not to hire, solicit, or accept solicitation (either directly, indirectly, or through a third party) for their employees directly involved in this contract during the period of the contract and one year thereafter, except as the parties may agree on a case-by-case basis.

1.4 Outsourcing Project Schedule

The following table reflects the schedule the ABC plans for this outsourcing project.

The ABC intends to pursue an aggressive outsourcing implementation schedule (if outsourcing is determined to be appropriate). The dates shown below are representative of the implementation schedule.

Outsourcing Project Schedule

Activity	Approximate Completion Dates
Receive Vendor notice of intent to bid.	January 13, 1995 *
Receive written questions from Vendors.	January 13, 1995 *
Distribute written answers to Vendors' questions.	January 23, 1995
Receive proposals from Vendors.	February 10, 1995 *
Evaluate proposals.	March 3, 1995
Determine scope of outsourcing.	
Re-evaluate outsource options.	
Select finalist/s.	
Conduct contract negotiations.	April 14, 1995
Finalize scope of outsourcing.	
Sign contract or a letter of intent.	

Activity	Approximate Completion Dates
Develop a transition plan. Assign project management personnel.	April 28, 1995
Execute the transition plan: Perform knowledge transfer. Set up hardware, software, and communications environment.	June 15, 1995
Contract-defined roles and responsibilities for ABC and the Vendor are in effect.	To Be Determined

* The Vendor question submission date and the Proposal Due Date are firm. All other dates are tentative and presented for planning purposes.

1.5 Questions Regarding the RFP

Any questions, exceptions, or additions raised by the Vendor concerning the RFP may be submitted, *in writing, via mail or fax,* to the attention of:

Ms. Jane Smith
ABC, Inc.
Address
Fax:

All questions must be received by January 13, 1995. Phone calls involving RFP questions will *not* be accepted or entertained. The ABC will answer appropriate questions in writing and mail the information to all Vendors on January 23, 1995. The ABC anticipates no other question sessions, and encourages Vendors to submit questions promptly, and only until January 13.

If the ABC deems it necessary to provide additional clarifying information, or to revise any part of the RFP, supplements or revisions will be provided to the recipients of the RFP. Vendor proposals shall then be considered predicated upon the terms and conditions of the RFP and its corresponding supplements or revisions thereof.

1.7   Outsourcing Rationale

ABC's Technology Services (TS) is responsible for the development of new and the maintenance of existing applications. These activities are key to the success of ABC's Lines of Business (LOBs)—and Internal Support Units (ISUs)—Corporate Services and Technology Services.

The existing applications have been developed using traditional methods on Tandem/Guardian and SUN/UNIX/Informix platforms. The ABC plans to redesign and migrate its legacy applications over a ten-year period to client/server technologies using the IEF CASE tool in a Sequent/UNIX/ORACLE environment. This migration effort began in 1992 and is progressing very actively. Several of the legacy applications, however, will remain on the legacy platforms for some time, and substantial staff resources will be required to support them. ABC's legacy platforms are detailed in *Section 2 (Current Environment)*.

The urgency of new regulatory rules and business opportunities continually presses the ABC to enhance its legacy applications rather than wait until these applications are migrated. Therefore, the effort and cost of maintaining legacy applications continue to escalate. The ABC seeks to reduce this cost. Also, while Technology Services has set an aggressive goal to retrain and redirect its application developers to new technologies, it recognizes that *supporting the legacy applications must remain a top priority.* Therefore, *ABC is seeking bids from Vendors to assume the primary technical responsibility for the software maintenance (e.g., emergency production support, ad hoc requests, and enhancements) of its Corporate Legacy Applications.*

1.8 Objectives and Scope of Outsourcing

1.8.1   Objectives of Outsourcing

The ABC has two primary objectives for the proposed outsourcing:

To enable its Technology Services' Software Engineers to transition from the legacy-applications environment to the new technologies.

To reduce the cost of maintaining legacy applications.

The ABC also expects to realize cost savings from a reduction in on-site staff; consequently, the ABC seeks to minimize Vendor on-site occupancy requirements.

It should be noted that the ABC has no intention of transferring any of its employees to the Vendor's payroll.

1.8.2 Types of Services to Be Outsourced

The ABC categorizes legacy applications maintenance and support services as:
    Baseline Maintenance, including:

Emergency Production Support

This service requires seven-day-per-week, 24-hour per day, "on-all" support. Support personnel must be available, on call in ABC's Data Center or other appropriate location, to resolve problems caused by abnormal program terminations. Responses to emergency calls must be made within two hours, with a fix or workaround provided within four to eight hours, depending on the severity of the problem and the number of applications affected.

Ad Hoc Requests

This type of service consists of on-site or off-site support during typical working hours (eight hours per day, five days per week) to fulfill end-user requests for minor enhancements, one-time reports, data conversions, file extracts, or other customized support. The ABC will discuss with the Vendor whether the work will be performed on site or off site. The required response time may range from hours to days, as determined by the requester. Priority conflicts will be resolved by ABC's Account Manager.

Enhancements

This type of service is expected to be coordinated on site, during typical working hours, and performed off site. It comprises projects to add or modify application functionality, as required by end users as a result of business opportunities, regulatory changes, and process changes. The required response time may range from hours to days, as determined by the requester. Priority conflicts will be resolved by ABC's Account Manager.

In Appendix C (Proposal Preparation Instructions), samples of the Service Provision Process (by support category) are given as a guideline. These procedures will be detailed and finalized during the Knowledge Transfer phase of the contract.

The Vendor must be capable of providing all the specified types of services for the applications selected to be outsourced. Detailed procedures for the provision of each of the above services will be developed during contract negotiations. Vendors are strongly encouraged to include their own proposed Service Provision Processes in their proposals.

1.8.3   ABC and Vendor Responsibilities

Technology Services will maintain its primary role as the information services provider to ABC's user community. To that end, Technology Services will continue to be responsible for project management, planning, functional analysis, quality assurance, and direct customer interaction for legacy applications and applications developed in new technology. *Vendors will not be expected to interact directly with the ABC end users.* ABC's Account Manager will designate Technology Services staff members to coordinate service requests with the Vendor. Their tasks will be specified in the Service Provision Process (to be proposed by the Vendor and approved during contract negotiations). *Under this contract, the Vendor is expected to perform technical design, programming, and testing activities.*

Vendor proposals must be developed taking into consideration the broad outline of responsibilities listed in the *Definition of Responsibilities* table.

Definition of Responsibilities

ABC's Responsibilities	Vendor's Responsibilities
Perform overall **planning activities and contract administration.**	**Adhere to** plans and agreements.
Provide technical **standards and guidelines.**	**Adhere to** these standards and guidelines.
Develop **requirements definition and functional specifications.**	**Review and understand** the information provided.
For enhancements or new development, prepare **project plans and negotiate** costs and schedule with Vendor.	**Respond** to requests for estimates, technical alternatives, and detailed plans.
Report emergency production support problems to Vendor.	**Respond** to service requests.

ABC's Responsibilities	Vendor's Responsibilities
Perform technical reviews.	*Develop technical designs and documentation.*
	Perform all programming activities, including code development, unit integration, and system testing.
	Provide review materials and incorporate changes.
Perform quality assurance reviews.	*Provide materials* for QA reviews and incorporate recommended changes.
Perform acceptance testing activities.	*Provide technical support* of acceptance tests.
Perform production testing activities (response time, capacity, restart, backup recovery, and other related activities).	*Provide support* for testing activities.
Transfer tested application into production.	*Provide appropriate support.*
Develop training materials and *perform* all user training.	*Support training* development by providing information, as requested.
Provide all *customer liaison* functions within ABC.	*Address all customer-related issues* included in this contract.

1.8.4   *Duration of Outsourcing Contract*

The ABC requests a three-year contract period, subject to cancellation for cause and for convenience. It should be noted that the ABC expects the amount of work involved in the maintenance of its legacy applications to decline gradually over the years as these applications are migrated into the new technology. The ABC may consider Vendor offers for alternative contract periods, but it requires all responses to address the three-year period to ensure a consistent, accurate, and fair evaluation process. Refer to Appendix B (Descriptions of ABC Corporate Legacy Applications) for the planned Retirement Schedule over the three-year period.

1.8.5 Pricing Expectations

The ABC will look favorably on Vendor responses that offer *flexibility* in pricing the defined service. The Vendor may propose a combination of pricing arrangements, such as:

Fixed Price
To furnish a specified number of effort-days to satisfy Baseline Maintenance (emergency production support, ad hoc requests, and minor enhancements).

Hourly Rates for Fixed-Fee Arrangements
To estimate and negotiate costs (e.g., fixed or not-to-exceed) for individual enhancements projects.

Cost Adjustments
To provide for credits to the ABC and/or incentives and penalties to the Vendor under appropriate work volumes, quality performance, or specified conditions. Include incentives and penalties in each cost.

1.8.6 ABC Maintenance and Project Activities in Scope

The maintenance activities which make up the scope of this RFP include a variety of legacy baseline support and enhancement projects from each of ABC's Lines of Business and Internal Support Units. Every activity requires the participation of individuals from each of ABC's Technology Services development groups (i.e., Product Development, Software Engineering, Quality Assurance). *For the purpose of this RFP, only the Software Engineering work component (i.e., technical design, construction, unit/integration/system testing, and technical documentation is being considered for selective outsourcing.*

Appendix A (Candidate Application Maintenance Activities for Outsourcing), includes a series of matrices listing the activities, by Line of Business, that are under consideration for selective outsourcing. Various information is provided in these matrices to assist the Vendors in preparing their proposal. *One important piece of information provided is ABC's Software Engineering level-of-effort estimate in effort-months.* This number was computed by ABC's Software Engineering staff during the 1995 ABC budget and planning process under the assumption that they would be performing this work rather than an outsourcing firm. It is anticipated that the Vendor will need this information to derive an accurate response to this RFP.

Appendix B (Descriptions of ABC Corporate Legacy Applications) contains a full description of the applications included in the scope of this RFP.

SECTION 2.   CURRENT ENVIRONMENT

2.1 ABC Applications

The ABC user community interacts with the public. ABC's business needs are supported by a variety of corporate applications of varying age.

The legacy applications for each Line of Business are described in:

Appendix A (Candidate Application Maintenance Activities for Outsourcing) which provides the details of the applications' size, age, programming language, number of programs, and the full-time equivalent (FTE) staff budgeted for production support and maintenance in 1995.

Appendix B (Descriptions of ABC Corporate Legacy Applications) which provides brief writeups of each application including description, user, and software/hardware environment (size, age, programming language, number of programs).

2.2 Legacy Application Platforms

The legacy applications reside on three different hardware platforms—Tandem, SUN, and personal computers (PC)—in both a mainframe and client/server architecture. For each of these platforms, ABC maintains separate environments for development, acceptance testing, and production. The ABC Quality Assurance configuration management staff use appropriate tools for version control of individual programs and files.

The Vendor Software Engineers will work on the development node. When an application is unit-, integration-, and system-tested, and is ready for acceptance test, the Vendor Software Engineer will submit the application to ABC Quality Assurance for acceptance testing. When all problems discovered during acceptance test have been closed, the Vendor Software Engineer will obtain appropriate sign-offs to allow turnover of the software to the production environment. Under the turnover process, the Vendor Software Engineer will present to the Quality Assurance configuration management staff a package that generally consists of the release contents, sign-off forms, and appropriate documentation.

For emergency production support fixes (i.e., fixes which are required immediately to ensure software stability and proper processing), the Vendor Software Engineer will test the fix on the development system, notify the Quality Assurance configuration management staff, and provide the turnover package with sign-off forms to waive acceptance test and move it directly into the production system. If the fix works as intended, it will be left in place; if not, it will be backed out, and the Vendor Software Engineer will be notified to continue working to correct the problem.

2.2.1 Tandem Platform

Refer to the following diagram for an overview of the Tandem system configuration.

By mid-1995, the Tandem configuration is planned to consist of CLX, Himalaya, and Cyclone processors running the Guardian D20 operating system. The migration to Guardian D30 is scheduled for the third quarter of 1995. The Tandems have NonStop SQL and Enscribe database management systems. Communications tools and protocols are: X.25, TCP/IP, and Tandem Expand. The systems support the Enform query language.

On the Tandem platform, the ABC Quality Assurance configuration management staff uses ControlJ (Version 11.54 by Network Concepts, Inc.) in the turnover process. The Vendor Software Engineer will develop and test the software on the Tandem development node. Following successful system test, the Vendor Software Engineer will be responsible for preparing the application and documentation for turnover to ABC Quality Assurance for acceptance testing and, later, to production.

The Tandem Platform

Tandem Nodes and
Planned Configuration June 1995

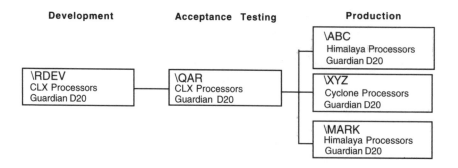

2.2.2 SUN and PC Platforms

Refer to the following diagram for an overview of the SUN and PC configuration.

SUN servers are SPARC 10, SPARC 5, SPARC 2, SPARC 1+, and ELC operating under SUN OS 4.1.2 and 4.1.3.

Informix 5.0 and 5.01 provide database management.

PC servers are AST 486/66 models running Novell 3.12.

By the third quarter of 1995, the configuration will be Pentium P90 system units running Novell 4.0.

This platform will move from Windows 3.1 to Windows 95 when available, with SMC Ultra moving to SMC/AST in mid-1995.

Microsoft Access 2.0 is installed for database management and will be upgraded to the release that is then current in the third quarter of 1995.

On both the SUN and PC platforms, the ABC Quality Assurance configuration management staff uses CCC/Harvest for version control in the turnover process. As in the Tandem platform, the Vendor Software Engineers develop and test the application on the SUN/PC development node. Following system test, the Vendor Software Engineers are responsible for preparing the application and documentation for turnover to Quality Assurance for acceptance testing and, later, to production.

The SUN and PC Platforms

SUN and PC Nodes and Systems
Planned Configuration June 1995

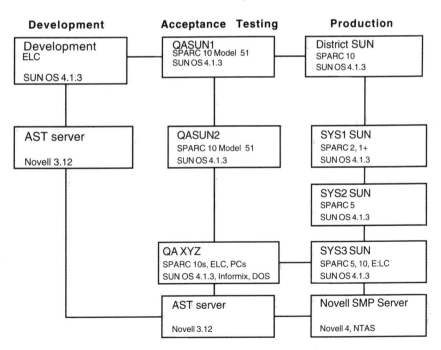

2.3 Documentation

The state of documentation varies from application to application. In general, the quality is about average for an installation with the number, complexity, and size of applications, such as ABC's.

The ABC will provide the Vendor with an index to the available legacy documentation and access to the on-site System Documentation Library during the Knowledge Transfer phase of the contract.

SECTION 3. PROPOSAL REQUIREMENTS

3.1 Proposal Delivery

All proposals in response to this RFP must be delivered to the ABC by:

> 5:00 p.m.
> DATE

The Vendor is required to deliver a total of ten copies, nine bound and one unbound. The proposal should be addressed to:

> John Brown
> Vice President, Product Development Department
> ABC, Inc.
> Address

The proposal must be signed by an officer duly authorized to make such an offer.

3.2 Vendor Selection Criteria

The ABC will consider the following factors in the selection of the successful Vendor. (They are not listed in order of importance.)

Completeness of Vendor proposal

Vendor's technical capability, as articulated in their proposal, to provide the specified legacy application maintenance and enhancement services based on:

Experience of Vendor's proposed personnel with this type of work and ABC's legacy platforms

Vendor's overall technical depth in maintenance of software applications and ABC's legacy platforms

Vendor's proposed Service Provision Process and Quality Assurance practices

Project management techniques (e.g., planning, estimating, progress tracking and reporting)

Vendor business history and Vendor corporate viability

References from customers with contracts similar to ABC's

Favorable pricing and terms for the ABC

The evaluation of the Vendors and the selection of the successful vendor/s will be based on the content of the submitted proposals. It is expected, however, that the processes, methods, techniques, tools, and configuration proposed by the successful Vendor/s will be further discussed, refined, and approved during contract negotiations.

3.3 Proposal Format

The proposal must be organized exactly as shown below to facilitate analysis and evaluation by the ABC; each section must be labeled and numbered as indicated. The proposal must be clear, complete, accurate, and in sufficient detail to enable the ABC to determine the suitability, practicality, and operational desirability of the services and methods proposed. To that end, Vendors may use narrative and/or diagrams, as they deem appropriate.

Vendors should make every attempt to use *terminology* in their proposal that is consistent with that of the ABC as indicated in the RFP. Comparable terminology may be substituted where appropriate if the Vendor provides clear and concise definitions.

It is anticipated that the proposal will become an important and integral part of the contract.

Detailed instructions for preparing the proposal are provided in *Appendix C (Proposal Preparation Instructions)*.

PROPOSAL TABLE OF CONTENTS

SECTION 1. UNDERSTANDING THE SCOPE OF THE ENGAGEMENT

SECTION 2. TECHNICAL PROPOSAL
2.1   Delivery of Services
2.2   Suggested Technical Environment (Hardware, Software, Communications)
2.3   Staffing Plan and Space Requirements
2.3.1   Staffing
2.3.2   Space Requirements/Facilities

APPENDIX A:
CANDIDATE APPLICATION MAINTENANCE
ACTIVITIES FOR OUTSOURCING

APPENDIX B:
DESCRIPTIONS OF ABC CORPORATE LEGACY APPLICATIONS

APPENDIX C:
PROPOSAL PREPARATION INSTRUCTIONS

ENCLOSURE:
ABC - INTRODUCTION BROCHURE

E

Example Outsourcing Agreement

Note: This sample contract is provided only to illustrate the typical provisions found in an outsourcing agreement. Do not use this example for your own contract. Get competent legal advice.

INFORMATION TECHNOLOGY OUTSOURCING SERVICES
AGREEMENT between
The ABC Company
and
The XYZ Outsourcing Company
May 23, 1997

This agreement is made on the 23rd day of May 1997 (the "Effective Date") by and between the ABC Company, a Delaware Corporation with principal place of business at 206 Holmard Street, Gaithersburg, Maryland (the "Customer") and the XYZ Outsourcing Company of Lexington, Kentucky (The "Vendor").

The Customer is in the business of running computer-based education, training, and testing centers at 48 sites in the United States from a central computing center in Frederick, Maryland. The central computing center is connected through communications links, to the company headquarters in Gaithersburg and to the 48 sites located in each state except Hawaii and Alaska. The central facility, communications links and the 320 desktop workstations located in the headquarters and the 48 sites are collectively the "Customer's Current Operations." The Customer circulated a Request for Proposal, dated January 10, 1997, which is set forth in Exhibit 1, soliciting proposals from potential vendors for the provision of information processing and related services of the Customer's Current Operations.

The Vendor, which is in the business of providing computer data center and network outsourcing services, responded to the RFP with a proposal dated May 10, 1997, which is set forth in Exhibit 2.

Based on the RFP and Proposal, Customer and Vendor have engaged in discussions and negotiations that have resulted in the relationship described in this Agreement.

The overall objectives of the Customer and Vendor in entering into this agreement are to reduce Customer's costs for Current Operations and improve service quality and responsiveness.

Customer and Vendor intend that the Customer transfer all of Customer's Current Operations to Vendor and that Vendor shall provide to Customer all the services provided by the Customer's Current Operations as described in this agreement and the applicable Site Schedule on the terms and conditions as set forth in this Agreement and the Site Schedule.

NOW, THEREFORE, for and in consideration of the agreements of the parties set forth below, Customer and Vendor agree as follows:

ARTICLE 1. DESIGNATED SERVICES

1.01 Description of Vendor Services. With the exception of the Excluded Services, as hereinafter defined. Vendor agrees to perform the following services (the "Vendor Services"):

All the services provided by User's IS department prior to the Effective Date (the "Prior Services") and more specifically defined in Exhibit 3 except the services specified in Exhibit 4 (the "Excluded Services");

User shall have no liability to pay any fees that exceed the Task Estimate by more than eight percent.

1.02 Vendor shall maintain time records for all time expended on the Additional Services and provide User with a copy of such records relating to each invoice.

ARTICLE 2. TERM

2.01 Agreement. The term of this Agreement shall commence on June 1, 1997 (the "Effective Date") and shall continue until the expiration or termination of all of the Site Schedules, unless this Agreement is terminated earlier.

2.02 Site Schedule. The term of a Site Schedule shall commence on the date specified on the Site Schedule (each, a "Site Effective Date") and shall continue until the expiration date specified in the Site Schedule (the "Site Term"), unless terminated earlier pursuant to Article 28 of this Agreement or the applicable Site Schedule.

ARTICLE 3. FEES

3.01 FIXED FEE. For the Vendor Services customer shall pay Vendor a fixed fee of $_____ per month in advance ("Vendor Fees").

    3.02 FIXED FEE ADJUSTMENT. Customer and Vendor agree that the Vendor Fees shall increase if transaction count exceeds 200,000 transactions in a given month. In such event, the fixed fee shall increase by $_____ for each transaction more than 200,000 transactions in a month.

ARTICLE 4. TURNOVER

4.01 TURNOVER TO VENDOR OPERATIONS. Customer and Vendor agree that customer's transition to the use of all the Vendor Services shall proceed in accordance with Exhibit 6 (the "Transition Plan"). The Transition Plan describes the customer and Vendor's respective obligations as well as the schedule for accomplishing the Turnover. Until the completion of the transition period, Vendor expressly agrees that customer shall have no obligation to pay for the Vendor Services consumed by the customer except in accordance with the section of the Transition Plan entitled "Phase-in of Fees"

    4.02 SCHEDULE. Vendor and Customer agree to perform their respective obligations in accordance with Exhibit 7 (the "Schedule"). The Schedule can be modified only with the written consent of both parties.

    4.03 POINTS OF CONTACT. Vendor and Customer agree that the following individuals shall serve as their respective managers and liaisons. They shall serve as a point of contact by which the parties may communicate on a frequent basis. Either party may change its liaison upon written notice to the other party. Customer acknowledges that the Customer Manager may accept goods and services provided under this agreement and thereby bind customer. Vendor expressly agrees that Vendor Liaison may obligate the Vendor in all matters pertaining to this agreement.

    Customer Manager is Frank C. Jones, ABC COMPANY.

    Vendor Liaison is James Franklin, XYZ OUTSOURCING COMPANY.

    4.04 EXISTING INFORMATION TECHNOLOGY EMPLOYEES. Exhibit 7 is a list of all of the Customer's information systems employees (the

"IS Employees"). Vendor expressly agrees to offer employment to certain IS Employees, in the same job categories as such IS Employees have with Customer, for a minimum of one year after the Effective Date of this agreement and in accordance with Section _____.

Vendor agrees to offer employment to such IS Employees listed or in job categories of people who are listed in Exhibit 8 (The "Transferred Employees"). Any IS Employee not identified as a Retained Employee shall be deemed a Transferred Employee.

Vendor agrees that Customer shall retain certain IS Employees. Such IS Employees (the "Retained Employees") are specified by name or job title in Exhibit 7.

Vendor shall offer the Transferred Employees employment with Vendor at the salary and benefits specified by the job description in Exhibit 9.

Vendor agrees for a period of three years not to solicit or to offer employment as an employee or as independent contractor to any person or job title designated as a Retained Employee.

During the first year (the "Guaranteed Period"), Vendor may terminate a Transferred Employee only for cause.

After the Guaranteed Period, Vendor may terminate any Transferred Employee upon two weeks notice; provided; however, Vendor shall make reasonable efforts to assist a Transferred Employee in finding other job.

4.05 EXISTING SOFTWARE LICENSES. Customer acknowledges that obtaining consent for Vendor's use of the Customer Applications as such are defined in Exhibit 10 is Customer's responsibility. Customer shall employ reasonable efforts to obtain such consent.

If there are any fees associated with obtaining such consent, Vendor shall pay such fees up to a maximum of $_____ in the aggregate for all Customer Applications.

For any Application for which Customer is unable to obtain consent, Vendor shall provide such application for Customer at Vendor's sole expense up to a maximum of $____ in the aggregate for such applications.

4.06 ASSIGNMENT OF EXISTING HARDWARE-RELATED AGREEMENTS. Vendor and Customer hereby agree that the Customer shall assign to Vendor the leases identified in Exhibit 12 for the hardware specified in Exhibit 11. Such assignment shall occur upon the Effective Date or as soon thereafter as reasonably practicable. Vendor agrees that as of the Effective Date it shall assume all of the financial responsibility for such hardware leases and that from the Effective Date on it shall pay such lease fees or negotiate with the appropriate lessors for termination of such leases.

4.07 EXISTING HARDWARE MAINTENANCE AGREEMENTS. Customer agrees to assign to Vendor or terminate hardware maintenance for the hardware maintenance agreements specified in Exhibit 13. As of the Effective Date, Vendor shall assume complete financial responsibility for such hardware maintenance agreements. If the assignments specified in this Section are not accomplished as of the Effective Date and Customer is obligated to make additional payments after the Effective Date, Customer may subtract such payments from all or any amounts due to Vendor.

4.08 VENDOR'S PURCHASE OF CERTAIN ASSETS OF CUSTOMER. Vendor hereby agrees to purchase from Customer, and Customer hereby agrees to sell to vendor the assets listed in this Section. Such purchases shall occur subject to the purchase agreements attached hereto as exhibits and described in this Section. The assets that Vendor shall purchase from User are as follows:

The land and improvements thereon that consist of Customers' data center in Frederick, Maryland.

Vendor shall acquire such assets pursuant to the agreements in the following exhibits. Real Estate Purchase Agreement in Exhibit 14; and Computer Purchase Agreement in Exhibit 15.

ARTICLE 5. PERFORMANCE STANDARDS

5.01 PERFORMANCE STANDARDS. "Performance Standards" means the measures specified in Exhibit 16. Vendor agrees to provide the Vendor Services in accordance with the Performance Standards. "Defective Performance" means Vendor's failure to perform in accordance with one or more of the Performance Standards.

5.02 REMEDIES FOR DEFECTIVE PERFORMANCE. In addition to such other remedies as are available to Customer, if there is a Defective Performance, Customer may avail itself of the remedies specified in this Section. Types of Defective Performance are defined as follows:

A "Defect" is any Defective Performance that occurs during a day.

A "Level One Defect" is any Defect that lasts for more than two hours but less than 24 hours.

A "Level Two Defect" is a Defect that lasts for more than 24 hours.

A "Level Three Defect" is a Defect that occurs more than once during any seven-day period.

A "Level Four Defect" is a Level Two Defect that occurs more than once during any thirty-day period.

For each Level One Defect, Vendor shall grant Customer a credit of $_____ against the Vendor Fees.

For each Level Two Defect, Vendor shall grant Customer a credit of $_____ against the Vendor Fees.

For each Level Three Defect, Vendor shall grant Customer a credit of $_____ against the Vendor Fees.

For each Level Four Defect, Vendor shall grant Customer a credit of $_____ against the Vendor Fees.

If a Level Four Defect occurs more than twice in any thirty-day period, Customer may terminate this Agreement upon prior written notice to Vendor.

5.03 PRODUCTION SCHEDULE. Vendor shall perform customer's daily weekly, and monthly production processing in accordance with Exhibit 14 (the "Production Schedule"). User may modify the Production Schedule upon thirty days written notice.

5.04 RESOURCE SCHEDULE. Vendor agrees to provide the resources and facilities described in Exhibit 15 (the "Resource Schedule") at the times specified in the Resource Schedule. The Resource Schedule can be modified only with the written consent of both parties.

5.05 OWNERSHIP OF DATA. Vendor expressly agrees that all data relating to Customer's business is the exclusive property of Customer. Vendor further agrees that all media provided to Customer or used for backup pursuant to the Section entitled "DESCRIPTION OF VENDOR SERVICES" is the exclusive property of Customer. Upon customer's written request, Vendor shall, within twenty-four hours, provide customer with a copy of all such data on the magnetic media of Customer's choosing. The fee that Vendor may charge for each such copy may not exceed $_____.

5.06 CONTINUITY DURING DISPUTE. In the event there is a dispute between User and Vendor, Vendor shall continue to perform the services described in the Section titled "DESCRIPTION OF VENDOR SERVICES." If such dispute relates to the payment of fees by Customer, Vendor may terminate this Agreement and cease to perform services only after six months notice to Customer.

5.07 CORRECTION OF PROCESSING ERRORS. In addition to such other remedies as may be available to Customer, Vendor shall, at its own expense, promptly correct errors that occur in processing.

5.08 RIGHT TO AUDIT. Vendor agrees that Customer, at Customer's expense, may engage an independent accounting firm (the "Auditor") to audit Vendor's records and operations relevant to this Agreement to determine Vendor's compliance with this Agreement. Upon three day's written notice, the Auditor may enter Vendor's premises and commence such audit. The Auditor shall use its reasonable best efforts to avoid disrupting Vendor's ordinary course of business. Customer shall pay Vendor for the Auditor's use of the Vendor Services in accordance with the Section entitled "ADDITIONAL SERVICES."

ARTICLE 6. DISPUTE RESOLUTION

6.01 DISPUTE RESOLUTION PROCEDURES. All disputes between Vendor and Customer shall adhere to the following procedures prior to the commencement of any mediation pursuant to the provision entitled "NON-BINDING MEDIATION" or any judicial proceedings.

The Liaison shall notify the other party's Liaison in writing of the occurrence of a dispute and shall establish a mutually convenient time and place to meet in order to discuss such dispute. In any event, such meeting shall occur within 48 hours of the time of the Liaison's notice to the other Liaison.

If the Liaisons cannot resolve the dispute to the satisfaction of both parties within 48 hours of their first meeting, then either Liaison may give written notice of the inability to resolve such dispute to the Management Designee, designated below, of the other party. The Management Designees of both parties shall meet within 48 hours of such written notice at a mutually convenient time and place.

If after 48 hours the Management Designees cannot resolve such dispute to their satisfaction as agreed in writing, then either Management Designee may give written notice of the inability to resolve such dispute to the Designated Executive, as designated below, of the other party. Within 72 hours of receipt of such notice, the Designated Executives of both parties shall meet in good faith to attempt to resolve such dispute.

If after one week the Designated Executives have not resolved the dispute to their satisfaction as agreed in writing, then either party may proceed in accordance with its remedies stated elsewhere in this agreement.

The Management Designees are

(1) Management Designee: <u>Joe Smith</u>

(2) Vendor Management Designee: <u>Barbara Walker</u>

The Designated Executives are

(1) Customer Designated Executives: <u>Joe Jones, CIO</u>

(2) Vendor Designated Executives: <u>Bob Brown, Account Executive</u>

6.02 NON-BINDING MEDIATION. If Vendor and Customer do not agree in writing that they have resolved a dispute, then after expiration of the periods referred to in the Section entitled "DISPUTE RESOLUTION AND ESCALATION PROCEDURES," either party may with written notice to the other (a "Mediation Notice") invoke the provisions of this Section.

Upon receipt of a Mediation Notice, both parties shall submit to non-binding mediation within ten days.

The mediator shall be mutually agreed upon in writing.

Each party shall bear its own costs and one-half of the mediator's fee, if any.

If Vendor and Customer cannot agree on a mediator, they shall use the mediator selected by the president of the Customer's state bar association.

ARTICLE 7. WARRANTIES AND LIMITATIONS OF LIABILITY

7.01 VENDOR'S WARRANTIES. Vendor represents and warrants the following:

That Vendor is entitled to enter into this Agreement and that by entering into this agreement it shall not violate any other Agreement to which Vendor is a party;

That Vendor is a corporation, duly organized, validly existing, and in good standing under the laws of the State of Delaware;

That Vendor has performed all necessary corporate action to have the appropriate authority to enter into this Agreement and comply with its provisions;

That Vendor shall perform in accordance with the Performance Standards; and

That Vendor's employees and agents shall perform their duties in a skillful and workmanlike manner.

7.02 CUSTOMER'S WARRANTIES. Customer represents and warrants the following:

That by entering into this Agreement, Customer will not be in default of any obligations pursuant to any other agreements to which customer is a party;

That customer is a corporation, duly organized, validly existing, and in good standing under the laws of the State of Maryland.

That Customer has performed all necessary corporate action to have the appropriate authority to enter into this Agreement and comply with its provisions.

7.03 LIMITATION OF LIABILITY. Customer and Vendor agree that this Agreement is subject to the following disclaimers and limitations of liability.

Except for the express warranties described in the sections entitled "VENDOR'S WARRANTIES" and "CUSTOMER'S WARRANTIES," neither Vendor nor Customer makes any other warranties, express or implied, including without limitation the implied warranties of merchantability and fitness for a particular purpose.

In no event shall Vendor Customer be liable for any incidental, special, indirect and/or consequential damages, even if Vendor or Customer was advised of the possibility of such damages.

In no even-shall a cause of action be asserted by one party against the other party more than two years after such cause of action accrued.

ARTICLE 8. TERMINATION

8.01 EXPIRATION. Upon the end of the Agreement Term, the Vendor and Customer shall proceed in accordance with the section entitled "PROCEDURES UPON EXPIRATION OR TERMINATION."

8.02 RENEWAL. Customer may renew this Agreement for an additional term of 7 years by giving Vendor 180 days notice prior to the end of the then current term.

8.03 TERMINATION FOR BREACH. If either party breaches this Agreement and fails to remedy such breach within 30 days after receiving written notice from the non-breaching party, the non-breaching party may terminate this Agreement upon ten days prior written notice. Upon such termination, the parties shall proceed in accordance with the section entitled "PROCEDURES UPON EXPIRATION OR TERMINATION."

8.04 TERMINATION FOR CONVENIENCE. Customer may terminate this agreement for any reason whatsoever upon 180 days prior written notice and upon payment to Vendor of $_____ times the number of months remaining in the Agreement Term. Upon such termination, Vendor and Customer shall proceed in accordance with the section entitled "PROCEDURES UPON EXPIRATION OR TERMINATION."

8.05 TERMINATION UPON ACQUISITION. If any entity not a party to this Agreement acquires a majority of the shares of Customer, Customer may terminate this Agreement upon six months notice. Upon such termination, Vendor and Customer shall proceed in accordance with the section entitled "PROCEDURES UPON EXPIRATION OR TERMINATION."

8.06 TERMINATION UPON DIVESTURE. If Customer sells or exchanges ownership of a subsidiary or assets such that Customer's use of Vendor Services is reduced by more than thirty percent, Customer may terminate this Agreement upon three months notice. Upon such termination, Vendor and Customer shall proceed in accordance with the section entitled "PROCEDURES UPON EXPIRATION OR TERMINATION."

8.07 CHANGE IN CONTROL. If more than thirty percent of the ownership interest in Vendor changes during the term of this Agreement, the Customer may terminate this agreement upon thirty days written notice to Vendor. Upon such termination, Vendor and Customer shall proceed in accordance with the section entitled "PROCEDURES UPON EXPIRATION OR TERMINATION."

8.08 PROCEDURES UPON EXPIRATION OR TERMINATION. If this Agreement expires or is terminated, then User and Vendor shall proceed in accordance with this Section.

The date this agreement expires is the "Expiration Date."

If this Agreement is terminated, the date on which termination is effective is the "Termination Date."

Customer either may immediately cease using the Vendor Services or, in the Customer's sole discretion, Customer may proceed in accordance with the provisions of the section of this Agreement entitled "TURNBACK."

Customer shall give Vendor express written notice of the election that Customer chooses in accordance with the following:

At least 20 days prior to the expiration of the Agreement Term;

At least 30 days after giving Vendor notice that User May terminate for breach;

Within 30 days after receiving Vendor's notice that Vendor may terminate for breach;

At least 6 months prior to termination pursuant to the Section entitled "TER-MINATION FOR CONVENIENCE."

At least 4 months prior to termination pursuant to the Section entitled "TERMINATION UPON ACQUISITION."

At least 3 months prior to termination pursuant to the Section entitled "TER-MINATION UPON DIVESTITURE."

8.09 TURNBACK. If Customer elects to proceed in accordance with this Section and pursuant to the Section entitled "PROCEDURES UPON EXPIRA-TION OR TERMINATION," then Vendor, in accordance with this Section, shall continue to provide the Vendor Services and charge the Vendor Fees for up to 3 months after the Termination Date or Expiration Date, as relevant (the "Turnback Period").

Vendor may cease providing the Vendor Services after expiration of the Turnback Period.

During the Turnback Period, Customer may terminate the Vendor Services upon thirty days notice.

At no additional charge, Vendor shall provide Customer with the following services in addition to the Vendor Services (the "Turnback Services"):

(1) Vendor shall promptly answer Customer's inquiries concerning the Vendor Services.

(2) Vendor shall coordinate the orderly transfer of communications to Customer's facilities as designated in writing by the Customer.

At no additional charge, Vendor shall provide Customer with the following items (the "Turnback Deliverables"):

(1) A copy of Customer's data and software in magnetic media specified by customer; or electronically transmitted to customer's facilities in accordance with Customer's written instructions.

(2) A copy of all run time documentation that Vendor has for the Customer's software.

(3) A copy of all job control that Vendor has for Customer's software.

(4) A written inventory and copies of all of Customer's third-party software and documentation ("Customer Licensed Software").

(5) A written inventory and copies of all of Customer's third-party software and documentation ("Customer Licensed Software").

(6) A written inventory of all of Vendor's third-party software and documentation used to provide the Vendor Services ("Vendor Licensed Software").

Vendor shall provide the Turnback Deliverables within thirty days after a written request by Customer, but in any event prior to the expiration of the Turnback Period.

8.10 CONTINUING RIGHTS TO USE CERTAIN VENDOR SOFTWARE. Vendor and Customer hereby agree that upon expiration or termination of this Agreement, Customer has the option to use the software specified in this Section in accordance with the provisions of this Section.

A. Customer's option is exercisable upon written notice to the Vendor prior to the Termination Date or Expiration Date.

B. Upon exercising the option, Customer may use the Vendor Software, and all associated documentation, specified in Exhibit 15.

C. Customer shall use the Vendor Services in accordance with the licenses agreement contained in Exhibit 16 (the "Vendor License Agreement").

D. Upon receipt of the notice and license fees due Vendor, if any, Vendor shall provide Customer with a copy of the Vendor Software in source and object code format in the magnetic media specified in writing by User.

ARTICLE 9. DATA CENTER MIGRATION

9.01 MIGRATION. As part of the Designated Services, Vendor shall perform all functions and services, including the functions and services described in the Site Schedule necessary to accomplish the migration to the Vendor data center identified in the Site Schedule of Customer's information technology operations and capabilities at the Customer data center identified in the Site Schedule. Vendor shall perform the Migration Services without causing a disruption to Customer's business. Vendor shall designate in each Site Schedule an individual at each Customer data center to manage and implement the Migration Services. Until the completion of the Migration Services at the applicable Site, such individual shall review with the Customer Project Manager the status of the Migration Services for which that individual is responsible as often as reasonably requested by the Customer Manager.

9.02 DATA CENTER CLOSURES. As part of the Designated Services, Vendor shall administer and manage the closing of information technology operations and capabilities at Customer data center as a result of the migration to a Vendor data center. In connection with such closures and as part of the Designated Services, Vendor shall, upon Customer's request, identify and solicit, upon terms and prices as favorable to Customer as Vendor would obtain for its own account, purchasers of Customer's data processing assets at the applicable Customer data centers.

9.03 MIGRATION ACCEPTANCE TESTS. As part of the Designated Services, Customer and Vendor shall perform the acceptance test described in the applicable Site Schedule in connection with the migration of a Customer data center to a Vendor data center (each, a "Migration Acceptance Test").

ARTICLE 10. MISCELLANEOUS PROVISIONS

10.0 ASSIGNMENT. Vendor may not assign this Agreement without Customer's prior express written consent. Vendor may not subcontract any of its obligations without Customer's prior express written consent.

10.02 GOVERNING LAW. Customer and Vendor agree that this Agreement shall be governed by the laws of the state of XXXX without regard to the state of XXXX'S choice of law rules.

10.03 CONFIDENTIAL INFORMATION. Vendor and Customer expressly agree that all information communicated to Vendor with respect to this Agreement and with respect to the services provided by Vendor pursuant to this Agreement, including, without limitation, any confidential information obtained by Vendor by reason of its association with Customer, is confidential. Vendor further agrees that all information, conclusions, reports, designs, plans, project evaluations, data, advice, business plans, customer lists, and/or other documents available to Vendor pursuant to this Agreement are confidential and proprietary property of Customer. Except as otherwise provided by law, Vendor and Customer agree that all proprietary and confidential information disclosed by the other during performance of this Agreement and identified in writing as proprietary or confidential shall be held in confidence and used only in performance of this Agreement. If such information is publicly available, already in the disclosing party's possession or knowledge, or is thereafter rightfully obtained by the disclosing party from sources other than the other party, then there shall be no restriction in its disclosure.

10.04 FORCE MAJEURE. Neither the Vendor nor the Customer shall be in default by reason of any failure to perform under this Agreement if such failure results, whether directly or indirectly, from fire, explosion, flood, acts of

God, or of the public enemy, war, civil disturbance, act of any government, dejure or defacto, or agency or official thereof, quarantine, restriction, epidemic or catastrophe (separately and collectively a "Force Majeure Event"). If there is a Force Majeure Event that prevents Vendor from performing a substantial part of it obligations under this Agreement and such Force Majeure Event lasts more than 24 hours, than Customer may terminate this Agreement upon 48 hours prior express, written notice.

10.05 NOTICE. All notices and demands required to be given pursuant to this Agreement shall be given to the parties in writing and by certified mail, return receipt requested, at the addresses specified in this Section or to such other addresses as the parties may hereinafter substitute by written notice given in the manner prescribed by this section.

Notice to Customer:

Mr. Joe Brown
CIO
ABC Company
206 Holmard Street
Gaithersburg, MD 20850

Notice to Vendor:

Ms. Barbara Smith
606 Anchor Street
Lexington, Kentucky

10.07 VENUE. Vendor and Customer expressly agree that this Agreement is entered into and performable in Frederick County, Maryland and that all, if any, suits arising under this Agreement shall be brought in courts located in that county, or, if in federal court, in the Montgomery County District

10.08 INTEGRATION OF AGREEMENT. Vendor and Customer agree that this Agreement and the Exhibits hereto embody the entire agreement in relation to the subject matter herein and that there are no other oral or written agreements or understandings between Vendor and Customer at the time of the execution of this Agreement.

10.09 MODIFICATION OF AGREEMENT. Vendor and Customer expressly agree that this Agreement cannot be modified except in writing executed by both Vendor and Customer.

10.10 LEGAL CONSTRUCTION. If one or more of the provisions of this Agreement are for any reason held to be invalid, illegal, or unenforceable in any respect, such invalidity, illegality, or unenforceability shall not affect any other provision of this Agreement; and this Agreement shall be construed as if such invalid, illegal, or unenforceable provisions had never been contained in this Agreement.

10.11 WAIVER. Any waiver by Vendor or Customer of any provision of this Agreement shall not imply a subsequent waiver of that or any other provision. And, further, any waiver must be signed in writing by the party against whom such waiver is to be construed.

10.12 BINDING EFFECT. This Agreement shall inure to the benefit of and bind the parties hereto, their successors, and permitted assigns.

10.13 AUTHORITY. Vendor and Customer hereby warrant and represent that their respective signatures set forth below have been, and are on the Effective Day, duly authorized by all necessary and appropriate statutory and/or corporate action to execute this Agreement.

10.14 CAPTIONS. All captions contained in this Agreement are for convenience or reference only and are not intended to define or limit the scope of any provision of this Agreement.

10.15 EXPENSES FOR ENFORCEMENT. In the event that either party is required to employ an attorney to enforce the provisions of this Agreement or is required to enforce the provisions of this Agreement or is required to commence legal proceedings to enforce the provisions of this Agreement, then the prevailing party shall be responsible for the payment of the other party's attorneys fees, including costs, collection agency fees, costs of investigation, or any other costs arising out of the litigation of this Agreement.

10.16 TAXES. Customer shall pay sales or user taxes imposed upon the services provided by Vendor pursuant to this Agreement; provided; however, in no event shall Customer be responsible for any other taxes, including, without limitation, taxes based on Vendor's net income and franchise taxes of Vendor.

10.17 MISSPELLINGS. Misspelling of one or more words in this Agreement shall not vitiate this Agreement. Such misspelled words shall be read so as to have the meaning apparently intended by the parties.

10.18 NO JOINT VENTURE. Vendor and Customer agree that each are independent contractors under this Agreement. In no event shall this Agreement be construed as creating any partnership, joint venture, agency or other relationship between Vendor and Customer.

10.19 COMPLIANCE WITH LAWS. Vendor expressly agrees that during the term of this Agreement it shall observe and comply with all relevant laws, including, without limitation, federal, state, and local laws, ordinances, orders, decrees, and regulations.

10.20 HIRING OR OTHER PARTY'S EMPLOYEES. Except as permitted in the section entitled "EXISTING INFORMATION SYSTEM EMPLOYEES," neither party may hire the employee of the other party while this Agreement is in effect without the express written consent of the other party.

IN WITNESS WHEREOF, Vendor and User through their duly authorized representatives make this Agreement effective upon the Effective Date.

User: _____

By: _____Title _____

By: _____Title _____

LIST OF EXHIBITS:

F

Major IT Outsourcing Vendors

There are hundreds of companies in the outsourcing business in functions, such as human resources, administration, customer service, finance, engineering, transportation, marketing and sales, and information technologies. This is a list of some of the many IT outsourcing companies.

Affiliated Computer Services
2828 N. Haskell
Dallas, TX   75204
214-841-6381

AmeriQuest Technologies, Inc.
Three Imperial Promenade
Santa Ana, CA 92707
714-437-0099

Andersen Consulting
69 West Washington Street
Chicago, IL 60602
312-580-0069

AT&T Global
Information Solutions
1700 South Patterson Blvd.
Dayton, Ohio 45479
513-445-5000

Cap Gemini America, Inc.
1114 Avenue of the Americas
New York, NY 10036
212-944-6464

Compass Computer Services
2085 Midway Road
Carrollton, TX 75248
214-944-6464

Computer Horizons Corp.
49 Old Bloomfield Ave.
Mountain Lakes, NJ 07046-1495
201-402-7400

Contemporary Computer Services
200 Old Knickerbocker Ave.
Bohemia, NY 11716

Convestrix Corp.
1100 Valley Brook Ave.
Lyndhurst, NJ 07071
201-935-8300

CSC
118 MacKenon Drive
Cary, NC 27511
919-469-3325

Cyntergy
656 Quince Orchard Road
Gaithersburg, MD 20878-1409
301-926-3400

Data General Corp.
4400 Computer Drive
Westborough, MA 01580
508-898-5000

Digital Equipment Corp.
111 Powder Mill Rd.
Maynard, MA 01754
508-493-5111

Electronic Data Systems Corp.
5400 Legacy Dr.
Plano, TX 75024
214-604-6000

Entex Information Services
6 International Drive
Rye Brook, NY 10573-1058
914-935-3600

GTE Information Services, Inc.
201 North Franklin Street
Tampa, FL 33602
813-273-4700

Hewlett-Packard Co.
3000 Hanover Street
Tampa, FL 33602
813-273-4700

IBM Global Services (formerly ISSC)
44 South Broadway
White Plains, NY 10601
914-288-3400

Inacom Corp.
10810 Farnam Dr.
Omaha, NE 68154
402-392-4456

I-Net Inc.
1255 West 12th Street
Plano, TX 75075
214-578-6100

Isogon Corp.
330 7th Ave.
New York, NY 10001
914-376-3293

Keane, Inc.
Ten City Square
Boston, MA 02129-3798
617-241-9200

Litton Computer Services
5490 Canoga Ave.
Woodland Hills, CA
818-715-5227/800-252-6527

MCI Communications Corp.
1801 Pennsylvania Ave, NW
Washington, DC 20036
202-872-1600

MicroAge Information Systems
2400 South MicroAge Way
Tempe, AZ 85282
602-929-2446

Octel Network Services, Inc.
17080 Dallas Pkwy
Dallas, TX 75248
214-733-2700

Policy Management Systems Corp.
One PMS Center
Blythwood, SC 29016
803-735-4000

Science Applications International Corp. (SAIC)
10260 Campus Point Dr.
San Diego, CA 92121
619-535-7900

SHL Systemhouse/MCI Corp.
50 O'CONNOR Street, Suite 501
Ottawa, Ontario, Canada K1P-6L2
613-236-9734

Technology & Business Integrators
50 Tice Boulevard
Woodcliff Lake, NJ 07675
201-573-9191

The Continuum Company
9500 Arboretum Boulevard
Austin, TX 78659-6399
512-338-7600

Unisys Corp.
Township Lane
Blue Bell, PA 19422
215-986-4011

Xerox Business Services
70 Linden Oaks Parkway
Rochester, NY 14625
800-835-9376

Index

A

Acquisitions, *See* Mergers and acquisitions
Agreement, *See* Contract
Analysis of outsourcing possibilities, 5, 9–10, 103–28
    costs, analysis of, *See* Costs
    personnel to involve in, 1, 74–75, 104–105
Asset specificity, 91–92, 152–53
Audits, 150, 220, 235, 262–63

B

Backlogs, 112
Bargaining power, *See* Contract, negotiation
Baseline, *See* Costs
Benefits of outsourcing, 26–30
Budget, 100
Business performance and outsourcing, 48, 111–12

C

Caldwell, Bruce, xxi–xxiii
Change, business and technological, 112–16, 179–80, 187–89, 213, 316–17 *See also* Mergers and acquisitions
Change in requirements, 147–48, 179–80, 184, 226
Change of character clauses, 180
Chargeback, 189
Communication, 133, 170, 227, 236–37, 243–44 *See also* Disputes; Personnel; Transfers
Competitive necessities, 84–85
Confidentiality, 206–207, 218
Conflicts, *See* Disputes
Consultants, 2, 107, 111, 119, 124, 145, 189, 211, 329–33
Contingencies, 121
Continuous improvement, 115–16, 218–19
Contract, 145–76, 260, 265–66, 365–79
    changes in, 150